Sex, Drugs & Economics

Also by Diane Coyle

Paradoxes of Prosperity

Sex, Drugs & ECONOMICS

An Unconventional Introduction to Economics

Diane Coyle

TEXERE

New York • London

Copyright © 2002 Diane Coyle

Published in 2002 by

TEXERE LLC
55 East 52nd Street
New York, NY 10055

Tel: +1 (212) 317 5511
Fax: +1 (212) 317 5178
www.etexere.com

In the UK

TEXERE Publishing Limited
71–77 Leadenhall Street
London EC3A 3DE

Tel: +44 (0)20 7204 3644
Fax: +44 (0)20 7208 6701
www.etexere.co.uk

This publication is designed to provide accurate and authoritative information in regard to the subject matter covered. It is sold with the understanding that the publisher is not engaged in rendering legal, accounting, or other professional services. If legal advice or other expert assistance is required, the services of a competent professional person should be sought.

Library of Congress Cataloging-in-Publication Data has been applied for.

ISBN 1-58799-147-0

Printed in the United States of America.

This book is printed on acid-free paper. ∞

10 9 8 7 6 5 4 3 2 1

Contents

Acknowledgments

For nearly twenty-five years I've been enthused by economics, so my first thanks must go to my own teachers, especially Peter Sinclair, Ben Friedman, Mark Watson, and the many other inspiring economists at Oxford and Harvard Universities in the late 1970s and early 1980s.

I'm also grateful to the following people, who helped me either in discussion or by commenting on specific sections of this book: Charles Bean, Alan Budd, Alison Cottrell, Nick Crafts, Partha Dasgupta, Meghnad Desai, Richard Freeman, David Hendry, Harold James, DeAnne Julius, Mervyn King, Paul Klemperer, Paul Krugman, Richard Layard, Richard Portes, Danny Quah, Amanda Rowlatt, Romesh Vaitilingam, and Tony Venables. The Centre for Economic Performance at the London School of Economics provided a welcoming base during my research. Of course, I myself am entirely responsible for any errors and omissions.

The book would not have happened without the efforts of Myles Thompson, Victoria Larson, and everybody else at Texere, or my agent, Sara Menguc, all of whom have given me tremendous encouragement and support. Special thanks must go to Peter Dougherty for all his advice.

And with much love, always, to Rory, Adam, and Rufus.

WHY ECONOMICS TRUMPS COMMON SENSE

Writing a book to popularize economics might seem to many people a madly ambitious project. There are many reasons for the subject's lack of general appeal. One fundamental reason is that it can seem so gloomy—after all, it earned the title "the dismal science" almost as soon as it was born in the late eighteenth century, thanks to one early practitioner, Robert Malthus, predicting the inevitability of mass starvation. The usual subject matter, recession, unemployment, debt, hunger, poverty, and so on, is quite simply depressing.

The unpopularity is in one way deeply unfair. For the aim of the economics profession is to extend the opportunities and choices available to everybody in their daily lives, aiding as many people as possible in their quest for well-being. Economics has its eyes firmly fixed on making this a better life, in the fullest sense and not just financially.

But in another way the subject's reputation is well deserved. Courting unpopularity is almost the raison d'être of economists, the dirty realists of the social sciences. Economists are the only people who warn about difficult choices and trade-offs—summed up in the catchphrase "there's no such thing as a free lunch." Choosing one course of action means closing off another: spending more now means having less to spend later. So economists can often seem like party poopers. What's more, they do it using a scientific approach and lots of difficult math.

Many of the tenets of economics also sound highly counterintuitive or counter to common sense. Cutting farm subsidies will make farmers better off? Financial markets reduce risk? And imports are better for the nation than exports? What planet are economists from?

In fact, economics is essentially about skepticism applied to human society and politics. Economists constantly ask questions: why is this happening, is that claim true, will a proposed policy actually work, who benefits from it? It is a subject born out of the Enlightenment two hundred and fifty years ago, the intellectual movement whose elevation of the power of reason shaped modern science and democracy. David Hume, the eighteenth-century philosopher and one of the founding fathers of economics, described the approach as "an attempt to introduce the experimental method of reasoning into moral subjects," to quote the subtitle of his great *Treatise of Human Nature*.

This book aims to demonstrate that economics is essentially a particular way of thinking about the world that can be applied to almost any situation affecting individuals, companies, industries, and governments. It is a way of thinking that involves having the highest respect for empirical evidence, for looking at charts and numbers and working out what the evidence means. Figuring out what it makes sense to believe is not only intellectually satisfying, it also offers an unparalleled understanding of what policies and strategies will make our societies function better. No other discipline can achieve the same enlightened pragmatism.

Economics also involves assuming that people are rational in the sense that on the whole they will act in their own best interests. The assumption gets taken to extremes in much formal economics, which is based on figuring out the behavior of individual "agents" who bear more resemblance to *Star Trek*'s Mr. Spock than to real, emotional, confused, and illogical human beings. Still, it is a good working assumption. People are certainly not totally rational in real life, but if you are going to argue that they consistently behave in ways that are not in their best interests, you had better have a convincing explanation for it.

So, for example, whenever the stock market crashes, economists are widely mocked for believing investors behave rationally and the financial markets are efficient—because in that case, why was a dot-com company worth $10 billion one day, worth only a few hundred million the next? How can any piece of news justify a 5 percent drop in the value of corporate America in a single day? There is no question that psychology and sociology have a crucial role to play in explaining what goes on in the stock market. However, it is always worth pointing out to the generally (but not always) innumerate critics that share prices are supposed to value the entire future profitability of a company at today's values. In other words, they have to discount for the fact that money in hand is worth a lot more than potential future money. A small change in expectations of profits' growth in ten or twenty years' time can as a matter of arithmetic have a big impact on today's valuation. What's more, there is also a deep truth in the economists' argument that investors are rational and will therefore compete away any lasting profit opportunities. For very few investors manage to beat the market for any length of time.

Similarly, people do not get married for purely economic reasons—well, not often, anyway. Yet economists' models in which people choose or ditch their partners in order to maximize their financial gains can illuminate trends like single motherhood. Welfare payments and the low potential earning power of inner-city fathers go a long way to explain how it became a financially sensible choice as well as socially acceptable. Or like the growing division between households with two high-earners and those with two low- or no-earners, which is an important explanation for the increase in income inequality, with more women taking on paid work outside the home. Those with high earning potential thanks to their background or education will have more success in seeking out similar partners precisely because they have more to offer. The economic explanation is never the only one, but it puts the backbone into the political and sociological explanations.

Some critics inside and outside the profession argue that the emphasis on rational behavior means that the use of complicated mathematical techniques has gone too far. Academics in other social sciences or the humanities do not like the attempt to apply the scientific method to human society and culture, especially when it leads to unwelcome (to them) conclusions. Others believe that the formalization now required to get anywhere in academic economics, using models based on unrealistic assumptions, is not only spurious when it comes to understanding the world, but also simply puts off many potential students. They prefer the realism of business school courses or the genuine technicalities of one of the natural sciences.

For the professional economists, working through the mathematics of a simplified model that isolates a particular issue is the way to gain new insights. But—and this is a big *but*—they have to be able to work out what the solution to the equations means. Economists must be able to explain their results to a wider audience, or there has to be a suspicion they don't actually understand it themselves. It is, after all, a social science whose findings have a social meaning.

I intend to demonstrate that economics is not a set body of knowledge about certain financial subjects. It is instead a method for thinking about any subject. There can be an economics of anything—marriage, sport, crime, drugs trafficking, education, movies, and even, yes, sex. Economics is one route toward understanding any aspect of human nature, and one of the most illuminating because of its analytical rigor.

Not that this means it is always possible to draw any definitive conclusions. A few things in economics are either right or wrong. If a country is importing more goods and services than it exports, it is also importing more investment capital than it exports, as a matter of accounting—the balance of payments deficit has to be paid for by foreign money, an inward investment surplus. A country's gross domestic product (GDP) is always the sum of its components. Heading onto thinner ice, moving from straight definitions to predictions, if something is in short supply or high demand, its price will tend to go up. Lower interest rates will usually stimulate investment. Beyond such basics, however, many supposed statements of fact in economics are usually controversial.

The reason is that finding the right policy, the one that's in the interests of citizens in general, will almost always require a comparison of the costs and benefits, which is an empirical matter. So in some of the chapters in this book, hard conclusions might appear to be missing; for the answer can vary at different times and in different countries. Sometimes economists will reach broad agreement on the empirical answer. At other times this will be difficult, as there is a lot of measurement error in the statistics, and sorting out cause and effect is intrinsically challenging in a complex and changing world. What's more, the analysis of what's in the public interest often involves trade-offs between specific groups of people.

As the empirical evidence is not always decisive, it is easy for different interest groups to make competing claims.

Indeed, economics is a deeply political subject. The old name for economics, *political economy*, is more appropriate than *economics*, despite the old-fashioned flavor of the word. Economists will often reach different conclusions depending on their own politics, as some of the past clashes between different schools of thought in the subject demonstrate. For example, two competing schools, often labeled monetarist and Keynesian, offered conflicting explanations of the stagflation of the 1970s, the grim combination of slow or negative growth with high inflation. The monetarists were mainly conservatives and the Keynesians progressives in their personal politics. The very fact there can be competing schools proves that a lot of economics is not hard science. On the contrary, it often involves grappling to keep on top of whatever happens to be going on right now in the world, whether that's recession, a technology-driven boom, high inflation or deflation, or globalization.

So if it changes with events anyway, and its conclusions depend on the politics of its practitioners, why bother with it? To start with, anybody who would like the world to be a better place should be able to think like an economist. Whether you are for or against globalization and trade, whether you think poverty is inevitable or an abomination, if you think there are too many people in prison or too few, economics will allow you to assemble the evidence and line up the arguments. This matters to the extent that you personally care about being right and it might also make a real difference because public opinion sways public policy. If more people could think economics, opinions might become less contradictory. As things stand, opinion polls show there are majorities in favor of both a cleaner environment and lower taxes on fuel, and for lower taxes in general and simultaneously better public services. Most people want to see an end to sweatshop labor and yet also want to buy their clothes as cheaply as possible.

What's more, some of the most interesting developments in economics have been taking place in the study of more detailed questions concerning one part or aspect of the whole economy, or microeconomics—such as how to structure welfare payments in order to create the best incentives for recipients to find work, or what explains why and how companies innovate. Here there have been genuine scientific gains in understanding.

The detailed economic arguments are vital in almost any public policy question, where success often depends on the triumph of realism over idealism. The war on drugs? It can't ignore the profit opportunities waging this war creates for organized crime. Guaranteeing the electricity supply in the face of constant new demands? The prices and investment incentives faced by the utility companies make all the difference between bright lights and blackouts. Protecting endangered species? Campaigns and policies will be effective politically only if they take account of the extra financial costs industry will face as well as the environmental costs.

Economics is central in government policy and all over the news. It affects each of us every day. It's important for our purely selfish concerns. Everybody cares about how much tax the government takes, anybody in business wants to figure out how much demand they might have to meet for their services and what wages they'll have to pay, and any working person is concerned about how best to save for tuition fees and retirement pensions.

The bottom line is that any informed and active citizen needs to understand the economic method of thinking. The more of us that can apply a little skepticism and an ability to weigh up the evidence to any public policy issue, the healthier our democracies will be and the wealthier our nations.

Besides, it's fun. Unless you're a hermit with no interest in the world, applying economic principles opens new windows on life day after day. It makes almost every article in the newspapers potentially interesting. It breathes life into dry tables of numbers and abstract charts.

Take the driest possible example—actuarial tables of birthrates, death rates and life expectancy. They paint a picture of an aging Western population and a workforce that will start shrinking. It takes only a little economics to turn the dusty columns of figures into vivid scenarios. Will taxes have to rise much to pay the growing old-age social security bill? Well, very high taxes have always fomented riot and revolution. Perhaps countries traditionally hostile to immigration such as Germany and Japan will have to start importing young workers from poorer countries with plenty to spare, a development that would have enormous political and cultural ramifications. So maybe the aging rich countries will opt instead for coping with population decline, say by working later or by developing technologies that make the shrinking pool of workers more productive. Yet in the past the strongest economies have always had growing populations. Maybe these tables therefore spell out Chinese dominance of the global economy in the twenty-first century. These are big questions, and in no way boring.

Economics is therefore the subject for you whatever your interests and concerns. The aim here is to provide a new light and refreshing appetizer that might satisfy delicate appetites but also encourage some readers to develop a taste for more.

The first part looks at some areas where it might come as a surprise that economics has anything at all to say, just to prove that it offers a rigorous analysis of almost any subject that might crop up in day to day life. Then follows a section on government intervention in the economy to shed light on a variety of difficult public policy questions of interest to all of us. The third part looks at the changing structure of the economy, at how businesses and whole industries thrive and decline, in the face of new technologies. The fourth addresses some global issues which tend to arouse strong emotions and where, therefore, economics can play a particularly valuable role. Even if these do not affect us directly, they do affect several billion poor people. The fifth part covers some traditional macroeconomic topics like growth and inflation. These are the subjects that many people think of as economics, but I hope to show that there is a lot more to it. Even such a wide range of topics can give only a partial view of the scope of economics, which is, after all, all of human life in its endless fascination and variety.

The book wraps up with a more general chapter about economics as a subject, a checklist of things to remember in order to think like an economist, and a glossary of the concepts used earlier in the book. These terms are in bold in the text the first time they appear.

Part I

SEX, DRUGS & ROCK 'N' ROLL

Economics Really Does Apply to Everything

The aim of this section is to make an unashamed bid for attention by showing that economics really does apply to everything in life, including some of the subjects that experience suggests interest people the most.

These first chapters cover the usual titillating areas—sports, sex, and all kinds of recreational behavior that are bad for you. But there's an economics of anything you can imagine, from embroidery to fishing, hairdressing to open-cast mining. The point is that what makes it economics rather than any other kind of analysis is not the subject matter, but the way you think about it.

Chapter 1

SEX

Can You Have Too Much of a Good Thing?

Sex sells. British tabloids, delivered to millions of homes every day, are notorious for their daily pictures of semi-nude women. The top shelves groan under the weight of magazines intended for consenting adults only. The number of new pornographic movies made each year is growing at a double-digit rate. Pornography is also the biggest success story on the Internet, and seems the one surefire route to profitability for a dot-com.

In short, sex is a big industry with a multibillion-pound, -euro, or -dollar turnover and a large workforce. Official figures do not list it as an industry in its own right, but it is roughly on a par with a sector like electrical engineering in size. It attracts a surprising range of people as workers, like the pretty army sergeant who posed for *The Sun* newspaper in just a small part of her uniform, or the official spokesman for the British prime minister who in a previous job wrote stories for a raunchy magazine. (Yes, it's true.)

Yet one economist who had been carrying out research into the size of the prostitution business (or so he claimed) mused that the real puzzle was not why so many women became prostitutes but rather why so few did. After all, the hourly rate of pay was so much higher than any alternatives, except perhaps for top female lawyers and management consultants—other professionals, in short. (In the U.K. the going rate is £1 a minute according to recent estimates, compared to a legal minimum wage of £0.06 a minute.) In addition, the hours are flexible and you can work from home. Why, then, aren't lots more women working as prostitutes?

Similarly with other branches of the sex industry. If it is so profitable, why isn't there an even bigger supply of magazines and prostitutes than we have already? You would expect enticingly large profits to be competed away and unusually high wage rates to be competed down.

Nevertheless, a recent *Economic Journal* survey of the economic literature on this subject (which has lots of equations but no centerfolds) concluded: "In the context of sexual services, economic theory is useful up to a point, but noneconomic incentives (or disincentives) must play a major role."

Still, economics can offer some insights into the sex industry. A lot of the participants are playing out the laws of economics without realizing it. It's all a question of **demand** and **supply**. This is the central concept in economics.

Start with the supply side of the market for sexual services. Part of the analysis simply mirrors the case of illegal drugs. A government ban keeps out competition and sustains a high rate of profit. So in countries where prostitution is illegal, for example, this can go a long way to explaining the puzzle about the impressive size of porn profits. Likewise with illegal hardcore or pedophilic material. The ban restricts supply, which is socially desirable because the consumption of such goods imposes negative externalities on the rest of us. But it boosts the profits of criminal entrepreneurs at the expense of consumers of such products who would otherwise have more choice and pay a lower price.

Legal pornography is a different matter. Maybe these sex markets are just not quite like markets for other goods, like candy bars, or other workers, such as bus drivers.

Take the job market in the sex industry, a market that in turn is an important determinant of the supply of services provided to customers. The conventional labor market is obviously segmented by the fact that people want to work within commuting distance of their home and have a certain set of skills it can be hard to alter. But you do not often hear complaints about shortages of skilled workers in the case of pornography. Indeed, perhaps we all think we could do it if pushed; after all there are (I am told) magazines that simply publish amateur photographs sent in by readers. It is therefore unlikely to be skill shortages that keep sex industry wages higher than those in local shops, offices, and factories. Still, there could be an **inelastic supply of labor** due to the social inhibitions attached to work in this field. That means a labor supply that is not very responsive to pay, requiring a large pay rise to increase the number of workers available whenever demand steps up.

A second possibility is that the job market for sex workers is similar to that for other workers with careers that will probably not last very long, such as sports stars or dancers or perhaps bond salesmen, with a pay structure that gives them high earnings but for a relatively short period. A wise blue movie star will therefore save a lot of his or her income to provide for a long retirement. High prices for the products of the sex industry could therefore reflect high costs, including wage costs.

Another contributory factor on the supply side is that, while there do not seem to be any conventional barriers to entry in the industry, such as high capital requirements, natural monopolies, regulatory restrictions, or a formidable amount of know-how, there are likely to be some less conventional barriers. The industry's criminal fringe and protection rackets will deter some would-be entrepreneurs. It is, after all, quite a violent business because parts of it are illegal. Again, social inhibitions might put off others.

What about the demand side? Just as the supply has some special features, the nature of demand in the sex industry is not quite like demand in many other markets either.

There is certainly a lot of **product differentiation**. One reason is almost certainly that consumers' desire for privacy prevents the kind of price comparisons that take place in normal competitive markets. The market is also highly segmented by individuals' differing tastes. In short, being turned on is not like going to the grocery store, where you can see all prices clearly labeled, and looking for the cheapest can of soup. Pornography, prostitution, and other branches of the sex industry are **monopolistically competitive** markets, as the textbooks would put it. The products offered in each branch of the business differ in small characteristics (do you prefer a schoolgirl or a dominatrix?), and different categories of customers will pay quite divergent prices.

There is some evidence that the range of prices is very wide. For example, a study of prices charged by U.K. prostitutes showed that location, duration, and special services had a big impact on price. Women could charge a lot more for visits to hotels or the client's home, for spending a long time with the client, and for services labeled kinky included as variables in the economists' regressions. The supply of certain services is clearly very limited, and such women also get a lot of return visitors despite their high charges. So the interaction of supply and demand can explain how the industry manages so successfully to part its customers from a lot of their money.

The Internet is likely to transform the structure of some parts of the sex market, as it has the markets for so many other goods and services. It has made it much cheaper, easier, and less frightening to become a sex industry entrepreneur. It has also made it easier, cheaper, and less embarrassing to buy pornography, boosting demand as well as supply. The porn industry and the Internet industry have in fact been mutually reinforcing as consumer enthusiasm for downloading pornographic material helped the Internet take off and spread so quickly to so many households.

Some of the demand will be accidental, as I once discovered when trying to find the website of the foreign policy journal *Foreign Affairs*. Many parents and employers are also installing screening software that might limit demand growth, although this doesn't seem to work too accurately at present. One well-known filter blocks access to the website of a piano music center; heaven knows what the programmers thought *arpeggio* means. At any rate, somewhere there already is an economist trying to estimate the impact of the Internet on profits from pornography.

The early indications are that the Internet has had a major impact on the supply of pornography, and there is indeed now enough overcapacity to have slashed profits from adult publishing offline. Trade sources estimated that U.K. circulation of pornographic magazines was 1.5 million in 1997 but down to 1.1 million in 2000. The decline has continued despite price cuts. Revenues from porn magazines are thought to have fallen from £5 million to £3.4 million over the same period. Not surprisingly, then, two of the biggest British publishers of such magazines sold off their magazine interests in 2001, one to concentrate on cable TV, the other on Internet porn. This parallels the way the Net has the potential to cannibalize some other types of printed publications that have in the past earned very high profits thanks to peculiarities of demand and supply—academic journals, for example.

However, although the supply shock of the Internet has had an adverse impact on profitability, sex is still a growth market. Of course, one peculiarity of the sex industry is that its customers are mainly men, so it is making its profits from only half of humanity. Whatever the gender-profile of the consumers, they are nevertheless buying more and more pornography as average levels of income rise. The **income-elasticity of demand** appears to be more than one, or in other words, spending on the sex industry is rising faster than incomes overall. Pornography is technically a **luxury good**. In this it is like many other leisure activities, including moviegoing, eating out, going to the gym, watching baseball, and so on, which have grown rapidly as our societies have grown more affluent. When hours were long, work hard, and pay low, few of us had the money or enthusiasm for a luxury such as pornography or visits to racy bars and strip joints. Now we're so much richer in leisure and money, it's a different matter.

Fun is becoming an increasingly important part of the advanced economies, which is something worth bearing in mind for anyone thinking about starting up a business. Of course there will always be demand for the basics of food, housing and shelter, but the big growth will come in markets where demand is growing even faster than incomes as we become more and more prosperous. These range from conventional luxury goods—such as designer clothes rather than cheap T-shirts—to services of all kinds. These include education and health care, hotels and restaurants, but also a whole range of others in the leisure sector that statisticians class as personal services. What they have in mind is personal trainers, manicurists, aromatherapists, counselors, and so on, but sex workers are in there, too: apparently, people think sex is fun.

Chapter 2

ILLEGAL DRUGS

It's the Economy, Man

Bill Clinton famously admitted during his first bid for the U.S. presidency that he had smoked cannabis as a student, but never inhaled. I have the opposite confession: I've never smoked it but have inhaled, at student parties where a number of other people were partaking and had filled the room with that characteristic pungent haze. Personally, I've never knowingly taken any illegal drugs, for purely rational economic reasons. As an impoverished student I could either pay £1.99 for a bottle of wine, albeit not the very finest, or pay a lot more for an illicit substance that did not seem to do much more for its users than alcohol did for me. And as the years have passed and I've grown richer, I've simply traded up to the £3.99 bottle of wine.

Some people will object to the idea that policies toward drugs should be anything other than a question of morality: drugs are just wrong. From this principle stems the "war" on drugs being waged in the United States, the United Kingdom, and other European countries. However, it didn't take Steven Soderbergh's movie *Traffic* for most people to realize that there was no chance of a zero-tolerance policy working when so many citizens of our countries use illegal drugs. A law that more than one in five people (almost one in three Americans over the age of twelve) breaks at some point in their lives, and none of their friends will ever report them for, is a failing law.

There are three broad philosophical approaches to drug policy. One is the ideal of a drug-free society, the approach that inspires so much of the rhetoric of the war on drugs. A second is the view that drug use is an illness, suggesting that warfare is not enough, and users need medical treatment and social programs as well. A third is the libertarian view that people should be free to use whatever they want as long as it doesn't harm anyone else, and in practice our day-to-day tolerance of friends, family, and acquaintances who do use drugs means politicians cannot ignore this principle even if they abhor it.

Economics can help shed light on the philosophical and political debate. There is, after all, a market in operation, one where government restrictions have some very predictable effects. What this implies is that price matters, as well as all the noneconomic considerations that apply to drug policy.

There are few firm facts established about an illegal trade, but consider what we do know. The use of drugs appears to be a permanent feature of human life. The ancient Greeks used opium, the Aztecs peyote and marijuana. Human beings have been taking drugs in one form or another throughout recorded history. Consistent government attempts to prohibit any of them are a twentieth-century phenomenon, a product of Victorian moral campaigners. One of the most famous efforts, of course, was the Eighteenth Amendment to prohibit liquor in the United States in the 1920s. Prohibition was a descendant of Victorian temperance campaigns that promoted alternative, nonalcoholic drinks like sarsaparilla or dandelion and burdock. They were a far cry from the drinks young people prefer today, such as trendy vodka cocktails or sweet "alco-pops."

Very many people today have taken illegal drugs at some time in their lives—up to a half in some Western countries—not to mention the millions of regular users of alcohol, tobacco, and caffeine. Use of illegal substances is often no more than a youthful experiment. According to surveys, three-quarters or four-fifths of people who have tried illegal drugs got their first samples free, often at a party or rave. Dealers try to build a customer base by giving away samples, just like a manufacturer trying to create a market for a certain shampoo or soup. Surveys—which probably underreport the true figures—suggest that about a third of American adults have tried soft drugs like cannabis, rising to 50 percent among college students.

In Germany and Switzerland the proportion of the population that has taken illegal drugs at some point seems to be about 20 percent. Can so many people be criminals in any meaningful sense of the word? Very many of us do not in our heart believe that the odd joint smoked in college, inhaled or not, makes someone a criminal or even a bad person.

Very few people are regular lifelong users or become addicted, moreover. The same survey evidence suggests that although 17 percent of the Swiss had tried drugs, only 2 percent had taken anything within the past year. Drug consumption falls dramatically among the over-thirties everywhere. Soft drugs are not addictive, whereas hard drugs are, although many people just quit them anyway. For example, studies of Vietnam veterans showed that many took heroin in Southeast Asia, but the overwhelming majority stopped of their own accord when they returned home. According to the U.S. National Household Survey on Drug Abuse, one heroin user in three is dependent—high but lower than the four-fifths dependency rate among nicotine users.

On the other hand, despite the fact that many illegal drugs are not physiologically addictive, the demand for them appears to be growing over time. As prices have been on a downward trend, this might well reflect increased supply. All drugs, however, can be damaging to the health (and that certainly includes the legal ones, too), so their use imposes costs on the health care system and perhaps also on productivity at work. Research indicates that an increase in the retail price of heroin, one of the most lethal, does result in a large and significant reduction in the number of deaths it causes. So the health costs are substantial. However, the illegal nature of the business means much of the drug supply is low in quality or adulterated, and it is often this that kills users rather than the drug itself.

The worldwide market for illegal drugs is known to be huge, but how huge is a matter of guesswork, because neither sales quantities nor prices are known for certain. One widely accepted United Nations figure is $400 billion (bigger than the global oil industry), employing around 20 million people and serving 70 to 100 million customers. Perhaps half of the customers are in the United States, the biggest single market for drugs, as indeed for everything else. Most of the fifty or so countries known to produce and export illegal drugs are very poor, and it is often their major cash crop. The earnings potential of the industry, combined with their other economic problems like falling commodity prices and heavy debt burdens, has probably led to a substantial increase in drug production by developing countries. Many big producers are also places of violent conflict—think of Colombia, Burma, or Afghanistan—although whether that is a cause or a consequence of the drug trade is not clear.

So if those are the broad facts, let's think like economists about the problem. In any **market**, there is **supply** and **demand**. Policies can tackle both the demand side and the supply side of the market, and even in supposedly liberal countries like the Netherlands both types of prohibitive policies have intensified since the early 1970s. Generally, there are much fiercer penalties for supplying than for using drugs, and countries take very different approaches to punishing users.

Prices vary widely between different markets, depending on the degree of **competition** among suppliers. For example, figures for 1993 show a gram of heroin ranging in price from $43 in the Netherlands to $196 in Switzerland. The prohibition on certain drugs in force in most developed countries restricts the competition to supply the substances concerned. In many cases there is, if not a monopoly on supply, something close to it, maintained by appalling violence and brutality. Illegality creates such huge profits that cornering this market is a reward seriously worth fighting for— think about the multibillion-dollar profitability of the legitimate pharmaceutical industry and multiply it several times to get an idea of the scale. Perversely (but in line with economic thinking), the tougher the prohibition, the more profitable the business becomes because the competition gets squeezed out. Police and customs officers end up helping the most determined and brutal suppliers by removing their competitors from the business.

There is a very real sense, therefore, in which the policy of absolute prohibition—enforced by most governments of countries that import illegal drugs—has created a parallel economy controlled by organized crime. The revenues generated by the drug trade need laundering, and extend the reach of the mobsters into other, legal activities. This is a global economy, too. In the opinion of many experts, ranging from U.N. officials to Manuel Castells, the respected Berkeley sociologist, the growing reach of the criminal multinationals threatens to undermine legal, democratic institutions. It also certainly prevents the developing countries from aspiring to greater prosperity through traditional economic and political progress. Why should they bother when there is an easy source of cash earnings for their farmers, and one that happens to provide generous kickbacks for corrupt officials and politicians who have to turn a blind eye to the trade? If they destroy the crops, they just have a huge headache about what alternative livelihood the very poorest peasants can find. It's not surprising that weaning Afghan farmers off the cultivation of heroin poppies is one of the toughest challenges in reconstructing that country's shattered economy.

What's more, prohibition creates criminality among buyers as well as sellers. The fact that prices are so high draws many drug users into crime to finance their purchases, while their regular contact with suppliers might well make crime seem normal or even in that milieu socially acceptable. Addicts have to finance their habit. German and American studies suggest that about a fifth of the income needed by addicts is earned legally, more than a third comes from drug-dealing, and the rest comes from either crimes like burglary and mugging or prostitution. A very high proportion indeed of crimes against property seem to be drug related. Drug use is certainly one of the complex of social problems that barricade inner-city ghettos with poverty and violence.

On the other hand, high prices will help restrict demand. If illegal drugs were much cheaper or if the legal sanctions were less severe, the number of users would be much greater.

How then can we weigh up the costs and benefits of different policies? Suppose a government were to consider liberalizing its policy on soft drugs like cannabis, permitting small amounts for personal use and licensing suppliers. On the plus side, the removal of tough criminal sanctions would increase the number of suppliers and weaken the grip of crime gangs. Retail prices would fall. There would be less crime to police, both on the part of suppliers and users, so the policing budget could decline. Social costs from burglary and violence would diminish. The health of users might improve to the extent that quality could be controlled. The government could also raise revenue from taxing or licensing a legal trade.

Against these gains would be set some costs. A lower price would increase demand and might create more new users. That would have adverse health effects and perhaps also reduce the productivity of users. (There is not much evidence on whether drugs hamper work effort, and some argue it goes the other way. Some great writers and artists have been notorious drunks, and rumor has it that the movie and TV industries would be nowhere without cocaine.) Some experts believe that tolerance of soft drug use also brings more people to hard drugs, which would amplify these costs, although others dispute this argument.

There have been a few experiments with alternatives to all-out war against drugs, and their results provide some suggestive evidence. One study reported by the Centre for Economic Policy Research compared heroin use in the U.K. and the Netherlands. The Netherlands continues to prohibit drugs, including cannabis; but it has a relatively liberal policy toward users possessing small amounts, which extends to allowing the sale of small amounts of cannabis in licensed cafés. Amsterdam's cafés are thus one of the city's prime tourist attractions, along with its equally famous red-light district and of course the canals. It combines this liberalism with the usual tough regime for anybody caught importing or exporting drugs, with large fines and harsh prison sentences.

The economists found that between 1983 and 1993 heroin had cost £28 a gram on average in the Netherlands, compared to £74 a gram in the U.K. Yet crime rates were lower in the Netherlands, and far fewer young people had used drugs of all types than in the U.K. Drug users were also given more medical help. By 1995, the Dutch had the lowest proportion of drug-related deaths in Europe, 2.4 per million inhabitants, compared with 9.5 per million in France, the next lowest. The Dutch have even opened a retirement home for junkies. So in terms of reduced public health and policing costs, the Dutch experiment suggests there could be big benefits from a more liberal regime. It's not too surprising then that in late 2001 the U.K. government announced it would introduce a Netherlands-style system for cannabis.

Another experiment in the conservative Swiss city of Zurich has been equally suggestive. Zurich is as straitlaced as Amsterdam is swinging. Yet despite heavily repressive policies, by 1987 drugs were being sold and used openly in the infamous "Needle Park" behind the main railway station. The place was filthy, the number of addicts in poor health was growing, and the supply was controlled by gangs who offered drugs to schoolchildren at special low prices. High profits meant new gangs were trying to gain a share of the market, so new entrants from Lebanon, Albania, and Africa started gang wars. And the property crimes committed by drug users to finance their purchases were rising exponentially. The police closed down the park, but the scene simply shifted to a disused railway station.

By 1994 the city authorities decided to experiment with a new approach. They now provide small, subsidized amounts of heroin to registered addicts, who must use the drugs in designated offices and accept medical or psychological treatment. Meanwhile the police have continued to crack down heavily on other suppliers but switched to a liberal approach to the consumption of drugs in private homes and parties. In many ways the new policy was a clear success. For example, the health of heavy users has measurably improved. More than half the registered participants got a regular job, and the vast majority of those who used to steal to pay for drugs no longer do so. In a December 1996 referendum the citizens of Zurich gave the policy an overwhelming vote of approval.

The liberalization approach has also made headway in the United Kingdom, which has the worst drug abuse figures in Europe. In 2002 the government effectively decriminalized the possession for personal use of cannabis, started experiments with the medical use of this drug, and started a debate on downgrading Ecstasy to soft-drug status.

The economic case for government intervention in the use of drugs at all is that health costs and social problems arising from consumer choices in the private, illegal market impose a cost on society as a whole that exceeds the private benefits of drug users' pleasure and drug suppliers' profits. This is known as an **externality**, which means that one individual's or group's behavior affects other people. Externalities offer the classic rationale for government involvement in the marketplace, because private choices lead to a less than ideal outcome—too much taking of illegal drugs, in this example. Other examples include noisy parties, driving in a congested city, or indeed, the taking of legal drugs.

The current solution is an outright ban on at least hard drugs in most Western countries. This is applied in the case of some other externalities. Some pollutants are banned or restricted, for example. However, it is relatively easy to tell when a particular factory is pouring toxins into the environment, but not so easy to keep tabs on the delivery of a portable product from a large number of potential sources. In logistical terms, prohibiting drugs is a bit like banning imports of any other small, portable product—cheese, say. A ban on cheese might make addicts desperate enough to pay a high price and therefore make smuggling worthwhile, but a customs duty on cheese that made it only a bit more expensive at retail level would probably not be worth the bother of avoiding. Such a ban would also be expensive to enforce. This is why America's war on drugs is estimated to cost $35 to $40 billion a year, and accounts for more than one in ten of all arrests nationwide.

So another approach to tackling the externality would be to impose a high tax on drugs. This is precisely the approach the British government takes to tobacco and alcohol. Both are very heavily taxed, raising more than £14 billion for the public coffers each year. More than half of the retail price of a bottle of wine goes to the government in tax revenues.

The tax is high because of the health costs of tobacco and alcohol consumption. The government would prefer a sober and clean-living workforce. But there are limits to how steep the tax can be, and because the duty imposed is high, it does still need policing. The human predilection for tax evasion is almost as ancient as the fondness for drugs. The demand for drink and cigarettes is sensitive to the price, for it appears that duty on spirits and tobacco—although not beer and wine—is now so high that further increases would reduce legal purchases and therefore tax revenues, according to research by the Institute for Fiscal Studies in London. The government has in fact now raised the excise duties to such a high level that it has driven some buyers of these legal drugs into the arms of bootleggers, with the associated costs of criminality and loss of tax revenue. This has also, thanks to the lower price in the black market, increased consumption. There is a level of retail prices, including tax, that maximizes the tax take and limits the demand. This would be true of a drug such as cannabis, too, were it to be legalized. How high the tax can go is an empirical matter that will depend on the size of the potential market, the costs of marketing the drugs, and crucially the **price elasticity of demand**, or how much demand responds to a small change in price. Still, consumption of cannabis might well be lower, the amount of crime and costs of policing lower, and tax revenues higher if it was legal but heavily taxed, like alcohol.

There are a lot of mights and maybes here. Partly because it is so hard to assemble the data, economists do not have good estimates of the advantages and disadvantages of different approaches, and the implications of the Dutch and Swiss experiments are hotly disputed. Yet an economist's reasoned **cost-benefit analysis** is not being considered enough in the policy debate, even though hardened nonusers like me can see the political gut reaction that there can be no let-up in the outright war on drugs is probably working against the public interest. The prohibition reflects the strength of feeling on the part of many voters and politicians. Still, it's a real shame. It's not that policymakers aren't putting a lot of effort into the problem—the European Union's officials on the

Horizontal Working Party on Drugs* in the Home Affairs and Justice directorate must be among the most dedicated—but the moralizing rules out some options that might make sense. A breath of economic pragmatism here would blast away the fuddled haze of a stale drug policy.

*Not a joke—this working party really exists.

Chapter 3

RISKY BUSINESS

Why Most Teenagers
Don't Act Like Economists

A lot of adolescents like to take **risks**. Unprotected sex, illegal drugs, legal but harmful drugs such as tobacco and alcohol, fast cars, gang violence—the list of options is long and alarming. The worrying point about teen behavior, to both their parents and the economics profession, is that by this age, they ought to know better. Fifteen-year-olds know roughly what the consequences of their actions could be. They are deliberately taking risks and making choices that they know with certainty might not be in their own best interests: tobacco kills; unsafe sex can lead to pregnancy and disease.

It's obvious why this would worry their parents. The reason risky behavior by adolescents bothers economists, too, is that it seems to undermine the foundation on which the subject rests: **rational choice**. This means that, given the information available, people will choose to behave in ways that are in their own best interests. They won't always have complete information. And their own interests can be interpreted fairly loosely. But at a minimum they shouldn't consistently harm their own prospects or do themselves damage.

Economists characterize people's behavior as making choices based on **maximizing expected utility**. It means that, just like *Star Trek*'s Mr. Spock, we should assess all the information we have and opt for the logical choice. Although we all know from the silly things we do when we're in love or in a panic or hung over that this obviously exaggerates human rationality, it seems fair enough as a general proposition that people know best themselves what's in their own interests. Any other assumption seems unpleasantly paternalistic; each person is the best judge of his or her own **preferences**.

Unfortunately, teenage daring poses a problem when it comes to assuming people behave rationally, because so much of what they do clearly is not in their best interests, and at some level even they know that. So, for that matter, does the midlife crisis, driving over the speed limit, or addictive behavior such as gambling or alcoholism at any age. The real trouble with this is not the well-being of irrational people, but rather the suspicion that such exceptions might undermine the very powerful tools economics gives us for analyzing and solving all sorts of other policy problems. For if economic analysis breaks down in some areas of human behavior, how can we be sure it works in others? For example, many people strongly doubt that rationality is an appropriate assumption to explain the decisions of investors in financial markets.

Fortunately, some researchers have begun to reconcile economics with behavior Mr. Spock would find hard to understand, and thus preserve the power and insight of economic analysis. To do so they have turned to other disciplines, notably psychology.

The marriage of these two disciplines, behavioral economics, produces a more powerful analytical framework than either economics or psychology does alone. While psychology can help us understand why people behave the way they do, the tools of economics are uniquely useful in the framing of public policies for helping the victims of their own stupid choices and for dealing with the wider social effects of their self-harm.

There is plenty of evidence that the principles of economics do in fact apply to some aspects of risky choices. For example, if the price of tobacco or marijuana goes up, demand goes down. Or to take another instance, when the job market is healthy and there is plenty of employment, or when the perceived risk of infection from a sexually transmitted disease such as AIDS, teenagers are more likely to use condoms. If there is any sign of people weighing costs and benefits, there is clearly some rational decision-making taking place. Furthermore, there is evidence from psychological studies that adolescents and adults are very similar in the attitudes they take toward the future consequences of various options. They are on average just as aware of the risks, just as well able to make calculations about complicated future possibilities, and just as disapproving about the negative consequences of drug use or gambling. Teenagers do not show any greater sense of personal invulnerability than adults—we retain that feeling throughout our lives.

The differences therefore lie not in how well or badly different groups are able to assess risks, but in their preferences for taking risks. While people as a whole are pretty bad at figuring out risks realistically, teenagers, like some middle-aged men, are more willing to take risks. Adolescents are trying to shape their independent identities as part of the transition to adulthood, and anybody in the throes of a midlife crisis is in search of a fleeting reminder of youth. Psychology therefore comes in handy as an explanation for the preferences of different groups.

However, we are all rather bad at assessing risks anyway. So even the most levelheaded among us tends to depart systematically from the ideal of rational choice. First, there is a strong human preference for immediate gratification at the expense of future satisfaction. In our psychological make-up we are all what an economist would describe as **time-inconsistent** in our preferences. The outcome we prefer at every moment between now and the future is not what we would prefer when we finally get to the future.

This can even be quite explicit. Addicts, for example, know very well that they would prefer not to be indulging in the same kinds of risks in the future but can't stop seeking the short-term gratification. The problem is one of lack of self-control, rather than poor risk assessment. And there are obviously different levels of sophistication possible. Some alcoholics don't even acknowledge they have a problem, while others try to control their current behavior by joining Alcoholics Anonymous.

The second systematic departure from rational choice is that many people are very bad at predicting how they will feel about different outcomes in the future, or what utility they will attach to the different possibilities, to use the jargon. It is impossible when you are young to appreciate that you might prefer different things when you are older: that a steady job and nice home will seem more appealing at fifty than hanging out on the streetcorner smoking dope with your friends. It's called a **projection bias** in people's preferences. We were all like that once.

We all know day to day how hard it is to act now according to future preferences: anybody who does the grocery shopping when he's hungry will know it's impossible not to walk out of the store without all kinds of extra items, generally unhealthy, than he had on his shopping list. At the other end of the triviality scale, suicide is an extreme example of an inability to predict future well-being, specifically an inability to believe that it will ever be possible to feel less bad in the future than right now.

The evidence is that young people have a stronger preference than older people for immediate gratification. And they are also not as good at predicting what their future preferences will be. This makes sense: experience does indeed teach us some valuable lessons. In sum, the young are more likely than the rest of us to depart from rationality.

This all adds up to a shortsightedness that results in overindulgence in risky behavior in general, especially by young people. Adolescents face objectively different costs and opportunities than adults do. They don't suffer the same costs from sleeping off a hangover most mornings rather than holding down a regular job. They derive greater benefits from impressing their peers (although of course some people never seem to grow out of this insecurity).

There is even a kind of rational fatalism about risk-taking, the idea that if you are going to go for it, you might as well be hung for a sheep as a lamb. It doesn't do all that much to alter the perceived balance of probabilities about future outcomes. Hence some teenagers indulge in risky behavior.

All this means that the usual tools of economics can easily be amended to take account of the psychological inclinations toward immediate gratification and misjudging future preferences. We can explain why teenagers, and others, don't show more sense and yet still be able to rely on the framework of rational choice and utility maximization for economic analysis.

There are several other potential threats to the power of economics, though.

One is the importance of **reference levels.** People care more about departures of their income or share prices or any other indicator from a reference level than about absolute value. People also care a lot more about avoiding losses than about achieving gains—about twice as much, in fact. So in assessing their expected utility in various future eventualities, there will be an asymmetry around the point they start from today.

Similarly there is a **status quo bias** or **endowment effect.** Anything that's already around is valued much more than something that's only potential. Or to put it another way, a bird in the hand is worth two in the bush.

There is also evidence of decreasing value being attached to additional increments of income or other indicators of well-being. Thus the difference between $100 and $200 is valued much more than the difference between $1,100 and $1,200. This is described as **diminishing marginal sensitivity**. If the figure is weekly income, this makes sense. But it could be wrong in some other contexts—say, the benefit derived from taking a drug. It could lead people to greatly underestimate the risks of something every time except the first that they do something.

Many people are also clearly altruistic, and they might have social goals that don't bear much relation to their selfish interests, that might even reduce their own incomes. This suggests that each individual's utility might depend on that of others also, that they are not just maximizing their own expected utility.

Last, but not least, there is clear evidence that people as a whole are very bad at forming coherent judgments about the probabilities of different future outcomes. For example, we all worry much more about low probability dangers such as a plane crash than high probability ones like being run over crossing the road.

These add up to a continuing challenge to the conventional economic approach in which rational individuals make choices that maximize their expected utility, and this is an area in which research is in its early stages. The rational choice model has no difficulty at all in incorporating **uncertainty**, the sheer lack of knowledge about what the future holds; but it is much harder to bend it to the existence of systematic bias in people's assessment of **risk**, or the probability of one outcome rather than another. However, behavioral economics has started to combine the analytical power of economic modeling, to predict how people might react to various policies, with the realism of psychological results.

Will it help us persuade adolescents not to take such silly risks? I doubt it, but it could help answer policy questions like whether or not giving out free condoms or syringes makes sense, or how much welfare support to give teenage mothers. Clever policies will take account of the way young people assess their expected future utility. For example, the State of California used a poster intended to discourage young men from smoking by showing a drooping cigarette, the reasoning being that immediate sexual dysfunction (a low probability result) as a result of smoking would affect their behavior of the activity far more than the distant future risk of lung cancer or another tobacco-related disease (a high probability result).

The assumption of rational behavior underpins much of economics, and it turns economic analysis into a powerful searchlight helping making sense of fog, of confusion and complexity in the world around us. Nevertheless, good economists always bear in mind the fact that some behavior is not fully rational, and we then need to turn to other disciplines like psychology and history for a fuller understanding of our fellow human beings.

Chapter 4

SPORTS

Better Than Sex

There is nothing more thrilling than the thwack of willow against leather, or so my husband tells me. No, not a bizarre sexual practice learned at his English public school involving caning and leather trousers, but cricket, the traditional willow bat hitting the traditional red leather-covered ball to the distant boundary of the pitch. Nothing more thrilling except perhaps the roar of the crowd as some enormous Neanderthal flings himself over a white line in the mud, clutching an oval ball. Or a World Cup penalty shoot-out between England and Germany, two countries doomed to fight old battles forever, at least in the minds of drunken soccer crowds. Yes, it's sport. A lot of people find it really exciting.

Somebody watching the Super Bowl or the Olympics on TV might not realize it, but there's a lot of economics involved in sport. It's certainly big business, especially in the United States. According to a European Commission estimate, trade in all sports-related activities amounts to 3 percent of world trade. At his peak, Michael Jordan earned $30 million a year for playing basketball for the Chicago Bulls and twice that from his product endorsements—just one sports star and just one sportswear company. On a generous definition, including sports clothes, TV and advertising revenues linked to sports, and gambling, as well as the actual business of people going to watch events, sport could account for as much as 6 percent of

GDP in the Western economies. That's bigger than farming or the auto industry.

So even to somebody like me who hates watching sport, any sport, it is nevertheless rather interesting. In fact, the sports industry is a wonderful test bed for economics. There is absolutely no shortage of statistics on performance, and all sorts of interesting twists to the structure of the job market and the industry. While some people like sport for its dramatization of the universal human struggle and the search for meaning in life, others among us prefer it for its demonstration of fundamental economic principles.

The really big money spinners are baseball, basketball, American football, and ice hockey, all in the United States; European soccer; and Japanese baseball. Only a few teams in any of these cases have managed to become truly global brands, like the Yankees or Manchester United, and only a few individuals like Michael Jordan or Tiger Woods are genuinely global stars. I couldn't name a Japanese baseball team if my life depended on it.

The team and league structures differ in each case, and the broadcasting arrangements, too. A country's sporting traditions are intertwined with its culture and history. So the institutional specifics vary quite widely. Nevertheless, two aspects make almost any sport economically interesting. One is the operation of a **labor market** where it is easy to tell how productive each individual is and how much he or she earns as a result. The other is the **industrial structure** of a business in which firms (the teams) need their competitors to remain successful enough to keep the competition interesting. A league won by the same team every year is really dull, so the weaker teams or players need to be good enough to deliver the bigger teams and star players their audience.

Take the labor market first. As every ambitious sports-mad kid now knows, becoming a top sportsman (not so often, yet, a sportswoman) is a potential avenue to unimaginable fame and wealth. Sports heroes rival, or surpass, movie stars and pop stars in their earnings potential. All of these are job markets in which **superstar** economics operates. This effect was first developed by economist Sherwin Rosen with reference to the entertainment industries and later extended to sport, and the idea has subsequently been popularized as the **"winner takes all"** phenomenon. Film stars or sports stars put in all the effort up front, and the amount of work they do is unrelated to the eventual size of their audience. David Beckham works no harder in a match for Manchester United when the TV audience is 20 million than when it is a million or none. The bigger the audience the better, in fact. There are spectacular **economies of scale** operating in the supply of sporting talent, like acting or singing talent, in the mass media world. What's more, audiences find it more convenient to watch stars than unknowns because they know what they are getting. There is none of the risk of disappointment you might get with a new face. So demand conditions reinforce the superstar effect.

The more important broadcasting revenues have grown in sport, the more striking the superstar effect. Top players' salaries have pulled way ahead of the average. It operates in almost every sport, not just team sports like soccer and baseball, but also individual sports such as tennis and golf.

This explains why a report by the accounting firm Deloitte & Touche in London found that players' pay packets had swallowed up virtually all the extra money English football clubs in the Premier League had gained from TV revenues. Manchester United spent £45 million on salaries in 1999–2000, of which its highest paid player got £2.8 million. The highest-paid player in the league got £3.6 million. Manchester United could afford it, but smaller clubs were having to pay high salaries to their players, too, and were making a loss. The league as a whole had a pretax loss of £34.5 million that year. The accountants recommended paying the stars as much as ever but cutting pay for the rest of the team.

To many people such high salaries are an obscenity. Actually, this attitude isn't new. In 1929, Babe Ruth earned $70,000. Challenged by a reporter to justify earning so much more than the president of the United States, he apparently said, "I had a better year." Still, the $10 million or more an American sports star could earn now compares favorably in real terms with Babe Ruth's modest income. Doesn't that make it all the harder to justify when teachers and nurses earn so little? What does the relative pay of Tiger Woods and a teacher tell us about our warped social values?

In fact, the evidence is clear that our societies value health and education far more than sport. Spending on either of these takes a share of GDP at least twice as big as sport, and considerably more than that in some countries. Many parents spend thousands of pounds or dollars a year on school and college fees but wouldn't dream of spending as much on attending baseball games or watching pay-per-view boxing on TV.

The difference in salary between a teacher and Tiger Woods is explained not by differences in how society values their contributions, but on the economies of scale operating in their respective professions. This is mainly due to the technology (the supply-side effect), and perhaps a bit to our greater willingness (demand side) to hero-worship sports stars than lecturers. Until we get to the point where a talented and effective teacher can reach a massive audience through TV or the Internet, the revenues that can accrue to an individual teacher will be limited by how many kids they can fit into their classroom. And indeed, some teachers in universities do have star status and correspondingly much greater incomes than their colleagues. The author of a successful textbook or a media don with newspaper columns and bestselling books is an example of superstar economics in teaching. The unit value per customer is probably similar in teaching and in sport, but the best athletes can reach a much bigger scale of audience than the best teachers. Sport is a low markup, high volume business.

Rather than proving different kinds of job are wrongly valued in our economies, the evidence from sport in fact demonstrates how well the labor market works. The pay of athletes can, uniquely, be linked to their performance as individuals. This is a huge contrast to any other industry, where figures for pay cover broad categories of people and where it is anyway hard to figure out what each person's or each group's **productivity** is. Even if a data set giving individual pay levels is available, productivity has to be proxied by other measures such as educational attainment, work experience, or family characteristics. With sports stars, there are objective measures of each athlete's performance.

The really satisfying news for economists is that the best players now get the highest pay! And this despite the fact that the job market in most sports is not fully competitive and open, at least after the initial signing. For example, until recently U.S. professional teams struck long-term exclusive contracts with players, with the sole legal right to transfer players to another team. In European soccer, transfers still involve large fees paid between clubs, a system at last under investigation by the European competition authorities. In no other industry except Hollywood have employers for so long been able to appropriate the human capital of their employees. The relatively recent switch to a system of individual contracts in U.S. sport has proven that wages are higher when workers, not employers, own the rights to the workers' performance.

Evidence from U.S. professional sports also revealed clear race discrimination in pay during the 1960s and '70s, which had mostly disappeared by the 1990s. The explanation for the change seems to be that fans started out disliking the idea of integrated teams—baseball had no nonwhite players at all before 1947—and were only willing to pay lower tick-et prices to see them play. (Up to a point; fans also like to see their team win.) By the 1990s fans had stopped caring; the consumer taste for dis-crimination in sports in America had evaporated, in a possibly encourag-ing signal of a wider shift in social attitudes to race. English soccer hasn't yet got to that point. Recent research has found that a team paying the same wage bill as a competitor but using more black players will perform better, or in other words, teams can pay a lower price for equal talent when the players are not white.

The introduction of free agency in sport might have raised pay for the players, but it does also give the teams less incentive to invest in talent. Just like the old Hollywood studio system, a team could formerly develop an unknown, lose money on many of them at first, but recoup the invest-ment in the rewards when they eventually develop a huge new star. Under free agency, players as a group do better, but as we've seen, some do a whole lot better than others. The others are probably losing out.

This will make striving to become a sports star an even bigger gamble than it has always been. It takes years of hard work to be good at a sport, with high risks of failure or injury or bad luck; but the probability of mak-ing a very large amount of money is indeed probably declining. The stars will do better, but there are fewer of them, and the typical player will do worse.

Whether this will shrink the supply of would-be players in future is an open question. Quality in sport has been increasing, but that too could cease if the supply of potential players diminishes. Recently U.S. team owners have used such arguments to strike a deal to restrict salary escala-tion among the top players, either on individuals or teams. Again, this is a unique phenomenon in the labor market.

It used to be argued, in defense of the old reserve contract system, that free competition in the sporting job market would allow rich teams to unfairly grab all the best players and make for a more boring contest because they would win all the time. However, a famous theorem in eco-nomics, first put forward by Ronald Coase, asserts that in terms of eco-nomic efficiency it doesn't matter who owns any given property right—ownership of players' human capital in this case—because any and every owner will want to achieve the most profitable outcome. The allo-cation of resources should be the same in either case. As long as teams could trade players freely, players would go to wherever they created the most market value, just as they would if they could compete directly in the job market themselves. In some sports the **Coase theorem** more or less holds. There is no decisive evidence in those cases that team quality has become less balanced than in the past. In others, like major league base-ball (so disgruntled fans have assured me), a clear gap has opened up between the best and the rest.

Meanwhile sports franchises sell for more than ever, so are clearly increasingly valuable despite the big wage bills. So it is hard to see the lat-est salary agreement between owners as anything other than a bid to recapture some of the economic rents they used to enjoy and lost with the advent of free agency.

At least two major areas of economic interest already, and we haven't yet touched on the fascinating industry structure in professional sport. Teams are not quite like companies in any other business. While most companies from Microsoft to the local café would like to destroy the com-petition, monopoly is no good at all to a sports team. It needs competi-tors, and it needs them to be good enough to keep the contest between them interesting. Otherwise potential spectators will watch *Big Brother* or *The Weakest Link* instead (and my goodness, these are much cheaper options for broadcasters than paying for the right to screen big sporting events). If football and baseball have been the twentieth-century equiva-lent of the Roman gladiatorial battles, these ghastly personality contests could turn into the twenty-first century equivalent if professional sport gets too boring.

Antitrust policies as applied to U.S. professional sports have long debated whether teams should be treated as individual businesses that should be competing but are in fact colluding; or whether instead a league is a single entity producing as its output a contest between teams, in which case the competition should be viewed as different leagues and different sports. (In the United States, teams compete in only one championship at a time; in Europe, typically in many at once, league and cup, internation-al and domestic.) The latter view has won out in practice, with a number of important antitrust exemptions granted to allow the collective sale of TV rights, for example, or to allow owners to reach collective agreements on pay structures. Similarly, the U.K.'s Restrictive Practices Court accepted the argument that the Premier League could sell broadcast rights to its teams' matches collectively because that would promote financial equali-ty between clubs, and stop the best clubs skimming off the bulk of the potential TV revenues by striking a separate deal with the broadcasters.

Whether fans mind imbalance all that much is a moot point—that is, an empirical question. As so many seem to support the best teams and want them to win all the time, collective well-being might be improved by less equality between teams rather than more. But of course supporters of the weakest teams would disagree. It is impossible to tell from theory alone. However, soccer-mad economist (not in fact a contradiction in terms) Stefan Szymanski has found that attendance has declined at matches in England's FA Cup competition, which have become more unequal, compared to the league matches, where the league structure means that like teams play like.

If it is right, then, to think of the contest as the industry's output, rather than the effort of individual teams, then the teams contribute jointly to the value they add to the game and might need to compensate each other. Sporting competition is the product consumers care about. Clearly if the weaker teams do not get the benefit of the value they add—if there is an **externality** in the pricing structure such that the private gains to an individual team are less than the social gains to the whole industry—they will have an inadequate incentive to compete. They won't invest enough in being good enough to keep the competition interesting.

Economists have not fully investigated the best way to solve this externality problem. A U.S.-style salary cap is one way to balance competition between weaker and stronger teams, but it punishes excellence. In European soccer the solution is punishment of weak teams by relegation to a lower league, which is very costly in terms of revenue loss. There is massive potential for future master's and Ph.D. theses in this area.

So, too, in the role of broadcasting in sport, a constantly evolving story. Market power in professional soccer, where Manchester United is without a doubt first among equals, is increasingly interacting with concentrations of market power in broadcasting. TV revenues are the most important source of income growth for the sport industry. For instance, the value of broadcast rights for American professional football doubled in real terms during the 1990s, mostly after 1997, when CBS reentered the bidding after the expiration of previous contracts from 1994–97, in which Fox had outbid it.

Similarly the cost of TV rights to English Premier League soccer matches climbed from £220,000 per live match in a contract starting in 1986 and £640,000 in a 1992 contract to £2.79 million in a four-year deal the league signed with satellite and cable broadcaster BSkyB in 1997. Competition among broadcasters for the rights to show sports that would attract lots of viewers has clearly gone too far, however. Another broadcaster, ITV Digital, decided that at £315 million it had overpaid for the rights to show the lesser-ranking Nationwide League soccer matches. Its owners put it into liquidation after paying the soccer clubs just £137 million of the total revenues they were banking on—a financial catastrophe for the many clubs already committed to high salary bills. What the outcome will be in the longer run for broadcasting revenues and star players' salaries is not at all clear.

So here, too, is wilderness territory waiting for pioneer researchers to stake their claims. If there is uncertainty about the competition implications of the structure of the sport, it is redoubled by the deals that are being struck with the less than perfectly competitive TV industry. This is a bigger worry in Europe, where not many people (apart from my husband and a few other sad cricket fans) care about any sport other than soccer and where the pay-broadcast market is more concentrated than across the Atlantic. But in both continents the sports industries clearly have the political muscle to be granted exemptions from the normal provisions of antitrust law. Can this be right? Not to an economist, not even one who really hates sports.

Chapter 5

MUSIC

The New Economy's Robber Barons

Bob Dylan turned sixty in May 2001. In an old BBC documentary rescreened to celebrate the great man's significant birthday, the young Bob—well, he would have been about forty then—said: "There was no money to be made in music when I started out. If you could support yourself, you was doin' good."

The music business has changed a lot in the space of two or three decades. There are, of course, lots of new bands, which are not nearly as good as the old bands I used to enjoy as a teenager. As my old dad used to say then, complaining about Dylan and Bowie, The Clash and Roxy Music, young people listen to absolute rubbish these days.

The technology of listening to music has also changed. When my husband and I were reminiscing about our favorite LPs, our ten-year-old said: "What's an LP?" They were as defunct to him as 78s and wind-up gramophones with big horns were to us. We have seen the invention of new broadcasting media, receiving and playing equipment, and formats. The Internet has joined TV and radio; big radios with valves gave way to portable transistor radios, to the personal stereo and CD player, and then to tiny MP3 players. Throughout each of these waves of astonishing technical change, the music industry has grown bigger and bigger.

According to industry figures, the global music market was worth

$38.5 billion in 2000, a 1 percent increase on the previous year. The United States accounted for the lion's share of this, with sales of $14.3 billion. (Japan trails a distant second, with about half the U.S.'s 37 percent share, followed even more distantly by the U.K. and Germany. No other individual markets are big enough to bother mentioning.) However, the Recording Industry Association of America (RIAA) reported for 2000 a small decrease in the value of sales compared with 1999, due to plunging sales of cassettes and CD singles.

Consumer preferences have swung decisively away from cassettes, whose share of the market dropped from 50 percent in 1990 to 4.9 percent a decade later, while the CD share rose from 38.9 percent in 1990 to 89.3 percent in 2000. However, the RIAA noted a "significant" increase in Internet sales direct from record labels' websites. Online sales, especially file-swapping services like Napster, hammered sales of CD singles, which plunged 38.8 percent in 2000 after trebling between 1995 and 1999. "Free access online seems to have had a dramatic effect on the singles sales market," the association's end-of-year report said. Who can doubt that accessing music online and storing on the new generation of portable devices like MP3 players is going to be the next wave?

It's also worth noting that along with the formats, although less visibly, the structure of the industry has utterly changed. Rather than shrinking like the technology, the music companies have been getting bigger and bigger. So the key change in industrial structure has been an increase in the degree of **market concentration**. Small, independent record labels are more marginal than ever; the music biz is highly concentrated among a few giant global corporations such as Sony, Bertelsmann, and EMI. Even some apparently independent labels are owned or partially owned by the big corporations as channels for the discovery of new talent.

Few artists have any market clout at all vis-à-vis the music corporations. One or two truly giant stars are the exceptions who prove the rule—David Bowie, for example, who was able to raise money by issuing bonds on the international capital markets, repaying investors with earnings from his back catalogue. However, few stars are big enough to be big businesses in their own right.

To the contrary, more artists are now very small businesses indeed, because they can self-publish. It is now very cheap and easy for artists to make their own music in the spare room and distribute it online. Yet what they lack as individual artists is the enormous marketing muscle it takes to turn a great song into a hit. The RIAA admits as much. In an article on its website about the costs of making a CD, it says: "Marketing and promotion are perhaps the most expensive part of the music business today." The scale at which the industry operates in marketing artists is what gives the corporations their power.

This isn't exactly the same kind of **scale effect** that gave the robber barons of American industry their fabulous wealth and influence at the turn of the nineteenth century. Then it took a lot of capital to build railroads or make steel. But it's really very similar. Now it takes a lot of capital to manufacture a pop star, or any increasingly all-purpose celebrity. The superstar effect that works for sports stars works for pop stars, too.

This, remember, means that audiences prefer known quantities rather than taking a risk on an unknown, and their preference can be satisfied when the **marginal cost** of transmitting the output of the favored performer is as low as the new technologies have made it. The rewards to being—and making—a star have been hugely magnified by the modern mass media. So along with the fact that new technologies have cut the cost of actually copying the music to zero, the importance of marketing and promotion means that the **economies of scale** exist in distribution and marketing rather than production; they are economies on the demand side, not the supply side. But they are big. Music is one of the core copyright industries (others include publishing, software, design, and film), which together accounted for 5 percent of U.S. GDP in 2000, more than any other industry group, including autos and auto suppliers. All the copyright industries tend to experience superstar effects. The giant corporations in these sectors are today's equivalent of the robber barons of the steel and oil industries in the heavy industrial economy of a hundred years ago.

In fact, the drive for domination is greater now than it was in the early twentieth century. The ideal for any of these companies now would be to capture the entire global market. Technological innovation has made manufacturing and distributing music very inexpensive. Once the backing musicians and studio technicians have been paid, copying CDs is cheap and distribution over the Internet is the next thing to zero cost. Operating at large scale is the most efficient. Ideally, Warner Brothers would like everybody on the planet to buy the next Madonna album because turning her into a star was a fixed cost and the ongoing cost of selling her music is very low. She enjoys huge economies of scale.

Music companies use their degree of **monopoly power** to charge a higher price than this low marginal cost, and split the difference between (in ascending order of size) royalties to the artists, the marketing budget and profits. The companies are able to use the monopoly power created by the large efficient scale of operation to set different prices to different types of customers. **Price discrimination** between national markets is the most common form (although it is outlawed within some national markets). The price of a CD by a popular group like U2 ranged in late 2000 from about $12 in New York to $13 in Madrid, $16 in Amsterdam and $19 in London.

No wonder, then, that Napster and similar Internet file-swapping services grew so popular. In fact, the same technology that is driving the music companies to try and grow bigger and more dominant in their market could also be the source of their downfall. It's not yet clear how the balance of market power between corporations and customers will settle—it is going to depend on the law, which backs the copyright owners, and the technology, which undermines the ability to protect copyrighted material. But there's some hope for music lovers. The music industry is one where rapid **technological innovation** is causing upheaval in the market. Technology is unleashing a tide of what the economist Joseph Schumpter called *creative destruction*, a period of great change that kills some businesses and gives birth to new ones. It poses a real challenge for **business strategy**.

Music fans have found they can store music on the hard disks of their computers as MP3 files and swap said music via Napster's servers for other people's collections. All of a sudden it was possible to build up a vast collection of free music. If you heard a song and liked it, you could just download it instead of paying close to $20 for that song bundled with a bunch of others on a CD. By the end of 1999 Napster had a million users a month.

It was at this point that the Recording Industry Association of America sued Napster, incidentally helping to publicize the service. A year later there were 9 million users a month, not to mention other file-swapping services like Gnutella and Freenet, Aimster and OpenNap, some using central servers but others not. The RIAA argued, mainly through spokesmen like the heavy metal band Metallica, that Napster was cheating artists of their rightful rewards for their creativity. Why, they asked, would anybody struggle to make a name for themselves, go on exhausting tours, work hard at new albums, take lots of drugs, and have sex with a different groupie every night (no, of course they didn't really say that last bit) if the financial rewards were going to be undercut by unlawful breach of copyright as kids swapped music files for free over the Internet? Eventually the courts found in favor of the RIAA, concluding that Napster was breaching copyright. Napster itself has been struggling to go legit since the February 2001 judgment, having signed a deal with Bertelsmann to ensure that only listeners who have paid can download files. The business is surviving but hardly thriving, with Bertelsmann providing an emergency financial restructuring in May 2002.

What about the 50 million plus young music lovers who have grown used to swapping files over the Net? Will they shrug their shoulders and return to the habit of buying CDs whose tracks they mostly haven't heard and with no flexibility about how the pieces of music they buy are packaged together? Will they be happy to once again start paying $20 for every one of these prepackaged items? To pose the questions is to answer them. As the industry figures cited earlier demonstrate, Napster and similar services have probably destroyed the CD singles market (although 56 million were still sold in America in 2000, as many as there are Napster users). The music industry declared war on its best customers in the Napster case. Even if we take a charitable view of what has happened, the corporate tactics have been heavy-handed.

Napster gave its users two things they really valued. One was free music. The other was more choice. Customers tend to like both lower prices and additional choice.

The industry could have taken a different tack without abandoning its defense of copyright by acknowledging that customers would prefer the new distribution method made possible by the new technologies. It could have welcomed the idea of selling individual songs online, perhaps for a registration fee, perhaps for a small charge per song. Music fans like to get music for free, sure, but most would be willing to pay something for the ability to swap files legally. It could even have decided to give them away online through the labels' own sites in order to attract customers for full-length CDs. After all, CD singles accounted for a small fraction of industry sales, $222 million out of $14.6 billion, or 1.5 percent of the market, in their peak year.

The strategy would probably give the music industry lower profit margins than selling high-priced CDs to a captive market that can't get access to the music any other way—but then it's a sad fact of life for the music barons that there is now an alternative means of accessing music, and there is nothing any of them can do about it. Popular technologies—and Napster's subscriber base of 50 million music fans counts as popular enough—do not vanish until something better comes along. A number of new Internet music ventures are therefore starting up subscription services, mostly backed by big corporations such as Vivendi and Sony. Napster gained lots of headlines, but it will prove to have been the tip of an enormous new iceberg.

The industry might actually have found that file swapping increases demand for music. For it is possible that free online access to some songs could eventually boost sales by allowing users to sample work by artists whose music they would never have bought on impulse but discovered they liked. In other words, free file swapping is equivalent to the free sachets of shampoo or face cream that manufacturers hand out to get you to buy their brand, or even the free sample CDs that sometimes come attached to magazines and newspapers. (It works, too. I've bought full-length CDs from several popular music combos I'd otherwise have imagined were far too young and trendy for me.) It's a tried and tested marketing device.

The worst fears of the big corporations are almost certainly overblown. Other technologies have been seen as posing a threat to earnings from copyright in the past. The early arguments about radio were very similar to those made now about file sharing over the Net, with free broadcasts expected to make it impossible for musicians ever to earn a living again. Photocopiers were seen as a fatal threat to book publishing, and VCRs were expected to undermine the movie industry. But in each case, when consumers value the final product, the issue has been the distribution of the profits rather than their existence. What's more, the pattern has been that the falling cost of reproduction of artistic output, whether acting or music or words, has favored the biggest companies and the biggest stars, because of the creation and reinforcement of demand-side economies of scale.

The Internet did unleash a wave of optimism about the scope for removing the need for intermediaries between performers and audience. While that is certainly technically feasible and cheap, creating the demand for specific performers is expensive, so there is no urgent threat to the record companies as intermediaries between artists and listeners.

The Internet does, though, pose a threat to the music industry's current system of distribution. The industry is still sticking with its hardball tactics to defend the status quo, however. The most recent figures available show worldwide music sales fell 5 percent in 2001, with declines in many big markets including the United States, according to the International Federation of Phonographic Industries. The reason for the fall isn't hard to find. Monitoring companies report that there are dozens of new file-swapping communities, post-Napster. According to one of the monitors, one single type of software that allows file swapping was downloaded 3.2 million times in one week, and 5.3 million users were offering a copy of Linkin Park's *Hybrid Theory*. What the industry wants to do is get lawmakers to make it illegal to sell hardware, such as the machines that burn music onto blank CDs, with the capacity to copy non-encrypted music and films. It wants anti-piracy measures hardwired, on the grounds that this is the only way to protect intellectual property and ensure musicians get paid.

But it's not the only way. There are many other ways to structure payment for music. The fuss about copyright theft and piracy is a red herring. Going forward, paying for music will simply have to be different from the industry's preferred structure of making customers buy a package of a dozen or so tracks for a relatively large amount of money. It might involve lower profit margins—it's hard to imagine them getting higher—in which case the corporations will need to try to increase the total size of the market.

Any set of institutional arrangements has supporters with strong vested interests in its preservation, and so it is with prerecorded CDs. Online music sales will not be good news for these people, who include the manufacturers, the shops that sell them, and the record labels that refuse to adapt. Metallica has claimed file swapping might stop them creating any more music, so a general move online would be bad for them and their fans, too. However, manufacturers of MP3 players and computers that can burn music onto blank CDs will do well from it. So will the record labels and musicians that decide to sell individual tracks for small sums over the Internet. Oh yes, and so will the customers.

So that's the choice facing the industry: give the customers what they want, or pursue anyone who dares try to do that through the courts. It's a tough one. The industry is still leaning heavily toward hammering consumers. But new technologies usually end up benefiting the customers, not the companies, although as past experience with robber barons shows, it can take quite a struggle to get to that point.

Chapter 6

FOOD FIGHTS

Helping Lame Ducks Waddle

If paper clip manufacturers were given a multibillion-dollar subsidy direct from the government, and gained as much again in extra revenues because the government restricted imports of cheaper foreign paper clips, you might imagine they'd be pretty contented about the state of business. Even better if the subsidy from the taxpayers took the form of a guaranteed minimum price per paper clip that exceeded the cost of manufacture. And if that meant there were mountains of unwanted paper clips dotted at sites around the country so the government switched to paying manufacturers not to make any more paper clips—well, that would be even more pleasing. Money for doing nothing.

It would obviously be a mad policy to apply to the paper clip industry. Yet we seem to think it makes sense for farming.

Few people realize the scale of farm support or the almost total degree of protection agriculture gets from international competition. In the European Union direct agricultural subsidies from the taxpayer amount to just under 60 billion euros a year, and farmers get an additional hidden subsidy of over 60 billion euros a year from consumers because import restrictions keep prices about a third above world market levels. This is enough money to buy every one of Europe's 45 million cows a round-the-world first-class air ticket. In the United States, the support amounts to

$100 billion a year, or about $370 per person. Total OECD agricultural support is worth over $300 billion a year. That's more than the GDP of all of Africa. It exceeds the annual profits of the twenty-five biggest companies in the world, from General Electric to Home Depot and Philip Morris. No other industry gets anything like the same degree of subsidy. In fact, all other industries put together do not get a state handout as big as agriculture's.

Not surprisingly, setting government-guaranteed artificially high prices for many agricultural products has led to overproduction—this is pretty straightforward economics. The market price of anything is determined by cost or supply conditions and demand, but if the government is going to pay a higher than market price, producers will supply more than buyers want at that higher price.

The result of oversupply in agriculture is a surfeit of all kinds of foodstuffs, from sheep to sugar beets. For example, the U.K.'s sheep population before the recent epidemic of foot-and-mouth disease had climbed to 21 million, or one for every three humans. New Zealand recently abolished sheep-farming subsidies altogether, but then it had long passed the point where it had more sheep than people. No longer does the EU's surplus butter mountain weigh more than the population of Austria, as it did in the early 1980s, but only because the Common Agricultural Policy has started to subsidize farmers to produce nothing instead of producing too much.

In short, farming, which accounts for between 1 percent of GDP (in the U.K.) and 3 percent (in Italy)—in other words, not much—is sucking in a subsidy equivalent to 38 percent of its output in Europe. In the United States, where average farm profits are higher because farms are bigger and can take advantage of economies of scale, agriculture still gets a 22 percent subsidy.

Who pays for the subsidy? We do, both as taxpayers and as buyers of food. There is in effect a tax of 25 to 35 percent on food prices due to government price support schemes and restrictions on imports. To spell that out, a $100 family grocery bill would be just $75 to $80 without the special protection for agriculture.

So why do farmers always complain that they are on the verge of bankruptcy? And if so many are feeling the pinch, what would it take to set this lame duck industry waddling on its own two feet?

The answer to the first question is that farming is tough for a very simple reason: there are too many farmers. Miners, steelworkers, and shipyard workers have all in recent decades been through the same harrowing experience of being surplus to the economy's requirements. In addition, farming in the U.S. and EU is divided into big agribusinesses, which are doing rather nicely thanks to economies of scale and huge subsidies, and struggling small farms, which can't compete on the same terms despite their subsidies. The big-business farms don't need the handouts, and the small farms are not going to be saved by them.

Industries decline because of changes in supply and demand. On the supply side, farming technology has changed, with more intensive methods and new breeds of crops (genetically modified the old-fashioned way by crossbreeding, and in the future, genetically modified the high-tech way), making it more productive. Productivity gains in agriculture mean the same amount of grain or pork or whatever can be produced with less labor and even a bit less land, too, which is why only 1 to 5 percent of the workforce in the OECD countries works the land now, down from between 25 and 50 percent a century ago. In addition, technical improvements and cost reductions in transportation mean low-cost supplies from other countries are able to compete with domestic farm output—when not kept out by trade barriers.

On the demand side, **consumer tastes** have changed. Consumers everywhere have developed more varied tastes and grown used to almost all produce being available at all seasons. Few would be happy to eat only what could be homegrown, never mind just locally grown, as some environmentalists would prefer. Even bananas were considered an exotic luxury in the postwar years, whereas now all kinds of tropical fruits are commonplace. Sushi has grown into a global industry, and a modified Indian cuisine has become a British staple, requiring imported spices and vegetables. Would anyone in Britain want to revert to the rightly notorious traditional cuisine of overcooked beef and boiled cabbage? Or give up lemons and bananas? I think not. Consumers are now used to a far more varied range of foods, despite the artificially high cost of imported foodstuffs.

These changes have occurred against a background of scant liberalization in agricultural trade. There has been little to no reduction in import restrictions on the shipment of farm products into OECD countries for decades. This is a real bone of contention for developing countries, which are becoming increasingly determined that trade liberalization will have to include agriculture in future. Their anger forced agricultural protection onto the agenda for the round of trade negotiations launched in Doha, Qatar, in November 2001, and reduced levels of protection are due to be negotiated. Trade disputes over food products flare up frequently, although often between the U.S. and the EU, by far the two most protectionist authorities when it comes to agriculture.

In farming, both in Europe and North America, the pain of long-term structural decline is being dragged out because the industry still experiences such high levels of protection from imports and domestic surplus capacity. Of course there are excellent political reasons for this. The experience of World War II made self-sufficiency in food seem imperative, at least in the starving European nations, right after 1945. Food also has an important place in every culture, whether it is simply a matter of different tastes or of deeper religious belief and social ritual. After all, even McDonald's has to adapt its menus to suit each country.

Farmers are also in every country a powerful and effective political lobby, with techniques ranging from emotional blackmail through campaign contributions all the way to dumping manure the length of the Champs Elysées. Small and focused groups are often the most effective lobbyists, especially when they can offer as their visual icons for the TV cameras cuddly lambs or golden prairies. Such images tug at the heartstrings far more than an economist with gray hair and glasses tapping away at a computer ever could. They are all the more effective because everybody feels genuine admiration for the smaller farmers trying to preserve our rural heritage while producing high quality food. That should not, though, divert us from the realization that profitable industrial farming has no need for our tax dollars.

What's more, government subsidies do make a real difference to farmers because the benefits cannot get competed away. If paper clip manufacture were subsidized, a lot of new firms would go into the business and compete prices back down. But with a more or less fixed supply of farmland and number of farmers, new entrants are not going to be attracted into the farming business by all that taxpayer largesse.

However, it is hard to believe the appropriate public policies should have changed so little in the past fifty-plus years. The economist's agricultural policy prescription for the twenty-first century is straightforward but radical. Liberalize trade; pull the plug on the grotesque subsidies; and if you must compensate the workers of the land until they can cope with commercial realities like everybody else in the economy, subsidize them to do something consumers actually want, such as running nature preserves or golf courses.

Trade first. Economists think about trade in a way that most people find strange and counterintuitive. Common sense says exports are better than imports. Economics says this is wrong: the benefits from international trade come from being able to import more things at lower prices, while the exporting is just what you need to do to pay for imports. Common sense says countries are competing against each other to increase exports, an idea encouraged by various competitiveness "league tables." Economists say that all countries gain from trade, that there are no losers. In fact, it is even worthwhile being the only country reducing trade barriers because the cheaper imports will increase consumer welfare. If you must compare countries in a league table, then something like income per head or the human development index is the best available ranking.

These contrasting attitudes come about because economics is about increasing the well-being of individuals, not about, say, having the biggest car industry or the richest farmers in the world.

As Adam Smith pointed out in *The Wealth of Nations*, it would be perfectly feasible to grow greenhouse grapes and make a very fine burgundy in Scotland, but nobody has ever thought it sensible to ban or tax imports of wine from France into the U.K. because the effort and expense of producing it at home would be too high. So the Scots export whisky and the French export wine.

The basic principle of international trade is that countries should export the products in which they have a **comparative advantage**. This is another of the cornerstone concepts in economics. If country A is better at producing shoes than clothes and country B better at clothes than shoes (even if country A does both better than country B), A should export shoes and B clothes. International specialization ensures global production is efficient, occurring at the lowest cost, which makes consumers in both countries better off.

International trade is simply a means for getting access to the technology and resources of another country, in the most efficient possible mix with your own. Trade is almost always a win-win affair for consumers— that is, people. Us.

Of course, domestic producers of those items in which another country has a comparative advantage don't see it that way. Often they will argue that their industry needs protection from "unfair" cheap imports to safe-guard jobs, because they are not able to match the low costs of goods produced in sweatshops or farmed on plantations overseas.

However, plentiful and cheap labor is precisely the source of comparative advantage in many developing countries. They *ought* to be specializing in the export of labor-intensive products like basic textiles or fresh produce, just as rich countries ought to be specializing in capital- and knowledge-intensive goods and services. Unless the developing nations can grow their economies, too, they will be stuck at cheap labor levels of income forever, so short of a magic wand the more they can export, the more they grow, and the faster wages rise in future.

Small European countries, short of land and densely populated, certainly do *not* have a comparative advantage in agriculture. It is a different matter producing grain in North America, but Americans and Canadians would be better off, too, if imports of many agricultural products were liberalized.

If protectionists in developed countries win the argument, they indeed save some jobs in factories or on farms that might otherwise vanish, but saving these jobs imposes a cost on every consumer who buys the product and also prevents the creation of other jobs. Restricting trade protects some citizens at the expense of others. It raises prices, fewer of the protected items are bought, consumers have less to spend on everything else, and the economy grows less. These costs can be high, depending on what's being protected, but they are widely spread and hard to assess, whereas it is easy to spot the 5,000 jobs that might vanish if a particular company goes bankrupt because of competition from abroad, or the small farms that will go under.

The general arguments about the benefits of trade and the allure of protectionism apply to agricultural output just as much as anything else. Substitute any agricultural products for whisky and wine or shoes and clothes, and the reasoning is the same. What makes wheat or butter any different from shoes and cars? The only possible reason would be food security, but the modern world has already gone far beyond national self-sufficiency in food. This mattered very much in a country like Britain when enemy U-boats blockaded the ports, but another naval war like that really does seem rather unlikely.

So farmers should be weaned off import protections. We'd pay less for our food—something low-income families especially would appreciate, as the food bill can make up half their family budget—and have more to spend on the services and goods produced by other industries. What about the direct agricultural subsidies? Is there a good reason why farming should receive more in government aid than all other industries put together, especially when the typical farmer is a well-off businessman, not a struggling son of the land?

The answer is no, and not only because the money could be used for better purposes. The price guarantees have harmed farmers, too. They have kept in business some less-productive farms and guaranteed an oversupply of many agricultural products. In their desperation to make a profit in these hypercompetitive conditions, farmers have been driven to increasingly environmentally damaging intensive production methods. This is especially true in Western Europe, where geography means the economies of scale enjoyed on farms in the U.S. Midwest or in some Latin American and Eastern European countries are out of reach.

The doomed quest for competitiveness in an industry with too many suppliers kept alive by the drip feed of taxpayers' money has led to the use of increasingly powerful chemical fertilizers. It can be blamed for the bovine spongiform encephalopathy (otherwise known as mad cow disease) epidemic, spread by farmers insisting on ever-cheaper feed for their cattle, a demand met by rendering scrapie-infected sheep carcasses. Similarly, Britain's foot-and-mouth epidemic was exacerbated by the practice of hustling thousands of animals around the country to centralized distribution centers and abattoirs—and also to other farms for short stays that would enable farmers to claim they had bigger flocks and were therefore entitled to bigger government subsidies.

Abolition of farm subsidies would certainly put many farmers out of business. That would be the point.

Easing people through the transition of the perpetual industrial restructuring that takes place in the economy is a valid use of public funds. So there's no doubt some of the tax money used for farm support would have to be used instead for some time to enable farmers to switch their land to other uses, or sell it for other uses such as forestry or country parks, or to retrain the people affected and help them move to alternative jobs. Land prices would fall directly when the subsidies were removed, and it might therefore be thought desirable to pay a one-shot amount of compensation, as a matter of political tactics if nothing else. Governments might also think it a good idea to subsidize different countryside activities—wildlife conservation for environmental reasons, for example. There is no doubt mistakes would be made in alternative uses of public funds, too, but they would be much less expensive ones.

The hope would be that farmers or other purchasers of the land would opt for commercially viable activities instead of milking the government. In other words, the countryside would be used for activities that reflected people's preferences as indicated by what they are willing to pay for. Tourism, after all, accounts for a bigger share of GDP than agriculture (more than 6 percent in the U.K. compared to just over 1 percent for agriculture) and is growing rapidly.

The bottom line is that if you believe farming is worth such massive financial support from taxpayers and consumers, when steel production or shipbuilding or coal mining was not worth a far smaller amount of subsidy, you need a noneconomic argument to justify it. National security will hardly do, as many countries have allowed their shipbuilding skills to vanish; if they need a new warship in future, they'll have to import it. (Nor were farmers notably supportive of the declining mining or shipbuilding industries twenty years ago.)

In the end, continuing farm support boils down to sentiment exploited by a powerful special interest group. And to ignorance, too. Few people realize just how expensive their food is because of agricultural subsidies. Do we really feel warm and happy enough about farmers to pay an extra third on top of the price of our grocery bills? Think about what you would do with another $25 or $50 a week, and see if it changes your mind about how big farm subsidies should be.

Part II

WHAT GOVERNMENTS ARE GOOD FOR

Public Goods, Externalities, and Taxes

Most economists, like any citizens, are interested in aspects of public policy, or in other words, what governments do. Government plays an important role in our lives, one that is continually developing and certainly not shrinking. Quite the reverse: public policies are becoming ever more significant in setting the framework in which we go about our work and business.

The following chapters look at some important and topical examples of what governments do, using a powerful intellectual tool kit that can apply to many kinds of policy. The aim is to demonstrate the particular kind of critical attention economics can bring to bear on some of the really stupid things people—politicians or pundits—often say about government policy.

Chapter 7

INFRASTRUCTURE

But I Never Travel by Train

Should the government own and run the railways? To a Continental European, the answer is obviously yes; to an American, obviously no. To a Briton, the formerly publicly owned, then privatized national rail system appears to have brought the worst of both worlds. It seems to offer the certainty of delay and disruption together with the alarmingly high risk of death in an accident, all at high prices, and there is a vigorous debate as to whether it should be renationalized.

The rail system is a good example of the difficulty of figuring out what governments can do better than the private sector. In theory this is pretty straightforward. There is a role for the government whenever there is a **market failure**. If the private sector would not produce enough of a particular good or service because the social gains exceed any private gains they might reap, then the government should step in. Thus in the case of big projects such as constructing a national rail network or building a tunnel under the English Channel, private sector companies might well not be able to recoup an adequate return on their investment from fares on any reasonable time horizon. The private sector incentives, and hence the need for government involvement, are likely to differ in different places and at different times. There can also be additional motivations such as social fairness in the provision of free or subsidized public services such as defense or education to people who could not otherwise afford them. But the basic justification for raising and spending taxes is the existence of an externality that means the market would deliver a less than ideal level of provision of the service in question.

In practice, however, different countries vary enormously in what activities take place in the public rather than the private sector. The size of government in rich OECD countries varies widely between the United States and Sweden, both, like all those in between, very prosperous economies. What's more, the boundary changes over time. A number of European countries have followed Britain's lead in privatizing certain nationalized industries, getting the government out of providing (although not out of regulating) those activities. At the same time, the scope of government has increased in other directions, mainly new or growing types of welfare spending such as housing and sickness benefits and pensions. The public-private boundary therefore clearly reflects voter preferences and historical accident, rather than any objective assessment of the existence of any market failures or indeed pure ideology.

That doesn't mean there are no economic principles involved in drawing the boundary, however. The long experiment in planned economies behind the Iron Curtain demonstrated comprehensively that the public sector is really bad at many kinds of economic activity. It's lousy at producing the right number of pairs of shoes in the right sizes and colors. It can't innovate in consumer electronics. It finds it really difficult to produce enough grain or vegetables. In many Eastern Bloc countries, it actually banned jazz, fiction, and other popular arts that consumers would like to have purchased. Almost everybody had housing, but the quality was dreadful. The list goes on and on.

On the other hand, the communist experience suggests the government can be reasonably good at the delivery of a high average level of education and health care, at basic scientific research, and at the development and popularization of high quality sports and the highbrow arts such as ballet and opera. Public transport in precapitalist Eastern Europe was cheap and frequent, and the quality was generally rather high, a legacy that lingers on. Any Briton waiting for hours today in a tatty station for a delayed commuter train can only dream wistfully of Budapest's trams or the Prague metro, so marked has been the decline of parts of the privatized U.K. system.

Rail systems are an example of the infrastructure, the physical skeleton of the economy. The national infrastructure includes roads, water and sewage systems, street lighting, telephone and electric cables, canals, bridges and dams, air traffic control, radio and mobile phone towers, hospitals and schools, parks, benches, art galleries, and many other things. Some of these are almost always state-owned and -run, others nearly always in private hands but highly regulated. They are also a subject of perpetual electoral dispute. If I never take the train, why should I want to see the government subsidize the rail network? People who are not parents think education provision is less important than health, and the elderly always want bigger pensions. However, what distinguishes all of these examples from goods and services that we'd all agree should be privately provided, run, and paid for is the existence of an important externality.

Externalities can take several forms, requiring different kinds of government response. Some of these goods and services are **natural monopolies**—for example, it would be inefficient to have more than one set of streetlights down each road or more than one hydroelectric dam across a river or more than one main electricity cable into each home or more than one set of rail tracks on the same line. Replication would be either physically impossible or simply highly inefficient because there are such huge economies of scale—either in supply, as in these examples, or in demand, as in the case of the **network externalities** involved in the telephone system, whereby having a phone is more useful the more other phones you can connect to.

Some are public goods and services whose consumption is **non-rival**: if I walk in the park it doesn't stop you doing so, too, so the additional cost of an extra visitor is zero. With this **zero marginal cost** the economically efficient price is zero, and unless the place becomes really crowded it would be inefficient for the park's owner to charge me an entry fee for each additional visit. Covering **fixed costs** like buying flowers and paying a park keeper is most efficiently done through a fixed fee such as an annual membership fee or a local tax. But determining what level that should be—what quantity of park services—is inherently collective. It depends on all the potential park users. Parks are one example of **public goods.**

Finally, some are goods and services where individuals do impinge on each other's use, but it isn't possible to prevent this. Transport and roads offer the classic example of this **nonexcludability**. Often they become congested, so each additional user raises the costs for all the others, in terms of delay, aggravation, extra gasoline, or whatever. Or there can be environmental externalities such as pollution. However, it is not often possible to exclude the "excessive" users. **Peak-load** and **off-peak pricing** can distinguish between people who value their time and space most highly, like business travelers on the railways as opposed to tourists or commercial users of electricity rather than households. New technologies mean commuters can now be charged more for driving into the city during rush hour. But beyond such broad-brush strategies (whose scope is nevertheless clearly being extended and refined by new technology), users cannot be made to reveal that they value a swift journey especially highly by paying more for it. There is no mechanism for distinguishing how much value each individual puts on the service and no reason to believe the market will provide the socially efficient amount of the service.

As the examples make clear, externalities are many and varied. Technology is constantly changing what is feasible in terms of solutions. And different countries have anyway opted for different solutions.

Here are three basic principles that always apply, however.

First, the government can almost always raise large amounts of money more cheaply than private sector borrowers. Whether it's done by raising taxes (which do nevertheless impose economic inefficiencies) or by borrowing in the capital markets, the cost of finance will be lower for a publicly funded than a privately funded project. This is because there is less risk involved in lending to the government, as investors count on a guarantee that it can always raise taxes to pay the interest. National or federal governments rarely default, although local governments are more likely to, and the fact that government bonds are not very risky means investors will be satisfied with a lower rate of interest on the money they have loaned. So government funding of a big investment project with social benefits in excess of private benefits will often be the most attractive financing option.

Second, the government almost always runs things more badly than the private sector. The "customers" (although more usually given a name reflecting their powerless status, such as *patients, pupils, users,* or *claimants*) can't usually withdraw their patronage from a state monopoly. Nor is there any profit motive to sharpen up employees' act. Public sector staff are less well paid and consequently sometimes less well qualified and dynamic than people working in the private sector, not to mention often more highly unionized and prone to industrial action. And a business run by planners will lack the diversity and speedy information flows of a business operating in the marketplace, the nimbleness to expand what's going well and pull the plug on whatever's doing badly. The admission of mistakes is usually prevented by bureaucratic politics. In many Western democracies, there is also ample public sector corruption, which probably has the edge over private sector corruption.

Third, wherever there is a significant social externality, the government will have to play a role anyway, whether providing the service directly or regulating whoever is providing it. Think of a mixed public-private education system, for instance. Democratic government is the mechanism we have for resolving social conflicts such as those potentially created by economic externalities, for balancing the interests of drivers and cyclists, parents and pensioners, and it is by far the best mechanism for doing so. The fact that such social externalities exist explains why there are few examples of privately financed and operated infrastructure projects anywhere in the world (although there are many examples of services that can be run successfully by the private sector as well as the public sector, and there is a huge amount of government subcontracting to businesses). While it is true that there is no obvious minimum level of public **ownership**, the idea that there could be radically less government involvement in the economy at all ignores the need to balance different interests through **regulation**.

Needless to say, it can be very hard to get regulation right, as California's dire experience of electricity shortages in 2000 demonstrated. The power companies were unable to meet surging demand at the height of the Internet frenzy, and the state suffered a series of rolling power cuts or brownouts. While the companies were clearly playing a game of brinksmanship with the state regulators, it is also clear that the state authorities were trying to achieve the impossible: they had capped retail electricity prices at a time when demand was surging and the oil price had jumped sharply. The generating companies were simply forbidden to pass on the increase in their costs or respond in the natural way with higher prices to an increase in demand given their fixed amount of capacity. The episode is a good demonstration of the fact that regulators have to balance a lot of different and often conflicting interests, such as consumers of electricity (many of them California voters) and investors in the power companies—but while California's electricity regulators were adept at the politics, good regulators must have a better understanding of the economics, too.

Regulation is so complicated that there is a huge and inconclusive economic literature on how to do it well. But there are good reasons for opt-ing for publicly regulated but privately owned utilities like electricity or telecommunications. The fact that public utilities owned by the state and run by bureaucracies provide a lousy service was one of the reasons Mrs. Thatcher's Conservative government in the U.K. was so committed to **privatization** during the 1980s. In many cases privatization did indeed improve service quality and innovation—the telephone system is the prime example. Previously Britons had had to wait weeks or months to have a phone line installed, often had to share lines with neighbors, and paid high charges. (It wasn't quite as bad as Ghana, where the waiting time for a phone from the state-owned telephone company is *seventy-five years*.)

British Telecom's (BT) first decade in private ownership brought huge successes and possibly contributed to an improvement in the whole economy's growth potential. Similarly the introduction of competition in a privatized electricity industry brought down prices paid by consumers and led to higher investment and better service quality.

Yet others saw little improvement. Some water companies found themselves unable to supply water during dry summers or to maintain water cleanliness in the rivers and streams. Rail passengers found themselves treated much more politely, but investment in the network fell to a literally catastrophically low level due to the lack of adequate incentives to maintain and upgrade track and signaling equipment, as a number of fatal accidents during the 1990s revealed.

Even the successes have not been unqualified, with questions now emerging over how effectively they have been regulated. For example, local telephone charges have remained high in the U.K. compared to the U.S. because BT, the former state monopoly, was not forced to open the local loop, the natural monopoly of the last bit of wire linked to individuals' homes, to competitors on commercially viable terms.

As for the failures, a proposal to **nationalize** the rail system once again would shock and alarm very few British voters, and we might yet get it. Interestingly, some water and energy utilities are starting to separate the regulated parts of their business from the nonregulated parts, to raise funds more cheaply for the former and free the latter to pursue broader commercial options. Thus Welsh Water has created a nonprofit water supply business, and British Gas has put its regulated gas supply business and its other activities into separate companies. BT, the phone company, recently announced plans to do the same.

Privatization is interesting because it amounts to a large-scale experiment in moving the public-private boundary. But the boundary is in a sense moving back toward where it was before. Shifting the *ownership* of utilities and infrastructure businesses, or even their *management,* from public to private sector appears to have been in some sense cosmetic. There is something special about these businesses that means they can't be just like any other private sector business.

The rail system is a good case study of the issues involved because it was the creation of the private sector and in the United States has stayed in the hands of the private sector, albeit with significant government involvement. Britain saw the building of its network in the mid-nineteenth century, followed by all the rest of the world. There was a massive stock market boom in the shares of both British and overseas rail companies. Finance raised on the London Stock Exchange funded a large proportion of the initial global rail network. The bubble burst in 1848, and many investors never saw a return on the cash they had put into this hot new technology, which would clearly boost economic growth in any country developing a rail network. In fact, it was rather like the 1999–2000 Internet share boom. Investors were voting massively with their money in an act of faith in the future. The stock market did what it is supposed to, and channeled finance to a high growth sector that held out the promise of high economic returns.

In the case of rail, however, these turned out to be social rather than private returns. For example, rail allowed the development of mass urban markets because fresh food could be transported into the cities from further afield. London no longer needed a large population of cows to provide milk, but could bring the milk in by rail. But these widely dispersed social spillover benefits could not be fully captured in the prices charged for rail transportation. The profits of the rail companies were disappointing and share prices plunged.

Britain was left, however, with an extensive but low profit rail network that was nationalized by the Labour government after World War II. Under public management it became decreasingly profitable and eventually came to eat up large amounts of public subsidy. In particular, investment in upgrading the track and rolling stock needed to be funded by taxpayers. But the large subsidies led to cost-cutting, notoriously in 1968 when many lightly used branch lines were closed down because more people started to be able to afford cars.

So by the time the Conservatives decided to privatize British Rail in

1996 there was an entrenched pattern of incessant cost-cutting, underinvestment, bad management, and dismal industrial relations. The sale to the private sector did not raise funds for the government. Rather, it had to hand over large sums of money to entice investors to buy shares in the new rail operating companies and induce these companies to bid for franchises to operate services on the different parts of the network. A separate company, Railtrack, was created with responsibility for track upkeep and investment. Even now the government has to continue feeding large sums of money into the ever-open maw of the rail system, for without a subsidy it is clear the private companies would not invest enough to provide the standard of service demanded by the public.

Contrast first the United States. Its rail companies were built privately, although with a not-so-hidden public subsidy in the form of favorable land deals and grants. They have always remained private. Today's operators were created by a series of mergers and operate as geographic monopolies except that they compete with the highway system. America's automobile culture, cheap gasoline, and extensive highway network, followed by its equally extensive air network, mean rail transportation has never been as important, any monopoly position never as powerful, as in the small and crowded nations of Europe. Its additional social benefits are much smaller than in the European case. In fact, if history had turned out a bit differently and the technology of the internal combustion engine had come before the technology of rail transportation, the railways might never have been built in America.

Contrast, too, Continental Europe, where no government has ever imagined it made sense not to subsidize the rail network in order to provide the service the public wants. With less land, crowded urban roads, and lower levels of income, there would probably always have been railways in Europe even if roads and cars had been around at the same time. Now most European countries have clean, fast trains, plentiful investment, and an extensive network that could never make a commercial profit but keeps all inhabitants within easy reach of affordable rail travel. Rail privatization has never been on the agenda on the Continent.

Britain's characteristic mid-Atlantic position is clearly uncomfortable. Should it now head in the American direction, and settle for a small but perhaps ultimately profitable private rail system? This would not reach all of the country and would probably be even smaller than today's network. After all, the profitable services are those taking commuters into cities and those connecting big cities. Some of the freight, as well as passengers, currently transported by rail would shift to the roads.

Or in the European direction? That would involve the recognition that a bigger and more comprehensive network will always need a public subsidy because the private return is smaller than the social benefits, in which case either public ownership or detailed government regulation of the service quality would be inevitable.

Public discontent with the current situation suggests British voter preferences point to the European solution. That certainly seems in line with my argument that the social benefits of a rail network are higher when alternative means of transportation like the roads, for unavoidable reasons of geography and history, do not compete directly with rail. Britain, too, is a small and crowded country with as many roads as it is ever going to have. Driving has a high private and social cost.

This highlights a broader point. The public-private boundary will always be fluid. It starts from where it is in each country anyway: the legacy of history is inescapable. The term often used to describe this is **path dependency**. But in addition technological change will shift the boundary over time. For example, mobile telephones have made fixed telephony look less like a natural monopoly; in Africa, there have been since 2001 more mobile phones than fixed lines in use because the new technology has allowed people to escape the clutches of inefficient state-owned fixed-line monopolies. Smart cards and electronic monitoring have made it feasible to exclude some drivers from the roads at certain times. Faxes and email created new forms of competition with the old postal monopolies. The social benefits of one service could also change for other reasons, perhaps changing assessments of environmental spillovers or the provision of an alternative public service like better roads in the case of the rail network.

Where to draw the boundary between pure private sector activities and those requiring public involvement through ownership or regulation is one question. How to manage publicly owned services or regulate privately owned ones involving social externalities is a separate question. There is little doubt we can't answer it. Whether it is electricity regulation in California or telecoms in Britain, there are vast pitfalls in setting up a regulatory structure. There might well be no such thing as a perfect answer because the provision of services involving big externalities necessarily involves multiple aims and inescapable dilemmas. What's more, despite the vast research carried out on the subject, we do not yet have any sys-

tematic appraisal of what kinds of institutional designs work well for publicly managed and regulated services, and which work badly.

There have clearly been some big successes in privatization, where big
gains in efficiency mean consumers are paying less for a better service.
Examples include telecommunications in many countries, gas and electricity in the U.K. and Sweden, the water supply in France, and many
industrial corporations once owned by European governments engaged in
businesses ranging from insurance to oil. The successes have also depended on subsequent good regulation of the industry, as in energy and telecoms.

Despite the favorable examples, Britain's privatization experiment
tried to answer the second question, about how to run utilities well, with
a solution to the first question, about the location of the private-public
boundary. It has been overall only a partial success. The lesson might well
be that some externalities are just too big for the private sector to handle,
and will always require government financing through taxation to provide
the necessary infrastructure and services.

Chapter 8

SCOREBOARD FOR ENERGY TAXES

Industry 5, Environment 1

Economics is often described as the dismal science, but nobody can beat environmentalists for gloom. Predictions of disaster and crisis are their raison d'être, because without an impending environmental crisis, why would anybody pay attention to them? Economists are relentlessly upbeat by comparison. They believe metaphorical time bombs, whether environmental, demographic, or anything else, never explode because human societies and economies adjust in response to pressures.

A famous example of this contrast between environmental pessimism and economic optimism was a 1980 bet between Paul Ehrlich, a biologist and an ardent environmental campaigner, and Julian Simon, a famously free-market economist. The dawn of the modern environmental movement was perhaps the publication in 1972 of a study called "The Limits to Growth," which predicted that at the prevailing rates of depletion the world would run out of nonrenewable natural resources within a century, at which point the economic system would collapse and there would be mass unemployment, starvation, and a soaring death rate. What's more, even if more resources were found, doubling known stocks, the resulting growth would lead to unmanageable pollution, economic and social collapse, mass unemployment, and so on. This approach was then given a tremendous boost by the huge jumps in the oil price in the early and mid-1970s. It was a commonplace by the end of the decade that the world's oil reserves would run out within fifty years.

So Ehrlich was confident he would win a bet with Simon that the prices of five metals would be higher, adjusted for inflation, in ten years' time. He chose a $1,000 combination of $200-worth each of copper, chrome, nickel, tin, and tungsten. The specified prices in fact more than halved between 1980 and 1990, and the $1,000 combination would have cost less in 1990 even without making the inflation adjustment. The value of the $200 components ranged between $56 and $193. Ehrlich sent Simon a check for $576.07, protesting that such a specific wager was not really meaningful. One of his arguments was that demand for some of those particular commodities had fallen—which was exactly his opponent's point.

The two men had agreed that if demand for a commodity grows far faster than supply, the price will rise. The environmentalist stopped there. The economist's argument, so conclusively proven, was that people would adjust their behavior in response. Higher prices in themselves would choke off some demand. They would induce suppliers to produce more—mine more ore or search for new reserves—because formerly unprofitable production would now be profitable. And it would also induce other profit-seeking entrepreneurs to try to find substitutes for the scarce commodities, introducing new technologies. Thus copper was replaced by glass fibers in telephone cables, cars no longer incorporated lavish chrome fittings, and so on. While specific commodities might be in limited supply in the short term, in the longer term, human adaptation and ingenuity make the supply of resources effectively infinite.

So for all their often-irritating claim to a monopoly of the moral high ground, environmentalists are not always right. In fact, I'd even say that usually they are not right. Most are guilty of having no understanding at all of basic economic principles, and caring less than they understand, a lack that makes many of their policy prescriptions doomed.

But this doesn't mean that they are always wrong. After all, the balance of probabilities is that climate change is taking place as a result of human activity, particularly CO_2-emitting energy use. There is too much pollution, damaging human happiness and health. A good deal of economic innovation has gone ahead, its environmental impact no more than an afterthought. In short, the economics profession had certainly overlooked some important **environmental externalities** caused by much economic activity until the green movement set the subject alight.

It is ironic, then, that pollution is one of the conventional textbook examples of an externality. A factory emitting pollutants as a side effect of its production imposes costs on other people in excess of anything it might cost its owners, and which the owners do not have to pay themselves. So, for example, dirty air that triggers many cases of asthma will drive down property prices around the factory, making home owners pay for the pollution. Households and all other businesses in the area will pay in higher charges for the costs of cleaning water extracted from polluted rivers and aquifers. The guilty factory's share of the cleanup cost will be tiny. Because it doesn't pay the external cost, it "overproduces" pollution, whose costs it then passes on to consumers.

It isn't just factories and power stations that pollute. All households discharge vast amounts of waste, and individual drivers plenty of emissions. There is noise pollution from aircraft flying overhead or builders playing loud radios. The residents of Tucson, Arizona, have complained about light pollution from electric lighting at night. Any of us can impose external costs on others by going to places that are already busy, adding to the congestion of a traffic jam or crowded art gallery.

There is also another well-known market failure affecting the natural environment, the **tragedy of the commons**. Why are certain kinds of ocean fish stocks dangerously depleted when there is no shortage of chickens? The answer is that the fish are owned in common, while chickens have individual owners. If a world dictator owned all the fish in the sea, she would have every incentive not to overfish in order to conserve supplies for future sales. The price charged would be higher, reflecting the investment in nondepletion of a resource that is not in **perfectly elastic supply**.

But individual fishermen have no incentive not to overfish because their individual contribution to the problem is tiny. If one or a few were to voluntarily reduce their catches, it would have little impact on the problem and the few would be vulnerable to all other fishermen **free-riding** on their restraint.

Governments therefore have to get involved and set quotas for each nation's fishermen, but even that is inadequate because governments battle for national interest, not global public interest. Eventually fish shortages mean the price mechanism kicks in, higher prices reducing consumer demand. But ideally prices would have been higher all along to reflect the **social cost** of depleting fish stocks.

Environmental externalities are pervasive. There is no market for clean air or quiet and uncrowded streets or species diversity. (How much would you pay to preserve a particular species of rain-forest insect?) Few governments collect data on the scale of the externalities either. The U.K.'s official statistics agency does publish an annual satellite account in an attempt to measure a variety of environmental impacts, but more data and further refinement are needed. Environmental policy is severely hampered by the absence of reliable and meaningful data.

So how should a concerned government tackle such externalities? It could ban emissions of various pollutants above a maximum level. Setting the right level is tricky. A total ban would often impose economic costs that were out of all proportion to the cost of the environmental externality—for example, only nuclear power stations can currently generate totally emission-free power at a price most consumers would find acceptable. Still, direct regulation is one solution.

Economists tend to prefer an alternative approach that clearly causes the polluter to internalize the external costs and brings the power of market forces to bear on the problem. This is the use of so-called **economic instruments**, or in other words, taxes, subsidies, and tradable permits.

Take the example of a government that wishes to reduce emissions of greenhouse gases by its businesses and consumers, as required by the Kyoto Protocol of December 1997. Individual countries committed themselves to reductions of up to 30 percent in carbon dioxide emissions compared to what they would have been on existing trends. (The average reduction was 11.5 percent for the EU compared with 24.5 percent for the United States. No wonder George W. Bush backed out of the agreement, to the outrage of Europeans, as one of his first presidential decisions.)

The countries that signed up agreed on an innovative emissions trading scheme. Companies would be required to set legal targets lower than current levels of emissions, but if they managed to reduce the level below the target they could sell the excess to a company that had not managed to meet its target. The price for the additional emission permission would be set by the market. The biggest reduction in emissions would occur where it was cheapest and allow the overall global target to be met in the most cost-effective way. The Kyoto scheme was based on the successful model of a sulfur dioxide trading scheme operating in America since 1995 as part of the Acid Rain Program and a scheme for trading nitrogen and sulfur oxide permits in southern California.

America pioneered tradable permits. European governments have in the past tended to stick to taxation. During the 1990s nine either introduced or proposed some form of energy tax designed to raise the price of energy to reflect the cost of the CO_2 and other greenhouse gases incurred in its generation. Norway, Sweden, Finland, Denmark, Austria, and the Netherlands went ahead with an energy tax first, followed by the U.K. (where it was called the climate change levy in a doomed bid to make it more popular with the businesses forced to pay it), then Italy and Germany.

Introducing a climate change energy tax has three advantages. First, it works through the price mechanism and is therefore likely to be more efficient, less distorting, not to mention easier to operate than direct regulation, although setting the tax at the efficient level is a challenge. Second, it can encourage companies to adopt more energy-efficient methods over time. And third, as a supplement, it can signal to companies that they need to take this environment business seriously in planning their long-term investments.

There are two ways to go about taxing energy. The tax could be applied to energy use by businesses and domestic consumers, so much per kilowatt-hour of electricity used. Or, for politicians shy of taxing every voter's electricity bill explicitly, it could be applied to suppliers of energy for passing on indirectly to final customers. This second type, known as a downstream tax, would also be easier to administer, as there are fewer distributors than final users of electricity. On the other hand, with lower visibility it might have somewhat less impact in altering consumer behavior in favor of energy conservation. The rate of the tax could be set differently for the different fuels used in energy generation, to reflect their varying carbon contents, as it is the carbon dioxide that's the chief greenhouse effect culprit.

The U.K.'s version was applied only to industrial and commercial companies, bypassing domestic energy use. Imposing a tax on home fuel bills was a complete nonstarter politically. The Labour government had, in opposition, humiliated its Conservative predecessor by overturning such a tax on the grounds that it was grossly unfair. Poor households spend a much higher proportion of their budget on energy than rich households do, and a domestic fuel tax is highly **regressive**.

The restriction on the energy tax nevertheless caused great bitterness among companies, even though the revenues were handed back through a reduction in other taxes on business. After all, domestic energy consumption exceeds manufacturing industry's use and amounts to about a third of total national energy consumption. The most intensive industrial users of energy thought it was outrageously unfair that they would pay most and demanded a special exemption to reflect their extra energy needs, rather missing the point that the aim was to discourage such intensive energy use. One sad case I know of was a local steam museum, which had to raise entry charges for visitors to see its fantastic eighteenth- and nineteenth-century steam engines in operation.

The energy industry in the U.K. would rather have seen a U.S.-style permit trading scheme. So would the investment banks in the City of London, which really liked the look of a new market to operate. But with no experience of such schemes and lacking the instinctive American preference for market solutions, most European governments remain hesitant about introducing tradable permits.

Another example of an environmental tax is duty on gasoline or petrol. The rates of duty vary widely between countries, from 22 percent of the wholesale price in the U.S. to 58 percent in Ireland (the next lowest among developed countries) up to 76 percent in the U.K. In October 2000 truck drivers brought Britain to a standstill by blockading wholesale gasoline depots in protest at continued planned increases in fuel duties, which won them a freeze in the following year's budget. But another tool used by the government has been the introduction of lower rates of duty for "cleaner" varieties. For example there is currently a three pence per liter differential between the duty on ultra-low sulfur diesel and ordinary diesel. An initial differential of one pence per liter introduced in 1997 was too low for the oil companies to be bothered with refining the cleaner fuel, but soon after its increase to three pence in 1999, the ultra-low sulfur share of the diesel market jumped from well under 20 percent to 100 percent. The government was encouraged to increase duty differentials for other types of fuel, including liquid petroleum gas and compressed natural gas, as a result, and will also encourage a switch to ultra-low sulfur petrol for nondiesel engines as new cars capable of using it are introduced from 2002 onward.

The most powerful environmental tools are those where it is possible to identify an externality and design a tax or other instrument that will address the distortion in the market directly. Indirect approaches are bound to be inefficient. To take one example, many campaigners argue that free trade is not all it's cracked up to be because it ignores a variety of environmental costs, notably the energy used in transporting goods long distances around the globe. The free trade regime is also criticized for encouraging companies to switch production to developing countries, where pollution standards are much weaker. There have been terrible examples of multinationals operating at lower standards overseas, like the notorious accident at a Union Carbide plant in Bhopal.

So environmentalists would like to see less trade, or at least minimum environmental standards written into trade agreements. But trade brings economic benefits to consumers, and restricting trade therefore means some of these would be lost: there could be a large **opportunity cost.** What's more, free trade will tend to shift production to the most resource-efficient locations, and lead to the most productive, least costly use of natural resources at the global level. If it is nevertheless correct to say the use of energy in transportation imposes a social cost through the emission of greenhouse gases, which is not reflected in the cost of transportation, the right policy is to raise the price of energy by taxing it. This tackles the externality without imposing additional and unknown economic costs by restricting trade.

In general, environmental problems need environmental solutions, not trade solutions or investment solutions. What's more, economic tools can offer powerful levers on environmental problems.

It's rare, however, to find environmentalists campaigning loudly for higher energy taxes. They know how unpopular these are with voters. In America even more than Europe, cheap energy is one of the basic demands of the people. After all, politicians in California would not allow power companies to charge a retail price for electricity that increased with the costs of generating it when oil prices jumped in 2000. The same year truck drivers across Europe blockaded gas stations and depots when higher oil prices drew attention to high taxes on gasoline sold at the pump. This means environmental campaigners have opted for softer political targets such as free trade, on which they can ally with unions protecting jobs and industry lobbies. It's altogether easier, but it does indicate that the green campaigners have failed to convince the public on their fundamental argument that humanity is using too much energy.

Sadly, the economic arguments do not often win friends. They spell out harsh choices too clearly. To take another example, one of the stumbling blocks in the Kyoto climate change agreement has been how much developing countries need to contribute to reductions in emissions. They argue that the rich industrial countries are responsible for most global emissions of greenhouse gases and should bear the main burden of reduction, because to make the poor countries reduce their emissions from current levels will prevent them from ever industrializing and reaching the standards of living enjoyed in the West. To developing countries, this is unacceptably hypocritical. However, on the other side of the fence, it looks essential to prevent the billions of the world's poor in the years ahead from contributing to similar high levels of emissions.

There is an economic solution to this apparently insoluble dilemma: tradable emissions permits. Allocate a certain amount of allowed emissions to every country through international agreement, adding up to a global total that shrank year by year—diplomatically thorny but possible. Poor countries could then choose between increasing the amount of polluting economic activity they undertook or selling the right to emit to a rich country, which would then have to struggle less to cut emissions. The poor country would be better off either way and worldwide emissions would be on a downward path.

However, many environmentalists seem to believe any use of the market mechanism is intrinsically immoral. When a World Bank research paper suggested a similar idea, whereby polluting industries relocated to developing countries, it caused complete outrage in the environmental movement.

Yet it is what is in effect happening as Western manufacturers switch production to East Asia or Latin America, mainly because these countries offer cheaper labor but also perhaps partly because it's cheaper to pollute to the extent that developing and middle countries have weaker regulation on emissions. The nations with a stronger preference for clean air get it, and those countries that prefer more industry to grow get that.

Indeed, there is a very strong relationship between levels of GDP per capita and indicators of environmental quality such as air and water quality and pollution levels. Rich countries are cleaner. That is surely because public concern for the quality of the environment in general grows when most people do not have to worry about food and shelter. Of course there are severe environmental pressures in developing countries such as a lack of clean water or soil erosion or extreme weather conditions, and many also have industries that are less energy-efficient and more polluting than those with high technical standards in the West. It is possible that the quality of the environment might get worse before it gets better for countries just setting off on the path of economic growth. But environmentalism itself appears to be a luxury good, one people demand more of as their incomes rise. Economic growth in the developing world, so that there are many more prosperous people, is likely to be a requirement for the adoption of higher environmental standards in those economies. If so, campaigners from the rich parts of the world will fail if they try to make higher environmental standards a precondition for graciously granting poor nations permission to grow.

Will such arguments make much headway with environmentalists? I doubt it. The basic philosophies of economics and environmentalism are too different.

Economics is empirical, searching for policy prescriptions that deliver measurable benefits. What matters is what works. Of course it is highly ideological, but it is a way of thinking about the world derived from the questioning, skeptical methods of the eighteenth-century Enlightenment. A good economist keeps an open mind. John Maynard Keynes, once accused of inconsistency, replied: "When the facts change, I change my mind. What do you do, sir?"

Environmentalism is a descendant of the nineteenth-century Romantic reaction to this rationalist approach. It is idealistic, not skeptical. Some of its beliefs are therefore dogmatic (to the economist, at any rate). One example is the environmentalist notion that the use of pesticides is always bad. Why? Because pesticides leave carcinogenic traces on the fruit and in the soil and groundwater. But they also make fruit cheaper so people can buy more, and that might reduce the incidence of cancer. To an economist, it's an empirical question in the end. Are the relevant cancer rates actually rising or falling, and is the incidence correlated with use of the suspect pesticides? Are there other potential causes of these types of cancer? What are the numbers? The environmentalists might be right about this, but they must demonstrate it using epidemiological evidence, not merely assert it. Similarly, recycling paper and glass is always good, according to dogma. Well, maybe, but plentiful supplies of cheap recycled material means paper and glass manufacturers have less incentive to plant trees or develop alternative means of packaging.

Humanity will inevitably have an impact on the planet. Ensuring that the impact is as beneficial as possible is genuinely complicated. The fundamentalist environmental approach that says any human impact is an unacceptable cost imposed on nature is equivalent to an argument for zero economic activity. Even less extreme green views can have significant implications for all of us as consumers, although these are hardly ever spelled out.

There is always an opportunity cost in any course of action. If economic activity has often ignored environmental costs, environmentalists often ignore the economic costs of their proposals. There are such costs even in the most innocuous of cases. Cycle or walk instead of driving? That imposes costs of time lost doing other things.

Romantic ideals versus rational choices? I can't see either side converting the other. But like many other economists, I do care about the environment, so I hope that governments do base their environmental policies on sound economics. And I would happily pay an energy tax.

Chapter 9

AUCTIONS

Call My Bluff

In 1990, just as the late 1980s boom had started to wane, a painting by Vincent van Gogh, the *Portrait of Dr. Gachet*, achieved the highest price ever paid at auction for a painting, $82.5 million. If you are not put off by the likely price tag and want to buy a painting by one of the Impressionist masters, you will probably have to bid for it in an auction, one of those intimidating events at a smart auction house like Christie's or Sotheby's, where a suave chap wielding a hammer starts the bidding at some figure in the millions. Auctions are a long-established way of selling rare things with competing potential buyers.

Auctions have also been long used by many governments for selling Treasury bonds, the financial instruments issued to cover government borrowing. These are downbeat events rather less glamorous than the art house auctions—in fact, often just involving the faxing of documents. Still, auctions have become newly fashionable in economics because of broadcasting and mobile telecommunications. The radio spectrum is a great example of a valuable asset in limited supply, just like Impressionist paintings.

Some countries started auctioning licenses to parts of the airwaves as early as 1989—the U.K., New Zealand, Greece, and India were pioneers. However, these were either modest successes or politically embarrassing flops. Auctions did not start to take off until, in July 1994, the U.S. Federal Communications Commission allocated ten nationwide licenses for narrowband personal communications services (PCS) in an auction designed by economists. A much bigger auction of ninety-nine broadband PCS licenses that took place between December 5, 1994 and March 13, 1995, was a huge success, raising $7 billion. By 2001 the FCC had raised over $32 billion for the government from thirty two auctions of radio-spectrum licenses. In recent years, governments everywhere have started following the example of the American authorities in auctioning licenses to telecommunications companies—and, increasingly, taking advice from economists about how to design the auction process.

The record of the spectrum auctions around the world is both mixed and controversial. Some have raised a surprisingly large amount of money for the government, others surprisingly little. Some have resulted in a vigorously competitive market; others have created monopolistic markets damaging to consumer interests. Governments prefer the first kind of auction in each case, companies the second. The controversy is inevitable because what's for sale is the right to the stream of income that will result from ownership of the rare asset, known as an **economic rent,** similar to the rent property owners receive from tenants on their land.

One of the most controversial of the recent auctions was the British government's sale in March–April 2000 of licenses to use parts of the radio spectrum for so-called 3G or third-generation mobile phone services. All the European auctions of that year involved the 3G technical standard, UMTS, because the governments sought the advantages of a common standard across the continent that had been so fruitful in earlier generations of mobile telephony.

For the British taxpayer the auction of five licenses was without doubt a huge success. It raised £22.5 billion, more than 5 percent of one year's total public expenditure and enough to build 400 new hospitals. The two academics who had led the team designing the auction were feted in the press, an unusual and heady experience for any economist.

The auction took place at the peak of the bubble in enthusiasm when share prices were high for technology companies, but before long there was a backlash as the companies grumbled that they had spent so much on the licenses that they had nothing left to invest in the service. After all, the estate of Ryoei Saito, the Japanese magnate who had bought the van Gogh at the height of an earlier investment boom, had to dispose of it at a lower price after his death. The telecom companies warned that because of the expense of the licenses, customers would have to pay more for their mobile calls. Worse, some experts started to warn of flaws in the 3G technology and predicted it would be overtaken by something better before the infrastructure had ever been built. One technology expert (who had for a long time worked for British Telecom, the U.K.'s dominant and fomer state monopoly phone company) described the auction as "a really good study in madness." Well, because the companies had spent so much money, their moans have to be taken with a grain of salt. They might be right to predict 3G phones will never take off, but if so it will be due to the technology, not the economics. To see why, we need a brief overview of auction theory.

If the government wants to do something like allocate licenses, it could ask companies to submit proposals and business plans, and choose whichever look best in its judgment—best for customers in the years ahead, yet commercially viable. This is known as a **beauty contest**, for obvious reasons. Or it can hold an **auction** intended to use the process of bidding, which reveals what the rivals think the business is worth, to determine the best companies to run the service. Politicians tend to like beauty contests because it gives them more discretion, but this is precisely why ever-skeptical economists tend to prefer auctions.

There are many different ways to design auctions, but two classical kinds of them. The art house type is an ascending bid auction, with successive rounds in which participants know everybody's earlier bids. The U.K. 3G license auction was of this form. The other kind involves an irrevocable sealed bid where nobody knows what the rivals have offered. But there are many variants—for instance, depending on whether bidders pay separate prices or uniform prices. In many Treasury bond auctions, all successful bidders pay the individual prices they offered for the quantity they bid for (a discriminatory auction). In other circumstances, all bidders pay the price set by the lowest winning bid (a uniform price auction), which is often used in markets auctioning many units of a standardized item like electricity.

The different approaches all have their pros and cons. An auction with successive open rounds of bidding makes it easier for companies to collude with each other. They can use early rounds to signal their intentions. For example, a 1997 U.S. spectrum auction that had been expected to raise $1.8 billion brought in only $14 million. Part of the explanation for the startling shortfall was that bidders turned out to have used the final three digits of their multimillion-dollar bids to indicate the identification numbers of the areas they wanted the license for. Such collusion is impossible in a sealed-bid auction.

Ascending auctions of successive rounds have another drawback. It is a fair bet that the auction will be won by the firm that values winning the most—in fact, that is precisely the great upside of an ascending auction, making it the best at generating both higher government revenue (as long as there is no collusion) and productive efficiency. However, this makes it less attractive for other competitors to enter the bidding. It might even make the auction unattractive to the company most likely to win, because if that company does, it might have the sneaking suspicion it has overpaid for something nobody else valued as highly. What if it has got its view about future revenues completely wrong? This is the notorious **winner's curse**.

In practice, the winner's curse does not seem to exist, which makes sense. After all, bidders are well aware of the possibility. This does mean that the danger of the winner's curse can mean participants bid very cautiously, resulting in a low sale price. This is especially true when the bidders know one of them has a genuine advantage. For example, in the 1995 auction of the Los Angeles broadband mobile phone license, Pacific Telephone had a well-known local brand and a database of potential customers because of its fixed-line service. There were other bidders, but the bidding stopped early and the price was low. Everybody knew the license was genuinely worth a bit more to Pacific.

The winner's curse operates in sealed-bid auctions too. However, the extra uncertainty in this type means weaker bidders—smaller companies, firms that are not already incumbents in the industry, foreign companies—stand a better chance of winning. So potential entrants will be more willing to participate, which is an important consideration for a government trying to boost competition in the industry.

So ascending auctions can raise more revenue and award the prize to the bidder who values it most. On the other hand, they are more prone to collusive behavior and are less attractive to new entrants. Sealed-bid auctions have the opposite characteristics. Auctions that combine elements of both, known as Anglo-Dutch auctions, get the best of both worlds. These involve rounds of ascending bids until only two bidders are left, and then a sealed-bid playoff where the bids must be no lower than the top price reached in earlier rounds. This generates high revenues and encourages competitors, who know the playoff gives one of them some chance of beating the most advantaged bidder.

However, governments can also influence the competitive structure of the industry in other ways. In the telecom case, for example, the number of licenses to be awarded is a key weapon. One option is to auction small chunks of spectrum, which winners could then trade to amalgamate into viable larger licenses. This has the merit of being a market solution. Unfortunately, in a high fixed cost network industry like telecommunications, the market solution is likely to be overly monopolistic from the consumer's point of view, with too few competitors left in the market. An alternative, chosen by the U.K. in the 2000 3G auction, is to issue a number of licenses that exceeds the number of incumbents in the industry and limit bidders to one each. This guarantees a new entrant.

Yet every situation is different, demanding tweaks to the auction design. The Dutch government, auctioning the same type of license a month after the U.K., copied the auction design in the important details, including issuing five licenses. Unfortunately, the Netherlands already had five incumbents, not four. This was a crucial error. The potential new entrants knew they probably wouldn't win alone, so they formed partnerships with the incumbents instead. The auction raised just £1.65 billion rather than the £6 billion the Dutch government had anticipated based on the U.K.'s experience just a month earlier.

A similar German government auction opted for selling off smaller bits of spectrum and allowing the market to decide on industry structure. The seven bidders had a choice: the dominant ones could push prices high, generating a lot of revenue for the government but leading to a more concentrated industry, or they could settle for smaller licenses at a lower cost but with more competitors. The government got lucky because the companies made a mistake: it got high revenues and a six-firm mobile phone market. The dominant bidders pushed prices up in the auction but then didn't bother to push the weaker firms out. As one of the U.K.'s auction designers observed: "It is hard to construct beliefs about opponents for which this is rational behavior." Like other fields in economics, auction design assumes rationality, which is obviously sometimes overrated.

To go back to the original question, then, was the U.K. 3G auction a success or not? The government raised a lot of money. It created a market with five strong competitors. But was the result flawed by the winner's curse?

The argument for an auction rather than a beauty contest was that the government and its expert panels would have no idea about the value of a 3G telephony license, whereas the companies providing the service would be able to value it. But in a fast-moving area of technology, perhaps there's no reason to expect corporate executives to have any clue either (although the market should know better). At best, they might have a handle on the relative value of the different licenses on offer.

In that case, a beauty contest combined with a regime to tax future profits might have done better at generating not only incentives for companies to carry on investing but also high government revenues. The government would then have chosen the lucky winners but would have guarded against their having underpaid for the privilege by taxing high profits in later years. This has proved the case with the licenses for oil and gas exploration in the North Sea for the past quarter century, the main example cited by fans of a profits tax. They were allocated at low cost in a beauty contest, but the accumulated tax revenues amount to £250 billion, or more than 4,000 new hospitals, in today's money.

There is a difference, however, between oil exploration licenses and spectrum licenses that makes the parallel inexact. The price of oil is set in a world market, and the North Sea tax regime doesn't affect the price the oil companies can charge for the oil they extract there. The world price means it is straightforward to calculate the profits that should be liable for tax. This is not true in a national telecom market, where companies set prices and have some power to simply pass on tax to customers.

There is anyway little doubt that the telecom companies would have moaned just as much if they had faced, instead of the spectrum auction, a special tax on profits from 3G mobile telephony. The right comparison to make for policy purposes is not auction versus beauty contest, but rather auction versus beauty contest with profits tax. In fact, I'm sure the moans would have been the same: that it would raise costs for consumers and discourage new investment in an industry for which incentives to innovate are the lifeblood.

It is hard to escape the conclusion that the telecom companies are just fed up that the government insisted on a transfer of economic rent from corporations to taxpayers. After all, in the U.K. the telecom companies were used to not having to pay much at all for licenses to use the radio spectrum. In the United States, numerous auctions have generated government revenues on the same sort of scale as the 3G auction, but the companies are used to it, so there is little fuss about it any more.

With five operators in the U.K. market it is hard to believe the telecom companies can carry out their threat to pass on the license costs in higher prices or to cut back on investment. As the FCC points out in its assessment of the U.S. experience, if the investment is economically worthwhile, it will take place anyway. The only possible risk is that if the company that first bought the license goes bankrupt, there will be a delay before somebody else incurs the cost of investment. The U.K. telecommunications market is just too competitive, and 3G mobile telephony is also going to be competing with conventional fixed lines, earlier-generation mobile services, and new technologies such as local and short-range wireless services (including 4G and Bluetooth).

Similarly, the Channel Tunnel never managed to recover its huge sunk costs because of competition from the cross-Channel ferries. The operators of services through the tunnel can only charge what the market will bear. It was the shareholders in Eurotunnel, the company that built the tunnel, who had to pay the price. Or to take a more prosaic example, the rent for an apartment depends on supply and demand in the area, not on the amount the landlord paid for it in the first place.

It will be shareholders in telecom companies who pay for the 3G mistake, if it does turn out to be a mistake. For we don't know yet whether the technology is going to be a success or a failure. It makes me rather suspicious that doubts about 3G technology began to emerge in the press, doubts raised by the companies that had just spent a fortune on it, in a matter of weeks after the auction took place, and in the run-up to a general election. If that wasn't an industry lobbying for an improvement in the terms and conditions of the licenses, I'm an Impressionist painter.

Making mistakes is actually rather the point about running a high-tech business such as a telecommunications company. It involves taking technical and commercial risks. Risk-taking is for businesses and investors, not for taxpayers. Perhaps the mobile phone companies got this particular judgment wrong. But even if they did, this is no reason for taxpayers to subsidize the next risk they take. Governments are right to opt for auctions that make companies pay for valuable licenses. Auction design is a fast-moving area of research, and it is clear that in the past, some auctions have worked rather well and others have not. Still, in principle and in practice, auctions save the taxpayer money, and if the design is right, they can also help consumers by ensuring competition in markets vulnerable to the exercise of monopoly power.

Chapter 10

TAX INCIDENCE

Only People Pay Tax

Tax is never popular. Nobody likes the chunk the government takes out of their paycheck, or the way a sales tax increases the amount they have to pay at the checkout. So politicians do their best to sugarcoat the pill. Income taxes are so visible that they are rarely raised. Sales and property taxes are unpleasantly obvious to shoppers and home owners too. Easier by far to increase the taxes that are not paid by individual voters, such as corporate taxes or business property taxes. This electoral logic means there is a vigorous corporate lobby against a higher tax burden on business. Vigorous but economically illiterate, because businesses don't pay tax. People do. Different people depending on which tax you're talking about, although working out exactly who—the **tax incidence,** in economics-speak—is sometimes difficult.

There are countless examples of how business taxes fall unnoticed on unexpected groups of people. For example, in 1997 the British government raised a lot of money by abolishing a tax credit that pension funds had been receiving for the tax withheld on dividend payments by companies in which they held shares. This is so complicated to just write down that it is easy to see why there was absolutely no fuss about the move. Who could care about some change in the tax rules for big investment funds? But what it meant was that the contributions people were making to their savings for retirement, invested by the pension funds, were suddenly being taxed at 23 percent. A couple of years on, when they were being advised by their accountants to boost their savings to make up for the shortfall, the penny dropped.

The incidence of many business taxes depends on the kind of market involved. The key is how sensitive demand for and supply of the product is to price changes. The elasticity of supply and elasticity of demand, in other words, determine how much prices paid and quantities sold change when a tax is imposed. Companies will generally be able to pass on some portion of the tax to consumers, just as they do their other costs. If demand is highly elastic so that sales drop off sharply when price goes up, they will be able to pass on less of the tax to customers than if demand is inelastic. Demand for cigarettes is inelastic because smokers are addicted, but demand for apples is elastic because apple eaters will switch to pears if apples go up in price. Companies will also be able to pass on less when supply is highly elastic, that is, increases a lot as price rises. This will be the case in very competitive markets, such as hair salons, with many companies eager to win customers. In less competitive markets, by contrast, businesses may be more able to restrict supply to keep prices high, and more able to pass on a high proportion of a tax to their customers.

Thus pure monopolists could if they chose easily pass on a tax on their revenues straight to their customers, who might buy less but have nowhere else to go for what they do buy. In a competitive market, companies will find it hard to pass on an increase in taxation by raising their prices, as that would bring in competitors. In that case, lower profits will mean lower dividend payments to shareholders because profits will be affected. Or the company could decide to try to cut other costs, perhaps spreading the tax burden to employees by firing some of them or cutting pay, or to suppliers by negotiating a lower price with them. Customers, shareholders, workers pay—all of them people of one kind or another.

Failing to understand tax incidence has led to some spectacularly flawed policies. More flawed than most, for example, was the 1998 settlement between the states and cigarette manufacturers, portrayed as a great victory for American nonsmokers and for smokers who might fall ill, and above all, as a justly severe punishment for the corporations.

On the face of it, this has nothing to do with taxation. It's about hammering the big bad purveyors of death, surely? Wrong. This is where the belief that companies, not people, can pay tax disguises the identity of the real losers. The tobacco settlement is a superb example of how important it is to think through the presentation of almost any piece of news to see what it really means. It's also a good case study for understanding tax incidence.

In a piece of deliberate obfuscation, what amounts to a new national tax increase of about 35 cents on a pack of cigarettes has never been described as such, but always rather as "damages" or "settlement payments." However, the deal, imposing an apparently staggering $206 billion bill on the cigarette makers, amounted to a tax to be paid by smokers—the very group supposedly being compensated by the settlement. Just $2.4 billion was to be paid up front by the tobacco firms (split between them according to their stock market valuations rather than any assessment of their relative guilt in killing and harming smokers).

How could this be? Well, it was in nobody's interests to admit the truth. The states had every incentive to appear tough on the tobacco companies. The companies could pretend to be feeling pain, when in fact they had sold out their customers in return for protection from a major category of lawsuits (the states' Medicaid suits). And the lawyers involved got fees amounting to $750 million a year for five years and $500 million a year indefinitely, payments estimated to have a **present value** (that is, added up and given a higher value the sooner they are received because people value getting money sooner rather than later) of $8 billion. (At one point during the debate on a proposed 1997 Federal tobacco settlement that subsequently collapsed, the Senate set a $4,000 *an hour* cap on legal fees, but that soon got overturned.)

In effect, the deal okayed a **collusive** price increase by the cigarette manufacturers in order to get consumers to fund their settlement of the lawsuits, to the benefit of the lawyers, plaintiffs, and defendants (especially the lawyers). It was possible because the cigarette market is a tight **oligopoly** dominated by four companies who between them account for 98.6 percent of sales, a fifth with 1.3 percent, and about a hundred with 0.1 percent of the total market between them. After all, it's a hard business to break into. Advertising is severely restricted, banned on radio and TV since 1971, and you can imagine the public outcry if a new would-be competitor announced plans to branch out big-time from cake mixes or fizzy drinks into cigarettes. As a result, it is an obscenely profitable industry, albeit one with a shrinking U.S. (and European) market. Profits as a proportion of sales revenue for the big four (Philip Morris, RJR, U.K.-owned

Brown & Williamson, and Lorillard) ranged from 26 to 45 percent in 1997, the year before the states' settlement.

What's more, smokers are addicted, so the **price elasticity of demand** for cigarettes is low. Higher prices squeeze off some demand, but not much. They are even hugely loyal to individual brands, depending on which appeals to their self-image. Only about one in ten switches brands each year.

With such inelastic demand, the industry would be even more profitable if the companies could cooperate fully in fixing prices. Of the $1.90 per pack price in 1997, before the settlement, 34 cents was state tax, 24 cents federal tax, 46 cents the margin for distributors and retailers, 23 cents marketing costs, 20 cents manufacturing costs, 10 cents other costs and 33 cents profit. The extra tax agreed in the settlement, another 35 cents roughly, would have the effect of pushing the price closer to the level a monopolist would have charged. A lower volume of sales would hit company profits but not unbearably—about $1 billion out of a total of $8 billion a year. Compared to the alternative, bankruptcy in a continuing hail of lawsuits, this looked like very reasonable terms for the settlement of a slew of cases. At the same time, the higher price would generate an estimated $13 billion in tax revenues to pay the lawyers. Oh, yes, and to meet the health bills for the sick smokers.

Not only do consumers bear the burden of the substantial tax increase negotiated in the tobacco deal, but poor consumers bear the heaviest burden. Cigarettes are an **inferior good**—people smoke less as their incomes rise. Taxes on cigarettes are therefore highly **regressive**, or proportionately much higher for those on lower incomes. People earning less than $30,000 a year could face an estimated rise of 9 percent in their federal tax burden as a result of the tobacco deal.

There is an extra twist to this extraordinary tale. The fifth company in the market, Liggett, is probably $400 million a year better off as a result of the settlement. It handed over secret industry documents to the plaintiffs' lawyers and argued successfully that turning in evidence to the state meant Liggett should be exempt from the new tax increase. Clearly giving one firm out of five a 35-cent cost advantage on a product that costs 20 cents to make is problematic, so the exemption applied only up to a 3 percent market share. But that was more than twice Liggett's market share in 1998. The company might have deserved some reward for helping turn the tide in the legal battle against tobacco, but an annual reward equal to four times its pre-settlement stock market value seems a touch generous.

Jeremy Bulow and Paul Klemperer, the two economists responsible for a magnificent intellectual demolition job on the multistate tobacco deal, put forward a couple of radical proposals they think would have made much better economic sense and been better for public health. One would be to sell licenses to make cigarettes, shrinking the number of cigarettes that could be manufactured each year, ensuring that the amount smoked continued to decline. Total consumption of cigarettes in the United States peaked in 1981, and consumption per capita even earlier in 1963, but the decline is quite slow. Licenses to manufacture would amount to government regulation of the quantity of smoking, which might seem an unwarranted intrusion on freedom of choice. But with the tobacco deal, it is already regulating prices sharply upwards. There is not a big philosophical difference.

The second suggestion is for the government to buy the U.S. tobacco businesses—in effect, to nationalize them—funding the acquisition through the tax. The benefit of this would be to take tobacco executives and shareholders out of the picture. Taxpayers, including smokers, would get the benefit of the industry's mega-profits instead. The two economists also speculate that there would be a public health benefit too, as they think a nationalized cigarette industry would lose customers faster: "If there is one thing government monopolies are traditionally good at, it is deglamorizing their products and making them as consumer-unfriendly as possible."

It's too late for radical moves, unfortunately. There is no political will to unstitch a deal that took years to put together. Nor is it obvious that the lawyers would benefit, in which case the radical proposals are definitely nonstarters. For another of the great lessons of the tobacco deal, as if it were needed, is the power of the American legal profession. In fact, that might be the one exception to the general principle with which I began, that only people pay taxes. Because, of course, lawyers pay taxes, too.

Chapter 11

WAR GAMES

A Government's Gotta Do What a Government's Gotta Do

Ever since September 11, 2001, defense has been one of the highest priorities in public policy. The defense of the nation is the classic example of a **public good** provided by the government. Even the most ardent free-market conservative—actually, *especially* an ardent free-market conservative—believes the government has to raise enough tax to pay for the military. Yet the apparently simple aim of making adequate provision for the security of the nation raises some difficult questions.

For defense is where foreign policy and economic analysis collide. The users of weapons need not only a military strategy but also a commercial strategy for procuring all that expensive hardware. Wherever strategy is important, either in defense or in less lethal areas of business, **game theory** is a natural way to think about what the outcome will be. Game theory is less fun than it sounds, but it's nevertheless a fascinating and powerful technique for understanding behavior in situations where the "players" are not operating in the perfectly competitive and static markets of basic economic theory.

One of the simplest examples is the famous prisoners' dilemma, in which two partners in crime are interrogated separately and offered a reduced sentence if they sell out their colleague. If neither tells on the other, they will each get five-year sentences. If one confesses the details, he will get just one year but his partner ten years, but if both spill the beans, both will go away for ten years. The outcome if they compete, by each implicating the other, is the worst.

Games in real life are much more complicated. And game theory has played a vital role in analyzing strategic problems of all descriptions, including defense. There is no more powerful way of trying to inside your enemies' minds and predict what they will do. As the opening line of the movie *A Beautiful Mind* puts it, "Mathematics won the war."

Let's start, though, with the most basic questions in national defense. For example, should you make all your own weapons or import them? A national arms industry has the advantage of security of supply and control over the technology, not to mention all the potential commercial spin-offs.

However, complicated weapons systems are very expensive to produce, involving a vast amount of research and development. So much of the cost is the initial fixed cost of development and testing prototypes that there are huge economies of scale in weapons manufacture. To give an idea of the figures, the development of a new air-to-air missile runs at about $1.5 to 2 billion. America, the world's lone superpower for the foreseeable future, does develop its own weapons, but for European countries it looks a lot more sensible to work jointly or simply import.

If a country does opt to make rather than import weapons, the next question is whether it should allow the export of the arms to third world countries to try and recoup some of the costs, because it is, after all, more efficient and profitable to manufacture the weapons on a very large scale. Governments and their commercial partners who have developed an expensive weapons system are in a position of monopoly power and could make a tidy profit—as long as they are happy for other countries to have access to the weaponry and the technology. These judgments are becoming all the more difficult as more and more military technologies have lucrative commercial applications, such as the Global Positioning System. This technology uses satellite information to pinpoint exact locations on the earth's surface, and has been pounced on by auto manufacturers, for example. Even email software was once at risk of a U.S. government export restriction because the National Security Agency objected to foreigners being able to encrypt their messages using the (then) spyproof methods developed by American companies.

The balance of judgment is rather different for different types of weapon. In the case of weapons of mass destruction or those classified as inhumane (as if there were humane ones) like land mines, considerations of security and morality tend to outweigh the economic arguments, for obvious reasons. For example, the nuclear powers are cautious about helping any other country develop the same capability, and few governments with the capacity to make biological weapons see this as a burgeoning export industry. There is a real fear that chemical and biological weapons could fall into the hands of terrorists, too. So ultra-strict export bans tend to apply. (It can still be difficult determining exactly what to ban, as a notorious British trial of three businessmen who had sold a big pipe to Iraq demonstrated. The government alleged it was part of a supergun. The businessmen eventually won their legal battle to prove it was in fact a pipe.)

At the other end of the scale, trade in light weapons such as rifles and machine guns, which are the main cause of death in conflict, is extremely hard to monitor. There is a substantial legal and illegal market, and many countries make their own small arms anyway because the technology is relatively simple and such arms are not costly to manufacture. In fact, some conflicts involve even more basic means of death, generally not imported, like the machetes that were the preferred method in the Rwandan massacres.

So the economically interesting part of the arms trade concerns the major weapons systems in between these two categories, items such as aircraft and warships, missiles, tanks, heavy artillery, and so on. Often they are packaged with services such as training and maintenance, which can be the most profitable part of a contract. Secrecy means there is no reliable source of statistics on this trade. However, estimates indicate that the five permanent members of the U.N. Security Council—the U.S., China, Russia, France, and the U.K.—account for about 85 percent of the world supply of arms. The United States exports about 15 percent of its production, the U.K. and France 25 percent and 20 percent respectively. About 80 percent of sales go to smaller and poorer countries, mainly in particularly troubled regions of the developing world.

This suggests that whether a country is an arms exporter or importer clearly has a geopolitical aspect. But there is an economic aspect, too. Even very poor countries produce light weapons and munitions for their own armies. Very rich or very big countries are self-sufficient in arms, and some are substantial exporters of bigger weapons systems. The main demand for imported weapons therefore comes from countries with middling levels of GDP, not big enough to produce all their own but still big enough (or badly governed enough) to have ambitions that require weapons that pack a bigger punch than machine guns.

However, the available figures suggest demand for arms imports has fallen substantially since the end of the Cold War, and is indeed negligible outside a few areas like East Asia and the Middle East. Falling prices and fierce competition for contracts suggests there is massive overcapacity. Given the size of government subsidies to some arms manufacturers, which must be offset against manufacturers' profits to assess the national economic benefit, it is doubtful whether there is a positive net return in the arms business. It looks a lot like a declining Rust Belt industry such as steel or shipbuilding, but one with a lot of strategic and political baggage. Certainly, there have been numerous mergers in the U.S. and European industries, in an effort to shrink the amount of excess supply. Making a profit is complicated by the fact that government policy prohibits the sale of major weapons systems to some potential paying customers.

For the manufacturers, the problem is relatively straightforward: how to make a profit in the teeth of stiff competition, subject to all kinds of government restrictions, but also with a captive market in the form of your own government and with a good chance of getting generous taxpayer subsidies through cheap export credit, funds for research and development, and so on. For governments, it's a different matter. They want to achieve several potentially conflicting objectives through the arms trade.

One such objective is to enhance national security. This points to spending a lot on arms. But if one country spends a lot, this can create military instability by making neighbors and enemies feel insecure—there is an externality, in other words. If every country spends a lot on arms, in an arms race, this can be much more stable militarily but involves an inefficiently high amount of spending on arms rather than on hospitals or schools. This is why politicians sometimes conclude it's worth putting a lot of effort into arms control regimes. Not just because it might save lives but also because a regime that involves less spending on defense is economically more efficient.

If a group of neighboring countries are allies, like the Western European nations since 1945 (but not before), then the ones with big defense budgets are providing a public good to the others sheltering under their defense umbrella. But that might tempt some countries to free-ride by underspending on their own defense and exporting what arms they do produce (although it will come to seem less like free-riding the closer the political integration of the European countries becomes).

Another government objective coincides with that of arms suppliers. It is to have a profitable arms export business, in order to reduce the amount of subsidy that needs to be paid and to create or save jobs, often in particular regions of the country. The arms industry is dominated by a few large companies, and also experiences big economies of scale, as described earlier. That means it is an oligopoly, or even monopoly in some categories of weaponry. There just aren't all that many companies that make tanks, nuclear submarines, or fighter planes. In such an industry restricting output and raising prices will maximize profits. The output of arms will in fact be smaller than if perfect competition prevailed.

Unfortunately, history indicates that it is difficult to make arms control regimes stick. Countries are all too willing to kill each other's citizens or their own. Oligopolies in general are not very stable. OPEC, the cartel of oil producers, is one example. For about a decade from the early 1970s it sustained huge oil price increases by restricting production. In 2000 this wildly successful policy had a brief renaissance. However, despite knowing how well it works in terms of increasing their revenues, most of the time OPEC is unable to limit how much oil its members pump out. There is an overwhelming incentive to free-ride by letting all the other members restrict their output while increasing your own in order to take advantage of the high market price. But once the free riders start to increase supply, the price will fall and the discipline breaks down.

Arms manufacturers have the same incentive to undercut their rivals, especially in a shrinking market, and one in which deals are generally kept secret. (After all, the oil price is flashed on screens all around the world all the time. It's difficult to hide any change in supply and demand conditions.)

So even at the purely commercial level, both arms buyers and arms suppliers have tricky strategic considerations. The relevance of game theory becomes still more apparent when we turn to military considerations. Game theory involves difficult mathematics. In general, though, all parties involved will benefit if they cooperate rather than compete (sometimes requiring that one compensates another); but there are clearly incentives not to cooperate, especially in the arms business. Even a noncooperative game can result in a stable equilibrium outcome. However, the arms market equilibrium often appears to be unstable, too, instability in an arms race implying war.

The antiballistic missile treaty that kept the Cold War cold was stable, thanks to its foundation on mutually assured destruction. If one side launched nuclear weapons at the other, it was guaranteed it would be attacked in return. The cost—atomization of major cities and much of the population and the economy—was sufficiently high to deter both the U.S.S.R. and the U.S. from starting a nuclear war. However, to keep up a credible threat of destruction required both to spend huge sums on nuclear weapons. The equilibrium was, like other arms races, stable but inefficient. Much of the intense concern outside the United States about President George W. Bush's proposed National Missile Defense (NMD) system is not a worry about a return to inefficiently high defense spending, however, so much as a fear that the new equilibrium might be unstable.

This discussion has so far assumed nation states are the relevant political units in analyzing warfare. But most of today's conflicts are civil wars—twenty-five out of twenty-seven big conflicts recorded by the Stockholm Peace Research Institute in 1999. Most of these occur in developing countries, which is just what you might expect looking at the pattern of which countries export and which import arms. In a civil war, the analysis of the game might involve different ethnic or religious groups.

On the face of it, it is both tragic and puzzling that the world's poorest countries are the ones squandering resources on warfare. Why is there more instability in these regions? Perhaps the absence of the credible threat of triggering a global nuclear winter helps account for it. That seems to be a real disincentive to starting a war, where it applies. It is certainly a threat nobody would much like to see someone like Iraq's Saddam Hussein wielding.

In some developing countries, there are natural resources to fight over, whether diamonds or oil or water. Plentiful natural loot of this sort tends to lead to a high level of conflict. However, so does extreme poverty, because this reduces the direct costs of warfare. If there is no abundant physical infrastructure or farmland to destroy, if soldiers have very low earnings potential in other occupations, then the opportunity cost of death and destruction is low. Opportunity cost is a way of comparing the actual outcome with what might have been, and in such cases the economic potential of peace is not all that much better than what happens to the economy during the conflict. A lack of hope for the future therefore means higher levels of conflict than in countries where there is a lot more to lose. Some recent research at the World Bank suggests economic conditions such as poverty or slow growth or economic decline or dependence on primary commodities are better predictors of war than any political or ethnic variables. Conversely, growth and prosperity tend to be correlated with peace and respect for human rights and political liberties.

The tools of game theory can be applied just as well to interethnic or other intergroup rivalries, however. In a divided country, there are two strategies that lead to peace, or a stable equilibrium. One is when the government spends a lot on weapons, so potential rebels would have to spend a lot themselves to win a war. So military regimes can be stable even when they expropriate to themselves large amounts of national resources, making it tempting for rivals to try and replace them. However, this is unlikely to be the most efficient outcome. Alternatively the government, perhaps faced with rivals likely to be good at fighting it, might decide not to spend that much on defense but instead promise to redistribute a share of the national pie to the insurgents. If they can make this promise credible, civil war can be avoided. However, the number of civil wars both large and small suggests this kind of credibility is in practice nonexistent in a divided society.

The number of civil wars has increased sharply since the end of the Cold War in 1989. It is as if the removal of the overwhelming threat of nuclear catastrophe has reduced the potential cost of going to war at a smaller scale. So while arms spending worldwide has fallen, suggesting the war game has been heading toward a more efficient level of defense spending, the stability of the low-spending outcome is not obvious. The American NMD plan is hugely unpopular among other NATO countries, but perhaps President Bush is right to worry about what all the foreigners are doing to each other.

Or perhaps not. Economics cannot answer these difficult questions of geopolitical strategy. But it does offer tools, such as game theory or the analysis of industrial structure when there are economies of scale, that can illuminate important aspects of the behavior of governments and arms manufacturers. Common sense says we should all live in peace and harmony, but as we clearly don't, any insight into why vast sums of money are spent on weapons and by whom must be welcome.

Part III

NEW TECHNOLOGY

How Business Is Coping with Change

What the government does crops up in Part IV, too, but here in Part III the focus is on business in a time of great change. New technologies certainly alter the framework within which policymakers, businesses, and individuals have to operate. Today's new technologies have characteristics that make them especially interesting in terms of economic analysis.

Yet even without a big technological development such as steam power or the computer revolution, any economy is in a constant state of flux and evolution, often described as creative destruction. Old industries decline, and new ones are born in different places and employing different people. With winners and losers, this means economics and emotions often clash—no prizes for guessing which usually wins out.

Chapter 12

MOVIES

Why Subtitles Need Subsidies

The hit film *Bridget Jones's Diary* was coproduced by three movie companies: Canal Plus of France, the independent U.K.-based Working Title, and representing Hollywood, Miramax. It was, not surprisingly, untypical of many commercial successes. The heroine was a then relatively unknown actress, nor were the two male leads the biggest stars around. In fact, as it was based on a bestselling book, which was in turn based on an English newspaper column, there was almost nothing of the conventional Hollywood recipe about it. Oh, except for one thing. With a plot spanning two Christmases, it showed a wintry England blanketed in fluffy white snow. Reader, it almost never snows in England at Christmas.

The dominance of Hollywood values and American culture in the global film industry, even in a movie like *Bridget Jones*, helps explain why nothing delights a wanna-be intellectual as much as art house movies. It's a mark of free thinking and sophistication. Beautiful French actresses taking their clothes off—fantastic! Subtitles—even better!

The chasm between commercial Hollywood films and arty European ones is all too often exaggerated, as the two traditions feed each other. Even so, successive French governments have time after time aggressively defended their right to protect French films, through measures such as minimum local content on television channels, on occasion even holding up all EU-U.S. trade negotiations specifically to safeguard the one industry against the titans of Hollywood. The French call it the cultural exception. Can there possibly be an economic justification for a cultural exception to free trade, though? After all, the case for the mutual benefits of free trade is so fundamental in economics.

Audience preferences certainly seem to suggest this fundamental argument applies in the movie industry, like any other. For the sad truth is that, despite the angst of the intellectuals, most French filmgoers are almost as likely as those of any other nationality to prefer the popular Hollywood blockbusters to the obscure and arty homegrown alternatives. Likewise in Britain, the gritty social realism favored by British directors does not do too well at the box office compared with the American hits. Drug addicts dying in stairwells in desolate northern British projects versus glossy feel-good romance or big-budget action? It's no contest. Some local films do very well, of course, but the people's choice is definitely Hollywood.

In which case, you might well ask how European politicians justify special trade protection for their own cultural industries. Surely in culture, too, free trade will deliver the best outcomes in this as in any other industry, the widest choice for consumers at the lowest prices?

Fan as I am of free trade, I do, however, think there is something to the cultural exception. It is partly to do with culture, which is really just a noneconomist's description of a certain type of externality, and partly to do with economies of scale.

In classical trade theory, the mutually beneficial effect of increased exchange depends on there not being any significant returns to production at a large scale and there not being high start-up costs in industry. In the usual terminology, there are assumed to be diminishing returns to scale, meaning that extra units of output cost more, not less, to produce. In these circumstances market mechanisms mean that small is competitive, that small producers can produce more efficiently than large ones. There will be an equilibrium outcome—only one—in which only the lowest cost producers produce and nations specialize in particular industries.

This was pretty realistic two centuries ago. Agriculture and basic commodities formed a high proportion of international trade. Farmers clearly used the best land first, so diminishing returns would set in as they put less fertile land to use, and similarly mines emptied the richest veins of ore. England could specialize in cabbages, Ireland in potatoes, and France in wine. The same conditions also applied in many traditional manufacturing industries such as textiles and footwear.

However, the classical trade theorists like David Ricardo did not give much thought to Hollywood, or even to the possibility of mass production and the assembly line in manufacturing. In the case of many manufactured goods, there are substantial start-up costs and hence economies of scale. The R&D, design, and setup costs for a new type of car or aircraft or a new medicine are extremely high. In such industries, there are increasing returns to scale. They exist, too, in new industries where the marginal cost of producing additional units is tiny, such as the software business.

For the most part, international trade now involves the exchange of manufactured goods like cars or washing machines or pharmaceuticals between the developed countries. However, there is a fair degree of specialization. Different countries lead in different sectors, especially in high-tech or advanced industries in which you might expect large economies of scale, and tend to hang on to their lead. It is clear that historical accident has played a part in the specializations that do exist, and that countries can develop industries despite lacking the obvious natural resources. For example, Japan is a significant producer of automobiles and steel, despite being naturally short on iron and energy, while the only reason the U.K. still makes any cars is because some of the key innovators in the early development of vehicles powered by the internal combustion engine were British.

Under conditions of increasing returns to scale, market forces can take the world economy to many possible combinations of output, depending on such happenstance, because it is hard to dislodge a particular country from an early lead. And it cannot be confidently predicted that any particular outcome will be the most efficient possible. Increasing returns introduce the conclusion that it all depends—on which countries' industries get to what size and when.

In such a world—the real world—the conventional conclusions of trade theory will still usually apply. It will not be efficient for an industrialized country to produce almost everything it consumes itself, splitting the workforce between many different industries. What's more, any country will benefit from its trading partners being equally successful in a wide range of industries because that will generate the prosperity necessary to create a big market for its own products. Poor, isolated countries do not make good trading partners; rich, integrated ones do. So there will continue to be gains from trade. In fact, there may be more potential for gains globally from trade precisely because there are increasing returns in many industries.

The hitch pointed out by theorists recently, as increasing returns to scale have become more characteristic in the advanced economies, is that in some cases trade need not be *mutually* beneficial. For if increasing returns benefit big producers, those producers will be located in particular countries. There might well be zones of conflict in which the success of one industry from one country actually damages other countries. It is likely that such conflicts arise between very similar developed countries or regions, like the EU and the U.S. An obvious example is aircraft production, essentially a two-horse race between Boeing and Airbus.

Another is the movie industry. The economies of scale are slightly different. They do not arise in production; after all, there are plenty of low-budget movies around. The costs of filmmaking are still plummeting thanks to continuing technological innovation like Apple's fantastic iMovie software. Instead, the returns to scale occur in buying in superstar talent, and in marketing and distribution, as discussed in the case of sports and music. Anybody can make a film as a hobby at virtually no cost, but few can translate their creative skill into box office success.

Now, I am highly skeptical of most industry lobby groups' claims that theirs is a special case and they deserve protection from overseas competition. Even though there is a potential theoretical justification, I'm certain it does not operate in practice as often as **special interest groups** would like us to believe. While exploiting economies of scale might sometimes offer greater efficiency and higher output in theory, the benefits from competition point the other way. Figuring out whether a given industry is in a zone of conflict with trading partners is an empirical question, and one highly vulnerable to political manipulation by rich and powerful corporations and lobbyists. Some economists in the late 1980s started out enthusiastic about the idea of managed trade, based on figuring out which particular national industries needed government help to exploit economies of scale or protection against competitors able to exploit them, but retreated somewhat from their enthusiasm when it became obvious the argument had given the usual suspects fresh ammunition to operate against the public interest.

In the case of the movies, I'd nevertheless be inclined to give the European film industry the benefit of the doubt. It might just be an exception to the rule that freer trade is always better. It seems very likely that the big Hollywood studios have an important advantage over European competitors even in European markets because of extensive increasing returns to scale. Hollywood has got into this position because the United States itself is the biggest single English-language market in the world, whereas language fragments the European market even though filmmaking had a head start there historically. Scale means Hollywood can always thrash British or French or Italian movies commercially. Yet the dominance of American films is not necessarily the most efficient and desirable outcome for the British or French or Italian economies—or cultures.

It is not as if movies account for a huge portion of international trade and GDP. However, the social benefits of having a domestic film industry probably outweigh the private benefits. The contribution to national culture exceeds the private return to moviegoers of watching pneumatic French starlets or scrawny Scottish junkies (especially the latter). In other words, there is a cultural externality, a gain unlikely to be realized by the operation of market forces.

It is with trepidation that an economist brings in a consideration as fuzzy and controversial as culture, even in the loosest sense, into the argument. Some economists would disagree altogether. However, I have put forward here the kind of argument you need to make to persuade other economists of the merits of special protection from completely free trade for European movies. In other words, it's not enough to say the film industry is part of the nation's cultural heritage, full stop. Defenders of subtitled films need to make a stronger case than that.

After all, in the advanced economies, culture, however defined, is an economic resource. If an increasing share of GDP is generated by services such as the creative industries, creativity and new ideas are important. It is impossible to say for sure where ideas come from, but a vibrant and distinctive culture is bound to play a part.

Personally, I feel that an afternoon spent watching something subtitled is as much hard work as a few hours sitting at the computer running regressions. One thing's for sure: Hollywood has the best special effects, but it's really not the place to look for the intellectual cutting edge.

Chapter 13

NETWORKS

"The Program Has Unexpectedly Quit"

That's just one of the things my computer says to me pretty often. If I'm lucky. Even more often it just crashes without bothering to warn me to save my work.

It's one of the everyday frustrations of modern life. But why? Why do we passively continue to use software that imposes on us such costs of lost time and raised blood pressure?

The answer, in short, is that I use it because you use it and so does almost everybody else. It is Microsoft's great commercial achievement to have made its software the near-ubiquitous standard in desktop operating systems and applications such as spreadsheets, slide shows, and word processing. Not to mention notoriously having a go at cornering the market in Internet browsers, too, at the expense of Netscape, which proved to be a step too far for the U.S. Department of Justice.

Microsoft's dominance is a classic result of a phenomenon that seems to be more and more common in the economy, **network externalities**. A network is a set of links connecting people and equipment. The Internet is one, as is the rail network or the telephone network. Some are a bit less obvious: automatic teller machines, for example, linking people and cash in banks. Money itself is another example—it's not much use my trying to spend cowrie shells if you use cows as a medium of exchange.

Network goods are accounting for a growing share of the developed economies, including information technology and communications, entertainment and finance. The share of GDP accounted for by these categories has climbed sharply during the past quarter century.

Network goods differ from conventional goods and services such as doughnuts or haircuts. Nobody wants a telephone for its own sake. The value to consumers lies in the telephone plus the link to another telephone. Or preferably to lots of other telephones. The more people are linked to the network, the more useful it is and the more consumers will want it. This is the network externality. It is a powerful effect. Suppose there are 10 telephones, with 90 potential links between different users. Add one more user, and you get 20 extra potential links. Moving from the 100th to the 101st user adds 200 additional links.

Traditional goods are **substitutes**: if I buy more of one out of a given income, I will get less of another. Network goods **complement** each other: the phone is no good without the phone line and the other users, or the PC without the printer, Zip drive, Internet connection, and so on. The value of the network good increases with the number of units sold. A network externality is in effect an economy of scale in demand.

What's more, many network goods fall significantly in cost the more of them are bought, because they are characterized by economies of scale in production, too. In developing software, for example, almost all the cost is up front in the programming and marketing. Making additional copies and distributing them is very cheap. So if the developer can sell a million copies rather than a hundred thousand the average cost and price can be much lower. The same is true of any high-tech network involving a lot of up-front research and development.

The presence of economies of scale in demand and often supply as well means network industries could be prone to dominance by monopolies. The scale effects mean it is hard for new competitors to break into the market—just as it is in aircraft manufacture or petrochemicals.

What's more, as with any externality, the presence of network externalities means the amount of the good produced privately is unlikely to be as high as the socially desirable amount. If the producers cannot capture the benefits of a bigger network, they will underproduce. This will be true whether there is perfect competition between producers or a monopoly. In fact, there is likely to be an even smaller network when there is a monopoly because the monopolist can increase profits by restricting supply. Competition is better for consumers even in these circumstances.

That is, unless the monopolist can find some way of clawing back those network benefits. It might be able to do so to some extent by setting different prices for different consumers. For instance, if businesses value the connectedness more than individuals, the company could try and charge the businesses a higher rate. Even so, whatever the industry structure, networks are likely to be too small.

In many cases, the desirable size of the network could actually be everyone. For example, telephones are most useful if you can get hold of absolutely everyone you might want to talk to. In fact, there does seem no limit to our demand for telephone connections as the growth of second and third lines, ISDN and broadband lines, and mobile telephony demonstrates.

In many a communications network, the ideal is ubiquity. It rarely happens. Even Microsoft, with its relatively high degree of monopoly power and drive toward world domination, wants Windows and Office to be ubiquitous only if everybody has paid them enough for it, *enough* being a lot.

Many providers of basic telephone services (often former state monopolies) are required to make lines available to anybody who will pay. In most other examples, however, the government does not step in to make the network's coverage universal, and its role tends to be restricted to making sure networks deliver the maximum possible benefits to consumers.

One method is by enforcing technical standards. Thinking about the ubiquity of technical standards actually reveals how many goods and services have network aspects. Battles over standards for new products spell the difference between huge profits and commercial disaster, and the history of technology is littered with casualties. Technological **lock-in** benefited Microsoft at the expense of Apple, and VHS videotapes rather than Betamax (and who remembers that now?), the gasoline engine, the voltage at which electricity is delivered into our homes, the shape of electric plugs, the QWERTY keyboard we English speakers still use because everybody has learned to type fast that way, the size of screw threads, and countless others.

As these examples suggest, the chance events of history can play a huge part in determining which technologies and which companies succeed. In addition, creating critical mass in the market for a new product very rapidly can be crucially important. The combination of the **first mover advantage** and the importance of cementing it with enough customers explains why so many Internet businesses have thought it was a good idea to lose a lot of money for a long time. It is a kind of special introductory pricing, common with many new products like green-tea-flavored cookies or a new type of cheese dip, but more important to technology companies. As it turned out, many of the dot-coms were wrong to think losing bucketfuls of money in order to buy enough customers would guarantee their success. But the jury is still out on some of the survivors (think of Amazon).

The "burst to be first" tactic has certainly worked in the past with many companies creating a genuinely new technology (as opposed to just using one, such as the Internet). For instance, in the 1880s and '90s, many manufacturers of electrical equipment gave away free electricity to attract consumers. This helped Westinghouse establish the alternating current rather than direct current as the standard in electricity transmission and equipment, and the resulting ability to transmit electricity safely over long distances was in turn a vital prerequisite for the widespread use of electricity.

Sometimes governments cooperate over technical standards, as in international telecommunications. European governments set the GSM standard for mobile telephones in order to ensure a big, continent-wide market for the blossoming new product, but the U.S. government opted for a different standard. It is often argued that this helps explain the greater success of European mobile phone companies, though the high and restrictive price structures for fixed telephony in Europe (legacy of all those state monopolies) must also have played an important part.

The individual companies might have an incentive to agree on compatible standards. They will all benefit from agreeing to a standard if compatibility increases the size of the total market by a large amount. In many cases, this is exactly what happens. Where there are network effects, cooperation between companies can be good for consumers, rather than damaging them, as long as the cooperation is helping develop a bigger market within which the companies will go on to compete with each other in the approved manner.

On the other hand, if they are big enough, they might do better by setting a proprietary standard and trying to monopolize the market. These countervailing forces have become very apparent in the computer software industry, where it has taken on a philosophical cast with the growth of the "open source" movement and the development of Linux as an operating system to compete with Microsoft.

What's best for consumers as opposed to companies is undoubtedly complete compatibility. There is nothing more frustrating than not being able to open or email a file or use a CD-ROM because it doesn't work with your machine's operating system. Perhaps the government's role in setting international technical standards should extend from the telecommunications industry to the computer industry as it becomes harder and harder to draw the line separating the two.

Some economists believe compulsory licensing of software or other proprietary technical knowledge is the best way to enforce competition in network industries. Others believe this is draconian and unnecessary because there are other strong forces for competition in high-technology industries, as discussed later.

Without legal force, the result will sometimes be incompatibility. As the many examples of past winners from being the technological first mover demonstrate, there are substantial profits in store for whichever company can face off the competition in terms of setting the standards. The first company in a particular network business (and often consequently the biggest if there are also big economies of scale in production) has every incentive not to cooperate in agreeing to a compatible standard—as long as its own standard is a good one. If it has a bad technology, the advantage will go to the second mover in the industry, which will have had chance to learn from the first mover's mistakes. But assuming the first mover has a good enough technology, it would rather rely on its dominant position and then perhaps license its own standard to any would-be competitors.

Better yet to eliminate the competitors altogether, of course. This is what makes network industries, often described as **natural monopolies**, so challenging for a government's antitrust authorities.

Take the Microsoft case. Its defenders argued that there was no genuine damage to the public caused by Microsoft's dominance. After all, they said, the company had invented and developed a fantastic product, one that benefited consumers precisely because they all used it and had created a market that hadn't existed in 1980; what's more, its prices had been falling over time. There was also a real threat of competition from innovation, from the potential for completely new technologies that would undermine the use of desktop computer operating systems altogether, the company argued.

The counterargument is that the product quality would have been higher and the price lower if there had been competitors in the market, but aspects of Microsoft's behavior prevented competition. Just because consumers have been able to buy good software does not mean they could not have bought better software for less in a different market structure.

Both Microsoft and the Department of Justice put forward good arguments. The competition dilemma in network industries is genuinely difficult. Consumers *do* gain from a common standard, whether set by governments or a dominant company, because it increases the size and value of the network to them and guards them against the risk of choosing the losing standard in a technical and marketing contest.

But there is no reason to believe common standards will evolve in a genuinely competitive market. That would happen only if none of the competing companies believed it had an edge over the others in terms of speed, product quality, or initial market size. In practice, that doesn't seem to happen very often.

This suggests that the emergence of a dominant company with a proprietary standard will bring consumers significant network benefits. Electricity once again offers a good example. In 1896, Westinghouse and GE entered a fifteen-year patent-sharing agreement, creating a duopoly in electrical equipment. But as they also gave away electricity to create the market for their equipment and in the process gave a decisive boost to the electricity transmission system, it is hard to be confident their duopoly acted against the public interest.

Even so, as we saw earlier, the network created by a monopoly (or small oligopoly) will be smaller than desirable, because the monopoly firm will restrict sales by charging a high price to boost profits. In this case, it would be in the public interest for the competition authorities to require a monopolist to license its technology to competitors (on nonprohibitive terms—and it is not easy to figure out what the fees should be). That will lead to the growth of a bigger network. Breaking up the monopoly instead—one proposal for dealing with Microsoft—might or might not benefit consumers. That would depend on which companies owned what parts of the network. In the case of the fixed telephone network, for example, the splitting of long-distance from local calls and the introduction of long-distance competition has certainly benefited telephone users. The crucial last bit of local link to people's homes and businesses is a natural bottleneck, because the costs of all that wiring are so high it cannot be replicated by a would-be competitor, which is why local telephony is everywhere so highly regulated. On the other hand, introducing long dis-

tance competition turned out to be easy, although the level of interconnection fees to the local network is a contentious matter for which different assumptions give different answers.

Of course, even the local telephone stranglehold has proved vulnerable. Wireless technology now exists to compete with the wired. In Europe
and also in many parts of the developing world where wired phone networks are inefficient and small, mobile telephony is now providing effective competition. The pace of technological change itself can undermine
the market power of dominant companies.

This is exactly what some economists believe will ensure competition
in network industries more effectively than anything else, the gale of creative destruction at a time of rapid technological change. Bill Gates was
famously nearly taken by surprise by the Internet, but the real technological challenge to a company with a monopoly in desktop operating systems will be the decline of ubiquitous desktop computing.

This kind of technological leapfrogging could yet happen. Some technology experts compare the desktop or laptop PC to the all-purpose electric motors sold to households in the early twentieth century. The modern
housewife would buy one motor and use it to run a whole variety of
domestic appliances. But eventually each appliance came with its own
internal motor and the consumer could simply forget about how to operate electric motors altogether. The parallel now would perhaps be the
pocket digital assistant/mobile telephone/email device, the TV/DVD/CD-
ROM player, and the smart household appliances. Computing power will
be distributed between communications devices, entertainment devices,
and appliances, or in other words used for specific purposes, making the
all-purpose desktop computer irrelevant.

Unfortunately, competition authorities cannot always rely on technological innovation to do their job for them, although the length of time a
company has held a dominant position can give useful clues as to whether
it is able to abuse its monopoly power or not. Bell, later AT&T, dominated the U.S. telephone network for well over half a century. It had started
out as the technologically superior long distance operator but faced stiff
competition in local markets. Its tactic was to refuse to connect to local
rivals, squeezing them out by offering callers a better service if they used
both the local Bell company and the long distance service. In the case of
telephones, the government-enforced breakup of monopolies in America
and elsewhere if anything paved the way for the development of mobile

telephony rather than the other way round. There was no urgent incentive for companies to invent mobiles, even though the technological building blocks were there, when the government ensured the fixed telephone monopoly was so profitable. Competition in any industry is an act of political will as well as commercial and technical pressures, because governments ensure the smooth functioning of markets, and that is more true in network industries prone to natural monopolies and first mover lock-in effects than in others.

What's more, network industries seem to be growing in importance. Partly this is because of the nature of recent technological advance. It has been concentrated in the computer and communications industries, which are innately subject to network externalities. There are plenty of examples of network formation, like instant messaging among AOL members, or eBay, which has grown more popular with sellers the more buyers it attracts and vice versa.

But in addition we are spending a growing share of our incomes on network goods, from financial services to cable TV, software to travel, as we become more prosperous. This will continue with the growing importance of international links. For example, the more people travel from country to country in their jobs, the more likely it is that educational qualifications will develop a network externality as a kind of common currency of ideas. As I suggested, there could also be an increasing network externality in actual currency, pointing to a natural monopoly of one global money. Let's just hope Bill Gates doesn't decide to take Microsoft into that market.

Chapter 14

THE INTERNET

The Economics of Dot–Bombs

The dot-com bubble seems so long ago. For a couple of years up to March 2001 a sort of millennial fever of excitement about the Internet swept the stock market, sending the share prices of high technology companies rocketing skywards. Silicon Valley sizzled. The number of initial public offerings on the three major U.S. stock exchanges leaped from 262 in 1998 to about 500 each year in 1999 and 2000. Many companies were able to print their own money in the shape of issuing shares they could use to take over other companies. At the peak of the bubble, there was a new millionaire made in America every ten minutes, although many unfortunately did not convert their paper wealth into more durable assets. For inevitably what went up later came down. The Nasdaq index lost two-thirds of its value in 2001. The flood of IPOs dried up. The dot-com dream was over.

To anybody old enough to have experienced several booms and busts, however, it looks inevitable that the backlash is as overdone as the initial enthusiasm. This is, after all, what stock markets are like, prone to exaggerating the shifts in real economy trends. You don't even have to invoke irrational investor behavior to explain some dramatic rises and falls in share prices. The basic arithmetic of **discounting** expected profits growth far into the future, to allow for the fact that we attach less value to earnings in ten years' time than today, means that small changes in expectations for the future lead to large changes in valuations now. And then there's the irrational hysteria, too, whereby we all get infected by the enthusiasm for the next big thing and by the bitter disappointment when it proves not quite such a big deal after all.

So the bursting of the stock market bubble does not spell doom for anyone with an Internet business plan. Economists are still excited about the Internet. It holds out the genuine promise of making markets work better because it is easy and cheap for people to find out information on things such as product prices and job availability. Lack of information has always been a major source of friction in the smooth working of markets. What's more, there is now enough evidence of a boost to productivity in the U.S. economy since the mid-1990s to have persuaded most economists that the new technologies do have the potential to trigger a faster rate of growth. In short, it is laying the foundations for increased prosperity in the future.

The experience of the dot-com bust does, though, mean a different kind of business plan will be necessary for commercial success. Entrepreneurs can no longer count on venture capitalists funding a business that plans to make a huge loss for several years, because the venture capitalists can no longer rely on getting their money back quickly through an initial public offering (IPO).

For, somewhat bizarrely in retrospect, losing a lot of money was for a while seen as the key to success for an ambitious dot-com. The reasoning was that building a big customer base and locking those customers in would secure for a business the first mover advantage. It almost didn't matter what you were selling as long as you won the customers and kept them loyal to your brand. Well, the strategy worked for Amazon, which stayed in the red year after year in order to continue its expansion from the original bookselling operation, and became one of the best-known Internet brands. A lot of entrepreneurs thought they would try the same trick.

It was inevitable that eventually investors would get fed up of businesses that continued to lose money, especially the more idiosyncratic ones. After all, how big a commercial prize could first mover advantage in the market for online knitting patterns possibly be? But that doesn't mean the "make a big loss" strategy was entirely dumb. The Internet does have some unusual characteristics that affect the underlying economics of an online business.

One feature is the fact that an Internet or information business more generally has high fixed costs and low marginal costs (or the cost of producing one additional unit). It is expensive to produce the first unit, whether it is a software program, a service such as online gambling, or a more broadly defined information good, such as a research-intensive drug or a design-intensive aircraft. That's because all the costs are up front and require a lot of skilled human input. However, subsequent copies are very cheap, or even zero cost in the case of copies of a program or online book. The copying can be done cheaply by computers and other machines. In other words, information businesses are inherently characterized by supply-side increasing returns to scale.

The Internet is also a network, obviously, and networks have the characteristic that there are demand-side economies of scale, otherwise known as network externalities, as discussed in an earlier chapter. Many Internet businesses could benefit from the same kinds of tactics used in older network industries such as telecoms, like setting technical standards that become the norm and thus locking in consumers.

Already we can draw plenty of strategic conclusions for dot-com executives. First mover advantage can be genuine, not hype, but it depends on being able to set a technical standard that makes it costly for consumers to switch to a rival later. So software companies and mobile phone operators might sensibly spend money on being first and biggest—look at the importance Microsoft attached to knocking Netscape from its first mover position in browsers—but it is not such an obviously wise strategy for an online retailer, as customers can switch from one "shop" to another easily.

Still, there are other potential justifications for high spending on marketing and customer acquisition. The structure of information industries means there are often several advantages to operating at a large scale. They are tied up with the importance of brand or reputation.

The cost structure of an information business means pricing policy has to be very different in such businesses compared to a basic old-economy business. The high initial costs are **sunk costs**, which can't necessarily be recovered. (To see why, think about the Channel Tunnel, the rail link under the English Channel between Britain and France. Customers don't care how much it cost to build or how fast the shareholders recover their investment, only how high the fare is compared to crossing by ferry.) Equally, the low unit costs of production (or reproduction) mean there is no natural limit to production capacity or potential sales.

Ideally, Microsoft would like to sell a copy of Office to everybody in the world. But how much to charge? The conventional rule of thumb, which is unit cost plus x percent, where x varies depending on the industry, is not much use when unit costs are very low. Prices have to be set depending on how much customers value the product. What the market will bear is the guideline. The ideal would be to charge every single customer the amount they personally think the product or service is worth, but in practice the price discrimination has to be a bit broader brush than that.

Possible techniques include offering different versions to business and personal customers; different prices for paper versus electronic versions of reports or software on CDs versus online; sending to regular customers for one kind of item money-off coupons for other products; selling the same information with different delays, such as access to share prices either instantaneously or after five minutes; customizing the product, as Nike now does with shoes ordered online or Dell with computers; and many, many others. It is easy for a company selling over the Internet to build up a detailed database that will help it target customers effectively.

Unfortunately there's a further difficulty with many information goods, which is that people often don't know how much they value them until they have already consumed them. Many are **experience goods**. You need to read a fair amount of a book or newspaper, see most of a video, or try running a program before you know whether it's any good. So publishers of information often offer samples—demo versions, first chapters, a couple of free articles, the abstract of a working paper. But as much of the information published on the Internet in the early days was free, there is a residual strong demand for free access and strong resistance to paying. So, for example, in newspaper and magazine publishing, only very strong brands, such as *The Wall Street Journal* or *The Economist*, have so far got away with meaningful online subscription fees. Most publications make a selection of the material in the print version available free online. Even such a popular author as Stephen King failed to get 75 percent of the readers who downloaded early chapters of an online book to send in payment, so he ended his electronic publishing experiment.

The fact that many information goods are experience goods is, nevertheless, another good reason for establishing a strong brand, which tends to involve heavy spending on advertising and marketing. Customers are more likely to take the risk of spending money on an experience if they know the company offering it has a good **reputation**, or in other words, a good brand image. If a lot of other customers had been disappointed, the reputation would not last.

The importance of reputation partly explains why some predictions that the Internet would wipe out intermediaries such as real estate agents or insurance brokers were wrong. Customers want a fallback in case a transaction goes wrong, the reassurance that there is somebody to watch out for their interests and perhaps complain to. What's more, with information plentiful, consumers are swamped with it. Bots that carry out searches and compare prices are far from perfect, being engaged in a technological arms race with retailers, who don't want to make price comparisons all that easy. Sometimes it is easier to go to a broker or an intermediary.

The **information overload** means businesses need to grab people's attention. Herbert Simon, a Nobel Prize–winning economist, summed up the problem long ago: "A wealth of information creates a poverty of attention." This is why just about all the most visited websites are search engines that sift through the oceans of online information to find the particular tasty plankton each of us desires.

The School of Information and Management Systems at Berkeley estimated that the amount of information produced in just one year, 1999, was 1 to 2 exabytes (an exabyte is 10 to the power 18 bytes, and 5 exabytes would take care of all the words spoken by human beings so far in history). That's about 250 megabytes for every person on earth, or the equivalent of 250 short novels each, 125 photographs, or 12.5 full floppy disks. The figures did not include the information produced digitally that year but not stored systematically, notably email. The report estimates annual email production at 610 billion messages, requiring roughly 11,285 terabytes if it was stored, or the equivalent of more than a thousand times the printed collection of the Library of Congress. Yet people are consuming the same amount of information as before, due to limits set by time and physiology. The Internet has not changed information consumption or even production, but it has revolutionized transmission and availability.

It has also made it possible for online businesses to **customize** their contact with overloaded customers. They can build up a detailed customer database and target advertising and special offers to suit the individuals. (That's the theory, anyway. Nobody seems to have told the online pornographers, who still seem to prefer to spray their advertising around randomly, if that's the right way to describe it. Or am I really one of only a select few getting those emails from BESTMEGAWEB—PLUG INTO A MEGA SENSATIONAL EXPERIENCE?)

In short, it is easy to understand why many dot-coms, and their investors, thought it made sense to spend heavily up front on product development, marketing and reputation. Where did so many go wrong, then?

Sometimes they forgot that the spending would be justified only by rapid growth in customer numbers, and therefore revenues. After all, there can only be one first mover per market; spending desperately on marketing gimmicks rarely makes sense for a slow-growing number two. Many were hopeless at customization, targeting, and price discrimination. For supposedly high-tech businesses, few appeared to know how to use the available tracking and database technology. They did not make the most of those customers they had managed to attract.

A lot of dot-coms also failed to understand that as the Internet is a means of doing business, they still had to have a viable business. It is a channel of distribution that has opened up new business opportunities in a few areas, but for the most part, it has instead changed the cost structure and market access in existing industries.

Gambling, pornography, software, auctions, and banking have been about the most successful Internet businesses. These are all genuinely weightless activities—there is no need for a physical product. In each of these cases, by reducing **entry barriers,** the Net has made it possible for new entrants to break into the market, albeit other big companies such as insurers in the highly regulated banking industry. It has also made the potential market bigger by extending its geographical scope. There have therefore been good business opportunities in such industries, as there would be in any industrial shake-up.

In other industries such as publishing and retailing, which are highly dependent on distribution channels that have built up in specific ways over a long time, the arrival of the Internet has been more problematic. A new means of distribution can simply cannibalize existing ones. The U.K.'s most successful online business is Tesco, the biggest supermarket retailer. Its online ordering and home delivery service has grown at the expense mainly of other supermarket chains but also because some of its own physical customers switched. In fact, many retailers have come to believe the only difference the Net makes to them is that it's one more means of

contact with customers they now have to provide along with physical presence, telephone access, and mail order. It hasn't increased the demand for
their goods at all. Shopping online for most customers means shopping
differently, not shopping more.

Newspapers face a similar dilemma: they might gain some of their
online readers only at the expense of purchases of the physical paper,
which is a problem when the former is free and the later paid for. Their
market has in fact continued to shrink in the face of competition from
specialist magazines, television, and other forms of entertainment.

Finally, let's face it, some of the dot-coms were just silly ideas that
could only have got off the ground at all during a wave of hysteria such as
the turn-of-the-century New Economy boom; or instead were perfectly
decent retail ideas implemented at indecent cost, with high salaries and
hip offices as well as glitzy advertising campaigns, because venture capitalists were throwing money away. Because the Internet has not abolished
the basic requirement that a viable business needs to generate healthy
growth in revenues. It certainly hasn't rewritten the rules of economics.

Some Internet businesses have got economists really excited, however.
They seem to have a business model that would be impossible without
this particular technology. One is eBay, the auction site that matches buyers and sellers of specific items, under an agreed set of rules, in a way that
would have been impossible without the Internet.

The other is Priceline, motto "Name your own price," which asks customers to suggest what they would be willing to pay for an item—often a
flight—and tries to match the offer to a supplier, such as an airline with
empty seats on particular routes. Again, there are clear rules and the company, like eBay, deals with the credit card payments. These two companies,
one very successful, the other getting there rather slowly, take advantage of
the technology to do things that would otherwise be impossible. Priceline
achieves perfect price discrimination by asking customers to specify how
much value they place on a certain item like a flight. Although airlines are
selling only a few of their tickets this way, it does mean more than ever
that planes are full of people who've paid prices ranging from the fortune
paid by a celebrity or top executive in first class all the way to the low
amount offered by someone who wanted a last-minute weekend away.
And they are more often full, with no empty seats that could and should
have been bringing in revenues.

Companies like eBay take both the differential pricing and also matching of buyer and seller even further by making it possible for almost anybody to auction almost anything. Buyers acquire items by paying exactly what they think those items are worth. Sellers find buyers for items they might not have been able to sell at all in the restricted local market.

Some business-to-business (B2B) online exchanges also take advantage of the Internet to match widely dispersed buyers and sellers. Although less visible to most of us, economists have estimated that businesses will be able to make significant cost savings through the use of B2B exchanges. Job recruitment sites also take advantage of this specific feature, the unparalleled ability to match demand and supply. They are making it easier for job hunters to find work, wherever it might be, and easier for employers to find staff with the right skills.

The beauty of such businesses to economists is precisely that they hold out the promise of making markets work better, removing obstacles like lack of information about prices and availability, or the whereabouts of potential buyers and sellers, and reducing the costs of search and carrying out transactions. Whether they and rivals will expand to account for a significant part of our spending is another matter.

Chapter 15

INDUSTRIAL CHANGE

Creative Destruction

In Britain's shambolic rail industry, the train companies face steep fines for every minute behind schedule the services run. The fines are imposed by the industry regulator, but the companies operating the trains and Railtrack, which runs the tracks and signals, have to parcel out the blame to decide who should pay them. After several dreadful accidents, by early 2001 many trains were running very late. The result was entirely predictable. It was the creation of an entirely new profession, the "delay attributor." Railtrack had 180 people in its delay attribution department in mid-2001, and the operating and engineering companies at least 120 between them. The numbers of delays were rising. That's just one example of the ability of an economy to create jobs where there is an unmet need.

There are countless others. For example, in the mid-1980s, I worked as an economist in the Treasury and was set the task of writing a short and simple explanation of financial derivatives, so short and simple that ministers would be able to understand it. The derivatives market was still pretty small, but the financial markets in the City of London were about to be deregulated and it seemed clear that derivatives would be one area of growth, as had already happened in New York. Only a handful of people working in the U.K. could be classed as derivatives traders. Within a decade, there were many thousands. However, as the trading is automated, the numbers will probably be back down in the hundreds before a second decade is over.

In fact, large-scale job creation and job destruction are basic characteristics of a capitalist economy. In any single year in the United States at least one in twelve people will change jobs, and the rate of turnover is similar in Europe. Britain is the only European economy where it is a little lower, and even there the turnover corresponds to 2 million people out of a workforce of 25 million changing their job each year. Some years in some countries the proportion is as high as a fifth of all jobs turning over.

When you think about it, this makes absolute sense. The structure of all the advanced economies has changed radically over time. Of course we don't need telegraph operators, hurdy-gurdy players on city streets, or Fortran programmers in 2002, whereas we do need call-center operatives, Britney Spears, and web page designers.

The basic change in every country is the decline in the share of manufacturing industry in the economy, and the rise in the share of services. (Going further back in time, the shift was from agriculture to manufacturing, the initial effect of the Industrial Revolution on work. The poorer OECD countries still have a big agricultural workforce, 25 percent of the total in Turkey for example, but in the U.K. just 1.2 percent of the workforce is employed in agriculture, in the U.S. 1.9 percent and in France 2.6 percent.)

The expansion of the service sector is a long-standing trend. The proportion of GDP and total employment accounted for by manufacturing peaked in the U.S. in the mid 1960s, and even in more heavily industrial countries such as Japan and Germany by the early 1970s. The proportion of the working-age population employed in industry now ranges between about 14 percent and 24 percent in the rich OECD countries, with Japan remaining at the top of this range.

According to the wonderful database maintained by the Bureau of Labor Statistics, freely available online, the number of employees in the United States has climbed from 47,230,000 at the start of 1951 to 132,167,000 fifty years later. Of this total, 34.5 percent were working in manufacturing at the start of that half century, compared with 13.8 percent at the end. (The absolute number of people working in America's manufacturing industries had climbed slightly, from 16.3 million to 18.2 million, whereas many other countries manufacturing saw an absolute as well as a relative decline.) There were corresponding increases in the proportion working in service industries—up from 14.6 percent to 17.6 percent in retailing; from 4.1 percent to 5.8 percent in finance, insurance, and retail estate; and leaping from 11.6 to 31.0 percent in a range of other services categorized together, including health, child care, education, motion pictures, and computer services. One of these miscellaneous services, health care, alone employed more than half as many people as all of manufacturing at the start of 2001. Oh, and of course, more people work for the government now—20.5 million people, or 15.5 percent of the January 2001 total, compared with 6.2 million, or 13.2 percent in January 1951.

Even within manufacturing there has been significant structural change, but less than you might expect. Not surprisingly, there has been growth in industries such as computers and electronics. The computer and office equipment industry employed almost nobody in 1951, a fraction of 1 percent of the manufacturing workforce. After half a century, the total was 363,000, or 2 percent of those employed in making things in America. Similarly, the workforce in electronic components climbed from 170,000 to 697,000, or 1.0 percent to 3.8 percent of the manufacturing workforce.

However, some traditional industries remain hugely important in U.S. manufacturing, although they account for a far less significant share of the economy as a whole. For example, in 1951, 5.5 percent of all jobs in industry, 893,000, were in the auto industry. In 2001, it was still 942,000, or 5.1 percent. After a dire slump in the early part of the 1980s, the American auto industry has expanded again. The textiles industry, clothing plus all other textile products, employed 15.5 percent of the manufacturing workforce in 1951, and 6.2 percent in 2001, a sharp contraction but leaving a substantial industry still employing more people than there are making cars and almost twice as many as are employed in the manufacture of electronic components.

If we look at these figures another way, one in every three American workers had a job in industry in 1951, compared with about one in every eight now. In the United States, like most other advanced economies, you're more likely to get a job in retail.

What do all these facts mean? They should help us put announcements about job losses in perspective. First, the net rates of job loss or creation are tiny compared to the gross turnover. In a typical year and a typical economy, the net increase or decrease in total employment is about a fiftieth of the workforce, equivalent to about 2.6 million people in the United States. But in a similarly typical year, a tenth or twelfth, 11 to 12 million in the U.S., will change their job.

There is no such thing as a typical year, of course. These averages smooth over the ups and downs of the **business cycle**. Almost all the job losses are bunched into **recession** years. For example, in the year to November 2001 employment in the United States had fallen by 1.5 million, with the impact of the terrorist attacks on top of the effects of recession. Often job losses are announced in big batches, too, when a company closes down a whole plant or call center, or decides it must axe 10 percent of its workforce. On the other hand, jobs are created more evenly, but more of them are created in years of economic expansion. Between 1991 and the start of 2001 the United States experienced the net creation of 25 million jobs.

This is the human face of the **creative destruction** of capitalism, in the famous phrase coined by Joseph Schumpeter. Some jobs and companies are destroyed, others, and more and more of them over time, are created. After all, the U.S. workforce has risen from just under 30 million in 1939 to 47.2 million in 1951 and over 132 million in 2001. It has nearly trebled during a half century that has brought dire warnings about jobs being destroyed by technology, by overseas trade, by the government—you name it. Such alarmist stuff flies in the face of more than two hundred years of economic expansion in the developed world. It has gone very badly wrong at some points, with the Great Depression in the 1930s in the United States (the 1920s were worse in Europe), the American Civil War, and two world wars, not to mention the economic calamity of communism. There are also persistent unemployment problems for specific groups such as black men in inner cities in the United States and elsewhere, or young people in France, reflecting social and institutional hurdles to employment. However, these vulnerabilities do not overturn the point that doom-laden prophecies about the end of work are highly unlikely to be true.

It isn't work as my parents would understand it, of course. They both started work in the cotton mills of northern England (interrupted by the diversion of World War II). The hours were long, often involving unsociable shifts, the work was arduous and boring, the conditions were grim in the hot and noisy mills, and the pay was low. Still, they both escaped into other jobs—my mum as a clerk for the social security department, my dad checking meter readings for the electricity company—and they were doing better than their parents. Their children did better yet. We all sit at desks and tap away into computers, in quiet air-conditioned offices, earning a decently bourgeois income. If we hadn't gone to universities and become professionals we might have got clerical jobs or been working in shops. Or trained in some skill such as plumbing or hairdressing and be running our own businesses. There are still some really lousy jobs, but fewer jobs are really lousy now. This pattern of improvement in the conditions of work generation by generation is a common story of our times. I have to admit that when I hear about another textile mill closing because of the pressure of competition from overseas or because investment in new equipment has made half a company's workforce redundant, I'm quietly pleased at one level. Boring, repetitive, uncomfortable jobs are surely jobs best done by machines.

If the economy is raising living standards over time and at the same time making the ways we have to earn our living typically so much more pleasant than in the past, that's great by me.

This is the big picture. How it happens in practice is more painful. Business cycles are not the smooth and regular expansions and contractions their name suggests. The expansions tend to be fairly long and steady, but a recession is always a short, sharp shock. A lot of people lose their jobs at the same time and naturally worry about finding another. Often they have to take work at lower pay and on worse terms at such a time, if they can find another job. As redundancies also tend to be geographically clustered, that can be harder than national average unemployment figures might suggest. What's more, people develop skills specific to the work they do, and those will not transfer easily. You can't work a loom one day and cut hair the next. Even if you are prepared to move to a different part of the country for work, it might well be the case that all the companies in a particular industry are in difficulty at the same time.

The trouble is that the people losing jobs and the people gaining jobs that are getting better over time are often different people. So the overall trend is not much comfort to anybody who finds that he or she is the wrong kind of person for today's economy. When the structure of the economy is changing rapidly, as it seems to have been during the past decade, a lot of the workforce can feel very insecure without any apparent objective reason for it.

There is a clear policy lesson here. Contrary to almost any public debate you'll ever hear, it is not jobs but people that matter. Governments should not make it their business to preserve specific jobs in particular industries and companies. That's a mission doomed to eventual failure. Could government policy have saved the horse-drawn carriage building business and all the jobs tied up in that? Should it have even tried when we know with hindsight that the automobile industry would create hundreds of thousands of jobs in the decades ahead? Clearly not. Governments have no special talent for predicting which technologies will succeed, how the terms of trade will change, what skills the economy will need, and what specific jobs might be created. Economists would be the first to admit they can't make those predictions either—after all, we can't even forecast GDP growth next year or next quarter with any great accuracy.

Could and should government policy help specific individuals through episodes of structural change? That's a different matter. It seems to me an entirely valid aim of the education system and the social security system to equip people to adjust to recessions and waves of industrial change. Governments could even devise radical new policies if they start thinking about the people—for example, grants so people can afford to move out of a declining area, apprenticeship schemes for older workers who need to retrain, job guarantees and so on. It's the workers who matter, not the factories or office buildings, not the industry (actually this is a nearly meaningless abstraction), not even the corporate shareholders.

It's pretty clear that most governments do not have good policies for helping people. The picture varies from country to country, but in general there is not much lifetime income and employment mobility. In other words, somebody with low skills and a bad or insecure job is unlikely to escape from the path of low pay and intermittent unemployment. What's worse, the trap is being passed from generation to generation. For example, in declining Rust Belt areas where factory or shipyard closures have put a generation of men out of work, there is also a high rate of unemployment and poverty among their children.

These generalizations hold true for the U.S., even though it enjoys much greater social and geographical mobility than the European countries or Japan. But the picture is worse in those European economies that have had through the 1980s and '90s high unemployment rates and little or no growth in employment outside the public sector. Much as many Europeans resist the idea, it's clear that long-lasting high unemployment rates of 10 percent or more in some countries are a price paid for a high degree of protection and high social benefits (like pensions and sick pay) for the 90 percent who do have jobs. It's expensive to employ people in parts of Europe, and expensive and difficult to destroy jobs, so fewer of them get created in the first place.

That leaves stubborn pockets of unemployment and poverty, or social exclusion, in the vogue European phrase, which pose a thorny problem. They are clustered often in areas of bad housing, high crime rates, an active illegal drug trade, high rates of chronic ill health and disability, and high proportions of ethnic minority or immigrant groups. In other words, the people concerned are likely to face not one or two difficulties, nothing so straightforward as not having a job, but a whole host of problems. This net of difficulties, cemented in place by lack of transport, bad schools and hospitals, and malign social norms, would trap even the most able and energetic person. No wonder governments have made little headway.

Yet part of the explanation for the policy failure must be that few policymakers have thought of the people as the policy target. The policy debate, at least until very recently, has been conducted in terms of abstractions such as jobs or industries. Companies form lobby groups to persuade politicians to protect their industries from foreign competition or to introduce tax breaks or whatever.

Preserving jobs is often one of the arguments deployed by these lobbyists. That might even be a beneficial side effect of whatever policies the government is persuaded to introduce. The U.S. textile industry, for example, might employ more people than it otherwise would had it not so successfully campaigned for protection from imports. (Of the $20 billion revenue raised by tariffs on imports into the United States in 2000, a full $9 billion came from tariffs on clothing and footwear.) However, fewer other jobs will have been created as a result—possibly even in the U.S. clothing industry itself, because consumers will be paying higher prices for their clothes and shoes. Actually, the jobs saved could well be specifically those of executives in the companies concerned, but the main aim of industry lobbying is to safeguard profitability.

Of course a thriving economy does need profitable industries, but there is nothing to tell us which industries they need to be. I have no doubt that a century ago the horse-drawn vehicle industry did everything in its power to lobby governments for assistance, but alas, it had become fundamentally unprofitable as consumers opted for trains, automobiles and eventually planes instead. You might imagine the fiber-optic cable industry would be a good bet for future long-term growth, but there is no need to help it create jobs if it is a fundamentally profitable business. The trouble with trying to pick winners as a matter of policy is that an official sitting in the capital city trying to figure out growth industries of the future is almost certain to get it wrong, in which case he or she will be creating a lot of vulnerable jobs—not a sensible policy. Or they might just get it right, but in that case private industry will create the jobs without any government help.

So it should not be an aim of public policy to preserve specific jobs. The right aim is creating a climate for the creation of many jobs, preferably in fast-growing sectors where pay and conditions will typically be good, and equipping people to fill them whatever they are. Doing so was the great success of U.S. governments in the latter decades of the twentieth century, and not doing so the great failure of many European governments, who will find they have created a stubborn legacy of unemployment for a large minority of their people.

I do hope, however, that the job of delay attributor in the British rail system doesn't survive for too many years. Now, there's a case where the government could wisely set out to destroy jobs.

Part IV

THERE'S A WORLD OUT THERE

Globalization Isn't All Globaloney

No guide to economics could ignore one of the main developments in recent history—globalization, or the increased extent and depth of the economic links between people in different countries. There were episodes of globalization in the past, but ours has brought new challenges demanding new responses. Indeed, the failures of globalization have played a big part in ushering in a frightening era of political instability and war.

Although the common perception is that economists have not covered themselves in glory in analyzing globalization and solving the world's problems, economists talk a lot less globaloney about globalization than many. That might not be saying much, but it's a start.

Chapter 16

DISEASE

No Man Is an Island

No man is an Island, entire of itself; every man is a piece of the continent, a part of the main. . . .any man's death diminishes me, because I am involved in mankind; and therefore never send to know for whom the bell tolls; it tolls for thee.

In this famous passage from one of his *Meditations*, John Donne, the metaphysical poet, insists on our connection to each other through our common humanity. Writing in the seventeenth century, he could have had no idea of the human capacity for mass slaughter, yet the huge numbers of deaths we have grown used to in the context of war, starvation, disaster and disease do not diminish the strength of his argument. On the contrary, globalization is weaving us together increasingly tightly. As Adam Smith, the founding father of economics, observed: "No society can be flourishing and happy of which by far the greater part of the numbers are poor and miserable." This is no less true for a global economy than a nation.

One of the most direct results of globalization is how much more likely we are to share diseases, with the explosion in foreign travel. Tuberculosis has reemerged in Western cities, cholera is in danger of once again becoming epidemic. And then there is AIDS, a disease that originated in sub-Saharan Africa and spread worldwide in the early 1980s. Even animal diseases spread more easily. The reemergence of foot-and-mouth disease, endemic in many parts of the world, that triggered the slaughter of millions of British sheep and cows in 2001 was traced to illegal meat imports.

All diseases are more prevalent and more often fatal in developing countries. For such countries have inadequate public health systems; the people in them are less well nourished and therefore less able to resist infection, they cannot easily afford medicines, and the climate makes disease control harder. But beyond that statement of the obvious, does economics have anything to say about epidemics? The answer is yes, as soon as you understand that a healthy population is a **public good**.

A public good is something that benefits everybody. It is also something that each of us as individuals has no incentive to acquire. A clean environment is a classic example. Everybody benefits, but if it is left to individual citizens or companies to keep the air and rivers clean, there will be too much pollution. Why would I bother with the cost of cleaning up the emissions from my factory if my competitors might not? They could free-ride on the back of my efforts without incurring the same costs themselves. The government needs to force all factories to meet minimum standards. National defense is another example. We all like to go to sleep secure in the knowledge some rogue tyrant will not be able to fire long-distance ballistic missiles at us, but how much would we each pay toward defense if it depended on voluntary contributions? As much as the price of a movie ticket once a week? Certainly not enough to build a national missile defense system.

To get back to diseases, public health is a public good. Disease control not only benefits those who are ill but makes everybody else less likely to fall ill in the future. Yet as individuals we would not want to invest enough to guarantee public health. Why should I pay anything toward somebody else's health unless I have to? Any direct personal benefit is hard to pin down, and I would also be suspicious that other people would not pay their fair share toward my health and well-being.

What's more, in a globalized world where international travel and trade are commonplace, public health is a **global public good**. It will be a benefit to anybody in any Western city if fewer poor Africans and Asians have tuberculosis, because it will reduce the risk that you or I will catch the disease. Several cities in the U.S. and the U.K. have seen tuberculosis outbreaks in recent years, some occurring in schools. And besides, the healthier and more prosperous the populations of developing countries are, the bigger the market for our exports—Adam Smith's point on a global scale.

Even though the concept of disease prevention as a global public good is new, the need to develop effective public policies is urgent; almost 20 million people died in the four years between the publication of a proposal to develop vaccines against diseases rampant in developing countries and the date of writing this chapter. The proposal would cost no government money at all unless a successful vaccine were to be developed. The idea, which has been gathering support since 1997, is an all-too-frequent example of a fresh insight from economic theory being ignored for too long by policymakers. It was not until 2000 that the United Nations agreed to set up a fund to tackle HIV/AIDS, tuberculosis, and malaria, and it was not inaugurated until April 2002, even then with only a fraction of the money it would probably need to succeed. Fast as this was in terms of the U.N. bureaucracy, private donors like Ted Turner and Bill and Melinda Gates were much faster in earmarking money for preventive health care.

It is a simple enough idea: world governments, whether singly through their aid budgets or together through the World Bank or United Nations, promise to buy a certain number of doses of an effective vaccine for any of the three main plagues of the developing world—malaria, tuberculosis, and the strains of HIV prevalent in Africa. While governments would have to spend money up front to reduce the prevalence of disease, if a successful vaccine is developed, they would no longer endure the continuing financial and economic burdens of illness and premature mortality.

Aside from the potential gains to the developed countries from preventing the spread of diseases, the potential economic benefits to poor countries of an effective malaria vaccine, for example, are huge. According to World Health Organization estimates, there are about 300 million clinical cases of malaria a year, and 1.1 million deaths. The impact on the workforce and productivity is a drain on the economy, and also ties up precious health care resources. U.N. and World Bank estimates suggest malaria alone slows growth by more than 1 percent a year, which is staggering. If correct, it means the elimination of malaria thirty-five years ago would have given Africa a level of GDP $100 billion higher than the current $440 million. Almost all the malaria cases occur in the developing world, and 90 percent in Africa, although global warming is helping spread malaria to new regions. Children and pregnant women are most at risk. There is also increasing resistance to the drugs currently used to treat the disease.

Other diseases add to the drag on the economies affected. HIV/AIDS, for example, mainly affects people aged fifteen to forty-nine, the most productive age group and those on whom many family members often rely. Gold Fields, the South African mining company, estimated that the 26.5 percent rate of HIV/AIDS infection among its workforce was adding as much as $10 to the cost of producing an ounce of gold. In early 2002 it therefore announced it would pay for treatment, despite the high cost of anti-retroviral drugs, in order to reduce the AIDS tax on gold production to about $4 an ounce. According to the United Nations, by the end of 2001, AIDS had killed 17 million people and infected 60 million worldwide. The toll from such diseases is one of the most serious issues in international development now.

Yet although this looks as though there should be a large and attractive potential market for a drug company to target, it is one subject to severe market failures. For one thing, individuals have inadequate incentives to take vaccines, as the individual risk of infection is often low but the cycle of infection is broken only if most people in a population are vaccinated. The social benefit is greater than the individual benefit. So the size of the potential market, without government intervention, is probably a lot smaller than the number of cases might make it appear. This is true of every vaccine, which is why governments either require or strongly encourage citizens to get their children vaccinated against measles, say.

In addition, the main beneficiaries of vaccination are often children. They will reap the economic benefits of not catching the disease as healthy adults earning money, but cannot earmark those future incomes to promise to pay for the vaccine when they are five. Parents are a good but not foolproof way of extracting today a child's future income; their heart is usually in the right place, but they are generally poorer than their offspring will be if he or she grows into a healthy adult. Indeed, as most residents in sub-Saharan Africa are too poor to afford an insecticide-treated mosquito net (often scandalously subject to high import duties by their governments) for their children, they'll be much too poor to pay for vaccination.

Third, consumers are often more willing to pay for treatment of a disease than possibly unproven methods of prevention. It takes time for the effectiveness of a vaccine to become apparent, and always involves a bit of an act of faith.

So an HIV vaccine, for example, would clearly be a global public good. The social benefits of bringing it to market will exceed the likely private gains. That means that private sector companies are underinvesting in its development. Without government involvement they will not recoup enough revenue to make the amount of investment the world really needs worthwhile. Indeed, in 1998 the global total for research and development into potential HIV vaccines was only $300 million, most of it publicly funded basic research rather than applied vaccine development. Of this total, only $5 million was earmarked for research geared toward developing countries. Without an additional stimulus, an effective vaccine is several decades away, even for the rich markets and certainly for the poor ones.

The development of a new drug is expensive because of the large-scale trials required and the length of time between the initial discovery and the first sales. When you also consider the political uncertainties surrounding anti-HIV policies and the challenging delivery of medicines in developing countries with weak health services, it is clear why the drug companies have not really been interested. The current market for vaccines in developing countries in fact amounts to just $200 million a year—too small to make any drug company think it worth bothering developing new products for the market.

On top of all these influences driving a wedge between the social benefits and the price individuals are willing to pay, there is a further problem in the fact that it is governments or public health services who for the most part buy vaccines. They are often tempted to use their purchasing power, or their control over patents, to force drug companies to sell at a price that is not high enough to cover the research and development costs. In effect, many developing countries have in the past expropriated corporations' **intellectual property rights** that are supposed to be protected by patents.

This explains why the big pharmaceutical companies in 2000 launched a case against a South African law that would have allowed the government to buy cheap copies of patented drugs needed to treat AIDS. After a high-profile campaign by organizations like Oxfam and Medécins sans Frontieres they dropped the case, realizing belatedly that taking Nelson Mandela to court in what looked like a bid to prevent South Africa tackling AIDS was disastrous public relations. But the issue remains a real concern to pharmaceutical companies.

There is a genuine policy dilemma with regard to patents. A patent gives the maker of a drug a temporary monopoly, even though consumers would be better served by enforcing competition that would lower the price. Better off in the short term, at any rate. For the longer term, no drug company would bother spending on the huge up-front investment need-ed to create new drugs. Patents are necessary to create long-term incentives to innovate. There's no way to be sure in theory what the right balance is—it's an empirical matter.

But while some patent protection is desirable, there is no reason why the big drugs companies should expect to have the same degree of monopoly power in all new markets that open up. If globalization is expanding their markets, they should expect to share the benefits by charg-ing a lower price for their drugs in developing countries. The only valid concern they might have about that is whether the drugs might end up being shipped back into their home markets at the lower price, but that is a worry shared by many industries now.

However, it would be worth overcoming these difficulties in order to get an effective vaccine against scourges such as tuberculosis, malaria, and HIV. The typical price of a dose of an on-patent vaccine sold in a devel-oping country is $2. Calculations by economists at Harvard suggest a pro-gram of malaria vaccination would still be cost effective—compared to the health care costs and economic losses imposed by the disease—at $41 a dose. That $39-a-dose gap is a measure of the social gains that could be captured by a program giving researchers the right incentives to develop an effective malaria vaccine; they add up to as much as $1.7 billion a year forever at today's prices.

The beauty of the proposed scheme to fund vaccine development via an international government guarantee is that it guarantees a big enough market to make medical success worthwhile for the private investors who would still be funding the research. The fact that the public purse pays nothing unless a viable vaccine is developed gives researchers the incen-tive to succeed rather than, say, concentrate on work that will enhance their academic reputation. The program, linked to the international aid effort, would also guarantee that the vaccines got to the people who real-ly need them. And, involving no public spending until it succeeds, the vac-cine guarantee proposal does not divert resources from current aid budgets, a problem with alternative proposals such as direct government funding of the basic research.

Disease: No Man Is an Island   129

A Global Alliance for Vaccines and Immunizations was formed in 1999 by the World Health Organization, Unicef, and the World Bank, along with a number of philanthropic foundations and research institutes. By 2001 the rich countries had agreed in principle to fund vaccine development, through the World Bank. This is a proposal whose time is nearly here, after its long gestation.

The idea's applications extend beyond developing countries and beyond diseases, however. There are many areas of public spending in which governments could pay the private sector by results for its innovations, thus getting round the classic problems of public sector management. If government is notoriously bad at picking winners and inefficient at management, why not set the private sector the problem and leave it to solve it? It is a question of creating an appropriate economic incentive. The government has to be involved in the case of public goods because there will by definition be too low a return to purely private effort. But if the reward for success has a government guarantee and the reward for failure is zero, success is a pretty likely outcome.

This reasoning about the power of incentives explains why economists are so keen on applying market solutions to environmental problems. A clean environment and natural resources are public goods whose benefits are cross-border: those who bear the costs of cleaning up pollution or gas emissions are often in a different country from the people who will benefit. On the global scale, financial stability, free trade, and knowledge have also been identified as public goods, those that create spillover effects whose benefit to society is greater than the private benefits, and whose social gains also spill over national borders.

The idea of global public goods is a powerful one for identifying issues where government involvement at the global level might be necessary to ensure enough of the benefit in question is produced. That could be public health, reduced emissions, international postal and telecommunications links, shipping rules, or financial stability. The fact that some of these goods have had international governmental institutions supplying them quietly for a long time, whereas others are buffeted by controversy, suggests there are difficult questions in some cases. For one thing, economists have to work out how much of the public good might be the right amount. In telecoms, the aim is clearly a set of rules enabling people to make calls abroad and setting the charges for operators to access each others' national markets. But what about public health? Obviously more should be spent on developing vaccines, but how much more? And who should pay? Should funds be diverted from other development spending and loans? Even trickier, in the absence of a global government, designing institutions to raise the money and deliver the goods is a major institutional and political headache, not to mention a challenge to economists.

Chapter 17

MULTINATIONALS

Sweatshop Earth?

It is easy to condemn multinational corporations—easy, but in the end wrong.

The taste of chocolate is very bitter, it turns out. In the spring of 2001 the news emerged that much of the chocolate made by big candy companies and consumed by us in vast amounts is made from cocoa farmed by child slaves in West Africa. The children are sold to traders by their parents in desperately poor countries such as Benin and shipped to other poor and desperate countries like Ivory Coast to work in the cocoa plantations. One such slave trade shipment was uncovered by the United Nations Children's Fund. One can only begin to imagine the harsh conditions and treatment the children are likely to experience working in a foreign land with no protection, not to mention the sheer loneliness and fear.

This was, unfortunately, just one example in a long line of revelations about working conditions in developing countries, whose workers are employed either directly by multinationals based in the developed countries or by local subcontractors to the multinationals. Whether it was children stitching footballs on the Indian subcontinent or young women in factories making sneakers or clothes in Indonesia or the Philippines or even relatively affluent Mexicans working in auto and electronics plants near the border with the U.S., evidence of the extent to which our consumer comforts depend on cheap labor overseas has made many of us uncomfortable. What's more, consumer protest has already proven quite effective in making multinationals pay much closer attention to working conditions way down their supply chain.

Giant international corporations have never exactly been popular, but their stock is particularly low at the moment. Naomi Klein, the Canadian journalist, hit the bestseller list with a passionate tirade against multinationals, capturing the widespread sense that the big bad guys are taking over the world economy, and that globalization represents the success of faceless and unaccountable private corporations in running the world in their own interests.

The trouble is that this left-of-center conspiracy theory is not entirely supported by the facts. It is very easy to track down some basic economic information published on the Internet by organizations like the United Nations and OECD that at the very least suggests the need for a more nuanced interpretation of globalization.

The basis of the argument, that companies are becoming more powerful, governments less so, is not necessarily true. The rhetoric since the era of Ronald Reagan and Margaret Thatcher has suggested that governments are getting smaller. As the U.K.'s prime minister Mrs. Thatcher launched privatization—the sale to private investors of government-owned companies—on the world, and many countries followed the British lead in transferring big state telephone and electricity companies to the private sector. However, there is no sign that the tide has in fact turned. The government takes a bigger share in the economy than ever in most countries.

For example, in the United States the share of government expenditure in the gross domestic product (GDP) was 34 percent in 1995, a little higher than it had been in 1980, when Reagan was first elected. In the U.K., Mrs. Thatcher stabilized the government's share of the economy at about 40 percent. In both countries, where supposedly a political revolution rolled back government, the proportions remain significantly higher than in the mid-1960s, when big government social programs started to unroll.

Elsewhere in the developed world, the share of government spending in GDP has been rising for the past twenty to thirty years, substantially in some cases. In the past few years there is tentative evidence that some of the big-government Scandinavian countries have started to reverse the trend. The government share has also increased in many developing countries, especially those in the middle income ranks, thanks to the introduction of state-funded education and welfare programs as these countries have become richer. Greater prosperity means people demand more and more from their governments in terms of public services.

In fact, the only group of countries in the world where there is clearly smaller government now than twenty years ago is the ex-communist bloc. These economies were almost 100 percent government-owned and -run in 1979. By 1999 they had transferred 40 to 80 percent of the economy into private hands. While there are big question marks over the process of transition from communism to capitalism in most cases, few people would argue it was wrong in principle to give the private sector a lot more say in those countries.

So in a very fundamental sense, private corporations do not have a bigger role in the global economy. They are not even paying less tax—the evidence doesn't back up the claim that multinationals (as a whole) can play governments off against each other to cut their tax bills. A lot of the enthusiastic free-market rhetoric has been just that: rhetoric, not reality.

What, then, is the reality? The answer is not privatization, but globalization. Two aspects matter in explaining the demonization of multinationals. One is the growth of international investment and sales by corporations. The other is the impact of a more open world economy on government policies.

Companies are increasingly not just marketing more and more of their goods across national borders, reflected in the continuing growth of imports and exports, but manufacturing more internationally as well. This is revealed by figures for **foreign direct investment** (FDI), which means investment in companies and factories in another country. It is not the same as portfolio investment in property, shares, and other financial assets, often described as "hot money."

Worldwide flows of such direct investment from one country into another have climbed from just $30 billion a year in the early 1980s to $800 billion in 1999. As a share of world GDP, that is an increase from 2.3 percent to 11.1 percent. Correspondingly, sales recorded by the foreign affiliates of multinational companies have risen from $2.4 trillion in 1982 to $13.6 trillion in 1999.

Most cross-border investment takes place between the developed countries, between two-thirds and four-fifths of the total each year. Countries such as the Netherlands, U.K., Ireland, and Australia are among the world's most open to investment by overseas companies. The most open developing countries include Singapore, Hong Kong, Panama, Trinidad, and Tobago, and about two dozen countries account for almost all of the investment flowing from the rich to the not-so-rich nations. Hardly any FDI flows into the world's poorest countries.

However, those foreign affiliates in countries like Indonesia, China, Malaysia, or Honduras that do attract a lot of inward investment by multinationals are increasingly making and exporting manufactured goods back to the rich markets. This is a significant change in the structure of their trade. As recently as 1990, only 40 percent of developing country exports were manufactured goods, with most of the rest either agricultural produce or commodities, but by 1998, nearly two-thirds of their exports were manufactures, and the proportion is expected to climb to 80 percent within five years. The shift has been most pronounced in the case of the United States, whose multinationals have been fastest to exploit the feasibility of production on a completely global basis. The proportion of manufactures in developing country exports, including those from U.S.-owned companies, to the United States jumped from 47 percent in 1990 to 75 percent in 1998

This, then, is perhaps the true underlying source of consumer concerns in the rich countries. It is clear that companies are transferring production overseas, a move made feasible by both new communications and computer technologies and by the slow but steady reduction in import duties on manufactured goods, because it is a lot cheaper. Why would they bother otherwise? The whole point must be to get away with paying exploitation wages. Or is it?

Labor costs make up about two-thirds of the total cost of manufacturing some low-tech goods (although much less in other cases), so there can't be much doubt that low wages in developing countries are attractive to corporations. So, too, with less stringent environmental standards.

But companies do not invest in the cheapest possible countries. In fact, they opt for middle-income countries such as Mexico or Malaysia. There is in addition overwhelming evidence that in most cases—not all—multinational investment in a low-wage country is good for the corporation and the workers. One survey of the evidence on working conditions in developing countries published by the OECD has a bibliography running to nine pages. The evidence was overwhelming that pay and conditions in factories owned by or working for multinationals based in rich countries are better than general local conditions. Even the controversial export-processing zones some countries such as Mauritius and the Philippines have established specifically to tempt foreign investors with special tax and legal breaks have better standards—higher wages, more unionization, shorter hours—than most alternative local jobs.

In some cases, the jobs created by foreign corporations have been taken mainly by women. Female workers are even cheaper than male workers and have additional qualities such as greater manual dexterity in assembling bits of microelectronic circuits or cutting and sewing garments. Is it any surprise that local men in quite traditional societies object to women acquiring greater economic independence and sometimes bringing home more money than anybody else in the household? For young women in rural China or even northern Mexico, however, a job in a foreign-owned factory is a form of liberation.

Similarly, caution is needed even before condemning the use of child labor in poor countries. Western consumer boycotts of soccer balls made by children in Bangladesh and Pakistan meant the children lost their jobs. Their parents sent them, not to school, but out to worse-paid jobs in other industries. Some ended up in prostitution. Banning child labor is highly desirable, but after, not before, a source of replacement income for their families is identified and school places are funded.

There is absolutely no doubt that parents stop sending their children to work (or selling them into slavery) as family incomes rise. In the poorest countries with incomes under about $300 a head, 10 to 12 percent of children work, compared with less than 2 percent in countries where average incomes are above $5,000 a head (remember, we still think children should do some work, whether tidying their bedroom for pocket money or delivering newspapers or working in a shop on Saturday afternoons). Most children work in agriculture, not in factories, often on family smallholdings. Adults tend to grab the factory jobs because these pay so much better.

A pilot World Bank scheme swapping food for school attendance may point the way to short-term reductions in child labor, but the best solution would be higher incomes. That means economic growth in the poorest nations. And selling exports is the best way, perhaps the only way, for an economy to grow.

That doesn't mean conditions are great in multinational-owned factories producing for export. And there are also many exceptions to the general rule that conditions are better than the local norm, concentrated in traditionally awful industries like manufacturing clothing or gem-cutting. It's no wonder that local workers are pressing for higher pay and better conditions; after all, so are workers in many developed countries. In fact, the sooner only robots work in factories, the better for humankind, because most are basically awful jobs, repetitive, hot, noisy, and even dangerous. Nevertheless, the past decade's surge in foreign investment, building up a manufacturing base, represents a source of greater prosperity in developing countries. Those wealthy multinational executives so criticized by campaigners have brought more jobs, more money, more technology, more exports, and more prosperity to developing countries. That's a lot more than the often corrupt and inefficient governments of such countries have achieved.

Where there is much greater controversy among economists about multinationals investing abroad is what impact it has on their home country. After all, switching production to cheap labor countries implies job losses in expensive labor countries. Corresponding to the increase in exports of manufactures by developing countries has been the decline of manufacturing's role in the developed economies. It is hard to believe the globalization of production has not cut jobs and wages at home. This was, of course, the great fear about NAFTA, that Mexicans would be putting Americans out of jobs, although there is no evidence that it happened. The 1990s was a great decade for employment in U.S. industry.

Foreign direct investment and overseas trade have probably contributed to net job losses in some developed economies, but it is hard to believe globalization is the only explanation for the scale of job losses in manufacturing and the decline in the relative pay of factory workers. Manufacturing's share in the U.S. and U.K. economies reached a peak in the late 1960s, and in more highly industrial countries like Germany in the early 1970s. That turning point long predates any noticeable volume of exports of manufactures by developing countries. Even the Asian tigers such as Korea and Malaysia, which are now substantial exporters of manufactured goods, only accounted for a minuscule share of world trade in manufactures before the 1990s. As Paul Krugman pointed out in a famous article republished in his book *Pop Internationalism*, imports from low-wage countries accounted for 2.8 percent of America's GDP in 1990, compared with 2.2 percent in 1960. How could an increase that amounted to just over half a percentage point of GDP have caused a 10-point decline in manufacturing output's share in the economy (from 29 percent to 19 percent of GDP)?

Many other studies have backed his conclusion that the scale of trade with developing countries is too small to explain by itself the scale of economic change in the developed countries. A majority of economists therefore believe that even if foreign direct investment is now playing a significant role, the introduction of new information technologies has had a more important part in the shift away from manufacturing in the advanced economies. In fact, the transfer of production overseas is more likely to be a symptom of economic change than a cause.

Still, symptom or cause, exploitative or not, multinationals do play a bigger part in everybody's lives. No matter where you live, you are more likely now than ten or twenty years ago to buy a product made by a foreign company or work for one. Foreign corporations have displaced not government but domestic corporations because of the increasing globalization of the economy.

However, there is one sense in which globalization has had an impact on government. It sets some limits on some government policies. Not, as we have seen, on the size of government. Sweden, whose government accounts for nearly 60 percent of national output, has no trouble attracting investment or borrowing money in the financial markets. However, the need to convince foreign investors, more skeptical than home investors, does limit the size of government budget deficits. Any country with high inflation, a big government budget deficit, and a big trade deficit will find it more expensive to borrow from overseas or attract direct investors. In extreme cases, a macroeconomic basket-case country will find it is experiencing a financial crisis when anybody who can get money out, foreign or national, does so. As Argentina has discovered in its recent trauma, globalization rules out bad macroeconomic policies.

More controversially, the Asian crisis in 1997–98 suggests globalization is starting to rule out really bad microeconomic policies, too. Foreign investors in that case were reacting to shaky banking systems and an unknown degree of corruption, rather than excessive inflation or government borrowing. When foreign investors seem to be wielding a power of veto over detailed economic policies or even the local style of doing business, it could look as if multinationals were trying to usurp the role of government (not that the democratic credentials of all the affected countries were of the highest order in the first place). Personally, having little confidence in the proposition that politicians and officials know best, I'm perfectly happy if economic good sense means governments are prevented from running stupid policies. You don't have to be a free-market fanatic to believe this: I'm all in favor of governments having policies, but would much prefer good policies to bad ones.

There is a genuine issue about democratic accountability, of course. But there is nothing new about powerful corporations trying to influence government policy. It would be naive to think it didn't happen in the past just because we didn't know about it. Big companies pay big bucks in direct political contributions and also hire lobbyists whose job is to help shape policy in the most favorable way by taking officials and elected politicians out for fine meals or rounds of golf, or hinting that a decision on a factory closure could be swayed by a helpful vote from the local representative. Perhaps I'm naive, but I think there is a bit less of this going on. The ubiquitous media and the Internet have made it much harder to keep channels of influence secret. The press is more likely to whip up a scandal about political donations.

In fact, the much greater scrutiny of corporate activity means multinationals themselves think they have less influence, not more. Some pay only lip service to concerns about their environmental policies or the working conditions in their third world factories, regarding it as a matter of public relations. But others are starting to take consumer and activist complaints seriously because they recognize that damage to the corporate reputation can and does affect their profits and share prices. They don't handle it at all well, on the whole, but that's only human. We all react rather badly to criticism, especially when we've been making a real effort.

For both multinationals and governments—for all of us, in fact—globalization has brought mixed blessings. Companies have the opportunity to produce more cheaply and efficiently but also face more competition and more complications in doing business. Governments have less power in some directions, more opportunities in others. It is easy to spot the difference between right and wrong when it comes to a slave ship packed with children moving along the African coast, but for the most part, there is no clear sight line between where we are now and the safe harbor of an ideal world; we can only try and figure out how to get from here to someplace a bit better.

Chapter 18

IMMIGRATION
The Missing Link

Every week, more or less, brings a ghastly piece of news. Three hundred young men drown when a rust bucket of a boat ferrying them from Albania sinks off the coast of Italy. A truck trailer in El Paso, Texas, is found to contain the bodies of forty-one young men and women, including a baby. A container ship sailing into Dover in England holds a cargo of tomatoes and the bodies of fifty-eight suffocated Chinese men and women. These are just the large-scale incidents. Daily there are individual deaths, of an African trying to cross the Sahara on foot to get into the Spanish enclave of Ceuta in North Africa and then into mainland Europe, or frozen to death clinging to the undercarriage of an aircraft, or a Kosovar trying to cross the Channel to Britain clinging to a high-speed Eurostar train and falling onto the rails.

Unless we think these anonymous people are disposable, the daily incidents must force us to recognize that something very terrible is happening, and try to understand it. Clearly many would-be immigrants from developing to developed countries believe it is worth facing a significant risk of death to circumvent the barriers to their legal movement. What pressures drive them to this, and what are the implications of the current structure of immigration controls?

The final years of the twentieth century brought a significant increase in the numbers of people crossing international borders, intensifying a slow upward trend that had begun after World War II. The flow is predominantly one of people leaving developing countries to enter developed ones, or in other words, out of Asia, Latin America, and Africa into the U.S. and Western Europe, but not entirely. There is also significant movement of people between countries in each category.

It is difficult to compare figures from different countries, as they are collected in various ways. However, with that caveat, the number of foreigners legally entering France, for example, climbed from 44,000 in 1988 to 102,400 in 1997, and the figures for the United Kingdom rose from 220,000 in 1988 to 330,000 in 1998. The inflow into the United States remained high throughout the 1990s, hitting a peak of 1.8 million in 1991 but not falling lower than 800,000 any year.

These far exceeded in absolute terms the numbers of immigrants in the 1900s, although they formed a far lower proportion of the total population, with under 10 percent of the U.S. population foreign-born compared to 15 percent in 1900. Illegal immigration has also increased, but of course there are no reliable statistics on it. It certainly numbers millions of people worldwide, possibly tens of millions.

Some countries saw also a substantial rise in the number of asylum seekers. These include Australia, Belgium, the Czech Republic, the Netherlands, Switzerland, and the U.K. As asylum seekers, fleeing war or famine, are by definition the poorest people on the planet and most in need of significant help from their hosts, they have aroused particular political hostility. Responding to this, some mainstream politicians in the U.K. have actually proposed interning people claiming asylum in concentration camps (not called that, of course) until their claims are assessed, a move lawyers argue would breach the Geneva Convention and the European Human Rights Act. The legal opinion had little effect on the popularity of the proposals, according to polling organizations. We're talking hot-button issues here.

To get a complete picture of the movement of people, it would be necessary to collect data on both inflows and outflows from every country on a consistent basis. This simply is not available. National data give some idea of the broad trends, however. One of the main sources of information for the U.K. is a survey of passengers entering and leaving at ports and airports—the benefit of being an island is that it's easier to count them. The number of Britons emigrating peaked in the early 1980s, when there was a net loss of population. The 1990s brought a net inflow, with increases in immigration from many sources: in descending order of magnitude: the rest of Europe; the Old Commonwealth (code for mainly white countries like Australia and Canada); the New Commonwealth (mainly Asian and West Indian); and other (mainly from the United States and China). Naturally, as in other majority white countries, the debate in the U.K. has a racist flavor. When populist politicians and commentators talk about "floods" of immigrants and asylum seekers, they are not referring to the young Australians teaching in British schools or the Americans and French working in financial services.

Other countries have somewhat different patterns, determined by their geography and history. The largest numbers of immigrants into the U.S., which always has a significant net inflow, come from the Americas and Caribbean, followed by Asians. Europe forms the third most important region of origin for immigrants into the United States. This is a great contrast to immigration in the nineteenth and early twentieth century, which was predominantly European and has contributed to a marked change in the ethnic composition of the American population.

However, although there has been an upward trend in the numbers of people on the move across borders, the past twenty years have seen nothing quite on the scale of the great mass movement of people that occurred between about 1850 and 1914, put as high as 50 million compared to a world population of 1.8 billion in 1913, or almost 3 percent of the 1913 total. In 1912–1913 the United States saw 3.3 million immigrants, when the country's population was 97.6 million, a 3.4 percent rise in the population due to immigration in two years. The 4.3 million immigrants in 1989–91, the three peak years in the recent inflow into the U.S., compare to a 1989 population of 248.8 million, or a 1.7 percent increase due to immigration in three years. The United States is one of the countries in the world most welcoming to legal immigrants, not least because of the part the earlier wave played in shaping the national identity.

Indeed, although other measures such as investment and trade flows, or the extent of overseas production by multinational companies, show the globalization of the world economy has now passed the benchmarks set in the wave of globalization that occurred in the late nineteenth and early twentieth century, the reverse is true in the case of immigration. The flow of people is the missing link in modern globalization. The rhetoric applied to immigration is completely different in flavor. Pro-globalizers have no problem with the idea that goods, services, and capital should be free to go anywhere in the world, but for some reason the same principle does not generally apply to people.

The forces of globalization have actually contributed to the increase in the movement of people. Transport costs have fallen, and perhaps even more important, so have information costs. Potential migrants are better aware of the rest of the world, of the opportunities, of what has happened to friends and family who have already moved. The more people move, the more family and personal ties will draw others behind them. What's more, as the rich countries have pulled further ahead of the poor, the images in the media of life elsewhere show a bigger gap than ever between what potential migrants have now and what is attainable elsewhere.

Another factor pushing migration has been an increase in military and political instability in many parts of the world since the end of the Cold War. Areas like Eastern Europe and sub-Saharan Africa have seen a dramatic rise in the number of vicious conflicts, creating millions of refugees.

Factors pulling potential immigrants include the much greater fluidity in the international job market in many industries such as financial services or computers. On top of that, some countries like the U.S. and U.K. enjoyed a long economic expansion during the 1990s, creating a lot of demand for workers. In some areas like Silicon Valley or the City of London, there was a dramatic rise in the foreign-born proportion of the workforce during the '90s. That includes not just financiers and programmers but also cleaners and restaurant staff. The demand for foreign-born workers could also stay high despite an economic downturn, as the populations of some Western countries are aging rapidly, pointing to potential shortages of native-born workers. While numbers of migrants do ebb and flow with the economic cycle, there is no reason to believe the long-term upward trend will cease. Not the least important reason is that many of the rich countries to which would-be migrants will move have stagnant or declining populations because of birthrates well under the replacement rate.

It is very clear that economic factors have been important in explaining the upturn in immigration, while deliberate government restrictions probably explain why the flows have not rescaled the heights they reached (in proportionate terms) a century ago. Will controls on immigration be able to tame the underlying economic forces? And should they? This is where the economics tool kit comes in handy.

A majority of migrants are of working age and seeking work. Their arrival therefore has the obvious effect of increasing the available supply of labor. Here lies one of the most common objections to immigrants: "They're taking our jobs." This is an example of one of the biggest chasms between economists and other people. Economists describe this as the **lump of labor fallacy.** The mistake is the assumption that there is only a fixed amount of work to go around, so if more jobs are taken by foreigners (or machines), there will be fewer left for the native-born (or humans). The fallacy has been completely discredited. It just doesn't happen. For if it were true, almost everybody would eventually be unemployed, given that the population has until just about now grown steadily. The existence of some pockets of high unemployment—among blacks in inner cities, for example—is not caused primarily by competition from immigrant workers, but by the too-high expectations and too-low skills of the people in those groups. High jobless rates in such neighborhoods are not correlated with numbers of immigrants.

What happens is that the arrival of immigrant workers shifts the labor supply curve out. For a given labor demand curve, the number of people in jobs will rise, but the wage will be lower. This is what induces employers to take on more workers. So in the short term, immigrants do not take jobs but could reduce pay.

However, over a longer time frame the economy will grow as a result of higher demand from a bigger population, employers will create even more jobs, new businesses will form—the labor demand curve moves out, too The weight of evidence suggests immigration rarely reduces wages in practice because migrants are moving to thriving regions with a growing number of jobs. What's more, at the bottom of the job pecking order—for janitors, child minders, care assistants, and so on—it is often the case that native-born workers will not take such jobs at any wage that makes them worthwhile for the employers. The very arrival of immigrants can therefore actually create these lowly and unattractive jobs.

Even at this first step in the analysis, it is clear that immigration brings benefits and imposes costs. Assessing its benefit to the national economy will obviously be a question demanding empirical research. It is not an issue that can be prejudged. The costs, if any, are borne by groups of workers in direct competition for jobs, which tend to be the very unskilled and the highly skilled, given recent immigration patterns. Countries allow in highly skilled workers most freely, and illegal immigration increases the pool of unskilled labor. The costs are not loss of work but potentially lower real wages for some unknown time period.

The benefits go to employers in the first instance, but later spread to everybody as the benefits of the boost to demand kick in and the affected wages start to rise again. The balance of evidence suggests immigration puts little or no downward pressure on wages in practice. For example, inflows of foreign IT workers have not depressed wages in the industry, indicating the industry has grown more relative to the rest of the economy than it would have if the labor supply had been restricted to the native-born.

A further, and immediate, gain stems from the fact that the economy as a whole can grow faster without leading to upward pressure on inflation when there is a significant addition to the labor supply. That means the central bank can allow interest rates to be lower than they might otherwise have been. This certainly seems to have played a part—how big, nobody yet knows—in the long economic expansions in the U.S. and the U.K. during the 1990s. The job market in California and London would have over-heated much faster without the influx of new workers from overseas.

There is a substantial body of research that shows that immigrants generally start out earning less than natives but eventually catch up and, for some groups, overtake. It's known as the **assimilation hypothesis**, and it holds true for the U.S. and the U.K., according to evidence available from earlier waves of immigration. This jibes with the observation that immigrants are often hard working and highly productive. To leave home, friends, and family, everything familiar, braving unknown hazards on the way and for an uncertain future suggests that they are either desperate to improve their lot or unusually adventurous and enterprising, or both. And when they find a new home and job they tend to set about ensuring their children have all the advantages they themselves did not enjoy. Such people might start with lower skills than typical of workers in their host country, and will often need to learn the language, but are subsequently likely if anything to improve the average quality of the workforce. By the next generation, it is harder to distinguish between the children of natives and the children of immigrants in terms of how they do in the labor market on average.

Certainly, there is no evidence that immigrants are a bigger drain on public services than natives. While refugees will tend to need special help with housing, health care, and welfare, for some time at least, economic migrants if anything make fewer demands than natives. They want work, are mostly young enough that they need fewer than average medical services, and pay taxes like everyone who goes shopping or has a (legal) job. Usually new arrivals are not entitled to many welfare benefits. The main difference will be in the case of immigrant groups with a higher birthrate, whose children will need schooling. Figures for the U.K. show immigrant groups recieve more child and housing benefits than natives but less in unemployment benefits and state pensions. A detailed Home Office study concluded: "On average and overall, *migrants are not a burden on the public purse*" (their italics). Research carried out in the United States and Germany reaches the same conclusion.

So on two of the main areas of the cost-benefit analysis, in which the balance could in theory tip either way, it looks like immigration brings at least no net costs and perhaps net benefits to the host economy. The balance will tilt toward net benefits to the extent that immigrants are filling jobs in which there are serious shortages of native workers. That includes many public sector jobs that are relatively low paid by comparison with private sector alternatives. Thus many European health and education workers are foreign born. It also includes highly skilled jobs in industries such as software and finance.

However, that's not the end of the assessment. We need to look at two other impacts. There is a general perception that immigrants are a drain on resources; this must have some basis in reality. It arises because new groups of migrants tend to cluster together, often in deprived neighborhoods where housing is cheap. Not only does this make their strange foreign ways highly visible, which in itself makes some natives uncomfortable, it also means the burden of finding houses and schools falls on relatively few local authorities and their taxpayers. It is in some cases associated with a higher rate of crime and drug use, typical inner-city problems. And more people, whoever they are, can put a burden on public transport, hospitals, police, social services, and other bits of the physical and social infrastructure. These **congestion costs** are very real.

On the other hand, immigration has had a tremendous and probably incalculable positive impact on society and culture. To take one example, consider British cooking. As a lifelong consumer of British food, I can vouch that immigrants from the Indian subcontinent, East Asia, Europe (especially Italy but excluding Germany), the West Indies, and Japan have had a fantastic impact on my well-being during the past quarter century. As a child and teenager I was restricted to the rightly notorious national cuisine of tough meat, overcooked vegetables, and potatoes. But by the late 1970s, the choice of alternatives had been vastly expanded by incomers. Thus curry—specifically the hybrid Anglo-Indian dish chicken tikka masala—has become the staple fast food in the United Kingdom. By 1996 there were 10,000 Indian restaurants and take-outs employing as many as 70,000 people, and with a turnover of £1.5 billion. That's more than steel, coal, and shipbuilding put together. This is not a frivolous example. It represents a serious improvement in consumer welfare. More choice is good for the economy.

The diversity introduced by immigrants has many other effects that are less easily quantified. However, they are highly visible. Immigrants often make hugely important contributions in cultural industries such as music, fashion, and art, in academia, in sports, and in science and medicine. In short, they are important in the industries that are playing an increasingly important role in the advanced economies. There are many historical examples, too. Would the City of London be the great financial center it has become without Jewish immigration in the nineteenth century? Would American universities dominate the global intellectual landscape without the influx of refugees from the Nazis? Or would Silicon Valley be preeminent without Indian and Chinese brainpower? Diversity could be valuable in itself by introducing new ideas and fresh ways of doing business, all important in an economy where growth depends on ideas.

The point of all this is to indicate that assessing the economic impact of immigration involves a cost-benefit analysis. There is no definitive answer in principle. In practice, the economic benefits, which tend to be ignored in public debate, seem to outweigh the costs. What's more, some of the perceived costs are completely spurious. The lump of labor fallacy is, as the name suggests, wrong.

If host countries gain from immigration, as I believe, does that imply that the countries losing people suffer an economic loss? That sounds logical. After all, in the context of emigrants from developed countries we often worry about brain drains. So it seems plausible to suppose developing countries are now losing out from the loss of economic migrants seeking to better themselves in America or Europe. Clearly if they are refugees, too, there is nothing much at stake, but there are concerns about the potential economic cost to countries such as India, the Philippines, Morocco, Mexico, and so on if they are losing many ambitious workers in their prime, especially those with specific skills such as medicine or IT.

These economies will make some gains from their overseas workers.

They will get remittances of earnings to the families back home. Some emigrants will return with valuable skills, experience, and capital. Many invest in their home country even if they never return. Some engage in large-scale philanthropy such as setting up schools or university institutes back home. The presence of groups of emigrants in another country will generally help to open up trade and investment and information links with the richer economy.

Again, the conclusion you reach about this is a matter of comparing costs and benefits. Looking at the example of the poor Mediterranean economies such as Italy and Spain in the 1950s and 60s, it seems to me possible that the benefits outweigh the costs for the emigration countries, too, but there is scant empirical research on this question. The preoccupation of Western economists has so far been the assessment of the impact of immigration on their home economies, not emigration on foreign economies.

Perhaps in the end the verdict has to depend on more than economics. In a world in which freedom is highly valued, it cannot be defensible for machines or dollars to be freer to move across national borders than for people. What kind of moral values would deny people any opportunity to make a better life for themselves and their descendants just because they have the misfortune to have been born somewhere in sub-Saharan Africa instead of somewhere in the Midwest? Call me a woolly liberal, but they are not my values. If freedom is good for me, good for investment bankers and oil companies, then it's good for everybody.

Chapter 19

DEMOGRAPHY

The South Has the Last Laugh

Half the people who have ever lived in all of human history are alive today. The world's current population of 6 billion is forecast to swell to 7 billion by 2015, and might not peak until it reaches a total of 8 billion. Population growth is a striking characteristic of modern times—until about 1750 it was scarcely above zero, but peaked at 2 percent a year in 1970.

One of the earliest economists, Thomas Robert Malthus, published a famous essay in 1798 about population growth, "An Essay on the Principle of Population as It Affects the Future Improvement of Society." He argued that faster population growth, as observed in England during the preceding few decades, would outpace the capacity of the economy to feed all those new mouths. After all, there were diminishing returns in agriculture— every extra acre of land brought into cultivation would be steadily less productive because the best land was used first. The resulting famines and disease would cut the population back to the level that could be sustained.

As it turned out, Malthus published his famous essay just as his analysis stopped being true. It was a fair characterization of the past but was overtaken by a new phenomenon, **technical progress**. New machinery and farming methods meant more and more corn per acre could be grown. Technical progress appeared in industry too, creating the non-agricultural wealth that meant demand for farm output per person grew as well. In a virtuous circle of productivity increases and wealth creation, more and more people could be fed more and more food.

Ever since the mid-eighteenth century, growth in population and growth in per capita economic output have been closely linked. When a country first embarks on the process of industrialization and economic development, there is a very rapid increase in the rate of population growth. Typically, the birthrate stays high (as it always is in poor countries, so parents can insure against the high risk some of the children will die in infancy), but life expectancy rises and mortality rates for children and adults decline. Once per capita incomes reach a certain level, however, the birthrate drops sharply. Mothers will have two or three children rather than six or ten. This is such a regular pattern that it is known as the **demographic transition**.

Now, for the first time in history, some countries may be experiencing a new kind of demographic transition. The richest nations for the most part have birthrates below replacement level, and life expectancy is increasing more slowly than in the past. So their populations are both on the verge of shrinking and already aging rapidly. The United States is an exception, mainly because of high immigration: it has immigrant groups with higher birthrates than the native-born population, and constant top-ups from new immigration. That small increase aside, all the growth in world population is taking place in the developing, not the developed, economies. By 2050 the rate of population growth in the developed world is likely to be -0.5 percent a year, compared to 0.5 to 1 percent a year in the developing world.

So it is that before another quarter century has passed, almost half the adults in Germany will be over sixty-five. Along with Japan, it has one of the world's lowest birthrates, just 1.3 children per woman on average. Italy and Spain are aging almost as rapidly. Some of these are also among the countries that have been least open to immigration—only 1 percent of the inhabitants of Japan are foreign born, 2 percent in Italy.

No wonder that these aging rich countries have been at the forefront of concern about what is usually called the **demographic time bomb**. This refers to the prospect of a shrinking workforce supporting an expanding population of pensioners. The ratio of people aged sixty-five or over to people of working age is called the **dependency ratio**, and it's going up throughout the developed world, including the United States. In Japan the dependency ratio is likely to climb from 10 percent in 1950 and 20 percent now to over 50 percent (if nothing changes) by 2050. In the United States, which has the smallest time bomb ticking away, the increase will be from 18 percent now to about 30 percent by 2050.

How worrying is this? Any economist will know that metaphorical time bombs never explode. The condition "if nothing changes" is always wrong. Something will change because of the incentives set up by the current trends.

Many developments could alter future dependency ratios. People will start to retire later—indeed, already have in many countries, aided by improving health and vigor in old age. The ratio of the population that is employed will increase. For example, more and more women will work in those countries—Japan and much of Continental Europe—where female participation in the workforce is still low. Other countries apart from the United States might liberalize their immigration policies and boost the growth of their working-age population that way.

Any of these, or a combination of all, would lead to declining, not increasing, dependency ratios. In Europe, for instance, only 60 percent of the working-age population actually works. If that were to rise to 75 percent, like the United States, there would be a 10 percent decline in the dependency ratio rather than the 25 percent rise predicted, with no change in the proportion in employment.

What's more, birthrates can change unexpectedly. Such shifts can alter the demographic landscape with a lag of just nine months. In the distant past, birthrates have gone down during and after wars, but actually rose after 1945. This postwar baby boom was expected to generate an echo boom in the early 1960s, but the birthrate fell sharply instead, probably because of social and cultural changes. The echo in fact came in the late 1980s and early '90s, when women born in the 1960s started having babies but much later in life than their own mothers. This wasn't just due to culture but also to advances in health technology. Who's to say our own children will not revert to starting early on larger families? The birthrate in the U.S. and the U.K. has crept up a little recently.

Still, scare stories are very compelling. Demographic change has widespread economic ramifications. It will alter the demand for all kinds of goods and services, especially housing, health care and education. It can affect economy-wide savings rates and therefore spill over into the stock market. It can boost suburbs at the expense of downtowns depending on whether there are many families with children.

However, the main concern about the rich nations' demographic time bomb has been how to pay for pensions, as—whatever the formal financial structure of pension arrangements—today's pensioners as a whole have to be supported out of today's economic resources produced by today's workers. For some years it was fashionable to argue that paying for pensions could be globalized: if pension funds invested in emerging markets in the rapidly growing developing world, then the workers in those countries would be supporting us in our old age. However, successive global financial crises have taken the shine off this option. The more likely solution is that working patterns will change until the ratio of dependent pensioners to workers is put on a more sustainable track.

However, there may be deeper issues raised by the world's changing demographics. Population growth will always go hand in hand with economic growth, but faster population growth is also often linked to faster growth in GDP *per person*, or faster growth in productivity in other words.

There are several possible theoretical explanations for this strong empirical link, none proven. Perhaps an expanding population creates incentives for technological advances to feed, clothe, house, and meet all the other demands of the growing numbers of people. Perhaps economies of scale are so important in economic growth, as suggested by research into economic geography in recent years, that a rapid increase in the number of people in particular places can trigger a virtuous circle of development and growth.

Whatever the explanation, history offers no examples of countries that combine declining populations with economic vigor. Over a timescale of many decades, it is hard to believe that Japan and Western Europe will remain among the world's economic leaders. After all, what kind of vote of confidence in the future is it that their populations are not replacing themselves? Some economists would dispute this, arguing that in future technical progress can substitute for population growth (rather than complementing it) in keeping GDP per head growing. I'm not convinced by them.

It seems to me more likely that either growing numbers of people will move from where they are being born to the already rich economies (that is to say, migration will increase substantially) or the centers of economic gravity will move to where the people are being born. All today's rich countries are close to much poorer countries with faster population growth—the United States has Mexico on its border, Western Europe has Turkey and

North Africa, Japan has Southeast Asia. If I had to bet on a particular outcome, I'd predict the rich countries will absorb these dynamic neighbors as
a matter of self-preservation. Indeed, this has already happened in Western
Europe, with the EU admitting Greece, Spain, and Portugal in the 1980s.

The deeper moral is that while fast-growing populations today seem a
Malthusian burden to many poor countries, people—not money, metals,
or oil—are nevertheless the key resource.

Chapter 20

DEVELOPMENT
The Triumph of Fashion

Insoluble problems offend our sensibilities. We have grown so used to the idea that technology and human ingenuity can provide solutions. Researchers find cures for more and more diseases, governments build new roads, auto companies make cars with reduced emissions—there's a fix, eventually, for everything. In the rich Western countries, most of us experience continuing improvements in health, longevity, and the quality of life, with caveats, of course; but in general things get better.

So it's all the more frustrating to see some countries lagging further and further behind American or European or Korean or even Mexican living standards. Across most of sub-Saharan Africa, much of South Asia, and pockets of Latin America it seems life has not been getting any better at all. This isn't absolutely true: even in the poorest countries life expectancy has increased. But it's true enough. Living standards measured by GDP per head are no higher now than in 1950 or even 1910 in too many countries.

Why is it that some countries just can't share in the solutions to the problems of poverty and disease that we know exist because we solved them in our own countries? Why is it impossible for so many countries to provide their citizens with clean water or electricity when there is no mystery about the technology and it's not even all that expensive? Why do some children continue dying for want of oral rehydration therapy when it is one of the cheapest, easiest to use, and most important medical advances (in terms of lifesaving potential) of recent times? Why was Afghanistan so dirt poor that a terrorist group managed to buy the government?

Sometimes the answer is in one sense pretty obvious: ethnic violence and civil war as in Afghanistan, Somalia, or Rwanda are never going to help when it comes to building prosperous societies. You'd hardly bother to even plant a few vegetables in your garden if marauding soldiers are likely to drive you out of your home (at best), never mind build a business. Often in Africa, intercommunity violence is a legacy of colonial boundaries. There's no easy fix to this.

Unfortunately, any answers that go beyond these basics are not at all obvious. In fact one of the basic questions in economics is one of the least well understood. Why do economies grow? This explains why the field of development economics, the study of how to set poor countries on the track toward prosperity, is one of the areas of the subject most characterized by intellectual fashions. The prescriptions economists in the developed world have devised for the developing world have swung wildly over the decades, but the challenge of turning base material into gold, uncovering the mysterious alchemy of growth, has proven irresistible. After all, it now seems our own peace and prosperity depend very much on sharing the secret with the poorest countries.

As William Easterly, a leading development expert, has put it: "Observing the sufferings of the poor and the comforts of the rich motivated us on our quest. If our ambitious quest were successful, it would be one of humankind's great intellectual triumphs."

He and others do think they perhaps now have some genuine insights into the process. This is progress because in the past development economists have been certain they knew the answer—and have been wrong each time. A greater degree of intellectual modesty is encouraging, therefore. It isn't that past theories of development contained no insights—on the contrary. But each has been presented as a panacea, and that is what turns out to be false.

What's more, it has embittered many people in poor countries, who have been promised that if only they do X or Y, even if it involves some sacrifices or political turmoil, then everything will be all right. Time after time, they follow one policy or another, only to find that the goalposts have been moved. This as much as the absence of economic growth explains the anger some very poor countries feel toward Western experts and the West as a whole.

It's worth running through some of the fashions in development economics to demonstrate the process. One of the earliest theories is that growth is related to investment in machines. Poor countries have low savings because they are poor, so if you work out how much capital investment they would need to hit a target growth rate, you can calculate their **financing gap**. Development experts did, for every country. Aid or loans from agencies such as the World Bank or the International Monetary Fund (IMF), or from rich governments, were meant to help fill the gap. Much of the money granted or lent to poor countries over the years has been spent on huge capital projects such as dams, roads, big factories, airports and the like.

Of course, growth must be related to investment in some sense. This is one of the basic workhorse theories in economics. But it shouldn't have been so hard to see it isn't the whole story. Machines need people to work them, people with certain types of skill and education. So eventually this realization gave rise to another panacea, education, or investment in **human capital**, as economists like to put it. There is a clear link between spending on educating the population and development: South Korea, one of relatively few countries to make the transition from developing to advanced, is the classic case study of the importance of education.

But again, human capital investment is an incomplete answer. This is why there's an array of other solutions to the development problem. Population control was once the height of fashion, based on the observation that poorer countries have higher birthrates than richer ones; but the causality is likely to run the other way, with rising incomes leading people to choose smaller families.

There was a strong and highly distinctive Marxist economics of development, as of other aspects of economic theory. It was popular in developing countries because it pinned the blame for underdevelopment on imperialism, and the search by capitalism for new territory to exploit especially in terms of extracting raw materials. But Marxist economics lost its remaining appeal in 1989 with the collapse of communism. Linked to the Marxist analysis, but logically distinct from it, was the theory that underdeveloped economies were deliberately kept in a state of subservience or dependency by rich and powerful countries. This is still a popular theory in developing countries.

Today there are other ideas more in vogue. One hotly debated question is the extent to which its climate and geography determine the fate of a nation, for after all most poor countries are in the tropics. Another is the role played by cultural factors such as the absence of the Protestant work ethic or attitudes toward gender. It is because we understand the process of growth so little that such debates can be so vigorous.

In terms of solutions to global poverty, there are at least two proposed cures in favor today. One is based on the all-too-true observation that in the past aid has been wasted because of corruption and bad government policies. So now, the argument goes, aid spending must be increased but must be conditional on good behavior by the recipients. Apart from the fact that few developing country governments will welcome even more interference from the IMF and other donors in how they run their countries, for there's plenty of it already, there are reasons to be skeptical about how rigorously the conditions will ever be applied.

Because suppose for the sake of argument we do know what constitutes good policies, and can tell when they're being applied (we don't fully). The poor countries that fail to deliver the good policies will be the ones with the worst-performing economies. They'll have slower growth, higher inflation, bigger government debts, and so on. And they'll be exactly the ones supposed to be penalized by having aid reduced or withdrawn in future. It might make sense to be cruel to be kind, but **conditionality** will never be an easy strategy.

A second fashionable solution for poverty is **debt relief**, or writing off third world debt. Often because of bad governments in the past, dictators prone to building palaces and stashing money in secret bank accounts in the mountains of Europe, some very poor countries have built up debts they can never possibly repay. If creditors know they won't get all their money back, it makes sense for them to write off some of the debt, and enable the borrower countries to grow enough to pay back a bit in future. So some debt relief was sensible.

But writing off the whole lot, as some campaigners wanted? Given the realities of how much tax revenue Western voters will pay for the assistance of developing countries, this would inevitably divert aid from very poor countries without heavy debts—in other words, countries like Bangladesh that have been running pretty good economic policies with relatively little corruption over the years. This is not a good incentive structure. What's more, debt relief frees up funds for governments to spend on other things; it's supposed to be for health and education, but that runs into the same conditionality problems.

Unfortunately, the debt relief panacea has been tried before and failed. The examples of debt forgiveness since the 1970s suggest that most countries with high debts borrow to the hilt again as past debts are forgiven. Indebtedness is not a natural disaster like being hit by hurricanes or floods; it's a policy choice on the part of rotten governments.

So where does the theory of economic development stand now? In order to embark on the path of economic growth, a poor country needs to invest in physical and human capital. It needs to stamp out violence and corruption. The government needs to operate good policies, whatever they may be, but certainly at a minimum provide a stable macroeconomic framework.

Economists seem to be continually discovering new requirements for a successful growth strategy, too. The Asian financial crisis of 1997–1998 taught that banking systems and financial institutions are important; corruption and favoritism do damage in the private sector as well as in government. There is a strong emphasis now on the importance of social and political institutions generally in economic development. People will not invest for the future if there is little protection for private property or no way of formalizing informal ownership, or if the police force and law courts are inefficient or corrupt. Often this is described as **social capital**, a new form of capital in which investment is needed. Amartya Sen, the Nobel Prize–winning economist, has made it clear that we also need to understand development as an extension of human capacities and freedoms, not just as more money.

The emerging consensus is that economic development depends on a complicated kaleidoscope of policies and institutions. Coordinating everything—getting all the ducks in a row—is very difficult. What's more, growth seems a matter of breaking into a virtuous circle, out of a vicious spiral of poverty. For instance, people in poor countries have little incentive to invest in their own education because there are not enough other educated people for there to be industries offering suitable employment. There's no point being an overeducated weaver of carpets or picker of tea. As in so many other areas of economics, the story is one of increasing returns, where success reinforces success and tough luck to the losers. It ties in to the revitalized field of economic geography, which uses increasing returns, and the bandwagon effect of markets thriving in some places and not others, to explain the unevenness of wealth and poverty within the developed economies. It isn't quite that geography is destiny, but bucking the forces of geography might well be as hard as overcoming history.

Still, the latest fashion—that there's no quick fix—is more encouraging, I think, than any of the previous ones. There's a much better chance of solving problems when you start out knowing how much you don't know as well as what you do.

Part V

LIFE, THE UNIVERSE & EVERYTHING
Macroeconomics

Most of the chapters so far have not touched at all on what many readers will think of as economics—namely, macro-economics or how economies work at the aggregate level. This fills the newspapers and broadcast news day after day—whether the economy is in recession, what the unemploy-ment rate has gone up to, how much interest rates have come down, what budget resolutions Congress has passed, and so on.

However, macroeconomics has always been and remains the most controversial branch of the subject, because there is so much economists do not understand about how the individual decisions of millions of people combine. Still, although it is a field of competing theories and controversy, these chapters try to shed some light rather than heat on how to think about the big picture.

Chapter 21

JAPAN

Kogaru versus One–kei, or Why Tokyo's Teenage Fashions Matter

Japanese teenagers might have come late to extreme fashions, but by all accounts they are making up for lost time. Since James Dean invented the idea of the teenager in the rock and roll era, one fashion wave after another has swept over young people in America and much of Europe, with some particularly outstanding examples such as punk in late 1970s London. But for much of that time, Japanese teenagers seemed conformist and demure, much more intent on studying hard than on fomenting rebellion.

No longer. The number and variety of teenage fashion tribes in Japan's cities are impressive. As I write this, one popular look is the cute *kogaru*, based on a character called Sailor Girl with teeny skirts, big wrinkled socks, and clunky shoes. The *one-kei* or "big sisters" look, at the other extreme, is a pastiche ladylike style. These had taken over from *yamanba*, a witch-like style involving white hair and lipstick. The passion for fashion has helped keep Tokyo's shops bustling and prosperous. Indeed, Japanese consumers' more conventional fondness for ultra-pricey Western designer goods shows no signs of letting up at all despite a decade-long economic slump.

What kind of slump is it that keeps some consumers shopping madly and Tokyo teenagers spending on a brand new look every few months? Sailor Girl offers some important clues, as we will see.

There is little doubt that Japan has experienced an economic catastrophe. The level of GDP or national output in real terms is in 2000 about the same as it was in 1991. The International Monetary Fund predicts it will fall in 2001–2002 and perhaps again in 2003. This will add up to more than twelve years of stagnation for the world's second biggest economy, which might have been expected to grow by at least 2 percent a year. Compounded over so many years, this implies the economy could have been about 25 percent bigger than it actually is today. As Japan is still despite its problems a $3.8 trillion economy (in current yen converted to dollars at long-term purchasing power parity exchange rates), a quarter of that is a vast amount of lost output. In fact, the lost potential is like losing an economy as big as Italy.

At the same time, unemployment in Japan has climbed to postwar records. Although these are low even by comparison with American standards, never mind European ones, the increase has been enough to mark the end of the Japanese worker's expectation that the first employment he chooses on graduation (a majority of Japanese women still stop work when they marry) would be a job for life. Nor is there much of a welfare system to cushion the blow of unemployment; it was never needed in the past.

In combination with zero real growth, prices have been flat or falling for several years. The **deflation** means the economy measured in current prices is actually shrinking. There is no historical exception to the rule that an economy does not grow unless prices are rising a bit, so a recovery in Japan seems unlikely unless prices stop declining. A contraction in the current value of an economy is something we haven't seen anywhere since the 1930s. The degree of hardship in Japan today is nothing like as bad as the United States in the Great Depression, thanks to the intervening half century of gains in prosperity, but in macroeconomic terms the Japanese slump of the 1990s is just as exceptional.

It is only as the years have unfolded that economists have come to realize the severity of the situation. Many countries experienced a recession in the early 1990s after the boom of the late 1980s, and Japan was thought to be suffering the same kind of hangover as everybody else. Its boom had been spectacular. However, unlike the U.K. and the U.S., it did not start to recover from that recession. Only one or two years mid-decade saw any real-term growth in the Japanese economy at all, and that very modest recovery turned out to be a false dawn.

What's more, it took a long time for economists to realize that conventional policies were not working. Everywhere apart from Japan there has been a remarkable consensus during the 1990s about how to run the national economy to achieve low and stable inflation and steady growth: a combination of a surplus, or not too big a deficit, of tax revenues over spending in the government budget, with a central bank that sets interest rates above all to keep inflation low. While it hasn't exactly been smooth sailing everywhere, economists' agreement in theory about how the macroeconomy works and what the appropriate policies should be has been striking.

All the more striking as it followed a fierce intellectual battle in the 1980s between monetarist and Keynesian theories. In a nutshell, Keynesians, followers of the eminent British economist John Maynard Keynes, believed in the power of governments to manipulate the economy over the course of the business cycle, by either monetary policy (raising and lowering interest rates) or fiscal policy (adjusting levels of tax and government spending). These tactics were described as **demand management** because they could boost or reduce demand in the aggregate.

Monetarists argued that even if these policies worked in the short term, they would make no difference to economic output in the long term, though, as that was determined by the economy's potential to produce goods and services—or the aggregate supply. All the government could achieve by trying to boost growth by raising demand would be higher prices.

The details of a debate that seemed all important at the time are irrelevant now. All that matters is that on the question of whether the level of demand in the economy can be manipulated successfully in the short run there was, in effect, a monetarist victory. Such attempts, sometimes called **fine-tuning**, simply affect people's expectations and behavior in ways that counteract the original policies. Monetarism enthused some governments so much they made terrible mistakes putting it into practice. (For example, Mrs. Thatcher plunged Britain into a recession that wiped out a fifth of the country's manufacturing industry by following slavishly fixed targets for particular measures of monetary expansion. Her simultaneous deregulation of bank lending rules made the measures and their growth rates a terrible guide to how tight or loose the policy was. It turned out to be strangulation tight.) After such early experiments, though, a gentler version of monetarism has delivered much better economic outcomes in the 1990s than in the previous two and a half decades.

Except in Japan, that is. And that single failure inevitably raises a question mark over how well founded the current macroeconomic consensus can be. If the standard policy measures do not work there, is that because of something unique to do with Japan, perhaps a question of culture or attitudes, or is it because the policies work only in certain types of circumstances? And if the latter, does that mean we should not be so complacent about the consensus economic policies outside Japan? Could the U.S. recession that started in March 2001, for instance, turn into a decade-long stagnation, too?

According to Keynes, the most important influence of all on the state of the economy is what he called "animal spirits," the general degree of optimism about the future, determined by psychological or political factors rather than economic ones. Economists cannot offer a policy to improve a country's animal spirits. When it became apparent that Japan was not recovering from recession, there were two standard policy levers that could be used to stimulate the economy, according to the conventional approach. If total demand in the economy is persistently falling short of productive capacity in a business cycle downturn, you can try, first, looser monetary policy, or second, looser fiscal policy.

A permanent monetary expansion in the long run increases only prices, not output, but in the short run (which might be years) a temporary monetary expansion can boost demand and growth by encouraging more consumer spending and business investment. In practice, looser monetary policy is implemented by cutting interest rates. Central banks usually achieve interest rate reductions through their interventions in the money markets, where the interest rate is the price of the central bank's transactions with commercial banks.

Japanese interest rates have been fairly close to zero since the end of 1995, however. In March 2001 the Bank of Japan cut its main interest rate back to zero after a controversial increase to 0.25 percent the previous August. In performing this U-turn it promised to provide as much money in the money markets as it would take to keep the rate at zero.

However, on several days in the summer of 2001, in an unprecedented money market situation, Japanese banks decided they didn't want any money even at a zero price. They couldn't think of anything they wanted to do with free money. The artist Akasegawa Genpei mocked the power of money by printing fake zero yen notes in 1967. He invited the general public to send him real yen notes in exchange, with the aim of putting the state currency out of circulation. Reality caught up with art in a most unexpected way thirty-four years later.

Economic theory does encompass a situation where monetary policy becomes useless because you can't push interest rates any lower than zero. It is the **liquidity trap** first noted by Keynes and his follower John Hicks in the context of the 1920s and 1930s depression. In this trap, the real interest rate (that is to say, the nominal rate less the expected rate of inflation) needed to raise investment in the economy up to the prevailing level of savings would be negative. Unfortunately a negative real interest rate is not possible unless there is inflation in excess of the nominal interest rate (for example, interest rates at 2 percent and inflation at 3 percent, for a real interest rate of −1 percent). If there is *deflation* instead, so there is a *positive* real interest rate when the nominal interest rate is zero, it is not possible at all. (Zero interest rates and prices falling at 2 percent a year makes for a real interest rate of plus 2 percent.)

Why? If prices are going to be lower next year, it still makes sense for consumers to save even if they get no interest because they can buy more with their cash next year. Yet there is a real cost to businesses if they borrow even at zero interest to invest because they will have to pay back next year an amount that would buy them more equipment than they can get for the money this year. Something else is going to have to stop prices falling if consumers carry on saving too much and businesses postpone investment.

Keynes's way out of the trap was fiscal policy. If monetary policy cannot work, then the government should be able to stimulate the economy by deficit spending. Leave taxes unchanged, or cut them to encourage consumer spending and private investment. Increase government expenditure on projects like building bridges or schools. This will boost demand and jolt the economy out of the liquidity trap. Keynes famously argued that even wasteful spending like paying people to dig holes and fill them in again would help by creating demand in the economy because the workers on such public schemes would spend their wages. This philosophy inspired Franklin D. Roosevelt's New Deal and seemed to work. The American economy had begun to emerge from its long slump when World War II gave an even bigger and better boost to demand.

The current economic orthodoxy, though, is that government deficits should not be too big. There are several reasons, corresponding to different archaeological layers of economic thought. First, there is the straightforward argument that if the government wants to borrow more from the national savings pool, it will bid up interest rates for private borrowers, so government spending will **crowd out** some private investment. This is less important if the government is borrowing relatively small amounts from the vast international savings pool.

Second, if the government borrows so much it drives the long-term interest rate higher than the economy's long-term growth rate, it could put its debt level on an explosive path. The economy will in some circumstances never grow fast enough to generate the revenues to pay the debt interest. This is a genuine, not a theoretical, worry. The governments of several countries have so much debt that their entire budget deficit consists of interest payments.

The most recent kind of argument against too much debt points out that taxpayers are not dumb. Sometimes this is described as **rational expectations**, which is the idea that what people expect about the future conforms to reality, at least in the sense that it is not possible to fool them systematically and permanently. Taxpayers will therefore realize—to a debatable extent—that government borrowing now means higher taxes in future. So they adjust their spending downwards now to compensate. In the extreme special case, higher deficit-financed government spending now is completely offset by reduced private spending as taxpayers earmark current income for future taxes.

Despite these arguments, economists accept that the government budget can help stimulate demand, so Japan has tried it. And tried again and again. Its government budget deficit has been as high as 3 to 4 percent of GDP throughout the late 1990s. Running such big deficits year after year has boosted the ratio of outstanding government debt to GDP from 60 percent at the beginning of the 1990s to 130 percent and rising by 2000. The fiscal expansion probably explains why there was a little growth in 1996–1997 and no doubt kept national output higher than it would otherwise have been.

However, even such a huge fiscal boost has not proven big enough to jump-start the economy. And now the accumulated debts have reached such an alarming level that there are serious concerns about continuing government deficits. Japanese taxpayers have certainly got to the point where they understand that future taxes will be higher and, crucially, that the government might not be able to pay their future pensions. So further government borrowing now is being offset by increased private saving. On a chart, government "dissaving" or borrowing is almost the mirror image of private saving. (The same is true the other way round, incidentally, in the United States, where big government surpluses in the 1990s have been mirrored by big private deficits.) Some economists now think Japan ought to put its fiscal policy into reverse in order to encourage taxpayers to save a little less. Others fear tighter fiscal policy would exacerbate the continuing slump and must be postponed.

If monetary policy doesn't work and fiscal policy doesn't either, what does that leave? Well, maybe Japan's problems lie in microeconomics, rather than macroeconomic policies. In recent years, economists have turned their attention away from policies aimed at manipulating demand in the Japanese economy to so-called structural policies.

These include measures like reform of the banking system to make it easier for businesses to borrow or to encourage a venture capital industry; labor market reforms that will make it easier for businesses to destroy old jobs but create new ones and will encourage workers to move more freely between jobs; abandoning the tradition of cooperative corporate networks (*keiretsu*) in favor of vibrant competition. In short, the prescription is for the Japanese economy to become more like the American economy of the 1990s. What worked for Japan in an earlier era, its big government-directed and bureaucratic corporations, is inappropriate for a time when technical change demands adaptability and risk-taking, the argument goes.

This is probably correct. Many Japanese policymakers and economists accept that the economic system needs to change. Banking reform in particular is widely seen as essential. Several banks have gone bankrupt because they had lent so much money to companies with which they had a traditional *keiretsu* relationship without applying basic commercial criteria to the loans: Were they being used to finance productive investments? Would they be repaid? The bad debt overhang is still immense and is preventing banks from lending to new customers. At the same time, consumer credit is vastly underdeveloped by the standards of the U.S. or Europe. Even credit cards are rare in Japan.

So advocating structural reform is perfectly good advice, but possibly irrelevant. It will certainly increase the Japanese economy's long-term potential. The problem, though, is that demand has fallen short of its existing potential. Structural reform might well only exacerbate the gap between demand and supply. The country might well have microeconomic problems, but it has macroeconomic ones, too.

Any measure to jolt the economy out of its current stagnation will have to get consumers and businesses spending more and will have to stop prices falling. This reasoning prompted Paul Krugman, an economist at Princeton University, to publish in 1998 a hugely influential article revisiting the Keynesian idea of the liquidity trap.

There are good reasons for thinking Japan is in a liquidity trap, apart from the obvious ones of falling prices and ineffective zero interest rates. The trap, remember, is the problem of too much saving and not enough investment (or too much supply and not enough demand in the economy as a whole) despite very low interest rates. In the past, Japan has been a high saving, high investment economy. It is plausible to suggest there might have been too much investment during Japan's boom years in the late 1980s, leading to overcapacity in some industries when growth slowed. This is a classic business cycle pattern, possibly taken to excess in Japan's case. Some economists believed the same happened in the United States in the late 1990s and are correspondingly gloomy about its economic prosepcts for the next few years (although, as I wrote, the American economy seemed to have begun to expand again).

More fundamentally, there are good reasons to believe Japan's long-term potential growth rate is now much lower than it was in the 1970s and 1980s. The main reason is the aging of the population. Tokyo's teenagers might be spending freely on platform shoes, mobile phones, Louis Vuitton handbags, and hair dye, but there are not enough of them. Instead, the ranks of the late-middle-aged are building up and the elderly are conserving their savings, fearful about how they can finance a retirement that might turn out to be longer than anything in past human experience. Throughout the rich world this aging is occurring due to a mix of longer life expectancy and lower birthrates. But it is at its most extreme in Japan, where the birthrate is far below replacement levels and there is next to no immigration. There are going to be fewer Japanese people and their average age is rising. It is easy to see why expectations of lower growth in future because of the demographic trends might lead people to save more than enough to satisfy the economy's need for savings to finance investment now. Perhaps the government should offer a special bonus payment to immigrants who are under twenty-five and will spend a lot.

Krugman went on to recommend that the Bank of Japan should bring about a reduction in savings by making the real interest rate negative. That involves guaranteeing there will be inflation. His suggestion was a permanent inflation target of, say, 4 percent, compared with a current inflation rate of about − 1 percent. That involves not just monetary expansion now but a promise of monetary expansion permanently into the future. For, in the end, a permanent monetary loosening will raise prices.

The trick is not only ensuring the permanence of the policy but also making sure everybody believes it to be permanent. Other creative suggestions for making monetary policy work again have included a proposal to time-stamp currency so that it would be worthless if not spent before a certain date. That amounts to an enforced rapid inflation; in a normal inflation it takes a currency a very long time to become completely worthless. So maybe this time-limited coupon idea is too extreme. Inflation targeting has worked very well in other circumstances as a means of setting monetary policy, and there is no reason to think it a bad idea in Japan's case just because it is suffering from too low rather than too high an inflation rate at present.

The Japanese economy might now have been in its trap for almost long enough for it to sort itself out, anyway. Eventually the economy will have adjusted down to the prevailing level of demand so that prices do not need to fall any further, and when prices stop falling, a zero nominal interest rate corresponds to a zero real rate and might start stimulating the economy in the conventional way. But that seems a pessimistic outlook for a country that until a decade ago was seen as one of the most dynamic and powerful in the world. Is there an optimistic scenario?

If Krugman is right about the reason Japan has fallen into a liquidity trap, its consumers are saving too much (except for the dwindling number of fashion-conscious Japanese teenagers in an aging population) and companies investing too little because they believe the country's growth potential is lower in the future than in the past. However, the United States has almost certainly seen an increase in its potential growth rate during the 1990s (despite the downturn since) because of the implementation of new technologies, and perhaps also because of sheer "animal spirits." If the Japanese started to see this kind of "New Economy" experience in their own future, pointing to favorable long-run growth prospects, the real interest rate that would bring saving and investment into balance would rise and the liquidity trap would fade away. To the extent that structural reforms would improve the economy's potential in the long-term future—and get people believing in it—this argument puts the spotlight back on the supply side of the economy.

Japan's unusually adverse demographic trends might outweigh the favorable effects of technological advances, or they might not. And it is not the only country aging so fast. Some European countries like Italy have very low birthrates and rising average ages, too, along with conditions far less favorable to productivity improvements—lacking, for example, Japan's impressive science base and leading high technology multinationals. On the other hand, Italy has a lot of immigration and a very different financial and industrial structure. The exact links between developments fundamental to long-term growth, such as demographic and technical change, and actual long-term growth form just about the least well understood area in all of economics.

The other point about this discussion is that it reminds us that thinking about demand and supply in an economy as a whole, as opposed to the market for apples or pins, is a bit of an intellectual convenience for economists. The idea of a price level for a "unit" of national output is highly abstract. The extent of this abstraction is actually revealed by the language of macroeconomics. It is much easier to write about individual industries or individuals' economic decisions without using any jargon, but it has been impossible to avoid all jargon in writing about macroeconomics. Any nonspecialist will start to glaze over a sentence that has *negative real interest rates* or *productive potential* or *liquidity trap* in it.

While we economists tend to fall into the habit of thinking about demand and supply and price at the aggregate level of the whole economy as being analogous to a market for a single good, this can be misleading. In particular, it is possible that for the economy as a whole, many levels of output and prices could prevail in a given set of objective circumstances, depending on what people expect to happen in future or how confident they feel. It sounds a bit woolly, but it is this indeterminacy that makes macroeconomics so interesting and, in the end, always controversial.

The pragmatic agreement about how to run macroeconomic policies that I described earlier has come about because for most of the rich OECD countries, the 1990s went rather well. It is real-life problems that generate controversy and change in economic theory. That earlier debate between monetarists and Keynesians was the fruit of **stagflation**, the 1970s experience of high and rising inflation combined with recession or stagnation.

Japan's experience in the past decade has looked like a return to the problems of the 1930s, especially the liquidity trap, which gave rise to the Keynesian prescriptions in the first place. Same problems, same policies? Unfortunately, that simple equation has not worked. And there is no professional consensus that Professor Krugman's updating of the policies would work. One of the lessons of this discussion is how little we still know about what makes economies as a whole perform well or badly.

Chapter 22

INFLATION

Targeting the Sleeping Beast

It is a long time since **inflation** was a serious problem for central banks and governments in countries like the United States, Japan, and the big European countries. Throughout the 1990s, and despite a record-breaking boom in the U.S. and the U.K., inflation—the rate of increase in the general price level—remained very low.

It wasn't always so, and still isn't true everywhere. In the leading economies the inflation rate climbed to near 10 percent in the last years of the '80s, and the 1970s and early '80s were marked by inflation rates of up to 25 percent.

In many other countries, ranging from Greece and Turkey to Brazil and Argentina, the Philippines and Thailand, the experience over the years has been far worse. Many suffered **hyperinflation**, with price levels climbing at annual rates in the hundreds or thousands of percent. In the statistical publications of the International Monetary Fund dating from the 1970s the charts down the side of each page of figures illustrating inflation showed lines that rose steeply on the graph, and then continued off the graph and over the rest of the page.

The worldwide acceleration in inflation dating from just before 1970, and exacerbated by the oil price shocks of that decade, was unexpected and alarming. For most of the postwar era policymakers had been firmly focused on ensuring their economies grew fast enough to keep unemployment low.

The people running governments and central banks remembered all too clearly the prewar depression and the political tensions stirred up by high unemployment. The economic failure paved the way for the political and diplomatic catastrophes that led ultimately to tens of millions of lives lost in World War II. John Maynard Keynes and other leading economists, who had spent a decade trying to figure out the causes and solutions to depression and unemployment, developed the tools of demand management that would allow them to fine-tune the level of output and employment.

For example, cutting taxes and raising government spending—levers of **fiscal policy**—would both put more money in the pockets of consumers and businesses, which would spend more, expanding the economy's level of aggregate demand. Reducing interest rates or increasing the amount of money circulating around the economy through central banking techniques such as buying up some government bonds—**monetary policy**—would have the same effect. Of course given the economy's **aggregate supply**, expanding demand would lead to higher prices and probably a higher rate of inflation, too. But for many years there was believed to be a trade-off between output (or employment, or with the opposite sign, unemployment) and inflation. The relationship linking unemployment and inflation even had a name, the **Phillips Curve**, a downward sloping line showing high inflation at very low unemployment levels and low inflation at high unemployment levels. Policymakers could choose where they wanted to be and adjust fiscal and monetary policy to get there.

Practice never quite works out like theory. The relationship turned out not to be stable and could be exploited in this way only in the short term. For suppose the government stimulated growth and cut unemployment at the price of a higher inflation rate. Before long people adjust to the new inflation rate and make higher pay claims, or expect higher interest on their bank deposits or increase the prices they are charging a bit faster. Nothing has really changed once people's expectations of inflation adjust, except for the fact that the actual inflation rate is higher than it was. The Phillips curve ignored the fact that expectations could change. (It was too mechanistic; in fact, the Phillips after whom it is named was an engineer who had literally built a machine to represent the economy. It sits now in London's Science Museum.) Over time, the trade-off became less and less favorable in the sense that to achieve a level of unemployment below a particular number cost more and more in terms of higher inflation. That particular number is called the **non-accelerating inflation rate of unemployment,** or **Nairu,** and varies between countries and itself shifts over time for reasons to do with the underlying structure of the economy.

This potted history of postwar macroeconomic policy takes only a few paragraphs, but was of course played out over several decades and causing much economic pain along the way. Many countries ended up with high inflation and high unemployment, a politically corrosive mix given the unlovely name of stagflation.

It is easy to think that it's unemployment that really matters. After all, depriving people of the opportunity to work undermines their ability to provide for themselves and their families, and also their dignity.

However, voters punish governments that give them high inflation even more. High inflation makes planning for the future harder because nobody is sure how much less their money will be worth in three or ten years' time. It redistributes money from savers to borrowers because it reduces the real purchasing power of savings and reduces the real burden of debts. It penalizes people on low incomes, or fixed incomes like pensions, because the low-paid never manage to keep their earnings rising in line with inflation. Their ability to purchase goods and services is steadily eroded as prices go up and their incomes don't match the increase. I still clearly remember the anxiety in my not-too-well-off family during the 1970s about what we would be able to afford with prices going up so fast, and my mother hoarding coffee and sugar because they would be so much dearer later.

Mervyn King, deputy governor of the Bank of England, labeled the cohort of U.K. citizens born in the mid-1960s the "inflation generation." For them, inflation had been the norm and affected every decision they made, from career choice (was the pension indexed?) to buying a house (was it worth taking on a big mortgage because inflation would erode its value?). The purchasing power of a £100 cash gift at their birth had shrunk to £1 by their thirtieth birthday.

Altogether since 1945 the level of prices in the U.K. had risen twentyfold by 1995. Before modern times inflation was virtually unknown (apart from one or two exceptional episodes). But if you imagine the U.K.'s price level to be represented by the depth of the River Thames, which was 8 feet in 1800, it varied mostly between 5 and 7 feet until 1914, and between 6 and 13 feet until 1945 (not a stable era in the world economy). But since 1945 the tide has risen to over 200 feet.

After this experience, a serious failure of macroeconomic policy, it would be foolish to think there will never be any danger of inflation again. Inflation matters, especially if it's long-lasting. A prolonged bout of inflation undermines investment, distorts people's decisions, and over time reduces the economy's potential supply.

Still, there isn't much to speak of across large swaths of the world economy. If anything, there is more concern about **deflation**, negative inflation or a falling price level. It is hard to achieve any real growth, actual increases in output, when the economy is shrinking in money terms because of widespread falls in prices. A little bit of inflation seems an essential lubricant for growth.

Nevertheless, it's worth pondering whether policymakers have a better handle on managing inflation—relying on there being no change in circumstances, or luck, does not seem a good policy. And the answer is yes, probably. It's what seems to have worked for the past decade, in admittedly favorable conditions. That is **inflation targeting**.

The U.K. was one of the pioneers of inflation targeting, which means setting an explicit target level of inflation without specifying exactly how it is to be achieved. Since the framework was introduced in 1993 the inflation rate has been low and stable, and there has not been a quarter of negative economic growth since.

Here's how it works. The government sets the Bank of England a target, currently 2.5 percent, for its chosen measure of inflation a range in which it is acceptable for it to vary—at present it's 1.5 to 3.5 percent. The bank is responsible for how it decides to hit the target, setting the level of interest rates month by month at regular meetings. Details very in other countries. Some choose targets that are not symmetric—they aim for inflation below a certain level rather than between certain levels. Targets can apply over various time horizons.

Public accountability is an important part of the process. The minutes of the meetings are published after two weeks to explain the reasoning behind the decision, and the members of the interest rate setting committee (five Bank of England officials, four outside experts appointed by the government) give speeches and appear before parliamentary committees to explain themselves. This is more than a matter of democracy, of bringing unelected central bankers to account. For **credibility** is a useful anti-inflation weapon in itself. If everybody believes inflation will stay around 2.5 percent, they will behave accordingly, by not making 10 percent wage claims, for instance, and thus help fulfill the target. Expectations worked against the successful use of the Phillips curve but are helpful to the inflation targeting approach.

Targeting seems better than previous policies for several reasons. In the past economists thought monetary policy was a matter of choosing between allowing the government or central bank complete **discretion**, which turned out not to be anti-inflationary at all, as we saw, and setting fixed **rules**.

The kind of rule tried widely in the late 1970s, as countries struggled to tame high inflation, was setting a **monetary target**, a fixed rate of growth for the money supply. This is not the place to go into definitions of money supply and all the other technicalities; the idea was just that inflation couldn't go beyond a certain rate if there wasn't enough money swimming around the economy.

Monetary targeting worked well in one sense. It did bring inflation down. However, there was in many countries an appalling cost—it worked by causing a deep and long recession. What's more, it became impossible to apply the rule because the deregulation of credit markets in many countries in the early 1980s made it impossible to find a measure of the money supply that continued to have a steady and meaningful link to economic activity.

There are other types of rule, however. One adopted in many developing and middle-income economies has been an **exchange rate target**. If you keep your currency in a constant relationship to the U.S. dollar, you can't have a higher inflation rate than the United States. In other words, monetary policy gets exported to a central bank that is better at it—namely the Federal Reserve. This too worked well for a while for many countries.

Argentina, for instance, had a very rigid link between its peso and the dollar, which did tame excessive inflation. Unfortunately, sustaining the link imposed a growing cost on the economy in terms of recession, while the government overborrowed to try and compensate by spending a lot more than it raised in taxes. In particular, provincial governments increased their spending by far more than the central government was able to raise in additional taxes. By late 2001, the country was in a catastrophic economic crisis. It mirrored many earlier currency crises in emerging markets, when it becomes clear to the financial markets that the exchange rate rule cannot be sustained, so they speculate heavily against the currency. It was no surprise to any economist that Argentina had to abandon the dollar link, devalue the peso, and default on the debt it had built up meanwhile. The crisis was an economic tragedy for the country and its people, and one that could have been avoided if the government had not over half a decade run a fiscal policy inconsistent with the tough monetary rule.

In short, monetary rules work well in some circumstances and not others. They do not work well if other policies undermine them. Not surprisingly, the ideal is to combine rules, which give people confidence monetary policy will keep inflation low, with discretion, so policy can be adapted when circumstances change.

Fans of inflation targets say they provide precisely this kind of constrained discretion. The framework is crystal clear: the authorities will do what it takes to keep inflation on track. But there remains enough flexibility to respond to changing circumstances.

So far the inflation targeting framework has not been tested by the kind of global economic shocks that sent inflation soaring in the 1970s. Nor is it the only option. The U.S. Federal Reserve is one of the world's best monetary authorities, and it doesn't have an explicit inflation target. It does, however, behave as if it has one. There are stable links between the economy's behavior and the way the Fed changes interest rates—growth above the normal trend leads to an increase in rates and vice versa. This kind of predictable policy reaction is known as a Taylor Rule after the economist (John Taylor, an official in President Bush's Treasury Department) who identified it.

There are some other promising experiments around the world. For instance, Turkey was launching a new inflation target, under the auspices of an IMF program to sort out its economic woes. It started with inflation around 60 percent, and so far the reduction has been encouraging. A number of countries along with the U.K., including Canada, New Zealand, Sweden, Finland, Israel, Sweden, Spain, and Australia, have adopted one form or another of inflation targeting.

Still, anybody aware of the changes in economists' and policymakers' consensus over the decades about how to keep inflation tamed will recognize that even the best policy frameworks don't last forever. Times change, and as Keynes famously pointed out, it then makes sense to change your mind.

Chapter 23

DEFENSE SPENDING

Farewell to the Peace Dividend

"My budget includes the largest increase in defense spending in two decades, because while the price of freedom and security is high, it is never too high." So said U.S. President George W. Bush in his State of the Union address in January 2002. The rise announced in the budget a few weeks later was $48 billion. No surprise, really, in the wake of the September 11 attacks just five months earlier and the subsequent war against terrorism in Afghanistan.

For a number of years American military top brass had been arguing that increased defense spending was essential, and coincidentally enough, the figure they had in mind was an extra $50 billion a year. In a series of reviews in the late 1990s the army, navy, air force, and marines had spelled out the ways they thought post–Cold War cuts in spending had undermined the defense capabilities of the United States.

America's defense spending peaked at $304 billion in 1989, as the Berlin Wall fell and the communist regimes of Eastern Europe crumbled. In 1999 the figure had dropped to $283 billion. This was a dramatic fall— from the equivalent of 6.5 percent of the U.S. GDP to 3.2 percent. In the months right after the West's victory in the Cold War, the realization that government spending on national defense could decline was labeled the **peace dividend**.

How important, then, was the outbreak of peace, and how much will it matter for the economy if the eruption of a new war, the war on terrorism, spells a rising defense burden in future? A saving in government spending amounting to 3 percent of GDP for a decade is a large sum of money—more than $250 billion in 1999 alone, and perhaps as much as $2 trillion in ten years. The exact figure depends on whether you assume the defense budget would have stayed at its 1989 level or risen or been cut back if the course of history had run differently. But in 1990, then-President George Bush had a $350 billion defense budget penciled in for 1994, whereas his successor actually spent $250 billion, a $100 billion gap. So a couple of trillion seems in the right ballpark.

Whatever precise number you opt for, it is a large amount released for either other government spending programs or deficit reduction. The state of the federal government's finances shifted from large deficit to large surplus over the course of the 1990s, in an extraordinary turnaround that would not have been possible without the defense cuts. The only other ways to start narrowing the chasm between government spending and tax revenues at the start of the decade would have been either increased taxes or cuts in other programs, both painful politically.

One important consequence of this substantial decline in government borrowing, a deficit of $290 billion in 1992 transformed into a 2000 surplus of $236 billion, was a fall in long-term interest rates set in the U.S. Treasury bond market—particularly in the later 1990s when investors woke up to the fact that the government was actually retiring some of its outstanding debt. For borrowing by the government crowds out borrowing by the private sector by competing for funds provided by investors. This may sound esoteric, but it had important ramifications because other interest rates depend on long-term government bond yields. For example, it became much cheaper for home buyers with lower mortgages rates or companies planning to borrow money for investment as federal surpluses grew during the '90s. While economic textbooks have long pointed out the existence of crowding out, budget deficits had been around for so long by the end of the Cold War that nobody could really remember what it was like when there had last been a lot less competition for funds in the capital markets from the government.

Alan Greenspan, the Federal Reserve chairman, was convinced crowding out was an important phenomenon. He believed that if the peace dividend could be directed toward deficit reduction rather than spending on other programs then investors would seek out other opportunities and put their money toward productive uses, which would have a big payoff for the economy. When Bill Clinton won the presidency for the Democrats in 1992, Mr. Greenspan struck a deal with the new president. He promised lower interest rates in return for reduced deficits. Mr. Clinton redirected the savings on the defense budget into a combination of increased spending on (mainly) Medicare and Social Security and a decreased federal budget deficit. Defense's share of total government spending dropped from 28 percent at the end of the 1980s to 16 percent in 1999.

Many traditional Democrats were nevertheless skeptical, and angry that they would not be able to increase spending on social programs as much as they had hoped—and all because a Republican at the Fed claimed the financial markets were all-important. How come the financial markets were more important than a democratically elected administration? James Carville, the director of the Clinton campaign, famously said, "I used to think if there was reincarnation, I wanted to come back as the president or the pope or a .400 baseball hitter. But now I want to come back as the bond market. You can intimidate everyone."

Others had a different concern about the shrinking defense budget. The government had been an important source of funds for research and development of new technologies through military and space programs— most famously, the Internet itself. Civilian R&D spending in the U.S. has long been much lower than in other industrial countries such as Germany and Japan—1.9 percent of GDP versus 2.5 to 3 percent. The fear was that nonmilitary companies would not make up for reduced military research and innovation (although economist William Baumol argues that America's military strength is based on the country's civilian technical expertise and economic vibrancy, not the other way round). Civilian R&D didn't, in fact, make up the for the drop in defense R&D. It's impossible to be sure at this point whether this is going to have made a big difference to the long-term competitive strength of the U.S. economy, because the whole process of innovation is so long and uncertain—and frankly, still so little understood by economists. There seems little reason for its citizens to fret, though, about America's economic strength and dynamism compared to other countries. It remains the world's undisputed technological leader in all but a few areas.

That one hypothetical concern aside, events favored the Greenspan view. Throughout the second half of the decade, interest rates in the

United States stayed low, investment in new businesses and technologies boomed, and the economy experienced its longest expansion since records began with a significant increase in the productivity trend. The good times came to an end, of course, but it's not too fanciful to see the New Economy investment boom as a part of the peace dividend.

It wasn't only the United States that enjoyed a peace dividend, however. Worldwide military spending fell from 3.6 percent of global GDP in 1990 to 2.4 percent in 1999, although the decline was concentrated in the industrialized and post-communist countries. Developing countries in general hardly cut their military spending at all, relative to the size of their economies, and some increased it. The worldwide peace dividend for 1999 may have been as much as $350 to $400 billion. That's the equivalent of an economy the size of the Netherlands. The International Monetary Fund reckons those poorer countries that did opt for a peace dividend were able to both increase spending on vital social programs like health and education and cut government deficits, too.

Throughout the rich world, too, other nations apart from the United States discovered the joy of deficit reduction thanks to a reduced defense burden. Britain's new Labour Chancellor of the Exchequer (or finance minister in plain English), took a leaf straight out of the Clinton book and opted to cut government borrowing before increasing spending on public services as so many Labour supporters would have liked. Gordon Brown was mocked for his obsession with "prudence"—yet the achievement of a surplus of revenue over expenditure meant he too could pay off some of the government's debt and save GBP 2 billion a year in on an annual interest bill of some GBP 25 billion. Just as in the United States, long-term interest rates in Britain fell to their lowest levels, in real terms, for many years.

Governments are always free to choose the level of spending and taxes, and the gap between the two. The state of the business cycle will make a difference because a recession will always lower tax revenues and lead to automatic rises in areas of spending like unemployment benefits. These types of adjustments are known as **automatic stabilizers** because they limit the impact of a slowdown in the private sector and occur without the government needing to make any decisions. But in the end it's a matter of politics, not mechanical choices. The point about the peace dividend is that it made the choices much, much easier because it was so obvious where spending cuts could fall. The military were, for a while, politically defenseless.

The peace dividend, then, has been large and significant. This should come as no surprise. War is not an inherently productive activity, to say the least. This points to a rather pessimistic conclusion about the likely impact of the resumption of war, and one that could, like the Cold War, be long drawn out and spread its tentacles throughout civilian life. After all, uncertainty about the world outlook is likely to keep investment spending lower than it might otherwise have been, as businesses opt for taking fewer risky bets on demand for their products or services. The new concern, not only in America but worldwide, about security, and higher insurance premiums, will raise businesses' costs. Even a small increase in costs can have a big impact on investment decisions and on international trade. Some specific industries—the airlines and tourism, for example—have been badly affected by the terror attacks. And there may be other ramifications, such as a drop in immigration to the United States, reversing a flow of skills and energy that had enormously benefited the economy during the 1990s.

As for the federal budget, it's up to the president to consider whether further increases in military spending will be needed in future, and also whether or not he should cap the budget deficit by raising taxes or cutting other areas of expenditure. To start with, he opted for tax cuts instead, arguing the economy needed a boost because it was in recession at the start of 2002. The Republicans like to cut taxes, but Mr. Bush will have to make a choice about how much the defense burden should be allowed to feed straight through to the deficit and hence long-term interest rates.

The other question that raises itself in the minds of non-Americans, even the closest of allies, is whether the U.S. really needs to spend $350 billion a year on defense. The spending will help the economy, for sure. New defense orders will help out many high-tech businesses that have been struggling since the dot-com bust. The military need is another matter. Before the Bush boost, the country spent as much on defense as the next nine biggest military spenders put together. Afterwards, although the rise is equivalent to just 0.1 percent of GDP, America's spending exceeds that of the next fifteen biggest countries, at current exchange rates. The $48 billion annual increase alone is twice Italy's entire defense budget. Is this perhaps taking superpowerdom to extremes?

Is it really going to take a lot more money to maintain the same military and diplomatic superiority over other nations—all other nations? It's hard to believe any other country, even China, could catch up on this overwhelming lead. Perhaps in a generation or two, if the Chinese economy lives up to expectations, but the People's Army has a lot of technological catching up to do. As for the old Cold War enemy, Russia, it is now a small economy, albeit one with nuclear weapons, and it has better things to do with its tax revenues than try to reclaim superpower status.

Indeed, is throwing a lot of money at the problem, buying even more aircraft carriers and warheads to add to the huge and overwhelming array of force already at the disposal of the U.S. military, the route to victory in the war against terrorism? The generals and admirals certainly think so, but they would say that, wouldn't they?

Chapter 24

WEATHER

Why Economists Care About
the Sex Life of Pigs

The British weather is a subject of endless fascination to the British people. Either it's terrible (most of the time and therefore deserving of complaint) or it's not (so unusual it's worth commenting on). As I write today we are enjoying one of the warmest June days in recent memory, with temperatures in London likely to hit 90 degrees Fahrenheit. The windows are all open. The builders across the way, drilling into old concrete, have a radio blaring out easy listening at top volume. Trucks and cars roar past. There are even people talking outside, for heaven's sake. How is anybody supposed to get any work done?

Well, the answer is that nobody much is working. In many continental European cities, where the summers are habitually very hot and uncomfortable but the offices don't all have air-conditioning, people start winding down their work as July arrives and go away for five or six weeks. Although less so than in the past, cities such as Paris, Rome, and Barcelona simply empty out during the heat and dust of summer, and the economy more or less slows to a halt.

Normally a near total cessation in economic activity would be regarded by pundits as a cause for alarm. Yet there are enormous seasonal swings that dwarf the kinds of variation typical of a business cycle, and nobody bothers much about them. Christmas shopping, for example: about a fifth of all the money passing through the retailers' tills in a year is spent in the four weeks ahead of the holiday. Much of the rest is spent in the months when retailers normally hold their sales. To put some figures on this, American consumers spent $219 billion in February 2001, compared with $311 billion in December of that year, a 25 percent difference. Average weekly retail spending in the U.K. was £3.6 billion in a quiet month like February 2000 and £5.5 billion in December the same year, a variation of more than 50 percent between the quietest month in the shops and the busiest.

The weather is the cause of much seasonal variation in the economic statistics, and it is scandalously ignored by most economists. Thus demand for heat or air conditioning affects power generation and has a knock-on effect on oil extraction or coal mining. People are more likely to buy new clothes when there is an onset of much warmer or colder weather. Construction is slowed or halted by rain and blizzards. And the weather affects harvests and thus the output and price of agricultural goods. Seasonality and other date-specific influences are too important for good practical economists to ignore.

Even the stock market is affected. Trading volumes on the London market always drop off on the days of one of the big summer sporting events such as the big race at Ascot or an international test match or an exciting Wimbledon semifinal. Many employers actually post the latest scores on their internal computer networks so all the staff are not constantly dialing premium phone lines or surreptitiously listening to the radio to keep up.

Trading is also much quieter—sometimes by more than 20 percent compared with the recent average—on days that are simply hot. This past summer month has seen daily temperatures 25 percent above average, whereas last year they were 7 percent below average. Okay, it has not been a stellar twelve months for the stock market anyway, but the daily number of equity bargains on the London Stock Exchange has been lower than last year on virtually every trading day for the past month.

A 1993 study found a weather effect operates on Wall Street, too. The author argued that the weather had important psychological effects on share prices, with sunshine making investors more optimistic. And a 2001 article reported that across twenty-six stock markets from 1982 to 1997, shares gained more than average on more than averagely sunny days, and less on cloudier than average days. On the New York market the difference was a 25 percent gain on a sunny day compared with a sub-9 percent rise on a cloudy day.

The explanation for lower volumes traded (as opposed to share prices) is no more complicated than the fact that traders are taking their lunch breaks out in the sunshine, away from their desks. It has been suggested that the Internet has increased the seasonality in trading. Private investors are particularly likely to spend an hour online if the weather is bad but hit the golf course instead on a fine day. It's not just sunshine, though. Some researchers have found stock markets do better around a new moon than a full moon, in 43 out of 48 markets analyzed. Explaining this werewolf effect is up to psychologists, though, not economists.

Statisticians do try to adjust most of the published data on the economy for seasonal variations, but it's tricky. They can only remove typical seasonal swings. For example, if December retail sales have been 20 percent above the annual average on average for the past ten years, they will roughly speaking remove 20 percent from the raw, unadjusted December figure. (In practice it is a lot more complicated.) Even though many of the commonly used methods of seasonal adjustment tend to overcompensate for seasonal swings, this approach works pretty well when seasonal patterns change little from year to year—but not so well when they are more erratic. Thus it works much less well for weather-related seasonal fluctuations because the weather isn't so predictable from year to year.

This can make a big difference to commentators' interpretation of the state of the economy, prone as they are to getting overexcited about shifts of a few tenths of a percentage point in the growth of industrial output or inflation. Moves of this size can often be due to nothing more than a seasonal change in the current year that is bigger than normal and therefore not blotted out by the statisticians' seasonal adjustment process. Many economists are often guilty of completely ignoring seasonality.

One of my favorite examples was the fluctuation in the reported price of pork and bacon over a couple of years when a very damp summer followed a hot one. According to the official statistician briefing journalists, pigs get much more amorous in hot weather—well, don't we all? A glut of piglets one year was followed by a shortage the next, with the logical consequences for pig-meat prices. Although it looked like an upturn in meat prices was driving inflation higher, it wasn't necessarily anything to get worried about once you had looked into the explanation for it.

Some weather-related effects on the economy go much further than mere seasonal fluctuations. The El Niño effect is one example. During normal seasons in the South Pacific, there is a high-pressure system off the western coast of South America and a low pressure system off the eastern coast of Australia. That makes the prevailing winds easterly (that is, from east to west). Warm surface water is blown from the east toward Asia and Australia, causing precipitation in these regions to the benefit of agriculture and industry, while in the eastern Pacific, cold but nutrient-rich water comes up from deeper in the ocean, making conditions for tropical fish ideal and boosting the South American fishing industry.

Unfortunately there are periodic variations in this pattern. During Las Niñas, the pattern intensifies, taking ocean temperature much lower. During Los Niños, the pattern is actually inverted, raising ocean temperature and blowing warm water toward the Pacific coast of the Americas.

The Los Niños tend to occur at three- to seven-year intervals and last for two years, and vary greatly in their intensity. There were especially severe examples in 1982–83 and 1997–98. The fishing industry in the Pacific waters of the Americas from Chile to British Columbia suffered enormously. In addition, global atmospheric disturbance altered high-altitude jet stream winds and affected weather patterns around the world. Both the severe recent Los Niños coincided with and perhaps contributed to periods of great economic turbulence, too: the Latin American debt crisis in the first case and the Southeast Asian financial crisis in the second.

There is plenty of anecdotal evidence (in other words reports rather than statistics subjected to formal testing of hypotheses) about the damage El Niño inflicts on the economy. In the recent one, Ecuador's rice crops were washed away, copper mines in Chile and Peru were flooded, Australia's wheat crops were damaged by drought, Indonesia suffered forest fires that also covered much of Southeast Asia in thick smog, and its hydroelectric output was diminished by drought, Californian vegetable growers were affected by damp-loving pests, and some heavy ships could not pass through the Panama Canal because water levels were too low.

A recent, more systematic study by the International Monetary Fund confirmed that Los Niños contribute to higher global commodity prices, and thus tend to increase world inflation and reduce world growth. In fact, a fifth of the variation in world commodity prices over four-year periods is accounted for by the fluctuating weather patterns. Not only the Pacific regions but also the predominantly Northern Hemisphere G7 countries are adversely affected. El Niño explains 10 to 20 percent of the movement in consumer price inflation and world economic activity, according to the IMF.

Not surprisingly, some researchers have started to look at the impact of climate change on the world economy. One of the aspects of climate change could be the unexpected creation of new medium-term weather systems or destruction of existing patterns.

However, a venerable strand of research dating back to 1884 looks at a different natural cyclical phenomenon: sunspots, the erratic patches of unusual activity on the sun's surface. The economist William Stanley Jevons found there was a strong correlation between increases in sunspot activity, which vary in cycles ranging from eleven years to a hundred years long, and commercial crises. The link was the weather and its impact on agricultural output, which was a far more important sector of the economy in the late nineteenth century.

Perhaps it should not be surprising that the bursting of the Nasdaq bubble in the twelve months after it peaked in March 2001 should have coincided with an upsurge in sunspot activity and solar storms so enormous it was feared they could put some of the web of communications satellites around the earth out of action. (The loss of satellite communications was a new economic vulnerability that would have been unimaginable in Jevons's day.) Following Jevons, a number of other studies looked at the impact of sunspots and atmospheric changes, so the global warming research follows in that tradition. And with climate change predicted to cause more droughts in some regions and more floods in others, and threaten an additional 290 million people with malaria as warmer, wetter times favor mosquitoes, this is an ominous matter.

Some researchers believe that climate plays an even more profound economic role than affecting the business cycle. In fact, they argue that geography is destiny. In his remarkable book *Guns, Germs, and Steel*, Jared Diamond, a professor of physiology at the University of California Medical School, argues that geography and climate explained different nations' economic destinies. Climate played a decisive role in the successful development of agriculture in some regions and not others, and explained why some societies were wiped out by disease or have never escaped its burden.

Africa, for example, has no native animals and relatively few native plants that could be domesticated easily. The tropics also harbor serious killers such as malaria, yellow fever, and cholera, all still impediments to economic development. Spanish microbes famously wiped out more Native Americans than the conquistadors ever managed; the decline in the

Indian population in the century following Columbus's arrival in the New World is estimated to have been as high as 95 percent. But while European diseases proved lethal to Native Americans, few Spaniards and Portuguese died of infections passed the other way. Diamond suggests exposure to domesticated animals meant Europeans had more resistance to pathogens, whereas the Americans had few domesticated animals and therefore scant resistance.

Some development economists (Jeffrey Sachs at Columbia prominent among them) have started to argue that the effort to reduce poverty and boost growth in the world's poorest economies—mainly in Africa—must take account of the specific problems of climate. Specifically, it affects agricultural productivity, a third to a half lower in tropical than in temperate countries, and human health. Sachs points out that only three out of the top thirty countries ranked by GDP per capita lie between latitudes 23.45 degrees north and south, and they are the tiny and atypical Hong Kong, Singapore, and Mauritius. Average incomes in the seventy-two tropical countries with a third of the world's population are only a fifth of the average for (nonsocialist) temperate countries. (Sachs adds that having avoided socialism and war are also important factors contributing to economic development.)

This approach is still somewhat controversial. In fact, environmentalists have gone the other way, campaigning (unsuccessfully) for a ban on the use of the strong pesticide DDT, sprayed over vast areas of the tropics to combat malaria by killing mosquitoes. Their arguments ignored the human and economic impact of the disease, one of the world's biggest killers. But even many economists still prefer to focus on traditional concerns such as the amount of investment or the infrastructure of roads and electricity in addressing growth in low-income countries.

And even economists with a firm belief in the importance of geography, like Princeton's Paul Krugman, believe that while geography might have been destiny in the past, explaining why economic activity is concentrated where it is because of the presence of a navigable river or predominance of a disease, it is not inevitably so in future. Other factors apart from climate and rivers could be the piece of accidental grit that sows the pearl of economic growth.

Still, it's clear those of us sitting in the temperate zones should certainly count our blessings. Even in London, where a June that brings a month's worth of warm, sunny days is a once-in-a-decade event.

Chapter 25

WORK

Why Do It?

"Remember that time is money. He that can earn ten shillings a day by his labor, and goes abroad or sits idle on half that day, though he spends but sixpence during his diversion or idleness, ought not to reckon that the only expense; he has really spent, or rather thrown away, five shillings besides." So Benjamin Franklin lectured his readers in 1736 when the first rosy fingers of the dawn of the Industrial Revolution were visible on the horizon. It was such attitudes that led Max Weber, the early twentieth century economist, to the famous conclusion that the work ethic lay at the heart of capitalism.

For all this emphasis on work, economics is actually based on the far more sensible assumption that people prefer leisure to work, and work mainly in order to earn income that will buy them the other things they want, such as food and shelter, or designer shoes and movie tickets.

There is rather a lot of evidence in favor of the leisure ethic rather than the work ethic. The main piece of it is that people have been working less and less as they get better off. More than a century after Benjamin Franklin's exhortations, in 1870 the typical worker in one of the world's leading economies was putting in an average of 3,000 hours a year. That's equivalent to nearly 58 hours a week every week with no holidays, or 6 days of more than $9^1/_2$ hours for each of the 52 weeks in a year. From 1870 until 1990, however, the amount of leisure time increased steadily.

Holiday entitlements were raised. The retirement age dropped. A higher proportion of the workforce in most countries started to work part-time. And average hours clocked by full-timers declined. At different times and in different countries, the most important reason for the falling off in working time varied. Nevertheless, the result was that average annual hours worked in the industrialized countries fell to 2,000 in 1990, with only a small upturn in a few countries during World War II interrupting the steady downward trend.

About a decade ago the trend did slow noticeably and even in some cases come to a halt, however. One or two countries, notably the United States, actually saw the first increase in hours worked for well over a century. In those countries that have seen a continuing decline in work, it has reflected either new legislation, like the maximum 35-hour week introduced in France in 1999 and being implemented in stages, or an agreement between government, unions, and big companies, as in Germany.

Looking beyond the rich OECD countries to those just outside the club, people work longer in the poorer countries, but especially in the ones where output is growing fastest. The pattern is that as countries go from low to middling incomes people work much longer hours—and also record big gains in productivity or in other words how much output each of them can produce per hour worked—so the economy grows rapidly and average standards of living rise. But when they grow richer still, hours of work decline and further improvements in living standards have to come from higher productivity alone. If they are not working longer, they can only get richer only by working better. This is more difficult to do: the economy's growth rate is typically far slower in rich economies than in the middle-income but catching-up ones, where hours of work are rising as well as effort.

Does this pattern make economic sense? Why should working hours rise, then fall as a country develops, and why should there be a long-term downward trend in many countries? And why might that trend have been halted?

The story concerns the supply of labor—how much people are willing to work, and how effectively they do it. Long-term trends are related to the supply side of the economy, not to fluctuations in demand. The most basic principles of economics can indeed easily explain the observed pattern. People want to work in order to have an income, because they value the goods and services that can buy. On the other hand, most people prefer leisure to work.

This statement has to be qualified, of course. Some professionals simply love their work, or perhaps want to get away from their families, so they face no dilemma at all. Having a job also brings status, company, and a sense of belonging. But you could get all those benefits from working far fewer hours than many of us actually put in. On the whole, most of us face a trade-off between leisure and income.

Economists can therefore draw an upward sloping labor supply curve on a graph representing the labor market. A higher hourly wage will draw forth more work because workers want an increased income.

But at very high wage rates this **income effect** can be outweighed by the **substitution effect**, when enough people choose to enjoy more leisure instead. They can sustain the same income on fewer hours when the wage rate is high enough, so they substitute leisure for additional income. The labor supply curve becomes backward bending (or downward sloping) at those very high wages.

This is what you'd get charting the combinations of average pay and average hours for many countries. At low to middle incomes, workers clock up more hours and incomes rise. At higher levels of prosperity, many workers might choose fewer hours and slower increases in income.

But that's not the end of the story. Surveys suggest the international differences also reflect different preferences. There are, after all, very wide variations between different countries at the same level of economic development. For example, the typical American or Japanese worker gets ten days of holiday a year (excluding public holidays), whereas British workers get twenty-one days and Danish ones thirty days. It was only at the height of the 1990s boom that some U.S. companies introduced extra vacation or innovations like time-off banks for scarce employees, and those experiments didn't last long once the economy turned down.

Likewise, about 40 percent of Europeans report a preference for fewer hours over higher pay, two-thirds of part-time workers say they prefer part-time hours, and one in eight full-timers say they would prefer part-time work, too, despite the fact that hourly pay amounts to less than three-quarters of the full-time rate on average. Opinion surveys in the United States on the other hand show a very strong preference for higher pay, not shorter hours, and for full-time, not part-time work.

Perhaps not surprisingly, half the new jobs created in Europe from 1987 to 1997 were part-time, increasing the proportion of part-time workers, whereas in the U.S. (which created very many more jobs in total), the share in part-time work declined. In Europe, it is mainly parents of young children who work part-time, while in the U.S. it is students and older workers. In 1999, 13 percent of Americans worked part-time, compared with 15 percent in France, 17 percent in Germany, 23 percent in the U.K., and as many as 30 percent in the Netherlands.

It's hard to escape the conclusion, then, that the Europeans simply like leisure more than the Americans and Japanese do. While the trade-off between income and leisure applies to all workers everywhere, the different underlying preferences lead different groups to make different choices. How this translates into actual differences in living standards depends in turn on how many workers out of the potential workforce are working and on productivity levels in each country, or in other words, how much output the economy is able to generate per worker hour. American workers not only work longer than others, but more of the adult population is in work.

The employment rate, or employment as a proportion of the population aged fifteen to sixty-four, in the U.S. is 74 percent. The U.K. comes close, at 72 percent, but in many other European countries the employment rate is as low as 50 to 60 percent. This reflects both stubbornly high unemployment and also low participation in the workforce by groups like married women, single parents, older workers close to retirement, and young people under twenty-five.

Not only do more Americans work, and put in longer hours, but they also work very productively. The average level of productivity in the United States is more than 20 percent ahead of the level in Britain. However, Britain is a bit of a productivity laggard. Both France and Germany, as well as Japan and a number of smaller European countries, have levels of productivity very close to the American standard, perhaps even a little higher on some measures.

The net result is that incomes per head are on average higher in America than almost everywhere else in the world. (Just a few smaller places like Monaco and Luxembourg can boast of a higher level, and they are scarcely typical.) The average American has $32,000 a year, compared to $26,000 for the average German and $18,000 for the Spaniard (these per capita averages include children).

That's the payoff to all those hardworking Americans. But is money everything? While nobody would argue that high unemployment is a blot on the economic and social landscape, or that it is important to have a workforce that works well in terms of having a high level of productivity, most Europeans would rather stick with their short hours and long holidays. After all, the Continent invented *la dolce vita*, café society. If Europeans are poorer but just as happy or even happier than those over-worked Americans, that's a good result as far as economists are concerned.

There is even some evidence about trends in happiness over time, gath-ered from surveys (which is just about the only way to measure happiness—by asking people). Being poor or unemployed definitely makes people unhappy, but the worst thing about unemployment is that it tends to make people poor. This is very clear to some of them. When unemployed French workers went on strike in 1999 (this really did happen—they blockaded government offices), they were striking for higher benefit payments, not jobs.

On both sides of the Atlantic there has been a slight upward trend in average reported levels of happiness over the years since 1970, but noth-ing like as big as the increase in incomes per capita over the same time. More money in the rich economies therefore isn't making anybody hap-pier. What's more, while people working part-time or working for them-selves at home report high levels of job satisfaction, contentment at work is dropping sharply among full-time employees.

In France (again) there has been an effort to tackle this dissatisfaction and simultaneously the high unemployment problem by limiting the legal workweek to a maximum of thirty-five hours. It has clearly made French workers much happier and proved a vote winner. It might well have created some extra jobs because the measure was introduced at a time when the economy was growing strongly, so employers did not use shorter average hours as a means to cutting back total output.

However, it is too early to declare the experiment a resounding eco-nomic success. For the government also guaranteed that nobody would suffer a pay cut from the shorter hours, and has so far subsidized employ-ers in order to meet that promise. Otherwise the reduction to a thirty-five-hour week would have needed a big jump in productivity per worker hour to justify the increased hourly wage. (If wages in real terms run ahead of productivity, then profits, output, and employment will fall.) Either pro-ductivity levels in France must rise significantly now, allowing the govern-ment to phase out the subsidy without denting levels of employment and output, or the taxpayer will have to continue meeting a pretty big bill.

So although money doesn't buy happiness, it is a precondition for it. As for work, that's the precondition for money. But economists want you to be happy, not just rich, and definitely not overworked.

IN PRAISE OF
ECONOMICS

An awful lot of rubbish is talked about economics on TV and radio, in newspapers and magazines, by people who are complete ignoramuses on the subject. I wouldn't dream of setting myself up as an expert on medicine or earthquakes in order to regurgitate whatever tidbits of information I'd picked up from my reading, but it appears no such qualms deter a lot of so-called economic pundits.

They get away with it because the economics profession has such a bad reputation, usually described as being out of touch with reality. Economists are criticized for becoming overreliant on abstruse mathematics. If you open any of the leading economics journals it is indeed full of frightening-looking algebra, symbolic models of the reality the author is seeking to analyze. Yet as one of the "out-of-touch" economists, I naturally feel this criticism is very unfair. After all, most economists are very practical researchers, who more than experts in any other social science and in fact, more than almost any other discipline at all, grub around in data and wallow in statistics.

In fact, professional economics is becoming less and less purely abstract, more and more applied to real-world issues. Partha Dasgupta, professor of economics at Cambridge University, counted how many articles in the flagship *American Economic Review* over a recent five-year period were theoretical rather than applied and empirical. The tally was 25 pure theory, 100 applied theory (trying to find a theoretical explanation for an observed fact) and 156 empirical or experimental. More than 90 percent of the total, in other words, was concerned with the real world. In a similar vein, Paul Krugman, at Princeton, has pointed out that there were just two theorists among the ten previous winners of the John Bates Clark medal, the American Economic Association's highly coveted award for young economists. Both of those specialized in issues of information and uncertainty. Three others had taken top policy jobs (Council of Economic Advisers, World Bank, U.S. Treasury), while the rest all concentrated on applied research of various kinds.

Economics as a subject isn't even a fixed body of knowledge or set of facts to learn. It is not defined by the questions it addresses. It's a social science, and the problems to be solved depend on what is happening in society, and change with society. So it is about things like money and jobs and shopping and trade, but looks at them in a particular way, as the earlier essays in this book have demonstrated. The eminent economist Lionel Robbins defined it as a study of how humans tried to attain their aims given scare resources that had alternative uses.

In other words, economics is about how and why people make choices. As this changes, the body of knowledge that makes up economics will alter too. John Maynard Keynes, one of the most famous practitioners of the subject ever, summed this up perfectly in reply to one of his critics: "When the facts change, I change my mind. What do you do, sir?" The conclusions are not fixed. Economics is an attitude rather than a set of findings, a process of applying intelligent scepticism to almost any issue. Its most fundamental question is why.

So it's a puzzle. Here's a discipline that is actually shaped by what's going on in the world and tries to understand it. It's becoming increasingly empirical. Why, then, the reputation for being remote from real problems? I think there are three aspects to the answer. In descending order of triviality they are:

First, a lot of the critics of economics can't do mathematics (and a lot of the equations in the journals are concerned with statistics and empirical research, not theory) and resent its use in a social science that they feel they ought to be able to contribute opinions on.

Second, the conclusions of economics often run against common sense and received wisdom, especially the conventional wisdom in other social sciences and the humanities. These scholars just don't believe the scientific method applies to the analysis of power or culture. Economists do themselves no favors by using impenetrable jargon.

Third, macroeconomics, the study of the economy as a whole and what most people think of as economics, has repeatedly overreached itself by pinning strong policy conclusions on elegant theories that cannot possibly capture the complexity of what actually happens in the world.

I want to address the second and third of these points. On the first, there's not much more to say, except to point out that many pundits and journalists, mostly arts graduates, still think it's a bit of a joke or perhaps even a matter of pride to be innumerate. There's even a vogue for claiming that mathematics has become too important altogether, creating in our societies an undue reverence for numbers. If only. Undue ignorance, more like. This attitude poisons public understanding of science as well as economics. Such people would be appalled by scientists who boasted about never reading a novel or having heard of Beethoven. They should be ashamed of themselves.

The Tyranny of Common Sense

The critics of economics get a far wider audience than the economists. Some of them are economists themselves, making a perfectly reasonable or even a profound criticism, but in a tone that suggests no other economist has ever thought of it before, which is very irksome.

Other critics, some of the most influential, have been published in literary or cultural magazines like *The New York Review of Books* and *The New Yorker* and are sometimes actively misleading. That is what you might expect of a critique written by an outsider, but the cultural magazines unfortunately reach an important intellectual audience that routinely belittles economics as a result of such articles. There is a wide gap between economists and other social scientists and intellectuals. Literary editors of course know literary people, not economists, and the lack of communication between the two species is compounded by the fact that so many

economists can barely write simple, readable prose.* In this they're exactly like some other academics, who all do much better in their careers by
writing for professional journals in obscure jargon rather than in newspapers and books for the general public (although they then grow bitter and
twisted about their colleagues who do gain a public profile by communi-
cating well). Just check out the recent academic journals on literary criticism or history for their obscurity.[†]

The criticisms tend to overlap on one point: professional economics is
"too mathematical," depends too much on writing down human behavior as algebra, in applying the scientific method to social life. It's hard to
avoid the suspicion, however, that many of these critics just find mathematics too difficult, but they don't dare criticize a natural science like biol-
ogy or physics for being too mathematical for fear of looking ignorant.
They can get away with it writing about a social science, though.

Is there any substance to the complaint? Does it make any sense to try
to capture the intricacies of human behavior in equations? Not all equations are algebraic representations of humanity—in fact, some equations
are essential. Paul Krugman, one of today's best and most accessible economists, repeatedly points out that there are the equations that capture the
fundamental logical truth that the things that add up must add up.

For example, some critics of globalization will argue that multinationals are relocating jobs in developing countries, producing cheap goods
they export back to their home countries while at the same time paying
exploitation wages to their poor employees. This will sound perfectly reasonable to the casual reader. But it can't be true that developing countries
are simultaneously attracting large inflows of foreign investment and running large trade surpluses because they're exporting to rich countries more
than they import. The point about the balance of payments is that it has
to balance. One bit of it is the capital account, or flows of finance into or

---

*Not for nothing is this one of the funniest professional jokes: What do you get when you
cross an economist with a Mafia don? An offer you can't understand.

[†]In one highly enjoyable practical joke, a physicist, Alan Sokal, submitted to the American
cultural studies journal *Social Text* a hoax article parodying the tendency of intellectuals
in cultural studies to sprinkle their writing with concepts and terms that were supposedly drawn from science but were in fact meaningless. *Social Text* published the parody in
all seriousness in 1996. Sokal went on to write a book with fellow physicist Jean
Bricmont, *Intellectual Impostures*, attacking the abuse of scientific concepts in post-modern
philosophy and cultural and literary theory. The charge was that these disciplines are,
absolutely literally, utter nonsense. The cultural theorists were not amused.

out of the country. The other bit is the current account, the flows of goods and services. A country buying more goods and services from abroad than it sells to foreigners (like the U.S.) has to pay for this deficit by borrowing money in various forms, such as bonds and shares, from foreigners. To put it another and more technical way, net inflows on the capital account must correspond to outflows—that is, trade deficits—on the current account. Typically, the two come into balance in the case of the rapidly developing countries because an inflow of investment creates jobs that boost wages and living standards, so they are importing capital equipment (investors building factories) and also consumer goods in greater quantities than they export them. Economists like Krugman—not all are as good or as intellectually honest—will bother to check the facts, and discover that real wages in many developing countries have been rising rapidly during the modern era of globalization. And recipients of foreign investment—not just developing countries but also the U.S. and the U.K. in the recent past—run trade deficits.

So while it's true that much of what economists say is based on ideology, not science, some of the abstract equations with which they dazzle everybody are genuinely important. In fact, many critics criticize the use of mathematics in economics precisely because they hate to let evidence and logic get in the way of a good story based on their own ideological or political views. This starts getting to the heart of why economists are unpopular, I think. A lot of economic truths simply don't tally with common sense, or conventional wisdom.

The economist David Henderson has labeled this sort of incorrect common sense "do-it-yourself economics." He has collected a list of such DIY notions, all wrong, and also prominent exponents ranging from business leaders to senior judges, the president of the World Bank to the archbishop of Canterbury. Consider some of its precepts (and why they are wrong).

- *Exports are good for a nation, imports bad.* The truth is the main gain from trade is cheaper imports and wider consumer choice. Exporting is what you do to pay for imports.

- *Industries can be ranked in order of national importance or priority, and the most important deserve government support.* Energy obviously is of national importance, but should the energy source be coal, which now accounts for only 6 percent of world energy supply, or oil? Or the increasingly important natural gas? Or renewables? Yes, solar power! Or perhaps hydrogen fuel cells? Oh, and food, also obviously vitally important. McDonald's is a clear case for subsidy, accounting as it does for such an important part of the national diet. Did somebody mention telegraphy? The point is that nobody, not even—especially— governments, can tell which industries will be important. Changing demands and technology will overtake any list.

- *A shorter legal working week will reduce unemployment.* In fact it won't unless matched by a smaller paycheck. It will raise employers' costs of producing a certain level of output and will therefore increase unemployment. The French thirty-five-hour week hasn't done so only because the government is spending a fortune in taxpayers' money subsidizing wage bills. However, French voters are happy for the time being.

- *More immigration will reduce the number of jobs available to native-born workers.* The truth is an extra supply of workers will reduce wages in some occupations and thereby increase the number of jobs. The cost of immigration to the native-born may be a lower wage for certain kinds of work, usually unskilled, although in practice only booming economies attract immigrants, so this penalty rarely seems to occur. There's no fixed number of jobs to go around—the total depends on the price of labor.

- *Laborsaving technologies destroy jobs.* The truth is that laborsaving technologies cut costs, and if they involve new products also stimulate demand. They therefore create jobs as long as the economy as a whole is expanding. It's the same as the previous error, known to economists as the lump of labor fallacy, the presumption that there's only so much work to do. There are whole books written around this basic DIY error.

The fact that in all these examples the truth is so counterintuitive demonstrates exactly why economics can offer rich and unexpected insights.

Getting a Grip on the Facts

One of the most important areas of economics is concerned with the factual realities: econometrics, which applies statistical theory to raw data using computers in order to try and uncover the way the economy operates.

The pioneer of programmable computers was Charles Babbage, an enormously creative and hugely obstreperous scientist who lived from 1791 to 1871. To celebrate the bicentenary of his birth, London's Science Museum built the first ever working version of Babbage's Second Difference Engine (his first was never built in his own lifetime either), and it is still on display in the museum, a beautiful array of gleaming brass cogs and numbered wheels.

To anyone under a certain age, the computers that researchers were using as late as the 1980s will seem almost as antiquated. It wasn't until the middle of that decade that desktop PCs started to become reasonably commonplace, and for another five or ten years those desktop machines were not powerful enough to cope with more than pretty small amounts of data. When I was a student we had to eke out accounts on big timeshare computers the size of large tables, which had rows of "dumb" terminals in the university science center hooked up to them. It was cheaper to run programs overnight, so that meant either staying up, or submitting batched programs and leaving them, but not finding out until the next day that they hadn't worked, and then waiting until the night after to correct the problem. Most big sets of data came on tapes that had to be loaded by specialist operators allowed into the inner sanctum, the cool white room that contained The Computer.

There was almost no off-the-shelf software, either. There was just one package available to do econometrics, as the practice of introducing economic theory to real-life data is known. It could do only the simplest procedures. Anything more sophisticated, and you had to program it yourself in a computer language like Fortran.

It's much easier now, of course. There are numerous software packages suitable for economists, and many of the professional journals carry software reviews. The packages make econometrics very easy: read in the data from a spreadsheet, try out a few equations. If they don't work, try out some others. Add a few extra variables, look for the equations whose diagnostic tests give the best results, and there you are. Econometrics at the press of a few buttons. Easy.

Unfortunately, it's all too easy. One 1996 study found that statistical inference had been incorrectly used in a large majority of the articles published in the previous decade in the *American Economic Review*, one of the premier professional journals. Most economists are rightly somewhat skeptical about much of the empirical research that is published. There is a lot of pretty bad econometrics around, based on the presumption that the computers make thinking redundant. Nothing could be further from the truth: computer power and thought are complements, not substitutes.

So the first step when contemplating applying economic theory to actual data is to engage the brain. Data come in different forms. Time series, often macroeconomic variables like GDP or inflation, have one observation per unit of time—day or month or year. Cross sections have observations for a range of variables all at the same time, such as income, job status, highest education qualification attained, number of siblings, ethnic origin, and gender for a large number of people . Panel data combine cross section and time-series information, such as all these every other year for ten years, or GDP, working-age population, capital stock, and investment for fifty countries over twenty-five years.

Theories usually contain some pretty broad-brush implications about life, and often you can tell whether or not a theory is going to work in practice by looking at a broad-brush outline of the data. Often, the best first step is to plot the data on a graph or just look at it in a spreadsheet. First, this will make it more likely that massive errors are spotted, like somebody entering the figures with an extra zero or missing a decimal point in a few places. Second, events like big strikes or earthquakes often lead to massive spikes in time series that bear no relation to any economic theory you might want to test, and need neutralizing (by including a dummy variable in the equations).

Most important of all, it is really vital just to get a feel for what the evidence is like. If you have no idea what size the economy is—the actual level of GDP—you have no means of assessing how important events are. If retail sales over the holidays are $100 million down from last year, how much does it matter? How big $100 million is depends on the size of total retail spending or the total economy. How outrageous a demand is it when farmers want an extra $50 billion in subsidy? Likewise, to know whether a tax cut worth $100 a year to each taxpayer will boost the economy, it helps to know what average income is.

The point is that looking at the data is about applying intelligent skepticism by the truckload. "Can that be right? What's the evidence? How important is that? Does it really go down that much?" and so on are key questions.

Plenty of "facts" bandied around in print or on TV are no such thing. For example, it is often claimed that income inequality is greater in the U.K. than anywhere in Continental Europe. In fact, it's not. Income inequality has increased faster in the U.K. since about 1980, but the degree of inequality is roughly similar in France and Italy. Another example of a bogus fact is the claim that since the Reagan era, privatization means the size of government has been shrinking. In fact it has not, not outside the former communist countries. In most places the share of government spending in GDP has continued to rise.

Many people who ought to know better, pundits and journalists, politicians and even some academics, play fast and loose with the facts or even ignore them altogether. To a good economist evidence is all-important. The search for evidence is what makes economics a science. Unlike some (but not all) natural sciences, the findings of economics are seldom capable of refutation. The possibility of disproving a theory is usually taken as the basis of the scientific method, because if a statement isn't capable of being shown to be wrong (as well as right) by other researchers there's not much to distinguish it from a nonscientific belief or intuition. Still, a lot of economic evidence is too broad-brush to be able to distinguish between competing theories, especially in macroeconomics. Experiments too are difficult in economics, although not impossible.

The heart of the subject is nevertheless a deep respect for discovering what's true about the world. Of course economists are as capable as anybody else, including scientists, of ignoring evidence that doesn't support their existing set of beliefs and ideology. Yet the very nature of the subject makes this bad economics.

Economists often talk about the "stylized facts," by which they mean the broad-brush outlines of reality with which a successful theory should be consistent. For example, real wages tend to rise when an economy is in an upturn and fall when there is a downturn. This was a headache for the kind of rational business cycle model (briefly fashionable when I was a student) that said economic ups and downs were due to supply-side shocks, meaning real wages ought to fall during an expansion to induce employers to hire more people. The fact that the actual moves went the opposite way rightly helped write off the theory.

Sometimes, though, theory can help write off supposed facts, as in the earlier example in about companies supposedly exporting jobs by building factories in low-wage countries and importing the cheap goods made there back home. It can't all add up in theory, and indeed some of the "facts" in it are incorrect.

Anybody going on to do much economics will soon find themselves plunged into the detailed statistical theory that underpins econometrics. This forms a big part of the abstract mathematics for which noneconomists often criticize the subject, although its purpose is precisely the opposite, and actually puts real-world flesh on theoretical bones. That is precisely the problem for critics who would prefer to cling to their preferred theories than have economists overturn them with evidence.

Flawed Macroeconomics

A lot of the generalized criticism about economics concerns macroeconomics, the study of the economy as a whole. It stands in contrast to microeconomics, the study of specific parts of the economy. These prefixes derive from the ancient Greek for big and small. Economies are made up of millions of individuals, hundreds or thousands of separate industries. In principle, adding up all the individual decisions by consumers or business executives or investors or government officials would give you the big picture.

Unfortunately, the top-down and bottom-up approaches don't actually meet in the middle. There is a chasm between macroeconomics and microeconomics; economists have yet to find a bridge between the two. Indeed, they remain two more or less separate subjects, and are in different states of health at present. Many of today's professional economists are very uneasy about making sweeping pronouncements on the future of capitalism or the nature of class struggle in modern societies. They know there's no empirical evidence, no refutable facts, to back up any pronouncements on such sweeping issues—in real contrast to the microeconomics, where they are confident about having a solid body of results that explains a lot about human behavior.

The lack of confidence among macroeconomists is justified. For all of my lifetime there have been competing schools of thought about how the macroeconomy works, a sure sign that nobody actually knows.

Looking back, these bitter disputes among macroeconomists seem rather quaint. Some of them are ancient history, unknown even to professional economists. In my adult life, the first great clash was Keynesians versus monetarists. It boiled down to a disagreement about whether wise policymakers could fine-tune the level of output or rate of growth of the economy by making monetary and fiscal adjustments (so-called Keynesians) or could only manipulate the rate of inflation by monetary adjustments (monetarists). The Keynesians lost when it became blatantly obvious that they could not fix growth and inflation as they had been confidently proclaiming. (Mea culpa, I was a young Keynesian, but then so was anybody with progressive politics in the 1970s.)

Next came a row between real business cycle or new classical or rational expectations theorists and post-Keynesians. The former argued that as people are rational, fluctuations in the level of demand in the economy must reflect supply-side changes such as a sudden improvement in technology to which everybody was reacting rationally. The post-Keynesians could be loosely described as anybody who didn't believe anything quite so daft.

The rational expectations idea wasn't totally mad. The presumption at its heart, that people will not be so foolish as to consistently ignore opportunities to profit or increase their incomes or whatever, is very powerful and has influenced much macroeconomic research to this day. It has something going for it. For example, many noneconomists mock the idea that the stock market is at all rational or efficient: although irrational psychology is obviously important in investor behavior, it's also true that investment managers do not on average beat the market, indicating that there are few opportunities for profit that are not already exploited. The marriage of the tools and insight of rational expectations (why would people consistently believe something that's false?) to a study of the imperfections and market failures of the real world has produced some very fruitful research.

Whatever the merits of one school or another, though, the point is that if there is scope for distinct schools of thought at all, this is not hard science. It's more like the debate about whether the earth is flat and held up by an elephant and four tortoises or whether it's round and orbited by the sun and the rest of the universe. There might just be elements of truth in one school of thought, but none of them is likely to have uncovered the full story. Analyzing a whole economy is always going to be difficult and controversial. For one thing, there isn't all that much data available to test competing theories: the economy changes so much it doesn't make much sense to take what happened before 1980, say, as good evidence for what might happen in 2005. At best an economist has perhaps twenty years' worth of statistics, some available monthly, or almost continuously in the financial markets, but some only quarterly or annual. Given that one month's price level is really very similar to the next month's, there isn't even all that much information in the separate pieces of data.

What's more, an economy consists of millions and millions of people and companies. In a global economy with so many international links through trade, investment and migration, anything that happens any-where is bound to involve tens or hundreds of millions of decisions made by people all reacting to whatever they can see happening in the world.

This is an insight that has led to an interesting line of thought that says it's possible to make some theoretical statements about the economy as a whole, but these do not translate into easily usable principles and policies. It stems from the application of complexity theory, developed in the nat-ural sciences, to economics.

Put simply, complexity sounds pretty obvious. It says people (or ants or molecules) influence each other in the many choices they make. This is a contrast to conventional macroeconomics, which assumes people make their decisions about what to spend, where to invest, how hard to work, independent from facts like the level of interest rates or level of company profits, and their own tastes and preferences. Adding something as sensi-ble as the natural human tendency to be swayed by what others are doing means, however, that a lot of standard economic presumptions don't work.

Fans of complexity theory overdo their claims about undermining all of past economics. Actually, economic thinking can easily take account of many of the phenomena beloved of complexity theorists. For example, increasing returns to scale in certain industries that arise from network effects (the price I pay depends on how many of you have already pur-chased the item), as described in an earlier chapter, certainly don't under-mine economics. Respected, and conventional, academic economists are doing a lot of research along these lines, especially in finance, trade theo-ry, economic geography, and industrial organization.

Complexity, however, does seem to pose a challenge to conventional macroeconomics. It torpedoes the machine metaphor that underlies most day-to-day forecasting and comment. Indeed, in the recesses of the London School of Economics there is a machine—called the Phillips machine after its creator—representing the flow of income in the economy, with colored water flowing along tubes to indicate the pace of consumer spending, and valves to indicate the tightness or otherwise of monetary policy. But it gives a bogus impression that it's possible to fine-tune the economy with a bit of twiddling here and there. Bogus because there will not be a fixed relationship between the amount spent by consumers and "levers" such as interest rates or government spending if you also factor in individual consumers being influenced by fashions, general "feel good" mood, or herd psychology in the stock market. The economy is not controllable, at least in any straightforward mechanical way. Perhaps a machine was a good metaphor in the immediate postwar era when even in noncommunist countries the economy was in fact much more highly regulated and controlled. It no longer holds good in modern, liberalized economies. Policymakers now are more like sports coaches than engineers, trying to psych the players—us—on to a good result.

Forecasting the Economy

Macroeconomic forecasting in particular is highly misleading, essentially because where the economy gets to in the future depends on what millions of us do between now and then. In general, this way of thinking about the economy introduces all sorts of self-fulfilling phenomena.

This isn't a new idea to economists. In a very famous passage in his most famous book, *The General Theory of Employment, Interest, and Money*, John Maynard Keynes, who was himself a successful investor, said investing in shares was like picking the winner in a beauty contest. You wanted to choose the contestant most likely to appeal to most judges.

> Professional investment may be likened to those newspaper competitions in which the competitors have to pick out the six prettiest faces from a hundred photographs, the prize being awarded to the competitor whose choice most nearly corresponds to the average preferences of the competitors as a whole; so that each has to pick, not those faces which he himself finds the prettiest, but those which he thinks likeliest to catch the fancy of

the other competitors, all of whom are looking at the problem from the same point of view.

This applies not only to stock market bubbles but also to general booms and recessions. A recession is a collective outcome that can feed on itself in a vicious spiral. It emerges in the way a storm does, if you're thinking about the weather as an analogy. Macroeconomic forecasting is really quite like weather forecasting. You can spot short-term tendencies and possibilities, might even be able to predict rain ahead with great confidence, but any greater precision in the forecast will be spurious.

Many macroeconomists are entirely comfortable with this conclusion, and indeed would quite like to educate the general public that sensible forecasts would be something like: "There's a 75 percent chance inflation will be above 2 percent by the end of next year." But we all feel rather comfortable with the appearance of confidence: "Consumer prices will be rising by 2.4 percent in eighteen months' time." The only thing that annoys them about attacks from fans of a complexity approach, or any other alternative, are critics' assertions that economics is hopeless especially in crisis because economists doggedly insist on stupidly reductive and simplistic formal models. Most practicing economists regard the models as a tool and are well aware of their shortcomings in the face of the complexities of real life.

Still, this leaves macroeconomic theory in an uncomfortable position. Any textbook will reveal it still rests on formal models of fixed equations—some of which capture genuine insights, but which don't add up to a tool for usefully analyzing or forecasting the economy as a whole. Unfortunately, there's nothing to put in its place that would satisfy the ambition some critics set for macroeconomics—namely, aggregating the behavior of millions of people who are not fully rational, who don't have complete information about everything, who make shortsighted decisions, who are all different, who sway each other's behavior, and who live in economies where there are all sorts of obstacles to free and competitive markets.

Since the ideological clashes of the 1970s and '80s, there has been an appreciation among economists that it might be a good idea to make far more modest claims to be able to understand and predict on the macro front. There is a greater degree of consensus now about what constitutes bad macroeconomic policy, thanks in large part to the disastrous results of putting once-fashionable economic theories into practice.

The professional consensus now about macro policy can be summed up as: don't make dumb mistakes. Keep inflation low, because it's economically damaging, unfair, and voters hate it. Get central bankers, who hate inflation too, to keep it low. They've been doing it pretty well for a decade now, using a variety of approaches (too well in Japan, where as we saw prices are falling).

A high rate of growth is good, but so is a steady rate of growth. The voters hate boom and bust, or at any rate the bust part of it. That means making sure government borrowing isn't too high or the government surplus isn't too big, because the government's not the point of the economy, businesses and consumers are. There are still heated arguments, of course, about whether interest rates or tax and spending have been set at the right levels. But the argument covers a much narrower range of options than before.

This new modesty must be an improvement on the macroeconomists' earlier incarnation as snake-oil salesmen. The failures of that overconfidence are demonstrated only too clearly by the dismal record of most macroeconomic forecasts, an important source of the disrespect in which economics is held by outsiders.

When the American economy was growing rapidly year after year in the late 1990s, the International Monetary Fund (with one of the biggest teams of macroeconomists working anywhere) for several years kept incorrectly predicting the rate of growth would slow next year. At one of the press conferences on its World Economic Outlook, a journalist asked Michael Mussa, then the IMF's economic counselor, about why after all this he was still forecasting U.S. growth would slow next year. "We're going to carry on forecasting the U.S. economy will slow down until the economy gets it right," was Mussa's answer. The economy, of course, overdid it. The IMF was forecasting 3.2 percent GDP growth in the U.S. in 2001 in October 2000. By May 2001 it had revised this down, and then it revised the figure partway back up in April 2002.

Expecting economists to forecast the future state of the world, in precise numbers, is slightly weird. No other profession faces the same demand. Besides, there's a good reason forecasts tend to be wrong. They are based on a series of equations in a computer model of the whole economy. The equations linking different indicators, like consumer spending to aftertax incomes and share prices, are estimated using about twenty years' worth of data. These relationships are then used to run the whole model forward into the future. But they inevitably capture a twenty-year average experience, and therefore inevitably predict the future will be a lot like the average of the past twenty years, unless the forecaster deliberately overrides the predictions using his or her skill and judgment. So models produce bland pictures of the future. They are very bad at forecasting extreme events like recessions. They are pretty bad anyway whenever the economy changes because what's new is not incorporated into the estimated equations—and just compare the American economy of 2000 or 1990 with 1980.

It's no surprise, then, that errors in making macroeconomic forecasts are typically large. Still, there is a need for macroeconomic forecasts in order to allow governments to design and implement sensible policies, or businesses to draw up profitable strategies. That inevitably involves trying to look into the future: "If we try this, then what happens? And what about if we try something else?" The demands for economists to produce forecasts are intense, and most of macroeconometrics is geared toward forecasting what's going to happen to output, prices, interest rates and currencies, unemployment, poverty levels, and so on.

Indeed, expectations of economic forecasts are simultaneously extraordinarily high and very low, for economists are expected to foretell the future with a degree of authority we'd never demand of a meteorologist or biologist, and—not surprisingly—are held in low esteem for often getting it badly wrong. Many forecasts are extremely bad—perhaps inevitably so, as we saw in the last chapter. As David Hendry, an eminent econometrician based at Oxford, has complained: "When weather forecasts go awry, meteorologists get a new supercomputer; when economists misforecast, we get our budgets cut."

The trouble is that consumers of economic forecasts are keen on certainty, even if it is bound to be wrong. We want to *know* what's going to happen! We are both unused to and unhappy about being told there are great uncertainties about how the economy will look a year from now. However, forecasts should spell out the uncertainties, in the form of ranges of confidence about their predictions. Many official forecasts, like those published by the Federal Reserve Board or Bank of England, do just this. The Fed will predict growth next year will be in a range—say, 2 to 2.5 percent.

Shockingly, many other forecasters have next to no idea what the confidence intervals are on their spuriously accurate predictions. Public understanding of probability is shockingly low, too, and there seem to be psychological barriers to being logical about it.

Still, the biggest difficulty in predicting how the economy as a whole will evolve is that the future is not at all like the past. The past forty-plus years have been completely different from any episode in human history beforehand. The real income of the average person in the world has more than doubled since 1950—unevenly, it is true, but nothing like it has ever happened before. More than half the people who have ever been alive since the dawn of time are alive now. Over the past two centuries, GDP per capita in the leading economies has grown by about 2 percent a year—but the standard errors in forecasting this growth are about 2.5 percent, or in other words, in excess of the thing being forecast. The trouble is that events—structural breaks, in economics-speak—keep butting in. Events like the Industrial Revolution, fascism, feminism, and world wars, or innovations such as electricity, the internal combustion engine, and the computer.

It's impossible to tell what it is about the present that will transform the economy, although many experts hold strong opinions about it one way or another. For example, the Industrial Revolution was seen by most contemporaries as a thoroughly bad thing, destabilizing society and covering the countryside with those "dark, Satanic mills"—not as a set of events that would, after fifty or seventy years, for the first time in history liberate most people from grinding poverty and short, diseased lives. The economy is constantly being shaped by technology, politics, and society. So how is it possible or sensible to take a long look ahead at how it will evolve?

We want to know. To echo Macbeth:

> *If you can look into the seeds of time*
> *And say which grain will grow and which will not,*
> *Then speak to me.*

The problem is, in the less poetic language of econometrics, that macroeconomic data are usually nonstationary. The mean or average value of the variable, and its variability around that mean, alter over time. David Hendry gives the growth of industrial output in Britain since 1715 as an example. The average rate of growth ranged from 0.86 percent a year in 1715–50 to 2.86 percent a year in 1801–50. The standard deviation (the measure of 'typical' variability) ranged from 3.5 percent in that early period to 6.3 percent in 1901–50, a period including the 1919–21 crash, the Great Depression, and two wars. Even the rate of change of growth in production, its acceleration or deceleration, altered a lot over time.

The frequency and importance of structural changes mean that most conventional econometric models are incorrect, in unknown ways, and in ways that change as the economy changes. There are some things we know we don't know, and some things we don't know we don't know. To make matters worse, we know that most economic variables are also inaccurately measured, so there is additional uncertainty introduced by the data used. Yet conventional forecasting assumes that the model used is a correct specification of a stationary economy, not an incorrect specificiation of a nonstationary one.

The Way Forward in Forecasting

Luckily, modern econometrics does offer techniques for coping, for narrowing the inevitable range of uncertainty attached to any forecast. Some of it is quite simple. First, forecast growth rates, not levels (first difference the data). That makes it less important to get the absolute level right, so any mistake you make here will show up as a one-off blip error in the forecast. Second, if you go one step further (second difference the data), so you are forecasting rate of acceleration, you can similarly neutralize any linear time trend in the series. Two simple steps can therefore tackle the most basic misspecifications of an econometric equation, getting the wrong intercept and the wrong trend.

Another good tip is to update estimated equations pretty often, using the most recent data. Many forecasts are in practice based on very old computer models, and the economists driving them deal with forecasts that are obviously going adrift by overriding the predictions with their own judgment. In the trade, it's known as adjusting the residuals or add-factors. The variable being forecast can be sorted into two parts, the bit that is actually produced by the equation for that variable, and the residual. In creaky old models the residual can easily be the most important component of a forecast value. Forecasters can also learn from their errors. If an equation turns out to have produced a big error last quarter, the error can be added to the intercept term in the equation for forecasting the next quarter.

A final point is that sometimes forecasts are wrong because they affect behavior, and sometimes they are self-fulfilling for the same reason. If an authoritative institute predicts a recession or a collapse in the currency, people might act on that, cutting their investment plans, postponing buying a car in case they lose their job, selling the currency if they are a speculator. On the other hand, the central bank might react by cutting interest rates to avert the danger of a slowdown, and the forecast would turn out to be wrong even if it had originally been right.

In short, economic forecasters have to stop believing—or allowing the rest of the world to believe—that what they do is set down a simplified but essentially true version of the structure of the economy. Macroeconomic forecasting is now a lot more pragmatic than that, a kind of guerrilla warfare waged against the tides of history, the ambiguities of the data, and the sheer unpredictability of all the millions of people whose behavior is being forecast.

There is also a much greater respect now for the gritty details of the real world rather than the abstractions of grand theories, and this must be good news, too. There has been a resurgence of interest in institutions and in economic history, kindled to a large extent by the process of globalization.

For example, why is the same person many times more productive the minute he moves from Haiti to the United States to do the same job? It can't be anything to do with the person, who hasn't changed, or the nature of the job, which is the same, so it must be something to do with America having institutions and arrangements that enhance the capacity of individuals. Why do countries that seem very similar in terms of the availability of technology and skills of the workforce, like the U.S. and Germany, have different rates of productivity growth? The answer seems to be that it depends partly on a host of details like their different traditions in raising finance, legal traditions, planning laws, openness to immigration, and so on. What is it about developing countries that keeps them poor when technology and finance for investment are more freely available anywhere than they have been for more than a century?

Such questions have generated a fascinating research agenda, because the broad answers stimulate a demand to know *exactly* what it is about, say, bankruptcy legislation, that helps or hinders enterprise. And the new focus on institutions is also a healthy reminder that successful economies as well as unsuccessful ones take many shapes. There is no such thing as a market economy or capitalism in the abstract, but only in specific forms. Therefore any macroeconomic principles will be generalizations, too, which will work in slightly different ways in different settings.

Similarly, economic history has enjoyed a revival thanks to the advent of today's new technologies such as the Internet and the question of whether or not it will lay the foundation for improved productivity in future. Previous episodes of technological change offer some of the only sort of evidence available. And one of the main lessons is that the economic impact of technology depends on the institutional and political context, too. Another is that, in a variation on the old joke about how to get into town from here, if you want to get somewhere a lot more desirable, some starting points are a lot worse than others. The past shapes the economy's possible futures.

The Success Story of Microeconomics

Reflecting on their failure to be able to explain or forecast the economy as a whole, macroeconomists lack a certain intellectual buoyancy at present. Their subject matter is as exciting as ever—more so, with globalization, financial crises, and the New Economy boom and bust to think about. But there are no hot new fashions in macro theory, nor do the brightest graduate students tend to flock to macroeconomics, as so many did in the 1970s and '80s.

On the other hand, most of microeconomics, the study of economic behavior at the scale of the individual, the household, the business, or perhaps the industry, has been enjoying an extraordinarily productive and even inspirational decade or two. It has a lot of answers to all sorts of why questions. The development of better statistical techniques and improved collection of data, not to mention the more widespread use of experiments, means economists have gained powerful insights into human behavior. Most of the examples earlier in this book have involved microeconomic analysis.

Economists know they can really offer a lot of insight on questions like these. Typical articles in the leading professional journals will look at issues like why businesses in one industry but not others will use a certain kind of exclusive contract with their suppliers, whether welfare payments work best in cash or as vouchers, what effect growing up in a public housing project has on earnings potential, whether maternal education cuts high birthrates in poor countries, and if so, how much, what kind of personality traits help people get jobs, what kind of interconnection charges in the telecommunications industry encourage use of the Internet, and so on.

Similarly, the government's most useful policy tools are all concerned with microeconomics, or the supply side, as it's often called in this context (as opposed to the demand side, which is what traditional macroeconomic policies try to influence). Supply-side economics got a bad reputation in some quarters because it was warmly embraced by President Reagan and Mrs. Thatcher and therefore seen as a veil for favoring big business and the rich. But two decades on, now the political heat has died down, it is clear supply-side issues are very important for the health of the economy, and are intimately bound up with government actions. Is the degree of regulation of a particular industry tough enough, but not too tough? Is it easy, but not too easy, to set up a new business? Is the banking system secure and well capitalized? Can damaging monopolies be forced to allow competition into their markets? Are certain tax rates so high they damage investment?

There are answers to many such questions, putting a figure on the size of the effects with fairly modest margins of uncertainty. And there are of course many more questions left to address, not least because the world keeps changing. The research agenda is incredibly rich and exciting.

Earlier scholars' focus on the traditional big themes of macroeconomics had a limited payoff in terms of our understanding of human economic behavior. On the other hand the payoff in applied microeconomics, applying the tools of economic analysis to all sorts of subjects outside the traditional boundaries of the profession, has been enormous. The research areas of a list of rising stars, mainly microeconomists, named in 1998 by *The Economist* magazine ranged from the transmission of AIDS to voting behavior, or the costs of the existence of urban ghettos to the impact of police numbers on crime rates. As the influence of economic analysis on other areas such as sociology and criminology spreads, it could really have a tremendously beneficial impact on public policy. Using economics to work out how to achieve better results is sometimes called evidence-based policy (which doesn't actually give one huge confidence in the past advice of sociologists, criminologists, political scientists, etc. What did they do before? Gut-instinct-based policy? Wild-guess-based policy?)

Some of the most interesting areas of economics now concern the overlaps with other social sciences. This interdisciplinary work has shed real light on phenomena such as inequality, educational outcomes, welfare and so on. As Matthew Rabin, a pioneer at the frontier between economics and psychology, points out, conventional economics does involve a psychological assumption, that of self-interested 100 percent rationality. But sometimes alternatives are appropriate, and that allows the powerful tools of economics to be applied to other sorts of problems. For example, addiction, procrastination, or risky behavior by adolescents have all lain outside the scope of economics before, but no longer. According to Rabin: "There was a distant past when psychology and economics were more connected, when all of social science was one, but things have gotten more specialized. So we're not addressing something that no researcher has addressed before. We're just bringing these things back together."

Much of this has been made possible by advances in the use of econometrics in microeconomic studies. The 2000 Nobel Prize winners, Daniel McFadden and James Heckman, won the award in recognition of the pathbreaking work they had done in applying statistical techniques to the behavior of individuals facing choices between alternatives about how much to spend or save, how hard to work, what to buy, how to travel to work, which job to train for, and all those other myriad everyday decision.

Two developments have made modern microeconometrics possible. One was the increasing amount of survey data from the 1960s on, resulting in some very large sets of information about thousands and thousands of particular people's characteristics and choices. The other was the steady improvement in computer power and decline in its cost, making it feasible to analyze all this information.

Much economic theory is built on the idea of the representative agent, a typical person with fixed preferences who would seek to maximize their utility with the choices he or she made. The economy was then the sum of all these identikit robots. Thus it is that introductory economics courses generate their first wave of dropouts. In the 1960s, however, McFadden drew on psychological research on how people choose to introduce a model where there are specific probabilities that people will choose between the various options open to them, and it then becomes possible to set out how consumer demand—for a certain type of transport, say—will depend on a given set of choices. This kind of setup is now called the multinomial logit model. One of its first big uses in practice was in the development of the Bay Area Rapid Transit in San Francisco. But although developed with reference to transportation choices, the model has a huge variety of applications and has become one of the most successful workhorses of applied economics.

One of the assumptions of the model, however, is that preferences between two choices stay the same whatever other choices are available—the so-called independence of irrelevant alternatives. This says, for example, that I am twice as likely to choose black shoes as red shoes when the other options are pink and beige, and also when the others are navy and beige, when in fact in real life I might well prefer navy to black. So the workhorse model has since been extended to accommodate this, and also to reflect the fact that preferences can change over time. Introducing time also means incorporating people's expectations about how their available choices will change in future.

A more fundamental issue turns on the inconsistency between the basic economic assumption that people have a given set of preferences, formed implicitly by their genes and upbringing, and the psychologists' view that instead people have attitudes that often change and depend on context, to the extent that it makes no sense to imagine anybody has a set of underlying preferences. In that case the economists' procedure of modeling individuals' behavior as making the self-interested choices that will best satisfy their preferences is deeply flawed.

McFadden's response draws on an analogy with vision. We know from the existence of optical illusions that we often misperceive the way things really are, but precisely because we know that we can adjust for it. Systematic illusions only rarely affect behavior such that we do things operating against our self-interest time and time again. On the whole, he argues, further refinements of the standard economic approach will provide the best means of predicting behavior and assessing alternative policies. The impressive catalogue of results from modern applied microeconomics backs up this claim. Besides, we have bumped up to the limits for now of what is computationally cheap and easy.

Fascinating developments in the laboratory, however, do confirm that sometimes people make decisions that do deviate systematically from the standard economic model. For example, experiments asking for answers to a question show that people's responses are heavily conditioned by any clues they are given in the question.

An influential experiment carried out by psychologists Amos Tverksy and Daniel Kahneman involved asking the subjects to say what proportion of African countries are in the United Nations, or similar nonobvious questions whose answers lay between 1 and 100. But they were asked after the spin of a wheel of fortune, which would randomly stop at a number between 1 and 100. The answers were always heavily influenced by the random number. If the wheel stopped at 10, the median answer was 25, and if it stopped at 65, the answer was 45. This phenomenon, known as anchoring, occurred even though the respondents knew the wheel was random, and even though the questions were meant to be emotionally neutral. There are now many other examples of how anchoring affects economic choices.

Robert Shiller has shown how anchoring affects financial markets. In his best-selling book *Irrational Exuberance*, he describes how it works in the case of share prices. Possible anchors are remembered past prices, nearby psychological milestones like 10,000 on the Dow-Jones Industrials index, past percentage falls if there is a stock market crash, the price-earnings ratio of other companies in the same industry, and so on. Thus the share prices of companies based in the same country behave more alike than the share prices of companies in the same industry, even though you would expect the fundamentals of demand for the product to have more influence on the value of the company than the location of its headquarters.

Similarly, people place too much emphasis on immediate context in other ways. We are heavily influenced by recent questions, or by events in the immediate past. We put far too much weight on pure coincidences. This is the appeal of the Kevin Bacon website, which plays on the "small world" phenomenon that very few links separate people in a network— the famous six degrees of separation, except that six is an overestimate in our connected times. Nobody can believe the number of links is so small and also so meaningless.

We all think we know more than we do. Overconfidence is another well-documented psychological phenomenon. Experiments asking factual questions that also ask people how confident they are about their answers have found that when people say they're certain, in fact they are right only about 80 percent of the time.

Robert Shiller has found from surveys he has carried out that investors are astonishingly confident. In a survey he conducted straight after the October 19, 1987 stock market crash, he asked: "Did you think at any point on October 19 that you had a pretty good idea of when a rebound was going to occur?" Nearly half of those who carried out trades on the day said they'd thought they knew what the market was going to do.

The overlap between psychology and economics is sure to be a fruitful and exciting area of research; it's unfinished business. A lot of the stylized facts uncovered in psychology have not yet been incorporated into economic theory, but thanks to the findings of behavioral and experimental economists this is starting to happen. Past greats like Irving Fisher and John Maynard Keynes placed a strong emphasis on the importance of psychological factors in explaining economic behavior. So in a sense this will mark a welcome return to an older tradition in economics, a true marriage of social with science.

In practice, as in theory, the transfusion of techniques along with ideas from other disciplines has started rejuvenating economics, making it one of the most exciting subjects you can possibly study.

Conclusions

It has to be admitted that not all attacks on economic theory are totally ill founded. Any kind of theory involves simplifications, or it's a description, not a theory. Setting out these simplifications as a formal set of equations can act as a powerful analytical tool. But being able to write down a set of equations isn't the purpose of trying to analyze the economy. On the contrary, the point is understanding the world we live in.

In one of his letters the early twentieth century economist and mathematician Alfred Marshall wrote:

> I have had a growing feeling that a mathematical theorem dealing with economic hypotheses is very unlikely to be good economics, and I go more and more on the rules: (1) Use mathematics as a shorthand language rather than as an engine of enquiry. (2) Keep to them until you have done. (3) Translate into English. (4) Then illustrate by examples that are important in real life. (5) Burn the mathematics. (6) If you can't succeed in (4), burn (3). This last I do often.*

For while writing down a formal model is a crucial professional tool, enforcing logical consistency, accounting truths and also bringing real insights, perhaps counterintuitive, that might be harder to reach with words alone, in truth a lot of economists rely too much on the formalities.

---

*Marshall is one of the all-time greats who did most to make economics very mathematical and technical, for example in the use of differential calculus to represent decisions at the margin. Yet as this quotation shows, he was well aware of the limitations of this approach. He also wrote extensively about phenomena that thrill complexity theorists, like increasing returns.

They need to publish academic papers for their professional advancement. Perhaps they are not too sure themselves about the practical implications of their research.

As Paul Krugman has put it: "Much of the criticism of formalism in economics is an attack on a straw man: the reality of what good economists do is a lot less formalistic than the popular image. Bad economists, of course, do bad economics; but one should not confuse a complaint about quality with a complaint about methodology."

Equally, at a minimum, we ought to do better as a profession in explaining to the widest possible audience what it all means in the real world. You can't blame the good economists for all the bad economics that gets done in universities. But perhaps there are too many bad economists allowed, because they're needed as fodder for the higher education machine, to get away with spuriously mathematical research that doesn't really amount to very much. There are certainly too few good economists engaged in outreach to the general public or business audience, despite the huge relevance of economics to public policy and private decisions.

The only possible conclusion is for me to encourage readers to go and do good economics. Oh, and enjoy it.

TEN RULES OF ECONOMIC THINKING

1. Everything has a cost.

Or as it's often put in the economics business, "There's no such thing as a free lunch."

This means more than the obvious statement that very often acquiring something will involve handing over money. Even activities that appear to be free will also have a cost, often called the opportunity cost.

We all make decisions weighing up various opportunity costs all the time. If I buy a new pair of boots this month, I won't be able to spend as much on other things. If I watch TV all evening, I won't write another chapter in my new novel. Most of us have limited financial resources and all of us a fixed amount of time.

The same constraints apply across the board, to all human decisions. Whether it's a university deciding which departments to hire new professors in, a company planning its next year's budget, or a government weigh-

ing up signing a new treaty or building a road, making one decision rules
out the alternatives.

2. Things always change.

This is another way of saying that economies are made up of millions of
people who, peskily, react to the environment in which they find themselves. Human initiative is bad news for policymakers because it means a
policy drawn up on the basis that people behave in a certain way can be
undermined if they change the way they behave in response to the policy.

Much economic theory is based on the so-called *ceteris paribus* assumption, that all other things will remain unchanged apart from whatever the
specific thing is that you're trying to analyze. The assumption is necessary
because without isolating certain aspects of a problem it can't be analyzed
at all. But it's essential at the end of the process to think about what will
change in practice and whether that sheds any new light on the analysis.

The deeper moral is that economic policy is not a matter of exercising
control over anything at all. For much of the postwar era, policy was based
on the idea that the economy was a machine about whose cogs and mechanisms we could steadily gain greater expertise, complicated but stable
and predictable. No such luck.

3. Metaphorical time bombs don't explode.

This follows from rule 2. Time bombs are all based on false *ceteris paribus*
assumptions, when in fact unsustainable trends always lead to changes in
people's behavior precisely because they are unsustainable.

Environmentalists are particularly keen on time bombs, which is why
economists so often seem to be anti-green. One example is the so-called
population time bomb. In 1968, environmentalist Paul Ehrlich wrote a
bestseller, *The Population Bomb*, predicting that overpopulation meant
hundreds of millions of people would die of starvation during the 1970s,
including many millions in the developed world. Not only did it not happen, but average caloric intake has increased by more than 50 percent
since 1961, food prices have fallen steadily in real terms, and the proportion of people who are starving has fallen dramatically to about 18 percent of those living in the developing world. Where did Dr. Ehrlich go

wrong? Birthrates decline as people become richer, and the world population is now expected to stabilize at about 11 billion in 2100. In addition, improvements in agricultural technology like the "green revolution" of the 1970s mean we are now more productive at feeding people. The main cause of starvation is not lack of food but lack of democracy, as it is in war-torn dictatorships that famines occur.

4. Prices make the best incentives.

Changes in prices are usually what defuses time bombs—and much else besides. People respond to prices. Everybody loves a bargain, and somebody always responds to a great profit opportunity. On the other hand, many people don't like to do something—or not do it—just because somebody in authority says so.

Government regulations are essential in any economy. Market economies work well only if they are based on solid institutions, the rule of law, the control of monopoly power, the adequate provision of public goods, and so on. The question is really how governments can best achieve all these desirable conditions. Often it is just by issuing instructions. The law is the law.

Often, however, price incentives can achieve the desired aims far better than any direct controls. Whereas people will try to get around regulations, they will respond to prices, and in ways that reflect their own needs and preferences, so the outcome is likely to be one that makes as many people as content as possible.

Critics often say the use of prices to limit demand is unfair because people cannot afford to pay equally well; but the real unfairness is the inequality of incomes, and that's a different question altogether.

5. Supply and demand work.

If you restrict the supply of some item, its price will go up at a given level of demand, whether it's Ecstasy or the construction of new housing in central London or Manhattan. If demand for something increases at a given level of supply, the price will go up. The example that leaps to my mind are those particularly coveted shiny Pokémon cards, or indeed whatever happens to become the most popular toy at Christmas when the item was made and shipped to distributors six months before kids start thinking about what they want as presents.

Following on from the last point, if the price can't adjust upwards for some reason, you will get shortages and long lines. This imposes other costs, such as time lost hunting around or waiting and general irritation on buyers. They pay one way or another. If it can't adjust down, sellers are left with unsold inventory, which imposes other costs, such as storage and wasted investment on them.

In fact, supply and demand are as close as social science gets to laws of nature. To translate many public policy problems into supply and demand terms is illuminating. Just think about a highly regulated market like city center housing, and the impact of rent controls. The effects of capping the price below the level the market would set are entirely predictable.

6. There's no easy profit.

This is a much-mocked principle of economics. The mockery is summed up in an old joke about an economist and her friend spotting a $10 bill lying on the sidewalk. The friend says they must pick up the money, but the economist says not to bother—if it were really there, somebody would already have picked it up. Or in another, about how many economists it takes to change a lightbulb. The answer is none, because if the lightbulb needed changing, market forces would already have done it. (There are many variants of the lightbulb joke, naturally. Another answer is: only one economist, but the lightbulb really gets screwed.)

The economist's valid point, however, is that somebody always takes advantage of opportunities for profit, even if it does not happen as fast and seamlessly in life as it does in economic theory.

The principle of arbitrage applies in many contexts. It is the process by which entrepreneurs of one kind or another see the chance to make a profit, but will not make vast profits for long periods of time, because if they do they will be imitated. If a new office complex opens, the sandwich shop will soon follow. If there are more and more busy two-earner couples, other people will set up dog-walking and take-out food services. And as long as the pioneers are obviously profiting, competitors will follow suit. There are almost always advantages to being first, but in general, any large excess profits will be competed away over time.

It is obviously not the case that every activity is equally profitable, though. People who take bigger risks, whether financial speculators or business entrepreneurs, tend to earn higher rewards on average. If they didn't expect to do so, there'd be no point in taking the risk. They might as well opt for a quieter life.

7. People do what they want.

All economic activities are equally desirable, or people wouldn't be doing them. There are caveats to this statement: it needs to add something like "at the current set of prices and given the constraints on technology and government rules and regulations." Still, it's basically a way of saying that people adjust to do what will suit them best given the current state of the world. This sounds obvious when spelled out but seems hard for noneconomists to grasp in many real-life contexts. There are countless examples of this principle.

House prices are higher in the zoning area of a good school, the house price premium reflecting the value people place on the better education. People choose between a cheaper home and weaker education for their children and a dearer home and better education. If the two sets of desires, based on different needs and preferences, were not in balance, the relative house prices would continue changing until they were.

Similarly, companies can choose to locate their factories in high-wage countries where productivity is high or in low-wage countries where productivity is low. If they are lucky enough to find a low-wage country where productivity is actually pretty high, they will be joined by lots of other manufacturers building factories, and wages will get competed up. And a country where wages are kept higher than warranted by productivity levels—by vigorous unions, for example—will find its industry relocating elsewhere, slowly but surely. If the roads become very congested, some people will switch to traveling by train or air until the congestion levels recede enough that people stop switching. Increase tolls, and some more people will switch. Raise train fares and people will become prepared to tolerate traveling on slightly more congested roads.

8. Always look up the evidence.

Economists have an unfair reputation for playing fast and loose with the facts. (As yet another joke demonstrates. Question: What does two plus two equal? Economist: What do you want it to equal?) Certainly, lots of economic pundits who speak on TV or are quoted in the newspapers fling around a lot of factual claims. Some of these are highly dubious. But for anybody interested in good economics, there are vast arrays of resources available on the Internet or in conventional publications.

Of course some sources are a lot more reliable than others. Official sources go out of their way to ensure accuracy because it is so important to them to preserve their reputation. The Federal Reserve, the Bureau of Labor Statistics, the Office of the Census, and equivalents overseas such as the U.K.'s National Statistics or the Bank of England, France's Insee, or the EU's Eurostat or European Central Bank post vast amounts of data online, along with press releases explaining the main findings. International agencies like the International Monetary Fund, the World Bank, and the World Trade Organization also do so. Whether or not you trust their policies, they too can't afford to publish incorrect factual information.

A huge number of other websites offer either data links or publish data, and like anything else online, you have to form a judgment about the quality of the information provided. This book ends with a list of websites I have found most useful. The blue-chip business press—publications such as *The Economist, The Financial Times, The Wall Street Journal,* and *BusinessWeek*—also offer pretty reliable information. Again, even if you don't like their attitude, for the sake of their credibility the statistics have to be accurate.

However, you need more than raw data. Sometimes you have to think about it, too. The basic question is, Can that statement be true? What kind of evidence would you need to prove or disprove it? What else would it imply? Is it logical or plausible, and is there any evidence as to that, too?

9. Where common sense and economics conflict, common sense is wrong.

Take the two most frequent examples. Contrary to many people's natural belief, imports are better than exports; and there's no fixed number of jobs to go around.

On jobs, we've already met the lump of labor fallacy, but it bears repeating. There were only 13 million people working in Britain in 1870 compared with 27 million in 2000. That's a doubling in the number of jobs in 130 years. Yes, sometimes unemployment has been high, when people who wanted to work couldn't find jobs. But in general, as economies grow, so do both employment and real earnings. Workers become more productive, so they grow more prosperous, and there are more of them, too.

10. Economics is about happiness.

Economic welfare is improved by being able to buy more and better goods and services with the same amount of work, or preferably less. And that is just what has happened over the decades. Living standards have risen to an extent our grandparents or great-grandparents would have found hard to believe, and average hours worked have declined (except for some Americans in the past decade or so—and that won't last).

Economic research into happiness has found that at a given time rich people are happier than poor people, although the level of happiness has not trended upwards as strongly as average incomes over time despite the corresponding gains in health and longevity. The biggest gains in happiness seem to come with economic growth from a low level of income, meaning people living in poor countries still have a lot of scope for growing happier as their economies grow.

In the rich countries, those who don't have a job are definitely unhappy, although that could be because unemployment goes with low income as well as loss of status and social connection. In other words, it might well be poverty rather than idleness that is the source of their unhappiness.

Winning the lottery makes people very happy indeed, but only for a year or two before the effect wears off.

The basic point is that economic welfare is about consumption, not production. Just as exporting is what a nation does in order to import, work is what the individual does in order to consume. Although everybody thinks work is the basis of capitalism, in fact, everybody having a good time and being comfortable is the key to a successful economy.

Why did anybody ever call it the dismal science?

Glossary

Chapter 1.
Sex: Can You Have Too Much of a Good Thing?

The **market** is where economic transactions take place, where some people **supply** goods or services to meet the **demand** for them by others. The quantity demanded and supplied depends on the price. A high price will induce more supply but less demand. So textbooks portray a market as a downward-sloping demand curve, on a graph with price on the vertical axis and quantity on the horizontal axis, and an upward-sloping supply curve. Most markets do not have a single physical location, and few behave just like the textbook version. There are markets for all kinds of goods and services, and many situations that seem to have nothing to do with economics can be thought of as markets, too—such as family life or the earth's atmosphere.

There are different types of elasticity, in demand and in supply, and in response to changes in price or changes in income. An **inelastic supply of labor** concerns supply and price; it means the amount of labor supplied— extra hours or workers—will not rise by much in response to an increase in the wage rate, or the price of labor.

A **monopolistically competitive** industry is one with lots of firms operating in it but yet not perfectly competitive because companies can create their own market niches by slight variations in what they are selling. This is **product differentiation**. It could take the form of slightly different technical specifications or design differences.

The **income elasticity of demand** measures the proportionate increase in demand for a product when income rises. If it is more than one (as with health care or designer clothes), it's a **luxury good**; if less than one, a **necessity** (like food, but also cigarettes). In other words, the technical use of these terms in economics is not quite the same as normal usage. (Cigarettes are actually now more likely to be **inferior goods**, demand for which actually falls as income rises, along with staple foods like maize as opposed to meat. If demand rises at all as income rises, it's a **normal good** instead.)

Chapter 2.
Illegal Drugs: It's the Economy, Man

Competition refers to the number of suppliers. If they are numerous, then not one of them is able to raise the price charged without losing all their customers. This is described as perfect competition. Imperfect competition is more normal in real life, and at the other extreme is monopoly, when there is only one supplier.

An **externality** occurs when there is a gap between the individual's private incentives and what would be best collectively or socially. There are many examples, one classic instance being pollution: it costs a company nothing to pour pollutants into the air or water, but there is a large cost to the local community. Similarly, drug use is not a private matter of comparing the health costs of taking drugs with the pleasure of doing so, but also involves the cost to the rest of society of antisocial behavior, and greater provision of health care. Externalities are often treated in introductory texts as exceptions to the norm, but they comprise all the interest and controversy in economic policy.

The **price elasticity of demand** is a measure of how much demand would fall if the price rose, or vice versa. If a 1 percent increase in price causes a 1 percent fall in demand, the elasticity is one. If the fall in demand is bigger, demand is highly elastic; if smaller, demand is inelastic.

Cost-benefit analysis simply means comparing the full costs of any policy or course of action or decision with the full benefits. In practice, it's very difficult to do well—who bears the costs and who benefits? Over what time period? And how are they all to be measured?

Chapter 3.
Risky Business: Why Most Teenagers Don't Act Like Economists

Risks are specific—unwelcome known outcomes that will occur with a certain probability. **Uncertainty** is general—the fog of obscurity that veils the future from the present.

Much social science assumes people's behavior is based on **rational choice**, or making decisions that will be in their own best interests given their **preferences** and the information available to them at the time. It seems more reasonable than assuming people make decisions that are against their own interests, but is nevertheless a controversial assumption with strong implications for people's behavior that are not always borne out by the evidence.

Economics is built upon the foundation of **utility**, the benefit or well-being of individuals. It's closely linked to happiness. Economics wants people to be happy. People are assumed to **maximize expected utility**, the terminology for making the decisions that will give them the greatest probability of the highest level of utility possible, which is the way the assumption of rational choice is formulated in economics.

A decision is **time-inconsistent** when it is the best, or optimal, decision for now, but not the best with hindsight.

People care more about departures of their income or share prices or any other indicator from a **reference level** than about absolute value.

The **status quo bias** or **endowment effect** refers to the higher value we put on something we already have compared to anything we only might be able to have.

Diminishing marginal sensitivity means the same absolute increase in money terms is less and less valuable at higher levels. So if I have only $100, I value another $11 much more than if I started out with $1,000.

Chapter 4.
Sports: Better Than Sex

The **labor market** is the market where people supply effort for wages and employers offer wages for work.

The **industrial structure** is a term for the pattern of what goods and services get made in an economy. What proportion of total national output is in manufacturing, such as electrical engineering or textiles, as opposed to services, such as software, finance, health care, or aromatherapy services?

In **superstar economics**, some individuals are able to turn a small advantage in talent or productivity to a huge income advantage, thanks to the existence of large economies of scale (see below) in the supply of their services. Sometimes known as **winner takes all.**

Economies of scale arise when the cost of supplying an extra unit of something, whether aircraft, a software program, or acting in a movie, declines the higher the quantity supplied. They can arise because of high start-up or fixed costs, like the expense of designing and testing a new aircraft or making and marketing a movie, in a market with a large number of potential sales. Economies of scale are therefore very common, but most people start out learning a textbook version of economics based on constant returns to scale, as the math is much easier.

Productivity is the increase in output per extra unit of input. Labor productivity measures increased output per additional hour of work, capital productivity measures rise in output per additional unit of capital (such as machinery), and total factor productivity measures, yes, increase in output per extra unit of all inputs. Actually measuring these abstractions, especially capital, is, needless to say, fraught with difficulty.

The **Coase theorem** says the identity of the owner of a given property makes no difference to the allocation of resources in the economy because any owner will seek the most profitable use.

Chapter 5.
Music: The New Economy's Robber Barons

Market concentration is a measure of how few companies dominate sales of a particular product or service, or in other words, how uncompetitive the market is. If the two biggest companies account for 80 percent of sales, the market is highly concentrated, whereas if you have to count the two hundred biggest companies before you get to the 80 percent mark, the market is pretty competitive.

Scale effect is another term for the presence of big economies of scale.

Marginal cost is the incremental cost of producing one more unit of output. **Average cost** is the average cost of producing all the units of output so far. They differ depending on the size of any initial fixed costs such as installing equipment or research and design, and on any other economies (or diseconomies) of scale.

Monopoly power is a description of a leading company's ability to dictate prices in the market because of the absence of effective competition.

Price discrimination means charging different prices to different categories of consumers in order to make a higher profit. It's a widespread practice: think of the different classes of air tickets, discounts for students, cents-off coupons to attract customers not willing to pay full price who can be bothered to clip the coupons, or higher prices to see the cinema in the evening. Price discrimination can occur in any less than perfectly competitive market: if there were an infinite potential supply of transatlantic flights, no airline would be able to charge businessmen a $2,000 premium for a little more space around their seat.

Technological innovation is the lifeblood of modern economies, the constant flow of new products and services, based on scientific discoveries and their practical application. The human appetite for innovations seems nowhere near its limits.

A company's **business strategy** is its basic outline plan for making profits. Is it going to grow by cutting prices in a bid for greater market share? By seeking new export markets? Does it care more about increasing the profit margin per sale rather than increasing the quantity of sales? Fewer businesses actually have strategies than you might expect.

Chapter 6.
Food Fights: Helping Lame Ducks Waddle

Supply, demand, and **productivity** are very familiar by now. **Consumer tastes** means just that, the tastes instilled by familiarity and culture: French consumers prefer wine to root beer, Chinese consumers don't have a taste for dairy products, and young consumers everywhere in the world like Harry Potter.

Comparative advantage is the term for one country being *relatively* more efficient at producing something, even if in absolute terms it is less efficient. It is measured by looking at the relative costs of two activities. Whichever country has the lowest cost ratio of X to Y has the comparative advantage in producing and exporting Y even if its cost is higher in absolute terms than in its trading partner.

Chapter 7.
Infrastructure: But I Never Travel by Train

Natural monopolies occur in markets that seem cut out for just one supplier, so great are the economies of scale. The power grid is one example. But in reality natural monopolies are rare. The grid can be regulated so that many suppliers sell electricity to it.

Market failure is a term for the presence of serious externalities. The normal mechanism of price adjusting to match supply and demand does not produce the best outcome.

Network externalities are externalities arising from the fact that the utility of a product or services increases the more other people use it too—like faxes or telephones or the Windows operating system.

A **nonrival good** is one whose consumption by me doesn't stop you consuming it, too, like the public park or a good idea or beautiful poem.

Zero marginal cost is when the production of an extra unit of output incurs no extra cost—like a software program, with high development costs but (almost) zero copying and distribution costs.

Nonexcludability in consumption occurs when it is not possible to prevent additional users from consuming the product or service. Once the road outside your house is built, anybody can drive along it. Once a piece of code has been published, it's next to impossible to prevent anybody using it.

Public or **social goods** are often both nonexcludable and nonrival. National defense is a good example.

Peak and **off-peak pricing** offer a way of dealing with congestion: charge more at times when overcrowding is most likely. Useful in transport, energy, movies, and bars—happy hour is off-peak pricing.

In the postwar years, public **ownership** was seen as the best way of dealing with many types of externalities, and governments in many countries **nationalized** chunks of their economies. Since the early 1980s, the balance has tilted away from public ownership because the absence of the profit motive created much inefficiency. Many governments have subsequently **privatized** a lot of what they owned; but those externalities make government **regulation** of those industries in the general public interest unavoidable. The debate, which will doubtless continue to ebb and flow, is not about whether governments have to be involved in the economy, but how best they can do it.

Path dependency means that where we are depends on how we got here. It's jargon for saying that history matters in explaining current circumstances. Often used to describe technological features like the QWERTY keyboard layout, first devised to minimize the chance of typewriter keys sticking together.

Chapter 8.
Scoreboard for Energy Taxes: Industry 5, Environment 1

Environmental externalities are those which mean private economic decisions take too little account of the costs they can impose on the environment. These are known as **external costs** because you pay to clean up my pollution.

The **tragedy of the commons** describes the depletion of resources held in common ownership because nobody has the (private) incentive to guard them even though that would be in society's best interests. Why is cod running out, but farmed salmon not? Why are cows in no danger of extinction, whereas tigers are?

Perfectly elastic supply is such that a small rise in price would trigger an infinite increase in supply. It's a limiting case, a horizontal line on the textbook diagram. At the other limit, perfectly inelastic supply is a vertical line—no more would be supplied at any price.

Free-riding is what happens when some people are able to take advantage of things that other people have paid for, because consumption is nonexcludable. The danger of free-riding is why taxes to pay for public goods are compulsory.

Social cost is an alternative term for total external costs.

Economic instruments are taxes, subsidies, and tradable permits that bring private costs into line with social costs and therefore create the right incentives to bring about the best outcome. Economists prefer economic instruments to alternatives such as bans, quotas, and rules, believing people respond better to incentives than to authority.

Regressive taxes fall proportionately most heavily on people with low incomes. The opposite is **progressive taxes.** A sales tax is regressive and an income tax is progressive. On the other hand, once you start tailoring taxes in any way to individual characteristics, you alter people's incentives (for example, about how hard to work) and therefore create inefficiencies. So most governments opt for a mix of different types of taxation.

Opportunity cost is a crucial concept. It is the value forgone from not having made alternative choices. Every decision has an opportunity cost as well as a direct cost.

Chapter 9.
Auctions: Call My Bluff

An **auction** is a market mechanism for allocating such scarce resources; it is likely to be more efficient, but it is not always easy to design well.

An **economic rent** is the income resulting from ownership of a rare asset. Land is one example. Natural resources are another. Government regulations often create rents by limiting access to something of value. Licenses are need for all kinds of activities, such as drilling for oil or marketing a new drug, as well as using the radio spectrum.

A **beauty contest** is a polite way of describing a decision by officials or politicians about which candidate should be awarded a valuable scarce resource like a spectrum license. We have every reason to be cynical about the quality of decisions made in beauty contests.

The **winner's curse** arises when the winner of an auction has only won by overpaying. Why did none of the other bidders put as high a value on the license? It doesn't seem to be common in practice, though.

Chapter 10.
Tax Incidence: Only People Pay Tax

Tax incidence is a description of who it is that ultimately pays a tax, because it's not necessarily the people who appear to pay it. Companies can pass corporate taxes onto customers in higher prices. A tax on property sales will get passed straight on to buyers in a seller's market.

In working out the value of something over a period of time, what's needed is the **present value**, which puts the future in terms of the present by **discounting**, or reducing according to a rate of interest, future sums. The reason is that mostly we prefer money now to money in the future— we are impatient, or to put it in economese, we have a **positive rate of**

time preference. If we have it now, we can buy more goods and services right away and enjoy consuming them. This is why banks have to pay interest when we deposit money.

Collusive describes companies that conspire together to boost their profits at consumers' expense. The companies simply agree not to compete.

An **oligopoly** is an industry with just a few big companies, whereas a monopoly has one, a **duopoly** has two, and then economists stop counting.

As described above, tobacco is an **inferior good**—people smoke less as their incomes rise. Taxes on cigarettes are therefore highly **regressive.**

Chapter 11.
War Games: A Government's Gotta Do What a Government's Gotta Do

Game theory is the branch of economics that portrays (or models) behavior as the outcome of the kinds of strategies that are used in games like poker or blackjack. There are several possible outcomes that occur with different probabilities and have different payouts. Game theory is incredibly useful for thinking about things like companies' behavior in different kinds of markets, or arms buildups, or any types of decision over time involving strategies. The basic example is the **prisoner's dilemma**: two prisoners are held apart and each offered a deal of a lesser punishment if they spill the beans on the other. If both stay silent, they get a short jail term for obstructing the law; if only one accepts the deal, he goes free and the other goes to jail; if both tell on the other, though, they both go to jail for the full term. What's the best strategy? In many situations in game theory, there will be both a cooperative and a noncooperative solution. Game theory sets out the prisoners' choices: either cooperate so that both would pay a little bit (jail time) but both would benefit (shorter jail term) in the long run; or take a risk on each other's behavior by not cooperating, and get either no jail or a long sentence.

Chapter 12.
Movies: Why Subtitles Need Subsidies

Diminishing returns to scale is the textbook situation whereby additional units of output cost more and more, not less and less. The classic example is agriculture, where farmers have to bring more and more land under cultivation or spend more on fertilizers to boost output.

Special interest groups are organized groups that lobby government for policies that will help their members, but not consumers, workers, or business as a whole. Examples include unions, industry associations, farmers' groups, and associations for retired persons. Arguments made by such groups about the economy are not likely to be unbiased.

Chapter 13.
Networks: "The Program Has Unexpectedly Quit"

The concept of **network externalities** came up in Chapter 6: they create economies of scale in demand because more users means greater benefits.

Goods that are **substitutes** suffer at each other's expense: if I buy more of one, I cut back on the other. Vodka and gin, for example. The relevant measure is the **cross-price elasticity of demand**. For substitutes it will be positive, meaning that if the price of gin goes up, I'll buy more (not less) vodka. **Complements**, on the other hand, are goods for which demand goes hand in hand, like gin and tonic. The cross-price elasticity will be negative, for if the price of gin goes up, I'll buy less (not more) tonic.

Lock-in is a term referring to the setting of technical standards that are extremely difficult to overturn, like those for mobile telephones or computer operating systems. Lock-in gives some producers a huge advantage, as with Microsoft and Windows.

The **first mover advantage** is the gain from being first in a market and thereby setting standards, reaping economies of scale ahead of competitors, establishing a formidable reputation, and so forth.

Natural monopolies were described earlier. But if a demonstration of how few are genuinely natural is needed, consider the fact that the mail used to be considered a natural monopoly, in the days before FedEx and UPS and all the other couriers. Now it's desktop operating systems.

Chapter 14.
Internet: The Economics of Dot-Bombs

Sunk costs is another term for fixed costs, one that makes the point that they can't be recovered. Once you've built the Channel Tunnel, that's it.

Experience goods are those like books and magazines you need to try out before knowing whether you want to buy them. This is why book-stores now encourage people to browse by putting armchairs in cozy spots.

Reputation is so valuable that companies can incorporate a measure of it in their published balance sheets—accountants call it goodwill, and it is closely related to brand value. Some dot-coms had no assets apart from their reputation, which is why they could suddenly become worth-less when customers and investors revised their views about reputation.

We all know about the **information overload:** more and more information and the same amount of time in which to make sense of it.

Customizing is tailoring a product to each specific customer. Long done on expensive cars, introduced by Dell for PCs and Nike for online running shoes, still waiting for it for most mass market products.

Entry barriers are any kinds of obstacles that make it hard for new companies to operate in any market. Barriers range from high start-up costs (making aircraft or cars, say) to government regulations (in banking or pharmaceuticals, for example) onerous for a newcomer to meet.

Chapter 15.
Industrial Change: Creative Destruction

The **business cycle** is the term for the expansions and slowdowns or recessions that characterize all economies. These cycles are not regular—expansions are generally long, and recessions short—but they last rough-ly seven to twelve years from peak to peak or trough to trough.

There is no technical definition of a **recession**, but it's usually thought of as either two successive quarters of declining GDP; or a year-on-year fall in GDP; or a general decline or slowdown in a wide range of economic indicators such as industrial output and employment.

Creative destruction is the term applied by Joseph Schumpeter to the turbulent process whereby a capitalist economy expands, with businesses starting up and failing, jobs created and destroyed, new technologies sweeping away old.

Chapter 16.
Disease: No Man Is an Island

Most discussion of **public goods** concerns national economies and governments. A **global public good**, on the other hand, is a concept that applies on a wider than national scale, as its name implies. There have always been some global public goods—international telecommunications standards and interoperability agreements, for example—and globalization has made the idea more relevant today.

Intellectual property rights are legal rights of ownership granted to creators of ideas or bits of knowledge, such as book copyrights or patents on new medicines or the specific design for a watch or industrial part. Users must pay a fee, a kind of rent for the use of the property, to the owner of the intellectual property right. The idea is controversial, though, with some thinkers arguing the concept of a property right is inappropriate for intangible ideas as opposed to tangible land or resources.

Chapter 17.
Multinationals: Sweatshop Earth?

Foreign direct investment is investment by a company from one country in another country. It can occur either by taking over an existing business in the host country or building a new business from scratch. Other kinds of cross-border investment, such as portfolio investments, are financial: buying bonds or shares issued by companies in other countries, or bank lending across borders.

Chapter 18.
Immigration: The Missing Link

The **lump of labor fallacy** assumes there is a fixed number of jobs to go around, and forgets that the labor market is a market in which demand as well as supply can vary. It crops up in many contexts—immigrants "stealing" jobs, technology "destroying" jobs, or a cut in the legal limit of working hours "creating" jobs.

The **assimilation hypothesis** says new groups of immigrants start out earning less than other workers in similar jobs, but later catch up or even overtake.

Congestion costs, remember, are a kind of externality in the (over)use of public goods.

And **cost-benefit analysis** is the systematic comparison of all relevant costs with all relevant benefits.

Chapter 19.
Demography: The South Has the Last Laugh

Technical progress is the increase in total factor productivity (that is, increases in output not attributable to increases in any of the inputs or factors of production) over time due to improvements in technology.

The **demographic transition** occurs when an economy has reached a modest level of prosperity, and death rates fall while birthrates decline even faster. This brings population growth down from the 2 percent a year typical of very poor countries, and the average age of the population starts to rise—from the mid-teens typical of poor countries to the mid or late forties in the rich countries.

The **demographic time bomb** refers to the fact that a population in the rich nations is stable or declining and average age rising fast. Who is going to do the work and pay the taxes to support all those pensioners in the future?

The **dependency ratio** measures the number of dependents below and above working age as a ratio to the working-age population.

Chapter 20.
Development: The Triumph of Fashion

The **financing gap** refers to the gap between what a country would need to invest to hit a target growth rate and the level of national savings.

Human capital is the set of skills, know-how, experience, educational attainment, and talents embodied in humans.

Conditionality is the term for the conditions attached to loans and grants by the International Monetary Fund, the World Bank, and other official lenders. Often criticized as onerous and intrusive, but hardly ever fully applied in practice.

Debt relief means writing off past debts because they are never going to be repaid in full. What matters is how much the write-off cuts interest payments that have to be made, as these are coming out of tax revenues that could be spent on education or health—or indeed arms and presidential palaces.

Social capital is a term even fuzzier than *capital* and *human capital*, shorthand for the institutions, habits, values, and traditions that characterize any society and might contribute favorably to economic growth. The definition and measurement of social capital are a subject of hot debate. But it is a useful concept because societies do differ so much in their economic capabilities, even if they have similar resources and similar degrees of physical and human capital.

Chapter 21.
Japan: Kogaru versus One-kei, or Why Tokyo's Teenage Fashions Matter

Deflation refers to consistent declines over time in the general level of prices in an economy—not just some prices, and not just a steady reduction in the rate of inflation, which is a **disinflation** rather than a deflation.

Demand management is the process whereby governments or central banks try to adjust the aggregate level of demand in the economy, to smooth out the ups and downs of the business cycle, or to boost growth.

Fine-tuning is demand management so excellent that it succeeds in eliminating business-cycle fluctuations. Often attempted, at least in the past, and never achieved.

Rational expectations says that what people expect to be true about the future is (by and large) correct, in the sense that their expectations about the economy will reflect the actual behavior of the economy. Taken too literally, this is obviously silly, but it captures the insight that people are not likely to get things systematically wrong. If the government is running policies that will lead to high inflation, people will tend to expect high inflation.

The **liquidity trap** is what happens when interest rates can fall no lower because they are already close to zero but that's still not low enough to stimulate demand. A reduction in interest rates should persuade people to spend more rather than hold on to cash and bank deposits, but in the trap they prefer this liquidity. The reason may be that if there is deflation, the real interest rate is higher than the nominal interest rate. The nominal rate is what your bank says it pays you on your deposit; the real rate is this nominal rate adjusted for what you expect inflation to be. If inflation is negative, the real return to holding on to your deposit is higher: goods will cost less if you buy them next year rather than now.

Governments can **crowd out** private investment by borrowing in the financial markets. The government borrowing drives up the interest rate all borrowers must pay, as they are competing for the same pool of savings.

Stagflation is the combination of low or no growth and high inflation. It is both unpleasant and has no place in conventional economic theory.

Chapter 22.
Inflation: Targeting the Sleeping Beast

Inflation is the percentage increase in the price level, usually measured at an annual rate.

Hyperinflation is wildly excessive inflation, running at thousands or tens of thousands of percent a year. There is nothing more corrosive to society than hyperinflation.

Fiscal policy refers to decisions about government spending and taxation; **monetary policy** to decisions about interest rates, credit conditions, and liquidity in the financial markets.

Aggregate supply is the economy's total supply capacity, and the missing link between demand management and inflation. Allow demand to expand without paying attention to the **supply side** of the economy, and the only result will be higher inflation.

The **Phillips curve** links the unemployment rate with the rate of inflation. It slopes down: the higher the inflation rate (y axis), the lower the unemployment rate (x axis). But bitter experience has taught us that this is not a trade-off governments can manipulate according to preference, because if they boost demand and hence accept higher inflation in order to cut unemployment, the Phillips curve moves. It slopes down short run, but in the long run is vertical at the **non-accelerating inflation rate of unemployment,** or **Nairu.** This is determined by supply-side conditions.

Inflation targeting is the outcome of this experience. Central banks now concentrate on keeping inflation low and steady at 2 to 3 percent a year. Sometimes they have an explicit inflation target; sometimes it is implied.

Deflation is negative inflation or falling price level.

Central banks have an easier task the higher their **credibility**. If people believe the central bank will always do what it takes to keep inflation low, the chances are they'll behave in ways that keep inflation low anyway, not making huge pay demands for example because they know that will drive interest rates higher.

A big debate in monetary policy is **discretion** versus **rules.** A rule like "always raise interest rates if the money supply grows faster than x percent" will help credibility but could be damaging in some circumstances—if, say, the excess growth is due to a technical change in the banking system rather than a change in economic behavior. The modern consensus favors constrained discretion, which means rules for when it's permissible to deviate from rules.

A **monetary target** is an alternative to an inflation target. They were popular in the late 1970s and early '80s, and took the form of target growth rates for the money supply—that is to say, cash plus different kinds of bank deposits. The rationale was that inflation could not occur if there was a limit on how fast the money to fuel spending became available.

An **exchange rate target** is the final kind of target for monetary policy, involving fixing the exchange rate with a major currency like the dollar. The rule is then in effect "have the same inflation rate as the United States." It is a great way of reducing very high inflation rates but can be disastrous when (a) the wrong exchange rate is chosen and/or (b) other policies are inconsistent with stabilizing inflation—for instance, when the government budget deficit is huge, so it has to borrow bucketfuls to finance its spending.

Chapter 23.
Defense Spending: Farewell to the Peace Dividend

The **peace dividend**: the government and national resources freed by not having to spend massive amounts on armaments and defense.

Automatic stabilizers are tax and spending devices that offset the direction of the economy without requiring an explicit decision—such as unemployment benefits (so the government spends more when the economy is weak) or sales taxes (so the government takes less tax when the economy is weak).

Chapter 24.
Weather: Why Economists Care About the Sex Life of Pigs

This one is about handling data, not concepts. Without well-based statistics, there's no picture at all, never mind a big picture.

Chapter 25.
Work: Why Do It?

The **income effect** is the effect of a higher wage rate on the work-leisure choice. It's negative: if you have more money, you need to work less to cover your bills. The **substitution effect** is the positive effect of a higher price for labor and is positive: if you are paid more per hour, you have an incentive to work more hours.

Selected Bibliography

Books

Diamond, Jared. *Guns, Germs, and Steel: A Short History of Everybody in the Last 13,000 Years.* Norton, 1999. A compelling big-picture view of human history and the reasons some countries have succeeded and others not.

Easterly, William. *The Elusive Quest for Growth.* MIT Press, 2001. This is an accessible history and critique of many of the past fashions in development economics.

Henderson, David. *Innocence and Design: The Influence of Economic Ideas on Policy.* Blackwell, 1986.

Hendry, David, and Neil Ericsson, eds. *Understanding Economic Forecasts.* MIT Press, 2001. See especially the Introduction and Chapter 1.

Krugman, Paul. *Pop Internationalism.* MIT Press, 1996.

———. *The Accidental Theorist and Other Dispatches from the Dismal Science.* Norton, 1998.

Nasar, Sylvia. *A Beautiful Mind.* Touchstone, 2002. This biography of John Nash is an enjoyable book that illuminates the importance of game theory.

Ormerod, Paul. *Butterfly Economics: A New General Theory of Social and Economic Behavior.* Basic Books, 2001.

Shiller, Robert. *Irrational Exuberance.* Broadway Books, 2001. This is a wonderfully readable introduction to the lack of rationality in financial markets.

Woodward, Bob. *The Agenda.* Simon & Schuster, 1994. An excellent account of the budget debates that took place when Bill Clinton became president in 1992.

Articles and Papers

Bourgignon, Francois, et al. "Making Sense of Globalization." Centre for Economic Policy Research, May 2002 (www.cepr.org.uk). This is a nontechnical overview of the evidence on globalization.

Bruner, Allan. "El Niño and World Primary Commodity Prices: Warm Water or Hot Air?" IMF working paper No. 203, 2000.

Bulow, Jeremy, and Paul Klemperer. "The Tobacco Deal." Discussion Paper No. 2125, Centre for Economic Policy Research, April 1999 (www.cepr.org.uk).

Caplan, Bryan. "Systematically Biased Beliefs About Economics." *Economic Journal* 112 (2002): 1–26.

Cline, William R. "The Impact of Global Warming on Agriculture: Comment." *American Economic Review* 86 (1996): 1309–11.

Dasgupta, Partha. "Modern Economics and Its Critics." Working paper posted at www.econ.cam.ac.uk/faculty/dasgupta.

Freeman, Richard. Freeman's course website, covering complexity theory, is at www.courses.fas.harvard.edu/~ec1818.

King, Mervyn. "Monetary Stability: Rhyme or Reason." Seventh ESRC Annual Lecture, 1996. (www.bankofengland.co.uk)

Klemperer, Paul. www.paulklemperer.org has much material on auctions, some difficult—some not.

Mishkin, Frederic, and Klaus Schmidt-Hebbel. "One Decade of Inflation Targeting in the World." National Bureau of Economic Research working paper, July 2001 (www.nber.org).

Sachs, Jeffrey. "Tropical Underdevelopment," 2000. (www2.cid.harvard.edu/cidpapers, under tropics_eha-1.pdf)

Sutton, John. 2001 Royal Economic Society Lecture. (www.res.org.uk)

"What a Little Moonlight Can Do." *The Economist,* October 20, 2001.

Websites

International Organizations
International Monetary Fund
www.imf.org

Organisation for Economic Co-operation and Development
www.oecd.org

World Bank
www.worldbank.org

U.S. Government Sites
Bureau of Economic Analysis
www.bea.doc.gov/bea/pubs.htm

Commerce Department
home.doc.gov/

Labor statistics for the U.S. and other countries
www.bls.gov/data

Council of Economic Advisers
www.whitehouse.gov/cea

Census Bureau
www.census.gov

Federal Communications Commission
www.fcc.gov

Federal Reserve Board
www.federalreserve.gov

Economists' Sites
Most academic economists maintain a website with their research papers, course material and popular writing. The author's favorite sites are:

Bradford DeLong at Berkeley, an excellent portal for anything in economics
www.j-bradford-delong.net

Paul Krugman at Princeton, who writes well for noneconomists
www.wws.princeton.edu/~pkrugman

Newspapers and Other Media
Bloomberg
www.bloomberg.com

The Economist
www.economist.com

The Financial Times
www.ft.com

Reuters
www.reuters.com

The Wall Street Journal
www.wsj.com

Bureau of Labor Statistics
www.bls.gov

Index

About TEXERE

TEXERE seeks to become the most progressive and authoritative voice in business publishing by cultivating and enhancing ideas that will illuminate the global business landscape. Our name defines the spirit of our vision: TEXERE is the ancient Latin verb "to weave." In an increasingly global business community, we seek to create an intersection where authors and readers can share the best thinking and the latest ideas. We want to leverage the expertise and insights of leading thinkers by weaving them with TEXERE's capability to deliver them to the marketplace.

To learn more and become a part of our community, visit us at:

www.etexere.com

and

www.etexere.co.uk

About the Typeface

This book was set in 10.25/14.25 Giovanni Book

Book I

The Safe Road to Prosperity

You are probably on the road to Financial Hell, and may not even know it. But as Yogi Berra said, "When you come to a fork in the road, take it."

It's never too late to change course. Now it's time to explore the first of two alternatives to a much better place than the Hell that awaits most middle-class Americans.

Book I outlines the steps on the safe road to prosperity. Its objective is nothing less than changing your life. It's for those who have concluded that they will never be financially secure, who have rationalized their lack of success. It's also for those who are doing OK but living way too close to the edge, with little hope of a decent retirement or a college education for their kids. It explains how your prosperous and secure neighbors got that way and how you can too. It opens up the prospect of a genuinely prosperous retirement for the wage slaves of America, and explains why many of the people you think are rich because of the big house and the boat and Mercedes in their driveways are really headed for Financial Hell. It tells you why "the mass of men live lives of quiet desperation" on that evil road, even if they appear to be really well off—and sometimes *because* of how they got that way. This somewhat embarrassing section also tells you why after years of huge income I'm not half as rich as everyone thinks I am and could have been.

Above all, it tells you how in 10 to 20 years you can build a financial basis for an enjoyable, independent retirement, with little or no risk, no matter what your current income or job status, simply by not making the stupid mistakes most people make.

Section I of Book I outlines the five most important and most universal mistakes that put you on the road to Financial Hell.

Section II of Book I outlines the most costly stupid mistakes that have cost amateur investors hundreds of billions of dollars and often have undone years of discipline and saving.

Book I is not about how to become Really Rich. The strategies and techniques for that blessed state are totally different, and are the subject of Book II. Book I will probably be more useful to more people than Book II, because it is risk-free, and prosperity is probably good enough for most people. There's nothing wrong with that. It means you will be debt-free, have a bit more income than you really need, and have a secure retirement. Your life will be secure and comfortable in Safe Prosperity Heaven.

Section I

The Dumb Mistakes
Almost Everyone Makes
with Their Money

I f there is any one piece of advice I could give you that expresses the spirit of this section, it is that the key to safe prosperity is avoiding the mistakes that lead to Financial Hell. There are five common mistakes that most Americans make every day. These mistakes are the principal reason most of them are living lives of quiet desperation, either because they are in chronic financial trouble or because they know they would be if even a minor emergency created big, unexpected expenses or their income were cut off for more than a month or two.

This section is designed to help you set up a program that will steadily strengthen your personal balance sheet and reduce your vulnerability. If pursued for enough years, it will also make you Safely Prosperous. It is no-risk and within the reach of everyone. Even those who are more interested in the goal of being Really Rich should take these chapters seriously.

It's also a bit embarrassing, as I learned most of these principles by stepping in them.

Chapter 1

Two Tracks, Two Heavens

The two very different roads to Safe Prosperity or Real Riches

When you finally decide to abandon the road to Financial Hell, you have the choice of two distinct and very different financial heavens and a distinct and different route to get to each one. You can choose either Safely Prosperous Heaven or Really Rich Heaven.

SAFELY PROSPEROUS

The road to Safely Prosperous Heaven is risk-free though unexciting, and smoothly paved with old-fashioned virtues. In fact, it's hazard-free, although sometimes downright dull. At the end of the road, you will be debt-free, financially secure, and able to enjoy your golden years without worries about money. Safely Prosperous Heaven is the place where most readers of this book should go, because it is secure and virtuous. It's the place the first half of this book is about. You will have a comfortable retirement with most of the pleasant things we take for granted we are entitled to—a Winnebago, visits with grandchildren, a nice home in a retirement community, an occasional cruise on a nice ship, weekly dinners out at a nice restaurant. It's the American dream,

25

and not to be sneezed at. All it takes is old-fashioned character and a willingness to postpone some gratification. It's the way to get rich slowly but surely.

The operative principle on this road is to be aware of and avoid several common stupid money mistakes made by most Americans.

REALLY RICH

Then there's the road to Really Rich Heaven. It's very different. It's strewn with rocks and pitfalls; 70-hour weeks on the job; worried, sleepless nights; humiliating failures that test your resolve as it has never been tested before; and marriage-threatening temptations. But it's downright exciting. At the end of this fast track is financial freedom beyond your wildest dreams. You will be able to fund your favorite charities generously and help down-on-their-luck friends and relatives. You will probably be honored by your community and asked to serve on various boards, because, as Tevye sang in *Fiddler on the Roof*, "When you're rich, they think you really know." You'll be able to buy anything you want without thinking about it or counting the cost. But the tough road on the way there will test your character and principles like nothing else in life can. It will be a tough route through a minefield between the transitory temptations that Mammon brings and the eternal happiness that comes from having a loving spouse and family to honor your name, and beneficiaries of your generosity that will rise up to call you blessed.

When you succeed, you will be the target of envy and the class warfare that paints all rich people with the political brush of unworthy selfishness and tries to use the coercive taxing power of government to take away your hard-earned money to give to the voting masses who want what you have but don't want to pay the price you did.

I will teach you how to exploit the principles and techniques that have created millions of fortunes. I have carefully mapped these two roads so you can follow whichever one you choose. They are both within your reach, and you do get to choose.

This started out to be a book called *The Ten Stupidest Things People Do with Their Money,* things I had done and observed others doing that kept them from becoming prosperous. It was to be my legacy to my numerous posterity. But as it unfolded, I realized that I knew about a lot more than just prosperity. I had been rich twice and lost everything twice, and *The Ruff Times* was really the perfect laboratory for watching thousands of others become not just Safely Prosperous, but Really Rich as well. So the book grew into more than just a prosperity guide. It was now also a how-to-get-rich guide, born in the real world of people who become Really Rich. This could really have been two separate books, one about prosperity, and one about real riches, so I have subdivided it into Book I and Book II.

Book I, "The Safe Road to Prosperity," is for those who really just want to be Safely Prosperous, which I define as living comfortably and then some, with no financial worries and a secure future even after retirement. It's in two sections.

Section I of Book I, entitled "The Dumb Mistakes Almost Everyone Makes with Their Money," is for the tens of millions of Americans who always have too much month left at the end of their money. It's about the foolish things they did with all the money that went through their hands day after day without sticking. It tells you why you aren't financially secure, and why some of your neighbors are, even though they may have no more income than you.

STARTING BELOW SCRATCH

Most stock-market or get-rich-quick books assume that you have money to invest, and ignore the crucial question of how to get it in the first place—and keep it.

Some years ago, on a promotional tour for my book *Making Money,* I found myself at a Chicago radio station that had a mostly black—and presumably poor—listening audience. After the usual opening pleasantries, the interviewer said, "Your book seems to be written for investors who already have money. What about those who are poor or barely making ends meet?" I responded weakly—but, I thought, cleverly—"I haven't yet designed an investment program for those who have no money to invest, and neither has anyone else."

Since I have grown much older and a little bit wiser, this book starts with the expensive mistakes you can avoid in order to accumulate a serious nest egg. It's about how to have a truly independent retirement, even if you're late starting and only a modest earner. It's about how to lay a nest egg out of current income, regardless of how small that is!

These expensive mistakes are well-nigh universal, and most readers, even those who are fairly well off, will at least catch a glimpse of themselves here.

In some cases, these strategies will take a few years to pay off, but don't write them off by telling yourself that you're too old for this sort of thing. The average life span in America has risen to 75 for men and 81 for women, so most of you have a few years to build an estate or add to yours to leave to future generations. Ten years is plenty of time.

Section II of Book I is entitled "Blowing Your Money in the Investment Markets." After you have eliminated the first six foolish mistakes and finally accumulated some money, I will teach you what I learned from some spectacular losers about the foolish things they did with their money that caused them to lose it in the market, especially during the current bear market. Most amateur stock-market investors have lost money, and I will tell you how they did it. These time-tested and infallible failure techniques have been implemented by millions of losing investors—

usually without them even knowing what they did and why they did it.

I wrote Book I for truck drivers and young married couples, small businessmen and Fortune 500 executives, retirees and their children and grandchildren, housewives, schoolteachers, and clerks, rich and poor. This is especially for all those who are struggling for survival every month and think it is because they didn't buy "a winning ticket in the lottery of life," as Bill Clinton said in one of the lower rhetorical points of his administration. Clinton meant that the rich were merely lucky, which is a crummy piece of class-war rhetoric. Luck had little to do with it.

BOOK II: THE REAL SECRETS OF THE REALLY RICH

Book II is a quantum leap beyond prosperity. It's about the most important things rich people have always done to get rich. This section teaches you how to leap the gulf between the Safely Prosperous and the Really Rich. One way to get rich is to choose your parents very carefully, but it's too late for that now. The rich really are different, and it's not just how much money they have or how smart they are, it's their attitude toward risk and fear, their understanding of when to break the rules of Book I, and their knowledge of a few simple capitalistic principles. It's also having the rich person's mind-set.

How do you define "Really Rich?" For the purpose of this book, I define it as having secure wealth that is way in excess of your real wants, with lots of discretionary cash flow produced from the assets on your balance sheet. You can afford to buy anything you want without a second thought, or to give away big chunks of money to causes you care about. It's a giant leap beyond Safely Prosperous. The truly rich can spend money or give it away whenever they want to without worrying about it and can give money to causes they care about without sacrificing any of their personal wants.

How do they measure their tangible wealth? Not by the cash in their bank account, but *by their balance sheets and the passive income their assets spin off.*

The Safely Prosperous are disciplined and make few mistakes with their money, but they take no risks, even calculated ones, live well within their means, and are very comfortable with a riskless lifestyle. That's OK, God bless 'em. But the Really Rich usually got rich by taking risks all the time and make a lot of mistakes along their journey. They aren't gamblers, except with a small part of their fortune just for the fun and excitement of gambling. They are comfortable with risk, but it is always calculated risk with the odds heavily on their side, usually where they can determine the outcome, and it has to return many times more than market rates. They are often driven—sometimes just by greed, sometimes to show someone they are someone too, sometimes by grand ideas. But most of all, they see risk as measurable and controllable, and they enjoy the game. And, ironically, they are usually heavily in debt. Their road to wealth is usually paved with failures, but their debts and failures aren't stumbling blocks, they are stepping stones.

In the parable of the talents, Jesus told about three servants who were given some money to care for by their master; one was given five talents (more money than a man could earn in a lifetime), one was given two talents, and one was given only one talent. When the master returned and asked for an accounting, the men who had been given five and two talents had both doubled their money, and were praised and promised great rewards. However, the man with one talent, knowing his master was a hard man, had buried it in the ground, and had no increase. The reward for his no-risk strategy? The master gave his talent to the man who had had five. Today's rich people go even farther than either of the first two; they earn 5-fold or 10-fold!

Book II teaches you the things rich people have always done to get rich that you don't do. In good times or bad—no matter how bad—smart people still get rich, and this book contains their secrets.

I'm not one of those ivory-tower experts in three-piece suits who say things like, "Given the inverted yield curve and rising GDP . . ." That is usually just gobbledygook that conceals the fact that they really don't have a clue. I love the English language, and it is most elegant when it is plain, simple, and direct.

Most people foolishly think the pursuit of prosperity or wealth is a sprint, not a middle-distance race or a marathon, so the get-rich-quick idea is very seductive, and get-rich-quick seminars draw big crowds. Is it possible to get rich quick? Sure, many have done just that, but the unvarnished truth is that no one magic secret will get you rich both fast and struggle-free.

"But," I hear you cry, "rich people are different from me; they're special." That may be so, but are millionaires especially talented? Are they all inventors or brilliant entrepreneurs? Are they financial geniuses? Are they NBA stars? Did they get rich quick? Not usually, although it often came faster than they expected. Most of them were just like you—no smarter, no luckier, and no more talented. They didn't do anything you can't do. But they understood and consistently and patiently practiced some old-fashioned principles of wealth growth year after year.

FORECASTING

I have made my living for a quarter century making financial and economic forecasts. Forecasting is not easy, but it made a lot of sense to me; if you can accurately forecast the direction of interest rates, you can make a lot of money in bonds and utility stocks. If you can forecast the direction of the dollar versus other currencies and the direction of inflation, you can make a lot of money in gold and mining stocks. If you can accurately forecast an imminent recession or recovery, you can make a lot of money investing in the stock market.

However, the techniques described in this book will work no matter what happens to the economy or interest rates or the stock market or the gold price, so you can achieve your objectives regardless of what the world around you does. However, for the record, I will tell you how the future looks from the perspective of late 2003.

First, we have been in the longest bear stock market seen since the 1930s, and despite the year-long burst of optimism from Wall Street in 2003, it's a long way from over. As this is written, the huge bubble of the 1990s is not yet fully deflated. The traditional standard measurements of value are actually higher than they were at the peak of the last bull market in March 2000. The price/earnings ratio (PE) on the New York Stock Exchange is now around 32 to 1. It was around 30 to 1 at its peak in 2000. No bear market in U.S. history has ever ended with such high evaluations. Not one! The PE at most bear market bottoms is about 7 to 1. That means that the Dow Jones will not bottom out until it falls below 4,000, or possibly 2,500. The Nasdaq doesn't have as far to go on the downside because it is already down more than 60 percent, so my downside target for the Nasdaq is below 1,000. There will probably be at least one more down leg to new lows, and it may take a few years.

This means the business environment will be chancy at least until late 2004, and possibly for several more years, with false rebounds in between.

But none of this matters much! The techniques I will teach you will work despite these uncertainties, and perhaps because of them. If I'm unduly pessimistic, I'll lead the cheering, and the techniques described herein will just be easier to implement.

DIFFERENT TRACKS

There are generic differences between the two tracks and those who abandon the road to Financial Hell to follow them:

- *Mistakes:* The reader who wants to be Safely Prosperous will have to avoid the most common mistakes and exercise some self-discipline and self-denial. Readers who want to be Really Rich must be willing to make mistakes as they launch their programs, some of which will fail and teach them much of what they will learn—but they are not the same mistakes prosperity seekers should avoid. To the Safely Prosperous, mistakes are stumbling blocks to be avoided. To the Really Rich, other mistakes are just stepping stones and business lessons along the road to real wealth.

- *Risk:* The prosperity seeker will be risk-averse and settle for modest but sure compound returns over the years. The wealth seeker must be willing to take calculated risks and sometimes shoot the moon.

- *Debt:* Prosperity seekers must avoid debt, and, indeed, liquidate the debt they now have. Wealth seekers will have to learn to use debt as an essential tool. In fact, they probably can't become rich without owing a lot of money under carefully controlled conditions.

- *Outside versus inside:* The prosperity seeker will always be a passive outside investor, buying the opportunities created and controlled by market forces and other business-people. The wealth seeker will be an insider, buying or creating investments at wholesale prices and selling them at retail to prosperity seekers.

- *Opportunity versus security:* The prosperity seeker has modest goals for financial security and values that security highly. The wealth seeker has little interest in security and is opportunity-oriented.

In summary, these are two different animals, and you could be either one of them. By the time you have heard me out to the end, you will have a lot better idea which one you are. It's too soon to decide.

WHO CAN BENEFIT FROM THIS BOOK

In the past, my financial newsletter, *The Ruff Times*, was most useful for upper-middle-class or wealthy families who already had cash to invest. Our surveys have told us that 49 percent of them were balance-sheet millionaires. They have tended to be personally and politically conservative and have seemed to enjoy my political commentary from the conservative/libertarian political side of the public debates. However, this nonpolitical book has little or none of that kind of content. It is conservative only in the sense that conservative financial principles cut across all political and philosophical lines. Money acts the same for Republicans and Democrats; liberals, conservatives, and libertarians; rich and middle-class.

Book I will be especially useful for young adults just starting their financial lives, and for the Baby Boomers and Generation Xers with 10 to 35 earning years ahead (30 to 55 years old). Many of them likely saw their paper profits decimated in the stock market crash of 2000 to 2002. While they are still in their peak earning years, they can most effectively use the long-term strategies herein to start now to prepare for their inevitable retirement—or for possible hard times while they are still over the horizon, if they are willing to face reality and stop spending money they don't yet have (borrowed money) so they can pretend they are already rich.

In the interest of full disclosure, I feel compelled to tell you that as a practicing Mormon, I intend to keep practicing until I get it right, but this is not a pulpit or a missionary tract; I save that for my Sunday-school class. However, Mormonism is not just a theology. It is also a classic nineteenth-century American culture with its roots in the old-fashioned self-sufficiency attitudes of that century, and those universal values have been planted in my bones and strongly influenced the content of this book. There is no overt or covert attempt to preach the unique

Mormon theology here. Tens of millions of non-Mormon middle-class mainstream Americans share these values down deep in their guts and will be comfortable with them.

Some of what you will read, especially in Book I, is very old-fashioned and probably politically incorrect. Successful people have practiced these principles for hundreds of years, and, in my opinion, they will never really go out of style, even if they periodically go out of favor.

I wrote this book to educate you, but as I have already paid your tuition, you now have a scholarship for only the cost of this book. Those of you who hire financial advisors to do the heavy lifting should make sure they read this book first so you can be sure his or her decisions don't undercut your newly honed guidelines. After you have read this, you will probably be smarter than your financial advisors are now!

All of these rules are very precious to me, and I hope they will be to you. They should be—I paid several million dollars in tuition to the school of expensive mistakes to learn them.

Chapter 2

Worshipping Mammon

The bad trade-offs of loving money more than God, family or country, and how to avoid them. How to have both money and true happiness.

The Apostle Paul wrote, "The love of money is the root of all evil." Not money, but the *love* of money. It is the archetypal two-edged sword; even if putting a misplaced love of money ahead of more important things often does lead to monetary wealth, it too often leads to misery.

The older I get, the less important getting rich seems to me, and the more intrigued I have become with studying the impact of money on character and true happiness. In fact, concern over the possible negative effects of the quest for financial security and wealth on the human psyche kept me from writing about how to become Really Rich until I sorted through the effects of the quest for money on me and my family. I finally decided I was not morally at ease with sharing what I have learned about the principles of wealth acquisition if I didn't share with you up front what I have experienced for myself and learned from others about the spiritual and emotional potholes along the road to wealth.

I have concluded that happiness is the real object and purpose of our existence, and the quest for riches and the sheer fact of the existence of excess money can either enhance or destroy it. That is a fact of life, and I have never read anything about what wealth can do for you and to you, so I decided to fill that void.

Those who are champing at the bit to join the acolytes of Mammon may be bored with this discussion and wonder why I even wrote it, but I believe it is the most important chapter in the book, and affects all that follows. That's why I put it near the front.

We usually think that money is impersonal, but in my quarter century as a financial publisher, I have observed that not much in life challenges us emotionally and spiritually as much as money—or the lack of it. More money and/or happiness has been lost because of misplaced devotion to money than most other causes put together.

Money—or the lack of it—profoundly affects you, depending on whether or not you worship Mammon, the heathen god who symbolized worldly financial success. Getting rich is not a sin per se, but it's a real test of what you are down deep inside, and how you react to money triggers a lot of genuine consequences. I have known some very happy rich men who left this life with a legacy of spiritual and moral riches and big estates, and I have known just as many rich but miserable men. I have also known some whose Mammon worship made them rich, but then cost them their fortunes and their families.

Mammon's evil, phony religion always leads to slavery, but you can become rich and also escape Mammon's chains before it is too late.

Out of my personal experience, I have included four real-life stories of men who all became very wealthy. Two worshipped Mammon and found misery; two defied Mammon and lived full and rich lives full of faith. They had the love and respect of all who knew them, and were great role models for their loving families. Their stories are instructive.

SAD EXAMPLE #1

Here is a sad but true extreme example of how worshipping Mammon (money) can lead to misery and loss of money at the same time.

Back in the 1920s, a very talented man was one of the founders of the chain of stores in Idaho and Utah which later became Safeway. He was their chief financial officer, and making money was his whole life. His favorite book, which he made into a kind of sacred bible for his life's guidance, was Napoleon Hill's *Think and Grow Rich.* He was also a mathematical genius; he could run his finger down a long column of figures six digits wide and give you a total at the bottom. He could inventory a store in his head and write down the figures accurately on the train on the way to the next town.

Getting rich was his one passion in life, but it was also his tragic undoing. He not only neglected his wife and family in the pursuit of business, but when his wife became pregnant for the second time, which he considered to be very inconvenient to his career, he forced her to have an illegal abortion, which was a source of great spiritual pain and guilt for her. When she got pregnant again, he tried to force her to have another abortion, but this time she refused. He was drinking heavily by now, and in a drunken rage, he beat her savagely to try to cause a miscarriage. She was injured so badly that her doctor recommended a therapeutic abortion to save her life, which she refused. She then went to bed for seven months to try to save the baby, and she gave birth in due time to a healthy son.

Flashing further back in time, some months earlier the man had made a decision to get *really* rich, so he liquidated his company stock worth almost $1 million and took the money to New York to make a real fortune speculating on margin in the stock market. The year was 1929, and he was wiped out in one day in the October crash.

He then turned to gambling in a single-minded effort to recoup his lost fortune, and gambled away the insurance money. Many months later, when his wife was nursing the baby, he walked into the room, put a gun in his mouth, and pulled the trigger. There was no insurance money.

He was my father.

I remember my mother's horror two decades later when she found me reading *Think and Grow Rich,* the book that my father called his "bible" and that I have enjoyed over the years. That was when she broke down and told me much of this story, which was later confirmed and added to by relatives. There are more informative details of my father's money obsession in Chapter 11.

This is not an anti-abortion tract, so let me leave it by saying that there are those who may think the world would be a better place if my mother had had an abortion, but I am not among them.

As I pieced this story together bit by bit from conversations with my mother and my aunts and uncles, it became clear to me that the unifying thread running through this story was "sacrificing on the altar of Mammon." I then vowed that I would never allow money to corrupt me as it had my dad, but, as you will see in later chapters, that was easier said than done, and when all is said and done, there is more said than done. Most of the real unhappiness I have experienced in my life came as a result of losing my focus—putting business ahead of my family, and allowing wealth and ready money to corrupt me—and amazingly, I was unaware of it. I thought I was the best husband and father in the world. I guess I was better than many, but I was nowhere near as good as I thought I was or should have been, and there was a price to be paid.

SAD EXAMPLE #2

Some years ago, the president and CEO of a Fortune 500 multinational company was a guest on my radio talk show. He was a

fan of *The Ruff Times,* and was also a well-known force to be reck-
oned with in publicizing and eliminating government waste as
the volunteer head of a government commission, as that was his
public service. We had a very cordial interview and went out
for a bite to eat afterward. He told me about his work schedule—
18 hours a day, seven days a week. He also required the same of
his management team. He flew all over the world in the company
727 and took his management team with him so they could work
on the plane around the clock. He was a great guy who liked me,
and I liked him in return, and envied his financial success—until
he asked me a strange question: "Do your kids hate you?"

When I told him I was pretty sure they didn't, he said, "My
kids won't talk to me and won't let me see my grandchildren. I
haven't seen some of them for years." Then, to my amazement, he
sprung a leak around the eyes and poured out his heart to me like
a dam breaking, releasing his pent-up misery. When I asked him
if his wife ever traveled with him on the company 727, he said
yes, but then he told me that she understood that he would be
working all the time with his staff and she also understood she
was not to interrupt him. She always brought a friend with her so
she wouldn't be alone, and he claimed she was happy with that.

I was planning to go to Bangkok, and since he was going to
Singapore in his 727, he invited me to go with him and fly to
Bangkok from there. I decided to go commercial anyway, as it
was obvious he wouldn't have any time for me.

This man has since died, which triggered a bitter fight among
his heirs over his fortune. Outside of his business associates, he
was mourned by few. Right now, I guess, he's doing a lot of
explaining.

THE OTHER SIDE OF THE COIN

In contrast, I have known some highly successful men who kept
their balance.

HAPPY EXAMPLE #1

J. Willard Marriott Senior was the founder of the Marriott Hotels, among other things. He was an important lay leader in his church, and always put family and church first. He was a dear personal friend, and one of my real-life heroes. He changed my life permanently one evening at a party in his home, which he had invited me to attend. (I was 20 years old at the time.) Out of the clear blue sky, he put his arm around my shoulders and said, "Howard Ruff, you're an entrepreneur. Never work for another man." So I didn't.

He lived happily and died greatly loved by his family and everyone else who knew him. He was one of the happiest and most successful people I have ever known. He passed his values on to his family, and his son, J. Willard Marriott Junior, is not only CEO of the Marriot financial empire, but has followed in his father's footsteps as a husband, father, and church leader.

HAPPY EXAMPLE #2

Another role model was one of my ancestors, Joseph Younger Mayberry. During the deadly Mormon persecutions in Missouri and Illinois in the 1830s and 1840s, he was thrown into jail because of his religion, never charged with a crime, and forgotten about for six years. When he was finally released, he made his way to the Rocky Mountains and was one of the first settlers in what later became Franklin, Idaho, where he became a very prosperous farmer, rancher, and businessman. Throughout his life he rarely turned down a request for help or a loan. Even in times of poverty and famine, he shared his wheat and wool and the lumber and firewood he dragged down from the canyons through the heavy snows. He even tolerated it without comment when he knew needy people were stealing from him, and he said repeatedly, "I can't seem to give it away as fast as God blesses me with it." He died a happy and greatly loved man—and a wealthy one by the standards of his day. And never at any time was he less than a completely dedicated husband, father, neighbor, and faithful church member.

UNREQUITED LOVE

The love of money is usually a composite of two things: (1) the love of wealth for wealth's sake, usually egged on by the greedy desire to be richer than the next guy; and (2) the love of the things money can buy that confer status and the appearance of success.

Some people may have made a lot of money by loving it to the exclusion of any and all other things. Maybe they have even become very rich, but are miserably unhappy, having lost a lot of things that they eventually learned to their horror were more important than money. And their money never loved them back. You can't cuddle up to it on a cold night.

A PARABLE FOR OUR TIMES

Many people are like the Guadalcanal Island monkeys. Our Marines who took the island from the Japanese thought these cute simians would make terrific pets, so they concocted a strategy to catch them. They would hollow out a coconut and fill it full of rice, leaving only a small hole, and secure it to a tree. The monkey would put its hand into the hole and grab a fistful of rice, but couldn't get its hand out without letting go of the rice, as its clenched fist full of rice was too big to get back out through the hole. The monkeys were easy prey for the Marines, as the greedy little animals were trapped. They had the rice they wanted, but they had lost something much more precious—their freedom.

This is a parable for our times. Poverty has corrupted people, but so has wealth and its accompanying greed. The older I get, the more positive I am that genuine, lasting happiness depends on intangible matters of character and spirit, and the pursuit of wealth tests them all.

Loving your money too much can also cause you to lose it, as I will show you in a minute. But although putting money ahead of much more important things—like family, church, and country—can and sometimes does lead to wealth, it too often also leads to misery. You may have the Midas touch for years, but if you love your money too much, the Midas touch can, to coin a new metaphor, turn everything into old mufflers. There is nothing sadder than a person who has sacrificed marriage and family on the altar of Mammon due to stupid, greed-driven decisions, or even uncontrolled spending on vices, only to find Mammon is a fickle god who often breaks his promises.

Conversely, love of money can lead to loss of wealth because it spawns greed, fear, and covetousness, which can lead to costly emotion-driven bad decisions.

All of these stories set the scene for my point. *Worshipping Mammon—loving money more than family, church, and country—can lead to misery.*

WORKAHOLICS

A letter to Dear Abby illustrates the point.

Dear Abby,

I didn't know I had a problem until the day my wife/lover/ best friend walked out on me two weeks before our 13th anniversary.

All our married life I worked a seven-day-a-week factory job on second shift, and in the mornings managed my own retail business.

I thought everything at home was great. Our house and cars were paid for. We even owned a boat. It turns out that all my wife wanted was for me to hold her, love her, and "be there" for her.

I learned my lesson the hard way. I closed my business, but it's too late. Abby, please warn your readers about the danger of becoming a workaholic. Material things are not worth the price of losing the one person who shares your life.

The ratio of unhappy people to happy people is at least as high among the rich as it is among the poor, if not higher. Money is a two-edged sword that can bless you or curse you, depending on the place you allow it to fill in your heart. Money can be the key that opens the door to all the expensive vices, or it can be a tool to advance the good things in your life, and this depends on your personal decisions. You can decide to be prosperous and miserable, or you can decide to be prosperous and happy, as I did after my bankruptcy. It's really that simple. Notice I said *simple*, not *easy*.

I have evolved some rules to help you put money in its proper place in your life so you can not only make it and keep it, but use it to enhance your happiness, not blight it.

The first set of rules, aimed at the fathers of traditional two-parent families, will insulate them from money's most corrupting influences and make it a source of happiness and a blessing to the whole family. I promise!

RULES FOR FATHERS

Rule #1: Choose a profession that allows you to spend plenty of dedicated time with your spouse and children, even it means less money and a step down in lifestyle. The lost years of your off-spring's childhood can never be recaptured. I know personally many men who have had successful careers and fulfilling family lives at the same time; they can and should go together. If you are struggling over the temptation to trade off riches for family life, let family win the debate. Maybe you need to settle for safe prosperity instead of real riches. Attend every major or minor event in your children's lives—dance recitals, soccer games, and so on— and elevate your wife to queen of your home, but don't be an absentee sovereign.

Rule #2: Set aside one night a week for a family night. We use Mondays. Use it for family activities and outings, game nights, family councils, and lessons in things that are important to your family's moral, spiritual, and ethical growth. This is your only chance to systematically pass on your family's values, history, and traditions so they become part of the family continuum. You can use this time to teach your kids the American history they are not learning in school, or old-fashioned virtues like work, worship, or the Constitution. If you fail to pass on the family baton, your children will grow up like a ship that is all sail and no anchor, drifting with every vagrant wind, and will be suckers for irresponsible peer pressure, as well as the vote-hungry politician's lawful prey.

This is the hardest rule to execute consistently as the kids are drawn in a million directions by school, their social life, and other activities on Monday nights. Our performance in the Ruff house has been less than perfect, but we have tried hard, and it has paid dividends in family togetherness and offspring with character and a sense of belonging to an extended family unit with standards and traditions.

Rule #3: Go over the family finances regularly with the whole family at least once a month. Don't just be a bank with what looks to the kids like an apparently endless supply of money. Make sure the kids know that hard financial choices are a routine part of life. In family financial conferences, you can implant in them a long-term perspective. The kids will moderate their demands on the Bank of Dad as they understand the family's financial parameters.

Rule #4: Don't have a secret financial life with unaccountable amounts of money to spend. No man would become a secret gambler or be tempted to have a mistress on the side if his personal finances were totally transparent. Not doing that can lead to divorce—which is always a financial catastrophe, as I will discuss later. Secret money that is available to finance secret vices can permanently crumble the character of a good man, and cover-up lies can become a reflexive way of life, turning a good man into a chronic liar.

Rule #5: Put aside at least 10 percent of what you make every month to earn compound interest (more about this in Chapter 3). This can be used for debt reduction, investments, bulk buying, entrepreneurial ventures, and bargain hunting, and it's the beginning of your retirement program. It's also a huge deterrent to irresponsible spending.

If you save at least 10 percent of what you make every month to build up a real nest egg, you will have found the antidote to greed and covetousness and the key to financial discipline. All of the Safely Prosperous people in your neighborhood (and there are probably several of them) have built up small or large fortunes by consistent savings over the years. The average American family earns about $3,000 a month, and $300 a month invested prudently can become a huge sum in 10, 20, or 30 years (how much is explored in Chapters 3 and 4).

Rule #6: If you must bring work home from the office, make it a rare exception, or save it until the kids are in bed. Making more money is not an acceptable excuse, and if you consistently spend family time working at home, your wife and kids will get the clear message that you care more about your work than you do about them—and they will be right.

Rule #7: Tithe to someone who can bless others. One evening we were having our regular family prayers, and one of our sons was leading us. Like a lot of kids, he had some ritualized catch phrases that are the easy substitute for genuine spiritual thought. With no real thought, He asked god to "bless the poor, the sick, and the afflicted," and I had an epiphany: "Why are we giving back to God the job he gave us?" From that time on, our prayers became, "God, lead us to those whose lives we can bless as thy servants." Giving away money may be the most important and effective way to eliminate greed and keep things in perspective, as well as to gain the genuine satisfaction and great self-image that comes from knowing that you have made a difference in the world. Do this off the top, or it won't get done. We tithe to our church; you can do it to any worthy cause. A tithe is a tenth, and is the cure for greed and selfishness. If you give away one-tenth of your paycheck every month, it will condition you to not love your money. Consider your income and assets, current and future, as a stewardship to bless others' lives rather than an entitlement.

There is a real payoff for this. When the Old Testament prophet Malachi promised us that if we will no longer "rob God" by not paying our "tithes and offerings," God will "open the windows of Heaven and pour out a blessing so great you can hardly receive it," he may have been talking about things that are more important than money. When your finances or your life are all messed up, you need all the help you can get—even divine help.

With the resulting stash, you can take advantage of bulk buying to save money. You can pay cash for a car or refrigerator, or you can pay the bills if you are sick or laid off. You can provide the seed money for that dream of a business you had. You can also swing for the fences on that great day in the future when the markets offer irresistible values with a terrific risk/reward ratio of at least 1 to10, as discussed in Chapter 16.

Rule #8: Be generous. This is the ultimate inoculation against the love-of-money disease. Never miss an opportunity to help someone in need. Who might that be? They are all around you. Be a soft touch, without thought of reward or even repayment (over and above your 10 percent tithe). My great-grandpa Mayberry learned the Law of Compensating Returns: You can't give it away faster than God blesses you with it. I really believe this works in the real world.

There is no happiness like that found in giving service or other help to someone. The recipient may not even appreciate it. There is an old half-true statement that says, "No good deed goes unpunished," but it doesn't matter: You know, and God knows, and peace of mind and serene nights of sound sleep are the result.

GET THEE BEHIND ME, GREENBACK

The Bible has some wise insights into the corrupting effects of money, such as, "You cannot serve God and Mammon." Those who put money ahead of family, wholesome family recreation, church, charitable works, and so on, usually live blighted lives. It has been driven home to me over and over that most very prosperous or rich people who got their money by single-minded dedication to making money at the expense of other much more important things are terribly unhappy. They are either divorced— sometimes several times—or have desperately unhappy marriages. They are usually estranged from their children and have become easy prey for gold-diggers less than half their age. What they have gained is dwarfed by what they have lost.

RULES FOR MARRIED WOMEN

Now, let's talk to married women.

You are the principal steward for your children, and you are your husband's conscience in keeping emotional and spiritual balance for your family. The following rules apply no matter how much or little your husband brings home.

Rule #1: If there are minor children, make sure one of you is a stay-at-home parent during the preschool bonding years, and I don't care which one—although in the early years, I think mothers are usually a lot better at it. I am not hostile toward working or professional women; I was raised by one. If you need a career, that's OK with me, but if you do, just don't leave your children with minimum-wage day care workers. If there is a great tug of war between making money and having a parent in the home, one of them will lose, although the damage to your children may not show up for years. They may seem to be coping just fine, but the latest research says that they are paying a silent price. Once you have a child, you are no longer a completely free agent. If one of you is not there during the day, you will miss out forever on all the important events of a child's life—the first crawl, the first step, and the first words. They will instead be witnessed by some emotionally uninvolved worker—if he or she is even watching. All those great teaching moments will be lost forever. Accept a smaller home; an older car; a smaller, older TV in exchange for a precious bonding experience. That's worth all the money, personal professional fulfillment, and prestige toys in the world. Some parents have worked it out by having staggered working schedules so one is always home when it matters. The rule is simple: kids come before all other supposed treasures.

Rule #2: Be the custodian and enforcer for the family savings account. Your husband is likely an overgrown kid on the loose all day. If he has unaccounted-for money burning a hole in his pocket, he'll spend it. You must save it and keep it out of his juvenile reach. Get him to agree on a small, fixed allowance he can spend as he chooses and not have to account for, and claim the same for yourself.

Rule #3: Train yourself to be a widow or divorcee. The odds are that you will not have a husband all your life. Statistics show that you will probably be alone for 5 to 10 years, and your adult kids will have to be a part of your financial life. If they have been taught well, they will be there for you when you need them. You have no idea how many new widows or divorcees call our consulting center begging for advice because their husbands had kept them in the dark about the family assets and income. You need to know the location of the insurance policies and the phone number of your agent as well as the location of the stock certificates, CDs, checkbooks, mortgage and payment books, and so on.

Rule #4: Don't let your husband become a workaholic. Insist on a weekly date to some inexpensive restaurant, movie, stage show, or sporting event. Gently but relentlessly suggest (demand?) that he preside over a weekly family night and/or family council and attend all the kids' special events and games and recitals, creating everlasting bonds that will become more and more precious as your lives wind down. Don't let him neglect his familial duties. Some day he'll thank you for it.

Rule #5: Stay out of the expensive social whirl. It will only lead to the keeping-up-with-the-Joneses syndrome, as it once did with us, and that will blow the family budget. It's just an ego thing, anyway. When Thoreau said, "The mass of men lead lives of quiet desperation," he must have meant the Joneses with their Mercedes, their boat, and their relentless, interest-laden credit-card bills.

RULES FOR THE UNMARRIED

Rule #1 through 10: Get married and stay married. A growing numbers of singles are postponing marriage until some undefined time in the future. Sometimes it's because they are getting lots of free sex without commitment in this increasingly permissive and sexualized world. Sometimes they are cohabiting with an undefined future—"We'll probably get married someday."

Often they give financial excuses, such as, "We'd like to get married, but we need to wait until we can afford children," or, "but we want to wait until we can afford a real nice home." They don't realize it, but they are sliding into a hell on earth on their buts.

Numerous studies have confirmed that married people are ultimately healthier, happier, and richer than singles. They are more emotionally stable, have more savings and investments, and make better employees and more successful entrepreneurs. Postponing marriage and childbearing does not seem to help people be more financially successful, perhaps because nothing concentrates the mind like having hungry mouths to feed and the emotional security of loving, being loved, and being committed to a joint future.

DIVORCE: THE FORTUNE WRECKER

Nothing is more devastating to your finances than a divorce; it's always a train wreck. It is an intolerable burden to the divorced husband, and there is rarely enough money to support two households. Poverty-stricken divorced women are almost a cliché, and many men don't make enough money to pay the court-ordered alimony and child support and also support a new marriage and family as they try to rebuild their ruined lives. They are society's most unsympathetic villains if they get behind. The chances for either party to ever have a financially sound future are small indeed.

I'll say it again: Get married and stay married, or be prepared to suffer from the terrible financial penalties that go along with a divorce.

Chapter 3

The Alien in Your Chest

Compound interest can be your best friend or your worst enemy. It is a two-edged sword—far more powerful than you thought.

Do you remember the gut-wrenching moment in the movie *Alien* when the horrible creature that had been quietly growing inside one of the spaceship crewmen suddenly bursts out of his chest? When I first saw that, my first thought was of compound interest on consumer debt. What is compound interest? It's interest earned or charged on top of interest, and, like fire, it is a powerful servant but a fearful master. Why is it like the monster bursting out of the spaceman's chest? Because that's what consumer debt does when your job is threatened in a recession, or when you wake up one day and find that your debt has grown until you cannot service it out of your income.

Compound interest is probably the main reason you won't ever be financially secure. Many corporations have become giants because of compound interest earned at your expense. It has burrowed deep into the lives of millions of families and individuals and quietly gnawed away at their substance 24/7—even while they slept—painlessly and surreptitiously eating their paychecks even before they were earned. Then, when these people

53

are laid off in a recession or over-committed and can't meet their compounding-by-the-second debt service, it can burst out in the form of creditor calls, sleepless nights, daymares, and irresponsible behavior they would never engage in if it were not for their debts.

Much of the money I don't have was lost because I arrogantly ignored my own rules for borrowing. Money already committed for paying compound interest for consumer debt is not available for earning compound interest for the future. I have evolved (usually the hard way) some inexorable rules, including some you may not have heard before, that you must never violate if you want to convert compound interest from your mortal enemy into your best friend.

The first step in doing that is to accumulate a nest egg out of current income by redirecting the money you are now paying out in compound interest on your debts into savings that will pay you compound interest instead. This will turn the power of compounding into your servant instead of the wealth-destroying master it is now.

So far, I probably haven't startled you with the novelty of my wisdom, but that is probably because you have no clue as to the power of this mathematical phenomenon. Albert Einstein, who is rumored to have known something about mathematics, said, "The most amazing mathematical phenomenon is the magic of compounded interest." Let's examine why.

THE INVISIBLE PROSPEROUS PEOPLE IN YOUR NEIGHBORHOOD

There are financially secure people—even millionaires—in your own backyard. They live in nice but modest homes, drive nice but modest cars, live very comfortably, are financially and emotionally secure and debt-free, and a lot better off than you might suppose. Bill Gates is not their kind of guy; they didn't make a big killing in the stock market or invent a super widget that everyone had to have. They took no risks and lost no sleep. They didn't even work hard at building their estates. They just quietly, year after year, used the magical power of compounding to build their fortunes. They are the Safely Prosperous. Compound interest is their friend, and they are on the right side of this powerful force.

Then there are some of your other neighbors that you may envy because they seem so successful. They may also live in nice houses and have nice cars—maybe even a ski boat—in their driveway, but they are living lives of quiet desperation. They have no savings and lose a lot of sleep worrying about their bills, and they are only one missed paycheck away from bankruptcy. And their marriages are battlegrounds—usually over money. Even while they sleep, compound interest is gnawing away at their wealth and their future income. Even a big raise or promotion only enables them to run in place a little faster so they can have a newer, more luxurious car and keep up the illusion of prosperity. Compound interest is their enemy, and they are on the wrong side of it!

COMPOUND INTEREST AS A FRIEND

Richard Russell is the newsletter publisher colleague I respect the most, and he is highly regarded on Wall Street. He is a wise, balanced, real adult who has been around a long time and seen it all, and shares most of my old-fashioned values. Not too long ago he wrote the most popular, most requested article he has published in 40 years of writing. It makes my point better than I could, so I obtained Dick's permission to reprint most of it here.

> Making money is not just starting a business, winning a lottery or a big NBA contract, predicting which way the stock or bond markets are heading, or trying to figure which stock or mutual fund will double over the next few years. For the great majority

of investors, making money requires a plan, self-discipline and desire. I say "for the great majority of people" because if you're a Steven Spielberg or a Bill Gates you don't have to know about the Dow or the markets or about yields or price/earning ratios; you're a phenomenon in your field, and you're going to make big money as a by-product of your talent and ability. But this kind of genius is rare.

For the average investor, you and me, we're not geniuses so we have to have a financial plan. In view of this, I offer below a few principles that we must be aware of if we are serious about making money.

One of the most important lessons for living in the modern world is that to survive you've got to have money. But to live (survive) *happily*, you must have love, health (mental and physical), freedom, intellectual stimulation—and money. When I taught my kids about money, the first thing I taught them was the use of the "money bible." What's the money bible? Simple, it's a volume of *the compounding-interest tables*.

Compounding is the royal road to riches. Compounding is the safe road, the sure road, and fortunately, anybody can do it. To compound successfully you need the following: **perseverance** to keep you firmly on the savings path; **intelligence** to understand what you are doing, and why; and knowledge **of the mathematics tables** in order to comprehend the amazing rewards that will come to you if you faithfully follow the compounding road. And, of course, you need **time**—time to allow the power of compounding to work for you. Remember, *compounding only works through time*.

But there are two catches in the compounding process.

The first is obvious—compounding may involve *sacrifice* (you can't spend it and still save it).

Second, compounding is *boring—b-o-r-i-n-g*, or should I say it's boring until (after seven or eight years) the money starts to pour in. Then, believe me, compounding becomes downright fascinating!

Table 3.1   The Power of Compounding, Part I

| | Investor A | | Investor B | |
Age	Contribution	Year-End Value	Contribution	Year-End Value
8	0	0	0	0
9	0	0	0	0
10	0	0	0	0
11	0	0	0	0
12	0	0	0	0
13	0	0	0	0
14	0	0	0	0
15	0	0	0	0
16	0	0	0	0
17	0	0	0	0
18	0	0	0	0
19	0	0	$2,000	$2,200
20	0	0	2,000	4,620
21	0	0	2,000	7,282
22	0	0	2,000	10,210
23	0	0	2,000	13,431
24	0	0	2,000	16,974
25	0	0	2,000	20,872
26	$2,000	$2,200	0	22,959
27	2,000	4,620	0	25,255
28	2,000	7,282	0	27,780
29	2,000	10,210	0	30,558
30	2,000	13,431	0	33,614
31	2,000	16,974	0	36,976
32	2,000	20,872	0	40,673
33	2,000	25,159	0	44,741
34	2,000	29,875	0	49,215
35	2,000	35,062	0	54,136
36	2,000	40,769	0	59,550
37	2,000	47,045	0	65,505
38	2,000	53,950	0	72,055
39	2,000	61,545	0	79,261
40	2,000	69,899	0	87,187
41	2,000	79,089	0	95,905
42	2,000	89,198	0	105,496
43	2,000	100,318	0	116,045
44	2,000	112,550	0	127,650
45	2,000	126,005	0	140,415
46	2,000	140,805	0	154,456
47	2,000	157,086	0	169,902
48	2,000	174,995	0	186,892
49	2,000	194,694	0	205,581
50	2,000	216,364	0	226,140
51	2,000	240,200	0	248,754
52	2,000	266,420	0	273,629
53	2,000	295,262	0	300,992
54	2,000	326,988	0	331,091
55	2,000	361,887	0	364,200
56	2,000	400,276	0	400,620
57	2,000	442,503	0	440,682
58	2,000	488,953	0	484,750
59	2,000	540,049	0	533,225
60	2,000	596,254	0	586,548
61	2,000	658,079	0	645,203
62	2,000	726,087	0	709,723
63	2,000	800,896	0	780,695
64	2,000	883,185	0	858,765
65	2,000	973,704	0	944,641

In order to emphasize the power of compounding, I am including this extraordinary study [Table 3.1], courtesy of **Market Logic** of Fort Lauderdale, Florida 33306.

In this study we assume that investor **B** opens an IRA at age 19. For seven consecutive periods he puts $2,000 in his IRA at an average growth rate of 10% (7% interest plus growth). After seven years, this fellow makes **NO MORE** contributions—he's finished.

A second investor (**A**) makes no contributions until age 26 (this is the age when investor **B** was finished with his contributions). Then A continues faithfully to contribute $2,000 every year until he's 65 (at the same theoretical 10%).

Now study the incredible difference between **B** who made only *seven contributions* but made them earlier, and **A** who made *40 contributions* but at **a later time.** The difference is that B had *seven more years of compounding* than A, simply because he started earlier. Those seven early years were worth more than all of A's thirty-three additional contributions combined. [Richard's lesson? Start today.]

This is a study I suggest you show to your kids. It's a study I've lived by, and I can tell you, "It works." You can work your compounding with muni bonds, with a good money market fund, with T-bills or five-year T-notes.

Let me interrupt Dick for a moment.

The amazing thing about his example is the small amount necessary to invest in order to achieve these results. The total net earnings weren't the real difference—$893,704 for investor A against $930,641 for investor B. But the out-of-pocket amounts invested were wildly different—$80,000 over 39 years for investor A, earning an 11-fold return, against only $14,000 over only seven years for investor B, earning a 66-fold return!

Because of compound interest, careless spending has a hidden cost. Due to the lost compounding, every dollar bill spent today for consumer goods or for compound interest on your consumer loans, instead of being invested to earn compound interest, could cost you as much as $20 at retirement time, depending on how many years until retirement. Borrowing at compound interest in order to buy things you could not otherwise afford devours your substance into the foreseeable future.

I have worked out a few more examples of the power of compounding to drive home the point. If you put aside only $40 a month, compounded yearly, and invest it at 8 percent, you will be astounded at how much richer you will be in the future:

After 5 years, you will have $2,980.
After 15 years, you will have $15,034.
After 20 years, you will have $24,763.
After 30 years, you will have $59,480.

If you blow $300 twice a year in Las Vegas for transportation, beer, smokes, or the slots, you just kissed off $71,397 thirty years from now.

Now, back to Dick.

[The typical investor] doesn't comprehend the power of compounding, and he doesn't understand money. He's never heard the adage, "**He who understands interest earns it. He who doesn't understand interest pays it.**"

But here's the irony; if from the beginning the little guy had adopted a strict policy of never spending more than he made, if he had taken his extra savings and compounded it in intelligent, income-producing securities, then in due time he'd have money coming in daily, weekly, monthly, just like the rich man. The little guy would have become a financial winner, instead of a pathetic loser.

So what investments can safely compound your money? As you consider these possibilities, remember that compounding by its very nature means earning interest on your interest. It requires that the interest be reinvested. It is important to maintain your stream of income from salary or business profits to live on as long as possible so you won't have to spend your interest until your estate is meeting your financial objectives and is earning enough interest to meet your needs—and, yes, your wants.

CHANGING OUTGO INTO INCOME

The first alternative is by far the simplest and offers the greatest guaranteed return. This can help anyone with a savings account, but it is especially useful for those who already have savings invested in low-interest bank deposits and money-market funds.

Let's say you have a 2 percent savings account and a 24 percent credit-card balance. If you pay off the credit card with the savings money, it's the functional equivalent of switching from a 2 percent investment to a 24 percent investment. It's the biggest riskless yield you can get anywhere. And there are other choices:

- Some "safe" investments offer no chance of either capital loss or profit—just a slow, steady, dependable, guaranteed yield and a guaranteed principal. These include bank savings accounts, T-bills, money-market funds, and mortgages. The bank and the money market fund will automatically reinvest your interest, making compounding easy and automatic. The downside? The yields can be very low (less than 1 percent as this is written) and, after taxes and inflation, offer a smaller return—even a negative real return—although these rates will not stay low forever. However, with T-bills and mortgages, you will have to actively put the interest immediately back to work earning interest to get the benefit of compounding.
- Some investments, such as Treasury notes, Treasury bonds, and corporate and municipal bonds, offer a fixed return and higher yield (around 4.5 percent as this is written)

with safety of principal but with a chance of capital gains or losses. These investments are all interest rate–sensitive, meaning that your principal can fluctuate up and down in market value as interest rates fluctuate. Generally speaking, when interest rates in the marketplace are rising, these investments tend to fall in value. When interest rates are falling, they tend to rise in value, and can even be more profitable than stocks. Let me explain why.

If you bought a $1,000 10-year Treasury note yielding 5 percent, you would get a guaranteed $50 a year in interest for the life of the note—no more, no less—and when it matured, you would not only have earned your interest, you would also get your $1,000 back. T-notes are risk-free if held to maturity.

However, if market interest rates rose to 10 percent, your note with a fixed contractual return of $50 a year would only be half as attractive to a buyer as a newly issued note paying 10 percent a year, or $100. Many people think that if you buy a 10-year T-note you have to hold it for 10 years until it matures, but that's not so. There is an active, liquid market for T-notes accessible through any broker, so you could sell the note whenever you wanted; but when market interest rates were higher than your yield, the note would have to sell at a big discount (as much as 50 percent) to make the effective yield competitive for the new buyer.

To illustrate this point, let's say that when interest rates were high, such as in 1981, you bought a T-bond yielding 14 percent—paying $140 a year. Interest rates subsequently fell to 7 percent just a handful of years later, so this bond as much as doubled in market value, as it was now yielding twice as much as a newly issued T-bond. This, of course, was affected by how close to maturity the bond was.

Even though the rule is pretty simple, let me say it again: *When interest rates go up, note and bond prices go down, and when interest rates go down, note and bond prices go up.* But whatever the investment, the interest, dividends, or capital gains must be reinvested, not spent, or there will be no compounding. Failure to compound can mean hundreds of thousands of dollars less when you are about to retire.

So, buy fixed-return debt instruments only when interest rates are rising, high and stable, or trending down, unless you are positive you will hold it to maturity. Lock in the high rates and compound them by reinvesting the earned interest, and enjoy some potential capital gains as well.

One of the most profitable calls in my quarter century as a financial editor and publisher occurred in 1981. After several years of steadily rising interest rates, new 30-year T-bonds were yielding a historic high of 16 percent. I believed interest rates would fall as low as 7 percent, so I urged my subscribers to buy 30-year T-bonds. We not only locked in juicy all-time-high yields, but a few years later when rates on newly issued T-bonds fell to 7 percent, we sold and reaped capital gains as high as 100 percent, in addition to our terrific interest. This "conservative" investment was much more profitable than even the most profitable stocks over the same period, with no risk of losing the capital.

The nice thing about investing in government securities is its simplicity; with stocks, you always have to evaluate the business prospects for the individual company and its industry group as well as the market as a whole. With corporate and municipal bonds (munis), you also have to worry about the credit rating of the issuer, as a drop in the credit rating by the organizations that rate them means an instant drop in value, and most of the credit surprises are to the downside. With Treasury securities you only have to worry about the trend of interest rates. But that's what guys like me are for.

Munis do have one great advantage over T-bonds—the interest is tax-free. But this tax advantage can be shared by T-bonds if you buy them for your IRA or 401(k) or other tax-free or tax-deferred savings account. And the interest on T-bonds or notes is not subject to state taxes.

A VARIETY OF CHOICES

As this is written, most people assume they can't get more interest than the pittance of less than 1 percent they can currently earn in a bank passbook account or a money market fund. But there are always lots of alternatives for decent yields of as much as 20 percent with reasonable risk. We will explore some of these choices in Chapter 5. They are only for-instances in a changing world and may not be good choices by the time you read this, but they are a great place to start looking, and there are always such opportunities, regardless of what the banks are paying.

I have little sympathy for those who complain about low passbook rates just because they are too lazy to dig a little bit for the luscious rates that are always there to be found with a little work. It takes at least 6 percent to make compound interest your real friend, and that's always doable.

WHAT TO DO ABOUT RISING RATES

So now you know what to buy when interest rates are falling or staying low, but what do you invest in when interest rates are rising? That's easy: a money-market fund. These funds invest your money in very short-term notes and bills, ranging from T-bills maturing in as little as 30 days to short-term (even overnight) commercial paper. As interest rates rise, the funds are rolling over their entire portfolios in as little as 30 days into paper paying increasingly higher interest rates, and most of that is passed on to your account, so you benefit from rising interest rates. Money-market funds have one other big advantage: You can start a money-market fund account with as little as $100 and keep saving until you have enough money to buy a bond or a T-bill or T-note when the time is right.

In summary, anyone can benefit from compounding, and total returns around 10 percent (interest and capital gains) can be earned year after year, even when interest rates are generally low. All it takes is a little discipline and the ability to keep your eyes firmly fixed on the future. Let me illustrate that principle with a true story.

When I was getting my pilot's license, my instructor would tell me to fly straight and level at a certain compass heading and altitude. That was easier said than done. I found myself wandering all over the sky—up 300 feet, down 200 feet, or with the nose of the plane swinging as much as 10°, 15°, or 20° to one side or the other while I switched attention from the altimeter to the compass or vice versa. Then my instructor gave me some very wise advice that has been useful in other areas of my life. He said, "Point the nose of the plane on the compass heading you want to fly, and then pick out the farthest landmark that you can see straight ahead—a mountain, a pass, a building—and keep your eyes on it and fly toward it." To my amazement, the plane settled down, and straight and level became automatic and natural.

So how does this apply to the subject at hand? Keeping your eye on the long-term objective will help you to avoid the bad short-term decisions that can cost you hundreds of thousands of dollars at retirement time.

NIBBLED TO DEATH BY DUCKS

Your personal balance sheet is probably pathetic compared to those of the truly prosperous people in your neighborhood; however, the erosion of your potential wealth by doing stupid things didn't happen all at once. It was a lifelong process, sort of like being nibbled to death by ducks. You have probably been nickel-and-diming yourself to death.

I have now taught you the importance of compounding your money, but how will you get the money to start saving and compounding? That's easy: Become a plumber and plug the leaks!

DOING YOUR OWN PLUMBING: BIG LEAK #1

First, you are destroying your future with the really big leak—compound interest payments on charge accounts, car loans, and credit cards. But even with a sudden rush of frugality, it may still be a while until you are far enough out of debt to be able to divert much of that interest money into a savings program to convert compounding from a ravening monster of an enemy into a faithful but powerful servant. So where can you start accumulating some money now to begin to get on the right side of compound interest, as it's obvious that time is of the essence?

THE WAGES OF SIN: BIG LEAK #2

You could change a few things right now with very little pain that could make a five- or six-figure difference in 20 or 30 years. Here are some cold hard numbers.

Alcohol

The average American family drinks two six-packs of beer and/or a dozen bottles of soda a week. This costs you at least $9 a week, or $35 a month. If you gave up the brew and started putting that $35 a month into an interest-bearing account at only 8 percent, you would have $23,096 in 20 years. Unless you are a chronic alcoholic, this involves only the most minor inconvenience or sacrifice.

I don't know just how much I have saved over 46 years of marriage by being a teetotaler, when I take my wife out to dinner and don't order wine, but it's a lot—a whole lot.

Smoking

Let's assume you have a one-pack-a-day habit. That means you are spending $4 a day, or $120 a month. If you had invested that in a money-market fund at only 6 percent, you would have—are you sitting down?—$70,682 in 20 years! And you are much more likely to be alive to enjoy it because you probably wouldn't have died of lung cancer, emphysema, a heart attack, or some other painful and loathsome disease. Yes, a real nicotine habit is hard to kick, and you may have made dozens of false starts, but maybe I have just given you a serious financial incentive to kick an expensive, dirty habit.

But what if you have no expensive vices to repent of? Is saving money hopeless?

CREATING SAVINGS OUT OF NOTHING

I know women who save their families $20 or $30 a month just by clipping coupons, learning to change their own oil, or sewing or mending the family clothing. That's enough to make a real start on building some real wealth through compounding.

How about going out to eat at an inexpensive Chinese or Thai restaurant every other date night instead of some ritzy joint where the food tastes no better and costs two or three times as much? You will save $20 to $40 bucks twice a month.

How about waiting until the biggest hit movies come to the local dollar theater or on video, instead of paying the $9 regular admission for each of you? That's worth about $35 to $70 a month.

There is hardly a family in America that couldn't save and put away 20, 30, or 50 bucks every month. They just need a clear picture of their long-term goals and a grasp of the power of compounding and the financial rewards of even a modicum of self-control and personal discipline.

Here are a few more suggestions gleaned from *The Wall Street Journal*.

Trim Your Insurance Bill

Stay clear of expensive whole life insurance, and buy cheaper term insurance instead, at least until your newfound prosperity makes it worthwhile to take advantage of the tax benefits whole life can provide. As you near retirement, reduce your coverage to lower your premiums; you don't need as much coverage as a young wage earner with dependent children. You can save the difference and earn compound interest on the money.

Redirect Your Education Dollars

Fifty-year-old people usually no longer have to spend money on education as the kids graduate from college. Invest the money and create a compounding cash cushion for yourself.

TAX-FREE SAVINGS

Because your plan can be aborted by taxes on your interest and other investment returns, cutting the money available to compound, you have to seriously consider putting as much of your savings as possible into a tax-exempt or tax-deferred account, such as an IRA or a 401(k). This can make a huge difference over time. Consider the following.

Stocks and Bonds

The real optimists assume there will be an average annual return of 8 percent in the stock market over time. I think that's a dubious proposition, but let's accept it for the sake of discussion. After you have paid 1.5 percentage points for taxes, your yield is down to 6.5 percent. Then knock off another 3.5 points for inflation and investment costs. You are now down to only 2 percent a year in a best case. If you dodge the taxes in an IRA, the real return is 3.5 percent. Not humongous, but still worth compounding.

With bonds, the results are more predictable because, unlike the case with stocks, the returns are guaranteed and riskless. A bond fund that owns a mix of corporate and government securities might start out with a 5 percent yield, but in a tax-exempt IRA, you will save about one-fourth of the bite from inflation, taxes, and investment costs.

The lesson is clear: Investing outside of a tax-exempt or tax-deferred account is like foolishly pouring real money down the toilet.

Tax-Deferred Retirement Accounts

Set up and max out your IRA account. The limit you can set aside now is $2,000 a year each for you and your spouse, but that will rise to $5,000 a year by 2008. If you are over 50, you can take advantage of a catch-up provision by adding another $500 a year, and as much as $1,000 a year starting in 2006.

The big savings will be found in a 401(k) account. You can currently invest $11,000 tax-exempt each year, and that will increase by $1,000 a year up to a total of $20,000 a year. Just make sure you diversify. Don't "Enronize" your retirement by putting all your eggs in one crumbling basket.

BIG OAKS FROM LITTLE ACORNS GROW

Table 3.2 can help you decide just how much you want to put away every month and for how many years. It shows you how unbelievably huge even small compounded amounts of money can grow to be at 8 percent in 15, 20, 25, and 30 years in a tax-exempt or tax-deferred account.

WHY THE POOR GET POORER

I recently saw a young mother at the supermarket with three children and a grocery cart full of beer, pop, cigarettes, frozen casseroles, and junk food that cost several times what the wholesome food in the same store would have cost them. After

Table 3.2 The Power of Compounding, Part II

Dollars Invested Monthly	15 Years	20 Years	25 Years	30 Years
$ 10	$ 3,460	$ 5,890	$ 9,510	$ 14,904
20	6,920	11,780	19,020	29,800
30	10,380	17,670	28,530	44,700
50	17,300	29,450	47,550	74,500
100	34,600	58,900	95,100	149,000
200	69,207	117,800	90,200	298,000
300	103,800	176,700	285,300	447,100

she paid for much of it with a credit card, she hauled it out to a 10-year-old jalopy and drove off.

I probably shouldn't judge her. Maybe she has an abusive, alcoholic husband. Maybe she's a divorcee or a widow or a deserted wife. The sad thing is that she doesn't have a clue about the principles we're talking about here. She's young, and in 20 or 30 years she could be very prosperous with a healthy balance sheet. The hard part would be to persuade her to change her whole perspective on money, and that is a monumental task.

We've all read the news stories of the manual laborer, maybe the janitor of the local school, who died and, to everyone's shock, left a fortune to a local church or charity—or pet cat. Where do such people get the money? They frugally and carefully saved, and usually the power of compounding took over.

This example strikes close to home. Kay's dad, Carl Felt, was the custodian at the local high school for years and managed to accumulate more than $45,000, which he was able to loan me at a time when my business needed it. (I doubled his money in a year.)

PAY YOURSELF FIRST

The biggest factor in your investment plan should be a generous savings program. Americans are saving at the lowest rate in history—just under 4 percent, up from only 3 percent in 2001. If you're serious about having a prosperous retirement, simply put aside in an interest-bearing account at least 10 percent of what you make every month! This may seem impossible to many of you, as there always seems to be too much month left at the end of your money, and expenditures tend to rise to meet income. The only way this will work is if you do it the minute you receive your paycheck. That will also discipline you to begin some of the economies I have discussed earlier in this chapter.

So what's the payoff for this kind of discipline? The average American family takes home about $3,000 a month. Saving 10 percent of that means $300 a month going into a money market fund or savings account. That's $3,600 a year. After 20 years of compounding at only 8 percent, that adds up to $176,700. In 25 years, it's $285,300. In 30 years, it's an amazing $447,100! Is that worth it?

This is pretty old-fashioned, fuddy-duddy stuff, and it's really out of style in today's live-it-up environment, but it has worked throughout history and it will work now and in the future. The math is inexorable—as sure as the rising and setting of the sun. The biggest problem is emotional: The payoff is long-term, and the sacrifices are right now. It takes maturity, a fundamental change of heart about the importance of material things in your life, a conscious decision to change your lifestyle, and a clear understanding of the value of long-term thinking as opposed to short-term thinking. It also doesn't hurt to have an attitude of gratitude for what you do have—an appreciation for the blessings that are so abundant in America. As you cultivate this attitude, you will find more contentment with less stuff, righteous pride in being increasingly debt-free, and a growing satisfaction in the security you are inexorably building for your old age. (And you won't be able to depend on Social Security to take care of you; see Chapter 6.)

As I wrote this chapter, I realized with a sinking feeling how few of the things I espouse here I have consistently applied to my own life. I have made really big bucks in my lifetime, and when the money was pouring in, it seemed endless and hard times seemed in another galaxy. But if I had saved 10 percent out of each paycheck and allowed the interest to compound, I would now have several million dollars more than I have now and would not have had to go through the financial roller coaster my life has been in recent years.

So, do as I say, not as I did. I don't have enough time left for the full power of compounding to work for me to the max (remember, sometimes I wish I was 72 again!), but Kay and I are now implementing the suggestions in this book. With a little luck, I might have 15 or 20 years to watch my own advice pay off. I have beaten cancer and a mild heart attack, so I'm pretty tough, and you probably couldn't kill me with an axe, and if I don't drive too fast and avoid sharp implements, I might live forever. Don't bet against it.

Chapter 4

The Great American Lie

Pretending to be rich by selling your future to buy the big house, the big SUV, the big home theater, the big boat, while living a life of quiet desperation when the monthly bills come in

Having a lot of consumer debt is the single most wealth-destroying mistake you can make because the compound interest you pay destroys your future even as you sleep. It's the turnpike to Financial Hell. Getting into consumer debt has demolished the futures of millions of people, because it's so easy to do. Merchants all around you will gladly loan you money to buy cars, furniture, vacation cabins, cruises, designer clothes, computers, appliances, cruises, jewelry, video cameras, home entertainment centers, motor homes, expensive dinners at fine restaurants. Anything the mind can conceive that you don't really need and can't really afford can be financed or put on a credit card; it's a kind of sweet slavery.

LIAR, LIAR, PANTS ON FIRE!

And it's a terrible threat to America! Why? Because our whole economy is built on a lie. Millions upon millions of people are big liars, only pretending to be rich. Maybe you envy them because they have two late-model cars, a big house, kids in college, a ski boat in the driveway, a home theater, two or three of the latest upgraded computers, and maybe even season tickets for major-league professional sports, at $50 to $200 per seat per game. And you can't tell the liars from the honest people by the medallions on their cars or the size of their houses. All that probably tells you is how far they are in debt. The truth is that they don't really own all that stuff; anonymous lenders own it. And sooner or later, all liars eventually get caught. In this case, they will be exposed for what they are if (or when) the economy really turns sour and they lose their jobs, their businesses fall on hard times, their investment portfolios take a dive, or their pension plans come up short. The liars' biggest enemy is a recession—or, Heaven help us all—a depression, because it rips away the facade and reveals the empty shell inside. Most of these liars are only one or two paychecks away from bankruptcy. Collectively, they have created the biggest bubble in human history—the debt bubble. Maybe we should rename it the liars' bubble.

DOES POLLYANNA HAVE A POINT?

"So what's so bad about debt?" I hear you Pollyannas say. "After all, it enables me to live as if I were rich, and it keeps the wheels of commerce turning. Without credit, I wouldn't own a nice late-model Lexus, a ski boat, a big-screen TV, and our lovely home in a nice neighborhood. Debt enables my family to have a much better life while we are young enough to enjoy it."

That's the seductive siren call of debt, and it seems to work out fine as long as the economy is moving upward so we have our jobs, our income continues to grow, our employer remains secure and solvent, there are no major health emergencies so we can't work, we don't get a divorce, and the present prosperity lasts indefinitely into the future.

But there are some growing clouds on the horizon. Millions of

Americans are beginning to worry about their debts and are calling companies that have sprung up like weeds that claim to help worried people deal with their debts. Even worse, bankruptcies have been setting new records every quarter, starting in the last two allegedly prosperous Clinton quarters, and the pace is accelerating. Millions of people are right on the edge of catastrophe, and living lives of quiet desperation.

Soaring debt has made us obscenely vulnerable if a recession or depression shatters our dreams of solvency, or if our appetites get bigger than our incomes can support. Enough people getting collectively in financial trouble will cause a debt implosion that will destroy the balance sheets of America's biggest banks and corporations that loaned them the money. And that's exactly what will happen when a recession becomes deep enough that millions of people lose their jobs, find they can't make their monthly payments, and finally file for bankruptcy. Millions of apparently prosperous families are so overextended that being out of work for only two or three months means the end of the big lie. When someone files for bankruptcy, an asset (their debt) is wiped out of some lender's balance sheet, and another chunk of America's wealth disappears as though it had never existed. A major debt implosion will be as deflationary as the Depression of the 1930s; wealth will disappear along with its purchasing power, the money supply will shrink, and lines may again be forming at Salvation Army soup kitchens.

For many years we have nurtured the delusion that the prosperous and dependable present will remain prosperous and dependable forever. As Neal A. Maxwell has said, "Too many of us seem to expect that life will flow ever smoothly, featuring an unbroken chain of green lights with empty parking places just in front of our destinations." History tells us that is an impossible dream. Every 50 to 70 years we have to live through a depression, and the last one began more than 70 years ago. All it takes to create a depression is for a recession to get deep enough to trigger mass layoffs and personal and corporate bankruptcies, taking our corporate dominoes and overextended consumers—first one by one, then by the millions. As this is written, despite apparent good times, we are flirting with such a depression, although I hope with all my heart that we can stave it off.

The bottom line? Corporate and personal consumer debt has created an increasingly vulnerable society as tens of millions of fragile balance sheets are built on an increasingly shaky foundation of consumer debt.

So why do we voluntarily rush to create and submit to such dangerous chains? Because these chains are like a tree that bears bittersweet fruit, even though the bitter usually lives on long after the sweet is history. This fruit is the by-product of a near universal human tendency—the craving for instant gratification.

RUFF'S RULES OF DEBT MANAGEMENT

Out of my own painful experience and the observed experience of others, over the years I have evolved Ruff's Rules of Debt Management to help you fight off this most seductive and carnivorous temptation and convert it into positive cash flow, earned compound interest, and a growing estate, thereby insulating yourself from the coming debt bubble implosion.

Ask yourself an honest question: If your regular paycheck was cut off for one, two, or three months, would you be in trouble? Are you really sure your monthly income would never be in danger? Do you really know your employer isn't another Enron, WorldCom, or United Airlines? Are you positive your pension plan is fully funded and earning enough money on its portfolio to stay solvent when the stock market is imploding and banks are paying 1 percent interest?

Even if there is no universal catastrophe, many of you are already sweating over your debts and considering a little of the hair of the dog that bit you. Maybe you are thinking of borrowing to the hilt against your home equity to maintain your standard of living, thereby increasing your debt total and turning an asset that should be your ultimate security into a bigger dagger aimed at your heart. Or possibly you have borrowed from relatives or friends, transferring your risks to them. Maybe you are only one or two missed paychecks away from bankruptcy.

According to government statistics, consumer spending is now exceeding income, and as the gap can only be bridged by more borrowing, total debt is growing much faster than the economy. I forecasted in early 2000, long before the bombing of the World Trade Center, that we were sliding into a deep recession or depression, which would have happened even without the New York catastrophe. Company after company was already laying off thousands of workers, and job security was slipping away at an accelerating pace. But conversely—and perhaps perversely—even in the face of that painfully obvious economic slowdown, in late 2003 Americans are still blithely borrowing to buy cars and big appliances, the Fed is pumping up the money supply and cutting interest rates to keep the credit ball rolling, and Wall Street remains mindlessly optimistic, just as it did between 1929 and 1932 as the world slid inexorably into the abyss of the Great Depression. Debt is so much a part of the national psyche that, perversely, the monetary powers that be look on rising consumer debt as a "positive indicator," and we have to run faster as a nation just to stay in place.

Let's face it, the old-fogy national philosophical and moral debate about debt is over, and instant gratification has won. In the wake of the World Trade Center bombing, we were even told that borrowing and consuming was "a patriotic duty." If we don't keep borrowing and spending, "the terrorists have won." What madness!

Let's look at some data so you can see if you have been as foolish as your neighbors.

MEASURING UP

- The average household has as many as five credit cards with an average balance of $4,000 each, at an average interest rate of 18.9 percent or more. That means that if you are that hypothetical average American, you pay at least an average of $756 in interest every year per card. If you make the minimum monthly payment, it will take you 41 years to pay it off. You will pay more than $12,000 in interest *per card*, three times your original principal balance. The typical minimum monthly payment is 90 percent interest and 10 percent principal.
- If you didn't have average credit-card payments starting at $80 per month, and instead invested that money every month in an 8 percent tax-free savings plan (such as an IRA) for 40 years, you would retire with $151,000 in the bank. At 6 percent it would total $78,000. So credit cards not only cost you thousands of dollars in interest, they also keep you from building a retirement estate earning compound interest every day, every hour, every minute. Those payments not only hurt you now, they destroy your future. Rather than giving your money to the credit-card company for the rest of your life, here is another opportunity to avoid the middleman and flush your money down the toilet.
- Americans paid out approximately $65 billion in compound interest in the year 2000, and despite the highly touted, alleged Clinton prosperity, a record 1.3 million Americans filed for bankruptcy, wiping out untold billions of dollars in lenders' balance sheets. That figure rose sharply in 2001 and 2002. If that has happened in good times, imagine what would happen in a really deep recession!
- The credit-card debt bubble may be deflating as I write, because payment delinquencies are rising. In the second

quarter of 2001, they rose one-third above the delinquency rate for the first quarter. In fact, delinquencies are at the highest rate since the government began tracking them in 1980.

We are suffering from a national infantile inability to postpone gratification. I remember seeing a sign of the times in a roadside diner in Arkansas that read, "Lord, give me the gift of patience, and I want it right now!" It's become the American way.

Following are the seven rules I have evolved over the years to keep you out of consumer debt trouble.

1. Borrow only to buy a home and one car, and in an emergency to replace a leaky roof or a necessary appliance, such as a washer or refrigerator, or perhaps for an education. Pay cash for everything else, or do without. Most homebuyers buy the biggest house the mortgage broker says they can afford based on the mortgage payment, and it's usually a lot more house than they really need. Less is more if you are trying to accumulate an investment stake. Also, the smaller it is, the sooner it will be paid off.

2. Use cheap mortgage debt only to pay off expensive consumer debt. I express this principle like porcupines making love—very carefully! If you have 18 to 24 percent nondeductible interest credit card or charge account balances, refinancing or taking out a home equity loan with 5 percent or less tax-deductible interest and paying off the credit card balances makes a lot of sense, depending on what you do with the money. If you use it to buy big-ticket consumer items like a more expensive car or a European vacation—or even worse, as a down payment to buy something you don't really need, incurring even more debt—it's a really lousy idea. More about this later. Use mortgage debt to pay off your high-interest debt, thus slashing your monthly

outgo and freeing up money every month to add to your wealth accumulation stash and maximize the power of compounding in your life. This is one of the smartest things you can do. Paying off your home mortgage should be your ultimate goal, although it is the last debt you will liquidate. This is a very old-fashioned idea. Six decades ago when I was a kid, I remember being at my Aunt Erva and Uncle Earl's mortgage-burning party. Mortgage burners are an endangered species, and it's a lot easier to reach that goal if you have a more modest house.

3. You need one good new or late-model car that you intend to drive until you have to shoot it to put it out of its misery. Unfortunately, a luxury car can be like a boat, which is a hole in the water into which you throw money. A BMW, a Lexus, or a Mercedes is nothing but a money-eating ego trip. If you buy a new car, prepare yourself mentally and emotionally to drive it at least 5 to 10 years. It will still get you from here to there sitting down in relative air-conditioned comfort, if you baby it. I love my seven-year-old town car when I'm on the interstate. If you start craving a new car, don't yield! Buy a lovely used car that is at least two to three years old. By the third year it will be about 40 percent cheaper than when it was new. I recently bought a two-year-old Yukon Denali for cash and saved about $18,000.

4. Seriously consider trying to get along with just one car. Just the money you save on insurance, if invested in safe, interest-bearing instruments, could mean as much as several hundred thousand dollars at retirement time. If you really need a second car—which can be a necessity for a young suburban couple with children—buy an older car for Dad to drive to work, preferably one you can pay cash for or at least pay off in no more than a year, then let Mom drive the newer family car.

5. Not all debt is bad; in fact, you will discover in Chapter 15

that the Really Rich are often heavily in debt. Borrowed money is an essential tool if you want to become rich, so it's not just okay to borrow to fund a new business or to buy income-producing assets, it's an essential tool on the way to real riches. But there is one fundamental rule: Only borrow if the borrowed money when put to work will produce enough dependable cash flow to service the debt from day one, so the debt will be self-liquidating. Then, when it is paid off, you will be left with more assets and no debt. When Ted Turner was asked how rich he was, he said, "I must be really rich, because I owe a lot of money." He built CNN, TNT, and TBS with borrowed money.

6. The most urgent short-term goal of your newfound frugality is to accumulate cash equal to six months of contractual obligations and living expenses, such as mortgage payments and living expenses like food and other real necessities. That way, if you lose your income stream for any reason, you can still pay your bills.

7. Get rid of your debts as fast as possible so you can redirect your former compound-interest-paying payments into compound-interest-earning investments.

A STRATEGY TO EMULATE

There's a couple I've known for several years. (I've concealed their identity at their request to protect their privacy.) The husband is employed by a company whose stock was red-hot during the bull market, and they had both stock and options. After a lot of prayer and soul-searching discussion, they took the counsel of their church leaders, liquidated their stock holdings, and paid off their house. Free of mortgage payments, they were now liquid with money in the bank, and were able to help when a relative became unemployed. They are very secure and happy with their newfound freedom from the tyranny of debt.

Their decision to sell their stock earned them the derision of the husband's coworkers during the hot stock market of the late 1990s, but after the high-tech stock collapse of 2000, the stock they sold is now worth a fraction of what it was when they liquidated. They managed to turn a paper asset into real wealth before the fickle stock market swept away their phantom profits.

"THOU SHALT NOT COVET"

Most, if not all, of humanity's ills are because of our failure to obey the Ten Commandments. We can all agree we shouldn't lie, steal, or kill, we should honor our parents, and so on. But why is there a prohibition against coveting among God's Top Ten, and what does this have to do with debt?

In modern times, to covet means to want something you can't or shouldn't buy just because your neighbors have one, and it is the root of irresponsible borrowing. Drive down any street in an upper-middle-class or wealthy part of town and look at the boats, cars, and big houses. I'll bet you anything that not more than 1 in 25 of these households is free of consumer debt and that many of them are sweating bullets over their monthly bills. Even so, you covet what they have. The irony is that you will be judging their apparent wealth not by how much they earn, but by how much they are in debt.

It's an almost self-evident truism that expenditures rise to meet income, no matter how much money you make. Even though you are probably already worried that there will be too much month left at the end of your money, when Jones has a new boat in his driveway you want one too. Jones gets a new Mercedes, so you trade in your two-year-old Ford for an Audi or a Lexus. Jones and his wife go on a vacation to the Caribbean, so you use your credit card to cruise the Baltic or the Mediterranean or Alaska. You mortgage your future to keep up with the Joneses. You covet!

It all seems harmless as long as your income is rising or stable and you can make your payments, but servicing as much as $70,000 to $100,000 in high-interest credit-card debt, as many big fat liars do, will cost you as much as $20,000 a year in interest and many hundreds of thousands of dollars at retirement time. You are a slave to those cards and charge accounts because your future revenue stream is no longer yours.

Also, this only works as long as we remain upwardly mobile as a society. In the last 16 years, millions have benefited from steadily rising incomes, which also has meant expanding lines of credit. We have accepted the credit card offers that stuff our mailboxes and used that expensive credit (18 to 27 percent, after the low "introductory rate" that sucked us in) to maintain an artificial standard of living better than the one we would otherwise have had. In some instances, when we have eaten up all of our current income with debt payments, we use our credit cards just to buy necessities. I am appalled and astounded to see how many people at the supermarket swipe their credit cards to pay for their groceries. I can only hope they are using a debit card or will pay off the bill in full when it comes due, but that's not the way to bet.

Today most newlywed couples start their married life heavily in debt with a house that's better than the one Kay and I had after two decades of marriage. They also drive two nice cars. Debt has become their American way of life, so deeply embedded that it is a negative economic indicator when people stop borrowing. The Fed accommodates by keeping interest rates low enough that people can qualify for bigger loans and buy bigger houses, bigger cars, bigger TVs, and home theaters.

Like most sins, the bill for covetousness (the monthly payment) keeps being presented month after month, long after you have committed the sin. I would suggest you repent of your covetousness.

LIQUIDATING DEBT

What I have suggested so far may be easier said than done. How do you get off the turnpike to Financial Hell by converting debt payments into investible cash flow, short of bankruptcy? Several ways. The following strategies should become part of your family life, mutually agreed on. Include the kids in the decision making, because this financial plan will affect them.

- Don't incur any new debt. The first step is to draw a line in the sand, say, "No new debt," and mean it. At least you are not digging a bigger hole for yourself. If you can't or won't do that, all bets are off. You should do what our youngest daughter, Terri Lynn (age 20), did. She realized that her paycheck was being eaten alive by credit-card and charge-account payments, and she was becoming increasingly addicted to impulse buying because her cards made it so easy. So last Christmas when she was home for the holidays, she gave us her cards. She, like many of her contemporaries, was becoming like the alcoholic who foolishly keeps beer in the refrigerator, and a radical plastic-ectomy (or plastic splurgery) was the only sure way out.
- Look your debts in the eye. Most people don't. Add up all your credit card balances and monthly interest charges and face reality to bolster your resolve. Organize them with the highest-interest-rate debts at the top to set your debt reduction priorities.
- First pay off the debts with the highest interest rates, starting with the smallest total balance. This is almost always your credit cards. You should pay more than the minimum payment on those you're targeting. The added amount will almost always be principal, and as the principal is paid down, a smaller and smaller portion of each payment will be interest. Pay only the minimum payment

on your lowest-rate cards until the more expensive ones are paid off.

- Economize, and apply the savings to an accelerated repayment schedule. Go to cheaper restaurants, movies, and vacations. Get a cheaper car. I am not asking you to take a vow of poverty or make huge sacrifices, but $10 here and $20 there a few times a month can make a huge difference over time. Don't think of these things as sacrifices; take righteous pride in sticking with your program and glory in your shrinking debt and your growing nest egg. Resolve that you will use your credit cards only for essentials, such as travel, hotels, and business expenses, and pay them off in full as soon as you get the bill. Even get a debit card from your bank.

- As a temporary expedient, get a new credit card with a low introductory interest rate and transfer your balance from your high-interest-rate cards to the new card so you can pay off the principal balance faster. Just make sure that the introductory rate lasts long enough to pay off your balance, or that the eventual increased rate is no worse than the one for the old card.

- Consider a debt-consolidation loan, but only if you have drawn that line in the sand and the consolidation loan carries a much lower interest rate. The ones offered by finance companies never do. Home-equity loans are usually the best.

- As each debt is paid off, apply the freed-up cash to an accelerated payment schedule on your other debts. Once they are all paid off, immediately start investing the monthly cash flow savings every month to earn compound interest.

- Give yourself a few rewards along the way. You might decide to devote some part (definitely not all) of the money you are saving as you eliminate installment payments in a modest, family-approved reward; perhaps a short vacation, or a new dog, or . . . well, I'll let you think of the possibilities. Just make sure you get right back on the program.

- Consider selling your home and buying a smaller one, preferably in a lower-cost area. That's what Kay and I did when we moved from Utah County, Utah, to Washington, Utah, where we live now. It's only a 3½-hour drive from the family and a lot more house for a lot less money. That will produce a big chunk of cash right away and some positive monthly cash flow to invest prudently and compound safely or to swing for the fences in the markets when the time is right. Smaller doesn't have to mean worse: $500,000 in capital gains on the sale of a principal residence is tax-exempt every two years ($250,000 for singles). You can buy a more modest home, pay off your credit cards, and add the remainder to your compound-interest-earning nest egg.

PROFESSIONAL HELP: YOU DON'T HAVE TO GO IT ALONE

As the tide of consumer debt and consumer bankruptcies has risen ever since the late 1990s, you may have seen and heard a flood of radio and TV ads from "non-profit" corporations offering debt relief. The headlines scream: "Reduce Your Debt Payments by up to 50 Percent," "Slash Your Interest Rates to as Low as 0 Percent," "Stop Harassing Calls from Creditors," "Eliminate Your Debts in ⅓ the Time," "Eliminate Late Fees and Over-Limit Fees," "No Loans Necessary," and "Past Credit Problems Are Not a Problem for Us." The organizations that make these claims are "credit-counseling companies," sometimes identified as such by name. They first sprang up in the 1970s, and now there are thousands of them—mostly "nonprofits," which doesn't necessarily mean they aren't designed to be profitable. It just means that profits aren't distributed to shareholders as dividends, but are paid out to managers and key employees in the form of high salaries or bonuses. Actually, these companies are immensely profitable. The term *nonprofit*, while an accurate legal description of their tax status, is really a stroke of PR genius for them, as customers flock to them, thinking they only have their best interests at heart, with no concern for profits. Not so!

The good news is that the reputable companies in this industry can usually make good on these claimed benefits, but the bad news is that much more often than not, your good credit will be seriously damaged, if it isn't already trashed. If your debt troubles are so bad that your credit score is already trash, you may have nothing to lose.

The bottom line? These plans are very helpful to some, but a big mistake for others. Let me explain.

The Good Side of the Coin

If you are already way behind on your payments, if your credit score would gag a maggot, or if bankruptcy appears to be your only other option, a good credit-counseling company can help you get out of debt much faster than you could on your own and keep you out of bankruptcy. There can be some very real benefits:

- Lower monthly payments. These companies can renegotiate your monthly payments down to about 2.2 percent of your balance owing. (If your payment is already this low, that is unlikely.)
- Reduced interest rates. In most cases a lender wouldn't even consider renegotiating your interest rate (or anything else) with you, but the credit-counseling industry has already pre-negotiated such deals with the big lenders, and can easily make deals that you couldn't that will mean huge interest savings for you.
- They can manage your "rollups." This means not reducing the total amount that you apply to your debt reduction

program as each debt is paid off, but instead applying the newly freed-up cash to one of the remaining debts to pay it off much faster. While in theory you could do this yourself, the credit-counseling company will rightly point out that nearly all of those who try this on their own fail to follow through to the end.

- They can "re-age" your accounts. This eliminates late fees and over-limit fees, which can be as much as $60 a month, until you are completely current on your originally agreed-upon schedule.

The Bad Side of the Coin

There are some very serious disadvantages to going with a credit-counseling company:

- Credit-counseling companies can only work with your unsecured creditors, such as credit cards, finance companies, old medical bills, old utility bills, or other unsecured debts that have been sent to collection. They cannot help you with mortgages, car loans, boat loans, or other secured debts.
- They will trash your credit. Most of your creditors will report to the credit bureaus that you are "not paying according to terms" or that your debt is "being paid by a third party." This will cause most, if not all, of your creditors to close your accounts. This is not necessarily all bad because it will help you make good on your commitment to stop adding new debt. But if you need a credit card for business travel for hotels and car rentals, it could pose a problem. And if you ever need to move, it will be nearly impossible to get decent terms on a mortgage for your new home.
- Their ability to legally re-age your accounts will not usually become effective until you have consistently made your payment to them for several months.

- Credit-counseling fees can vary widely. Up-front set-up fees average around $200 to $400 but range from zero (or voluntary) to over $1,000. Many require you to pay the company your next monthly payment as a set-up fee while they skip a payment to your creditors during the renegotiation month. Sometimes this is not disclosed up front. Monthly fees can be as low as $20 a month or as high as $100 a month. These companies derive some of their compensation from a commission, called *fair share*, paid by the lenders, that averages about 8 percent of each monthly payment.
- On the positive side, the credit-counseling industry has been a win-win deal for lenders and borrowers. The borrower gets out of debt, and many unsecured debts have been paid in full (with reduced interest) when they might have been discharged in bankruptcy. The debtor can also preserve his or her personal integrity in honoring his or her financial obligations.

But don't choose credit counseling unless your credit is already trashed and you have little or nothing to lose!

Debt Settlement Companies—Aggressive Debt Retirement on a Faster Track

There is another class of companies, called debt settlement companies, that help you eliminate your unsecured debt more aggressively; the only faster way is bankruptcy. They can lower your payments more than credit-counseling companies and usually promise to eliminate your unsecured debt in a short 24 to 36 months. The downside is that the damage to your credit is significantly worse than with credit counseling.

Here is how debt settlement companies operate: You send your new lower monthly payments to the debt settlement company. Instead of sending it on to your creditors, they let it accumulate for several months. Then they start negotiations to settle with your creditor for approximately 20 cents on the dollar and keep working at it until each of your debts is settled. They charge you about 40 percent of the savings that they negotiate for you. They usually keep your first two payments as a retainer against the fees they will charge you.

The downside is that your creditors will usually not cooperate with them. They will continue to press you for the full amount of your obligation and they will proceed with judgments against you, which will be devastating to your credit—sometimes worse than a bankruptcy. Avoid debt settlement companies at all costs!

Debt Plans for the Creditworthy—By Far Your Best Choice

A few companies offer comprehensive debt plans that have no negative impact on your good credit, and can get you out of debt, including your mortgage, in nine years or less! They are by far the best choice if you have a mortgage, at least $15,000 in non-mortgage debts, still have good credit, are a homeowner, and have some equity. Some of them start off with a debt consolidation loan against your home, while others simply manage your existing debts. If you have a lot of debt, these debt plans will save you tens of thousands of dollars in interest (as much as $100,000) and have you completely debt-free (including your mortgage and other secured debts) in less than 10 years. You make one monthly payment to them and they implement a roll-up plan that eliminates all of your debts in the most efficient manner possible. Set-up fees range from $3,500 to more than $9,000, which is usually not out of pocket, and monthly fees range from $20 to $100 per month. Since the typical savings on one of these plans usually exceeds $100,000, the cost turns out to be a tiny percentage of the savings. It can be well worth the fees to have professionals handle the whole program for you. This will not increase your monthly outgo.

The company I am most familiar with is No More Mortgage,

founded by my son Larry. In the interest of full disclosure, I do have a financial interest. I am such a passionate believer in this concept that I loaned the company some money and serve as chairman of the board.

When you call the company, the first thing they will do for you, even before you commit to them, is give you a comprehensive, personalized seven-page debt analysis of your individual situation generated from the information you give them over the phone. You can see a specimen of a typical debt plan on their Web site at www.nomoremortgage.com, which illustrates how the plan will work, how much you will save, and when each debt will be paid off. It will also show you how to transform your debt into retirement wealth. Your personal plan will project your financial status 20 years from now compared with the results of the track you are currently on. The typical client's 20-year window can change from $100,000 in debt if they do nothing to $200,000 in the bank and growing when they take advantage of the plan.

No More Mortgage's fees are the lowest in the industry, and if you decide to proceed, you will also receive a comprehensive financial education in the form of a Money Mastery Financial Kit, complete with videotapes and workbooks and a monthly newsletter to help you stay on track. Next, the company will arrange the most advantageous financing for a debt consolidation loan to save you the maximum amount of interest and get you completely free of debt the fastest. This may be a low-interest refinancing of your home or a low-interest home equity loan. The proceeds will be applied to your debts. Set-up fees are based on a small percentage of what the company will save you and come out of the proceeds of the loan at escrow, meaning there will be no out-of-pocket costs.

Then the company will manage your payment schedule with a monthly draft from your bank account. Your funds are protected by a bonded third-party administrator who disburses the debt payments and provides a monthly statement showing the progress of the debt elimination plan and an annual summary, complete with an audit of each of your creditor statements to ensure you have not been overcharged by a creditor. (The FDIC has reported that interest miscalculation by creditors has caused debtors more than $8 billion in overcharges.)

Perhaps the greatest value to you is that No More Mortgage stays with you until you are completely debt-free, and you can call them anytime for financial advice. If you relocate, replace a vehicle, or add to or restructure your debts, they will make appropriate adjustments to your plan with no additional fees. They will also help you to take advantage of your improved credit scores by lowering your interest rate, shortening the time it will take you to be debt-free.

The best thing about the plan is that it has no bad effect on your credit because it does not involve any negotiation with creditors. There is no out-of-pocket expense or increased monthly payments. If there is such a thing as financial salvation, assuming you have some home equity and your credit is not thoroughly trashed, this is it!

BIWEEKLY MORTGAGE PLANS

Biweekly mortgage plans focus on your first mortgage only. Instead of making your usual mortgage payment of, say, $1,000 per month, you pay $500 every two weeks. This results in 26 half-payments each year, which is the equivalent of 13 full payments each year. I know this is hard to believe, but this extra payment each year usually results in the mortgage being paid off in about half of the normal time and results in savings of tens of thousands of dollars in interest, because the extra payments are applied to your principal, thus steadily reducing your interest. If you are paid biweekly, such as every other Friday, this program can be ideal. If you are paid twice a month, budgeting is a lot harder. You can do this yourself or work with a management company. Set-up fees range from $250 to $3,500. Monthly fees range from $20 to $40. These plans are also available from No More Mortgage.

DO-IT-YOURSELF DEBT PLANS

But, couldn't you do all of this on your own, eliminating the fees that the companies charge? Sure you could, but few of us have the discipline or the know-how to follow through on our own, month after month and year after year. It is too easy for the initial resolve to be honored for a while and then for the discipline to fall apart when "things come up." Things always come up—car repairs, Christmas, weddings, veterinary bills, clothes, and other non-budgeted items. If you have tried and failed before, the external discipline of a good plan with a good company is more than worth the investment. If, however, you decide to go it on your own, here are some suggestions:

- Stop adding new debt right now. A firm resolve from both you and your spouse is essential.
- Start off with a realistic budget, one that you can really live with. If it is not realistic, you will soon find a way to undermine it. Don't forget to include in your monthly budget the things that come up annually, like Christmas, tires, car repairs, car registration, birthdays, wedding gifts, family vacations, honeymoon trips, prescriptions, insurance premiums, and so on. Realistically estimate these expenses on an annual basis, divide that number by 12, add it to your monthly expenses, and then set the money aside in a savings account every month without fail.
- Apply at least the same amount to your debts every single month, adding to it as debts are eliminated, freeing up some cash flow, until you are completely debt-free. Never decrease this amount because one of your debts is paid off.
- Do not count on future windfalls to wipe out your debts.

Anytime you experience a modest windfall, apply at least half of it to your debts and enjoy the rest. Consistency wins this race, and trying to go too fast can soon undermine the discipline of consistency.

- Target smaller debts first for early payoff, even if they are not the ones with the highest interest rates. There are two reasons: First, it gives you an emotional boost every time a debt is paid off; and second, when you pay off a debt, there is more money every month to apply to other debts or to give you a bigger margin of financial safety. The bigger your margin, the more easily you can withstand an unexpected financial emergency by lowering your debt payments if you absolutely have to.

- As you pay off each debt, consistently add the newfound money to the highest-interest-rate debts first. Work from the top down—highest interest rate down to the lowest. Your shortest path to becoming debt-free is to target the highest-interest debt for early payoff.

HOME EQUITY LOANS AND REFINANCING

All of this new thinking will inevitably bring you to the question of whether or not you should take out a home-equity debt-consolidation loan or refinance your home. There are several advantages to doing so:

- This is the only kind of loan where the interest is tax-deductible. For example, if you are in the 30 percent tax bracket, you will save in taxes 30 percent of the amount you pay in interest on that loan.
- This type of loan will carry a much smaller interest rate than your credit-card balances and charge accounts, so you could use the proceeds to pay off those debts and immediately cut your monthly overhead.

But there are some avoidable booby traps here. Home-equity loans are usually stretched out over a much longer time than the old debts. You should insist on no prepayment penalty, then, as each old debt is paid off, start immediately applying the old payment to another debt and pay it off sooner. Work down from the highest interest rate to the lowest, and your mortgage(s) will be the last paid off.

A Test of Character

The biggest booby trap in home equity loans has a lot to do with character.

First, you will be sorely tempted to abandon your debt-reduction program when the home-equity loan eases the pressure of the old debts. Only do it as part of your total debt-elimination program. Second, I have a visceral fear of further encumbering my castle. It is my security blanket, and I might start thinking of it as my cash cow. Borrowing against your home should be done like porcupines making love—very carefully. Make it a critical part of your debt elimination plan, and use any cash proceeds only to pay down other higher-interest-rate debts. It's also an emotional security decision. You will have to decide that for yourself.

There is competent professional help for debtors, but this burgeoning industry is loaded with booby traps. At a minimum, check them out with the Better Business Bureau (BBB) at bbb.org. Proceed with extreme caution into your debt-free future; there is a brighter day ahead.

Many readers just don't have the mental and emotional discipline or knowledge to carry out a long-term debt reduction program, so they need some professional help to see that they really do it. Do not despair, because the professionals can help you do just that. Some are very helpful to those who are way behind in their payments with ruined credit. Others can be really helpful to those who still have good credit and are current in their obligations, but have taken my message to heart and want to get rid of their consumer debt to get off the turnpike to Financial Hell.

BANKRUPTCY

Bankruptcy is a last-resort strategy. You may have borrowed yourself into insolvency, your debts may far exceed your income and/or assets, and many of the things you bought may be depreciating faster than you are paying for them. If the recession comes to roost on your doorstep, you may lose your income and be unable to meet all of your monthly payments without a desperate juggling act, like using your high-rate MasterCard® to pay off your high-rate Visa®.

In Great Britain before our revolution, if you owed money and couldn't pay it as agreed, you would be put into debtor's prison. Finally the government figured out that people in jail couldn't make any money to pay their debts, so America created the bankruptcy laws that say if you can't pay your debts, society will give you a chance to legally get rid of them and start over. There are two types of bankruptcy for individuals:

- Chapter 13 of the Federal Bankruptcy Code allows you to work out a plan to pay your creditors because you think you can do it. These plans are more complex and require the approval of all your creditors.
- Chapter 7 of the Code is your most realistic bankruptcy option. It says that if you can't or don't want to pay your debts as agreed, you can wipe them out and start over. Another name for this is "stiffing your creditors," and it has a devastating impact on your credit rating. However, there are legitimate times, either because of past indiscretions or

circumstances beyond your control (such as the loss of a job or the failure of a business) when you simply can't meet these obligations. As this is written, there is a bill before Congress that will change the bankruptcy laws to make it harder to cancel your consumer debts. Lobbying by lenders paid off for them big time.

What about the morality of stiffing your creditors? Bankruptcy has only one moral use: Rather than spending your life fighting off creditors and going nowhere on your comeback road, you can ethically use the bankruptcy laws as a temporary shield between you and them while you rebuild your wealth, with the goal of eventually paying them back. After all, it's hard to make forward progress with your eyes on the rearview mirror.

I filed bankruptcy back in 1968 when my speed-reading franchise was abruptly canceled and I was left with no income and a half a million dollars in business debts that I had personally guaranteed. I should not have been in debt in the first place. Kay and I were living very well indeed, taking home a lot of money and spending all of it. We gave big contributions to the Oakland Symphony. I bought Kay a $1,000 designer original dress to wear to pre- and post-concert receptions so we could get our pictures in the society pages. When my speed-reading franchise was canceled, my doors were padlocked and I had a pile of debts with no income to pay them, and we were forced to file bankruptcy.

As a practicing Mormon, I have to be interviewed every year by my stake president (the Mormon equivalent of an archbishop) to see if I am worthy to renew my Temple Recommend. This card entitles me to enjoy the additional spiritual benefits of attending the temple (for sacred ordinances during the week, as opposed to regular public Sunday services in the ward chapel). In the interview, members are always asked routine questions about our moral and ethical behavior to verify that we are worthy to enter a place kept clean and sacred by attempting to exclude all those who don't meet certain moral and ethical standards. After all the routine questions, my Stake President said to me, "I understand you have filed bankruptcy. When are you going to repay your debts?" I was stunned because I was worried about buying food for my family, and paying off half a million dollars in debts seemed totally ridiculous. I was even looking for a job, something I thought I would never do. It hadn't yet occurred to me that I could simply come back and start a new business and that my prior business success was at least partly a result of my talents. When I told my stake president that I had been legally discharged of these debts, he replied, "Well, the court may have forgiven your debts, but the Lord hasn't, and you should pay it back."

After I recounted the conversation to Kay, we decided that even though there was nothing mandatory about accepting this counsel and we might have to spend the rest of our lives paying off the debt, we would do just that. That ethics-based decision actually laid the foundation for the much bigger fortune that I created later, but the initial motivation was simply to meet the moral commitment to pay for that dead horse.

I knew that if I was going to pay off half a million dollars, I couldn't do it in installment payments out of wages. You can't cross a 10-foot ditch with six-inch jumps. I had to get rich! So I did. This was the most important money decision of my life to that point because I had made an irrevocable decision to become rich.

Bankruptcy was a shield that kept creditors off my back while I started and built my financial newsletter; it bought me time to mount a comeback. It was tough telling people I couldn't give them my first hard-earned seed money. Kay and I had to drastically alter our spending habits, and I had to reinvest the money I made into direct mail to build my business. I pyramided the subscription money as it came in and poured it back into more subscription mailings.

The end result is that we balanced the books with God and all those creditors. It took 12 years to pay back every penny with interest. I cannot tell you the satisfaction I felt as I wrote that last $12,000 check, and I won't tell you how much money I made later as a result of that simple decision to pay for a dead horse.

If you have to file bankruptcy, do it with the intent of eventually paying off your debts, even if it takes everything you have later on. I would rather die broke but even with the world, and face God blamelessly, knowing I couldn't take any of it with me anyway.

This is a plea that, if you use bankruptcy to get out from under your debts, you do so with an honest intent. You can inform your creditors that even though you are no longer legally obligated, over the coming years you will pay them back somehow, sometime, someplace. If you are not able to, at least your creditors will know you made a good effort.

Bankruptcy and Credit: The Good News

But won't bankruptcy leave a permanent stain on your credit rating? Yes it will, for 7 to 10 years. That is probably the best thing about it, because it was borrowing that got you into trouble in the first place. Bankruptcy will make it much harder to borrow again. If ethical principles are important to you, bankruptcy is just a tool to help you meet your moral obligations.

SUMMING UP

To recapitulate, start now to get out of debt. Start a whole new lifestyle. Cut your artificial standard of living so you can start rapidly accumulating a nest egg to invest. Drive an old rattletrap of a car if necessary. Live in a smaller house; perhaps even rent. Save and set aside at least 10 percent of your income every month—possibly more—to eventually pay back your debts and build a nest egg, and work your tail off to meet your moral obligation to pay for that dead horse.

This will require a total change of attitude. You must be willing to simply burn up all those mail offers that come to newly minted bankrupts from credit-card companies, department stores, and so on, offering you a chance to start "re-establishing your credit" (i.e., begin a new debt cycle). They know that because you can't file bankruptcy again for at least seven years, you are a pretty good credit risk. Don't go near that old debt trap. However, I have one word of caution: Be sure these offers are all burned or shredded, or at the least put into the trash just before the garbage collector comes. Such documents are treasure to the identity thieves who can use them to pretend they are you, and run up purchases in your name or loot your bank accounts.

Chapter 5

How to Prosper by Earning 15 Percent in a 1-Percent World

In early 2003, interest rates on riskless investments fell to 1 percent or less, torpedoing compounding programs below the waterline. Savvy investors still compounded their portfolios at 15 percent or even 20 percent in investments that were almost as riskless.

N ow that you've decided to get on the right side of compound interest, it becomes obvious that the percent of return on your savings is a really big deal. There is a huge difference down the road in the results for money compounded at 2 percent as opposed to money compounded at 15 percent or 20 percent.

As this is written, too many people assume they can't get more interest than the pittance of less than 1 percent they can get currently at the bank or in a money market fund, but Safely Prosperous or even Really Rich people never surrender to this assumption because they know they don't have to. In fact, your prosperity depends on getting a decent compound return on your money. If you don't get at least 6 percent, your compounding program is aborted. There are always lots of alternatives for decent yields, sometimes as high as 20 percent with acceptable levels of risk. ("The times they are a-changing" so all of the following examples are for-instances, which may not be good choices by the time you read this, but they are a great place to start looking.)

You can start with 10-year Treasury notes, which in late 2003 are yielding 4.25 percent. Long-term T-bonds or T-bond funds are yielding 5 percent or better; however, they are exposed to greater capital risk if interest rates should turn around and head the wrong direction—as I explained in Chapter 3—which will lower the market value of all bonds. The risk is higher with the 30-year treasuries than it is with the 10-year notes, and the 10-year note returns are close enough to make them an acceptable compromise. If you invest through your IRA, there are no current taxes, as taxes are deferred and the interest is exempt from state and local taxes.

What if you want a better yield than Treasury securities offer? As yields go up, risk increases, but there are still reasonable compromises.

One of the best places to look is real-estate funds. Fidelity Mortgage Securities Funds (FMSFX) returned 7.74 percent in 2002, and is probably still in the 6-percent range as this is written. Alpine Realty Income and Growth Funds (AIGYX) has yielded 13.08 percent. The fund invests in big real estate companies, such as malls and La Quinta hotels. Then there is the Security Capital European Real Estate Fund (SEUIX), which yielded 24.02 percent in 2002 and has yielded 21.9 percent to date in 2003.

Next are international bond funds. The average year-to-date yield for mutual funds in this sector is *9.6* percent. Most of the funds are producing *double-digit returns year-to-date. Five funds* in this sector have yielded between *19.53* percent and *18.76* percent in 2002, and are very close to that in early 2003. There are lots of big-name bond funds and fund families to choose from. You probably ought to *throw a few darts at the sector* and *invest in the holes* to diversify.

Then there are long-term government bond funds. As of May 2003, the average yield year-to-date for all funds in this sector is 9.42 percent. *The top-yielding eight funds* are between *16.08* percent and *14.12* percent, all of them in the American Century Mutual Fund family. *Among the big-name funds,* Vanguard and T. Rowe Price have *good performers here in the double digits.* This again is a dartboard, but if the stock market takes off, these funds will crash and burn. I think it is a pretty good bet that *won't happen,* although there will be market *rallies.*

There is another choice you should at least look at: Stable value funds are in a category *between money market funds and bond funds* where there is more yield and lower risk. However, *these are new,* so they have a very short history.

If you choose a bond fund, look for low duration, which means low sensitivity to rising interest rates—but the trade-off for that is *lower yields.*

Real estate investment trust (REIT) Funds can give you *diversification,* but not always high yields, although some individual REITs have high yields, including Equity Office (EOPRG), Simon Property Group (SPGGRF), and Liberty Property Trust (LRY).

There are also some very interesting high-yielding preferred stocks you can look up at www.forbes.com.

You can also invest in first or second mortgages, safely secured by real estate. Most mortgage brokers will have some suggestions with yields above 6 percent. I will also monitor some of these opportunities in *The Ruff Times.*

There are really intriguing opportunities to get some unorthodox high yields, such as real estate tax liens from county tax assessors or written-off loans from lenders. These usually yield more than 15 percent and are often secured by the property. I consider them virtually riskless, but they do have some limitations.

As I am finishing my last edits for the publisher, I haven't completed my research, so you can get a current list on a one-time basis by calling *The Ruff Times* office at 1-801-224-3660 or e-mailing us at service@rufftimes.com. These opportunities are extremely interesting.

Even 20 percent yields will not make you Really Rich, as described in Book II, but they can accelerate your drive toward prosperity and cut years off your program. They are also great places for the Really Rich to put their money once they have made it.

That's what I've dug out so far in late 2003. There are always similar possibilities, and you don't have to be a Sherlock Holmes to find them. Many are listed every day in *The Wall Street Journal*. All such choices need fairly close monitoring; they are not sock-it-away-and-forget-it investments. In this market where rapid reverses are possible, you have to stay right on top of things either with your broker or on your PC.

The bottom line is that only fools will settle for near-zero yields when they don't have to. It just takes a little homework that anyone can do. I also monitor the yields in the "Investing for Income Portfolio" section of *The Ruff Times* every month.

Chapter 6

Social Security, the Ponzi Chain Letter

Why you would be much better off by not counting on Social Security, the biggest scam in the known universe

Don't be alarmed by this chapter if you are now getting Social Security benefits or are over 60. The big problems described herein will not occur until after you are gone, and it's too late to do anything about it anyway. If, however, you are under 55 and worry a lot, take this chapter very seriously.

Millions of people are betting that Social Security will be there for them when they retire and will provide enough for a comfortable life. Financial planners build this assumption into their financial plans. For millions of Americans, this is a lie, and it is a very expensive mistake to bet on it!

Every time I express my politically incorrect views on this subject, I rub a lot of people the wrong way. Social Security is a sacred cow that we are not supposed to question. It is also called the third rail of politics. But, as the saying goes, "Fools rush in where angels fear to tread." I guess I'm a fool.

I may be beating a dead horse here; many of you already

know in your heart of hearts that Social Security is a big ripoff, but you still bet on it, hoping that the day of reckoning will not come until after you have gotten yours. But if you are under 50, you may never see your money, or it may be so inflation-ravaged that it won't buy much. Social Security is by far the biggest Ponzi pyramid ever conceived, and, like all Ponzi schemes, it will have its day of reckoning.

PONZI REVISITED

Social Security is a perfect reflection of a classic fraud case some years ago in which a man by the name of Ponzi raised funds from investors by promising huge payoffs as high as 40 percent a month. He did nothing productive with the money and earned no real profits for his suckers, but he paid huge "dividends" to previous investors by using the money raised from new investors. The Ponzi pyramid eventually collapsed of its own weight, and Ponzi went to prison. This type of scheme is considered a crime when private citizens do it, but it is considered compassionate social engineering when the government does it.

As long as there are enough new suckers to balance the books, the fraud holds up. But if the number of paying "marks" diminishes until they cannot or will not balance the books, then the scheme collapses spectacularly. Just understanding this truth may give you more incentive to begin preparing for a retirement that does not depend on Social Security—even if it somehow hangs together until you die. You can be far better off when you retire than if you just keep betting on Social Security. You will also learn here why Congress will never fix Social Security before it is too late to save it.

Most Americans believe that Social Security is supposed to take care of them in their old age, and they plan their lives accordingly, but Social Security wasn't even intended for that in the beginning. It was only to be an income supplement to your personal savings and other pensions. Under the most optimistic scenario, Social Security alone wouldn't allow you anything but genteel poverty when you could no longer earn a living. Here are some hard truths: In the most likely scenario, either Social Security won't even be there when you need it, or the money the government will have to print to pay you your monthly check will cause saber-toothed inflation that will so diminish the purchasing power of the money that it will be next to worthless.

So here are the rules to help you avoid a monumentally stupid mistake.

Rule #1: If you are under age 50, plan your future without Social Security. If you are over age 40, plan on progressive benefit cuts after you retire, steadily increasing FICA deductions from your paycheck, and growing inflation that shrinks the value of your benefits when (and if) you actually get them.

Rule #2: Don't retire at age 65 unless you are physically, mentally, or emotionally unable to be productive. Maintain your income stream as long as possible.

Rule #3: Accept personal responsibility for your own retirement income by becoming frugal and starting now to build a nest egg big enough to live comfortably on the interest without Social Security, following the guidelines in Chapters 3 through 5.

Let me explain the Social Security scam.

The following exchange took place 25 years ago during Senate Social Security hearings between Senator William Proxmire and a Mr. Cardwell of the Social Security Administration.

Proxmire: "There are 37 million people, is that right, who get Social Security benefits?"

Cardwell: "Today between 32 million and 34 million."

Proxmire: "I'm a little high; 32 to 34 million people. Almost all of them or many of them are voters. In my state, I figure there are 600,000 voters that receive Social Security. Can you imagine a senator or congressman under those circumstances saying we are going to repudiate that high a proportion of the electorate? No.

"Further, we have the capacity under the Constitution, the Congress does, 'to coin money as well as to regulate the value thereof.' Therefore, we have the power to provide that money, and we are going to do it. It may not be worth anything when the recipient gets it, but he is going to get his benefits paid."

Cardwell: "I tend to agree."

Just to bring you up to date, 49 million people received Social Security benefits in the year 2000, 25 years later.

Social Security is the most dishonest, reprehensible, deceitfully unsound scheme ever foisted by a government on a trusting public—a fraud so huge that the imagination is unable to grasp it—and the politicians have made us willing accomplices to the fraud. (Someday I will tell you what I really think!)

Try this short true/false quiz:

T F Payroll deductions for Social Security go directly into the Social Security Trust Fund "lockbox," where they are saved for your retirement.

T F Money deducted from *your* paycheck will be used to pay *your* retirement benefits.

If you marked both of these true, you score 0 percent. All your basic assumptions about the Social Security Trust Fund are probably false.

The national economy has become dependent on the Social Security system. It disburses more funds than any other governmental subdivision. FICA is the biggest single tax paid by most Americans. The impact of changes in Social Security payroll taxes or benefits is immense, and if we increase or decrease either, the effects on the economy are complex and ultimately negative.

Pensioners are trapped in the system. Many are totally dependent on it. According to the Social Security Administration, their Social Security check represents more than half the income of 64 percent of the recipients. Millions of people would be in for genuine suffering if the Social Security system were to go broke, or if benefits were to be cut, or if they were not increased to accommodate cost-of-living increases. Even worse, though, is the easily demonstrable fact that rather than saving for their retirement—a good old-fashioned, time-honored American tradition—millions have spent everything they earned (usually on debt payments) and placed a touching level of faith in Uncle Sam to take care of them.

I have a tough question for you. What would your life be like if you were forced to retire at age 65, you were heavily in debt, and your principal income was your Social Security check?

Well, I am about to make a big dent in this faith in a beneficent uncle in Washington with the unpleasant, unvarnished truth. You are about to learn why you must not make your retirement totally dependent on government promises.

THE LOCKBOX MYTH—A GRIM FAIRY TALE

Let's reexamine your true/false quiz: "Payroll deductions for Social Security go directly into a Social Security Trust Fund 'lockbox' where they are saved for your retirement." During the 2000 presidential election, Al Gore made a big deal of the lockbox into which he would put your Social Security Trust Fund. It was a crock!

If that's a crock, what is the truth?

When the government forces your employer to deduct Social Security taxes from your paycheck, all of this money, along with your employer's "contribution," goes into the General Fund. It is all used for current government expenses, and current Social Security checks are just a part of it! It is not held separate from other funds. The Treasury borrows all of it by issuing illiquid, non-negotiable IOUs to the Social Security Trust Fund, and they constitute the whole fund—just under $1 trillion as of December 31, 2000. The Trust Fund has never seen any of that money, only these pieces of paper that represent that the government has taken the money and spent it, and will print more if necessary. All there is in the Trust Fund "lockbox" is a mountain of government IOUs.

The government uses a rhetorical trick to make this palatable; they tell us that, "in the interest of safety," the Social Security Trust Fund is "invested in the safest possible instrument—U.S. Treasury Securities." These securities are a liability of the United States Treasury, secured by "the full faith and credit of the United States government," which means the printing press. When the fund disburses its monthly benefits, it merely calls on the Treasury to issue checks. The government would do this even if there were no government IOUs in the fund. The cost to the taxpayer would be the same. It is just that everyone feels more secure if there are pieces of paper saying the government promises to do this. That's what makes the scam work and the public feel secure even as they are robbed, but it really doesn't make any difference; the so-called Social Security Trust Fund is nothing more than a glorified set of bookkeeping entries.

Just for form's sake, if it should issue more money than was collected for FICA, the Treasury merely retires some of those notes and the "Trust Fund" shrinks. If it issues less money than was paid out in current benefits, the Trust Fund is in "surplus," and the pile of IOUs grows.

How valuable is a Treasury security held by the Social Security system? If you were to write yourself an IOU for $1 billion, add it to your financial statement, and take it to the bank to obtain a loan, you would be laughed out of the bank. We cannot create real wealth by giving ourselves our own IOU. The Social Security Administration is a division of the United States government holding IOUs of another division of the United States government that has spent all the money and has no assets of its own for collateral. This paper represents no value at all. It is not an asset. As a result, the political debate in the last election over whether the Social Security trust fund should be put in a "lockbox" is simply a discussion of cosmetics—the appearance of things. Already the current Social Security payments are paid from the General Fund. The so-called "depletion of the Trust Fund" or "dipping into the Trust Fund" is not the real threat to the system, nor is it new; it's the way it has always been. The real threat is the ever rising tide of pension payments supported by fewer and fewer workers.

There used to be 90 workers supporting each person in the system; now there are three. Within five years, there will be only two. You are making a monstrous bet on your children's willingness to bear that increased burden, which in a few years will have to be more than 30 percent of their paycheck, until they won't dare take any more out of people's paychecks, lest it cause a war between the generations.

The Social Security system depends on the people believing that their payroll deductions will pay for their retirement, but that's not true, and it never was. The government plays games, and we are conned. Social Security payroll deductions are simply another method of raising money to fund the government's alleged needs. Your FICA payroll deduction is a slush fund to pay for Defense, Agriculture, FTC, EPA, and the rest of the alphabet soup of federal government, as well as current Social Security benefits.

THE GOVERNMENT-CERTIFIED CHAIN LETTER

But the real fraud is the fact that the system is really a gigantic chain letter. Chain letters operate under the assumption that when you add your name to the bottom of the list and send your dollar to the top, other suckers will add their name under yours so eventually your name will rise to the top and you will get money from the bottom. It pays off only if a continual new supply of workers continues to fall for it. Sooner or later, as the number of contributors shrinks and the number of recipients grows, it sputters to a stop, and the last guys in lose out.

Everyone now receiving Social Security will get payments until the day they die, so if you are a current recipient, you have nothing to worry about. The real victims are those young workers who are paying into the system now through FICA deductions. They will pay rising and increasingly onerous FICA taxes, expecting to retire in 15, 20, 30, or 40 years. They will be ripped off when they retire, or they will be paid with inflationary funny money.

The money taken from you is also used to pay benefits to many who have paid nothing into the system, as the system is being used to achieve social benefits other than the original intent, such as Medicare and subsidized or free prescription drug benefits. Because of that, plus cost-of-living increases in benefits that have outstripped increases in payroll deductions, it is now being operated on a pay-as-you-go basis. The result? The supposed "dipping into the Trust Fund" we have already discussed, which we have always done anyway. If this were honestly labeled, the admitted federal surplus under Clinton would have been far smaller, or maybe even in deficit.

Democratic Minnesota Senator Paul Wellstone (since deceased) asserted that Social Security "will be able to pay all promised benefits until 2038 without any changes." That sounds like good news, but even if it turns out to be true, all that means is that someone entering the workforce today can look forward to paying Social Security taxes for 34 years only to find there is nothing left when he or she retires.

This Trust-Fund fantasy is worse than false—it is dangerous, because it creates a huge political obstacle to sensible, fiscal policy, and lends itself to demagoguery. It has turned Social Security into the third rail of politics—touch it and your re-election hopes die a sudden death.

Meanwhile, you hope the system will hang together long enough that when you reach retirement age, others entering the system will be willing to pay enough in FICA taxes that you can be paid when you get to the top of the chain letter. You are totally dependent on a continuous flow of new money from those new workers entering the Social Security system.

GOOD MEDICINE: THE ENEMY OF THE SYSTEM

More people are living longer into their golden years, and they vote in disproportionate numbers; and this great voting bloc is treated very carefully by our legislators, who continue to increase their benefits faster than payroll deductions. The irony is that medical advances that prolong life are actually an enemy of the system. An effective, widely accepted cancer cure or an end to heart disease would devastate it, because as people live longer than expected, each unanticipated recipient is a financial threat to the system. Even without them, too few will soon be paying for too many.

The baby boom of the 1940s and 1950s, which brought a large number of workers into the system in the 1960s and 1970s, is about over, and fewer worker bees will enter the hive, while the number of recipients will increase enormously. If the government continues to increase the payroll deductions to maintain the appearance of solvency, the economy will grind to a halt because of this terrible drag on the spending power of the American worker.

Our senators and congressmen are pretty smart, however. They know how unsound the Social Security system is, so they have their own sound, healthy, fully funded pension program with generous cost-of-living escalators. Let me give you an example: When they retire, no matter how long they have been in office, they continue to draw their regular pay (unless increased by cost-of-living adjustments) until the day they die. Former Senator Bill Bradley (D, New Jersey) and his wife can expect to draw $7.9 million over their lives, assuming they live out a normal life span. It costs them nothing! You and I pick up the tab. We would have to collect Social Security benefits for more than 46.5 years to do as well.

This leads to a suggestion that would trigger some honest changes—cancel Congress's wonderful plan and put them on Social Security, then watch them rush to fix the system! However, on second thought, they might just increase the payoff on the scam and place demands on it that would topple it sooner. Then they can continue to cynically vote for spending programs and more Social Security taxes and bigger monthly checks to buy votes because they are insulated from the problem they have caused. Just remember that the next time you vote for a big-spending "defender of the Social Security system."

I'm not so much worried that the Social Security system will collapse but that the Social Security system will be the cause of the nation's bankruptcy, because it is the single largest obligation of government and the debt defies description. According to *Business Week,* the Social Security system's unfunded obligations (the excess promised to future recipients over the amount to be collected) amount to an almost unimaginable $20.6 *trillion* over the next 75 years. That's twice the expected output of the entire U.S. economy this year. The amount of unfunded obligation grew in excess of $1 trillion in 2000, and is accelerating.

Put another way, it's now a rotten deal getting worse every year. Workers who earned average wages and retired in 1980 at age 65 recovered the value of the retirement portion of their and their employer's contribution, plus interest, in only 2.8 years. Every month they lived beyond that was pure gravy. It was a pretty good deal for them, even if the return was only 2 percent per annum. However, those who retired at age 65 in 2000 will need 16.7 years to recover their money. If they die before age 81, they are shortchanged. And younger Americans who don't retire until 2025 will really take it in the shorts. It will take 27.4 years to get your contribution back. Just be sure not to die before age 93!

And that, of course, assumes that the system will still be alive and well then.

WHY SOCIAL SECURITY WILL NEVER BE REFORMED

During the 2000 presidential campaign and the first few months of his administration, President Bush proposed that two percentage points of your FICA contribution be yours to invest in market securities at your option. Historically, that money would produce a return double the 2 percent yield you now get from Social Security, and the principal would be yours at retirement. This proposal was immediately attacked by Gore and other Democrats as "a risky scheme" allegedly opened up to market risks, such as the bear market we are in as I write.

Do you want to know the real reason they oppose this fresh idea? It's because Social Security is a huge slush fund for government, and the big spenders will never let it out of their hands. Can you imagine what would happen to federal spending if all of a sudden the Congress could not borrow the Social Security Trust Fund and spend it on their favorite programs? They'd be about $175 billion short every year! And what would happen if you could invest 2 percent of your FICA as you choose? There would simply be that much less money in the slush fund.

And how "risky" is the scheme? That depends on what you invested the money in. If you invested it in Treasury securities or a T-bond fund, that is riskless.

SELF-FULFILLING PROPHECY?

I have been accused of destroying the very confidence in the system that keeps it alive by telling you this, but I trust the truth.

What choice do I have? The present Social Security System is the real risky scheme. Sooner or later the problems will be recognized and the jury-rigged, dishonest system will collapse of its own weight, whether or not I talk about it. My concern is for you. You must plan your life on the sure premise that Social Security will be of very little help to you, and may have done a lot of harm. It has discouraged saving, because it takes money away from you that you might have saved for yourself and gotten a return at least twice as high while continuing to own the principal. Also, most people believe that Social Security will take care of them. That's what the AARP tells its members as it lobbies for more benefits, and that's what our national legislators and political candidates tell us ad nauseum. They have made Social Security junkies out of us because even the most sophisticated financial planners seldom seriously question that Social Security will be there when needed.

Those who will be hurt most are those who were promised the most. The system is immoral, dishonest, and unethical, and we have bought the big lie and become hooked on it. The only honest way to save the system and the economy would be to slash benefits, which would not only be cruel at this point, but politically impossible. But the greater cruelty is yet to come when the system collapses under its own weight.

Section II

Blowing Your Money in the Investment Markets: The Turnpike to Financial Hell

The next four chapters assume you have accumulated some money to invest, perhaps because you took the advice in Chapters 3 through 6, perhaps because you are a high earner, perhaps because you have had a windfall. Millions of Americans have laboriously accumulated a nest egg over the years and then decided to invest in something—maybe the stock market, perhaps real estate, perhaps a business started by one of their offspring—and they have blown all or part of the money.

All of this pain could have been avoided if they had understood and practiced the few simple principles in this section.

Chapter 7

Listening to Wall Street

Wall Street's conventional wisdom has been 180° wrong almost forever. Here's why, and how to tell.

For four years back in the late 1950s, I was the soloist and announcer with the Air Force Band and Singing Sergeants. That was government work, however, so we only worked two hours a day when we weren't touring about a quarter of the time. So I got a job with a New York stock exchange brokerage. I learned some enduring lessons:

- The firm made recommendations for us to sell to our clients that were in the best interest of the brokers; sometimes the trading department had stocks in inventory and had higher-than-normal profit margins, and promised higher commissions.
- We were under constant pressure to sell higher-margined financial products, such as front-load mutual funds, tax shelters, and other financial-planning instruments.
- The firm's more mainstream recommendations were always aligned with the consensus of Wall Street, which turned out to be pretty darn wrong more often than not.

- No customer would buy a stock if you weren't bullish on it, so it was easy to convince yourself that you were bullish because you were a commissioned salesman. No bullish recommendations would mean no buy orders and no commissions.

After I finished my four years with the Air Force, I tried to continue in that business, but I determined to become more discriminating and use my best judgment. Until then, I had just been a loyal employee and I trusted the house, believed their recommendations and sold them. But when I started exercising my own judgment, there were a lot of high-profit items I couldn't make myself sell, so I didn't sell much, and I didn't make many commissions, and my family was near starving. That's when I decided to get out of the business.

Since I became a financial newsletter editor 25 years ago, my respect for Wall Street has sagged year after year, until now it is nearly nil. The worst thing you can do is blindly accept the consensus of opinion on Wall Street and follow their advice. Most of the brokers' recommendations are—sometimes subtly, sometimes not so subtly—in line with their self-interest.

THE DINES SAGA

Back in the 1960s, James Dines was one of the stars on Wall Street. He was a gifted technical analyst, and, in fact, he wrote books that are still classics of technical analysis. He was everyone's fair-haired boy.

During that time, however, his technical analysis told him that gold was headed for a bull market in the not-too-distant future, so he began recommending gold and became bearish on the stock market. This did not sit well with his employers or his colleagues on Wall Street who didn't sell gold, so he became a pariah and eventually lost his job.

I've known Jim for many years, and you just can't intimidate him that way, so he created a new career for himself as "The Original Gold Bug," and founded and wrote a very successful financial newsletter. He was dead right during the gold bull market of the 1970s (and so was I, by the way), making a lot of money for a lot of people.

Despite his Gold Bug status, Dines has also been bullish on the stock market when it was appropriate, and he was usually right. He is a financial newsletter legend.

The lesson I learned from Jim Dines' history is: If you want to get along with Wall Street, you go along, and it doesn't matter if they're right or not. And there is very big money for talented people who go along.

If you were watching the financial channels, like Bloomberg or CNBC, during the late lamented bull market bubble of the 1990s, you heard many bullish stock recommendations, all assuming that the bull market would continue and that trees grow to the sky. In fact, the bullish recommendations peaked on the day before the market peaked. On that watershed day, 90 percent of the recommendations were "buy" and 8 percent were "hold." Only 2 percent were "sell." The next day the bubble started to deflate and the panic began that has lasted more than three years—the biggest bear market in the history of the New York Stock Exchange. We have since found that Wall Street had been recommending stocks that not only were not profitable, but that contained nothing in their pro-formas to indicate they ever would be profitable. They were stock promotions pure and simple. Many of those companies are now gone, simply because they needed continuing rounds of new capital just to stay alive, and the venture capital markets dried up as panic-driven capital investors ran for the hills.

I had become bearish in November of 1999 when I spoke to a major investment conference and told the audience we were in the middle of a bubble and it was time to start averaging out and soon be completely out of the market. I was laughed at, and there were a few boos and hisses as everyone in that audience was caught up in the bull market mania. Of note, I haven't since had any calls from people telling me how right I was when the market peaked in March of the next year and began its long downhill slide.

So, do I watch CNBC or Bloomberg? Sure I do, but I only want to track market performance and to see what Wall Street believes, so I can consider whether or not to be a contrarian that day.

What's the bottom line of all this? Wall Street is no different from you; we all act in our own self-interest and Wall Street needs to be bullish whether it is appropriate or not because bears don't sell stock, produce commissions for salesmen, or accumulate profits for the company. The bullish attitude is essential to the very life of Wall Street brokers, so like a stopped clock that is right twice a day, there are periods when they are right on, but only when it aligns with their self-interest or they get lucky. Wall Street is not the place to look for objective or accurate financial advice.

When you attempt to make money on Wall Street, you are competing against cold-blooded professionals, and they really are a separate breed. Most are short-term traders; very few are long-term investors like Warren Buffett. They tend to be in early in upswings in individual stocks, and out before the top—just about when you're excited that that tree will grow to the sky and you start to buy. The average investor can't make any money in the stock market competing with those hard-nosed professionals. Because of the emotions described elsewhere in this book, most investors lose money even in bull markets.

To top it all off, in my lifelong experience with wealthy people, I have only found one who became rich in trading the stock market, and thousands who have lost a lot of money in the market.

We were once on a cruise ship with a group of my subscribers. As always, they would ask me to look at their portfolios and make recommendations. One gentleman, whom I believe was 90 at the time, showed me his portfolio, and I gasped. He had averaged more than 30 percent a year for two decades, which was better than I had done—a heck of a lot better! The interesting thing is that his portfolio consisted almost entirely of disasters. When Wall Street was bearish on something because a calamity had occurred and the stock had nosedived until no one wanted it, that's when he bought. He bought Union Carbide when its Bhopal, India chemical plant blew up and killed hundreds of Indians, and Wall Street was heading for the hills. My friend bought it cheap, hand over fist. It was basically a sound company and when the inevitable comeback materialized, he quadrupled his money. And just about every stock in his portfolio had a similar story. In other words, he made a fortune going the opposite way of Wall Street, and he's the only person I have ever met who had the ego strength to consistently do that.

Wall Street is also subject to some malign influences within management. We now know that many of their recommendations were fraudulent simply because the financial consulting arm of the firm wanted a fat consulting contract with the company under discussion. So their analysts became bullish on that stock, which pleased their employer, and the brokerage house was rewarded with a fat consulting contract. I'm not saying that some of this was not sincere, but a lot of it was just flat-out crooked. Again Wall Street operated in its own self-interest, and now some of those people are going to prison along with some accounting firms, and there are a lot of them walking the streets that should be in the pokey.

In addition, brokers are as human as you and I. They are as prone as you to get caught up in manias and in their personal self-interest.

In the final analysis, is Wall Street the place to get your financial advice? With their track record? Where should you get such advice? Is there such a place? Should you even be in the market? I will deal with those questions later.

Chapter 8

The Bigger-Fool Theory of Investing

The stock-market bubble of the late 1990s inflated because investors (speculators?) assumed that if they paid a foolish price for a stock, they would be able to sell it to a bigger fool.

Ignoring the importance of intrinsic value in picking stocks to invest in during the 1990s is by far the most foolish thing done by the most investors during my quarter century as a financial publisher. It was a universal epidemic! It worked for awhile as the market soared to unsustainable heights, driven by investors (speculators?) who assumed that even if they paid a foolish price for a stock, a bigger fool would come along and pay them an even more foolish price. Understanding the importance of real value made fortunes for a few investors who were lucky enough or smart enough to sell at or before the peak of the bull market in March or April of 2000. They understood that at those prices, most stocks were worse than lousy values, and they would go higher only if investors were willing to pay ridiculously higher prices. But most Americans who bet on the biggest stock bubble since 1929 when it was full of lousy values still own their deflated stocks and mutual funds in individual investment accounts as well as in their 401(k)s, and have been hurt big time. As this is written, the carnage is far from over, and millions of investors are still holding onto their big losers like grim death, emotionally incapable of admitting they made a terrible value judgment, and hoping to just break even.

Sooner or later, stocks always "regress to the mean." If they get too far out of line, either up or down, sooner or later they go back within the historic range of traditional measurements of value. The further they go above intrinsic value to the upside in an investment mania, the further they will overreact to a level well below intrinsic value on the downside near the bottom of a secular bear market. I will teach you how to measure these values so you know whether you are really investing or just counting on the bigger-fool theory to bail you out. I will also share my strategies for determining when the values are real and not illusory, and the world is truly on the bargain table.

For most of the 150-year history of the New York stock market, investing was a matter of selecting the shares of the companies that had the best management and business prospects for sales and earnings. It was assumed that if management took good care of the business, the price of the stock would do fine, and the investors would share in the profits through dividends and capital gains. Yes, speculators and traders would bet strictly on stock movements, using charts and other technical tools, and these speculating traders served the useful function of creating the short-term, in-and-out trading volume which created the necessary good liquidity for everyone else. But the speculators were a tough and hard-bitten bunch who knew exactly what they were doing and got an exciting emotional high from the potentially profitable risk. The vast majority of shareholders were conservative investors trying to make a good return from owning a piece of a successful business over the long term.

Sometime in the last two decades, however, investment slipped away from the Wall Street center stage, and speculation became the order of the day. Most people didn't sense the sea change, because they still called it "investment." Actually, it was insanity, a mania that was near to a mass psychosis. Millions were subscribing to the bigger-fool theory. Those who should have been investors were really speculators and didn't know it. The Nasdaq bubble was created by this mentality. The hottest high-tech stocks had zero chance of profits in the foreseeable future; profits weren't even in their projections, but if they were, the underlying assumptions would make Pollyanna blush. If speculators' price expectations were met, those prices were way beyond levels that could have been supported by even the most wildly optimistic business scenarios. Buying stocks had nothing to do with investing in a company's drive toward a healthy bottom line; it only had to do with a soaring stock price, totally disconnected from the reality of true business success. Stock prices were totally detached from any objective measurement of business success. It had nothing to do with value. It was mass stupidity, speculating on price movement.

For some lucky ones, the road to financial heaven seemed to be paved with initial public offerings (IPOs) that only a few favored wealthy clients were able to buy as the companies apportioned them out to the brokers who used their allotments to reward their biggest clients. Money was doubled and tripled overnight, based on an airy foundation of dreams, hopes, and speculation, unfounded in any kind of reality. Some people got in at the start and sold out before the bubble burst. A few of the companies would become real businesses, but most of them started out as dot-coms, and now they are dot-gone!

During the late, lamented bull market of the 1990s, the term *value* was a hiss and a byword to most investors, and especially to analysts on Wall Street. It was a quaint, fuddy-duddy word that had no relevance to the market. Stocks were going up just because they were going up, and "momentum investing" was the new catchword of the day. Traditional measures of value, such as price/sales, price/earnings, and price/dividend ratios and profits were simply ignored. Many of the hot stocks of the last few years didn't even have a profitable bottom line built into their spreadsheets and projections; they would worry about that in the sweet by and by. All management wanted now was share of market and a soaring stock price at any cost, as they would only make their killing with their options if prices soared. Dividends now or in the future weren't even being talked about. If they ran out of cash, they assumed they just had to go into the hot venture capital market and get more. Then, when the market started its death spiral in April 2000 and the portfolios of the venture capitalists were devastated, the capital gravy train jumped the tracks, stung venture capitalists pulled in their horns, and company after company went under, starved for lack of cash, or became a mortally wounded, crippled basket case. People like me who refused to participate in the mania looked like fools for a long time; we seemed to be the stupid ones.

A lot of this phenomenon was created by our dysfunctional tax structure. For example, dividends are taxed twice at the highest rates—first by the corporate tax and second by the personal income tax when you get your dividend checks. Corporate executives did not want dividends; they wanted the company to retain its earnings (if there ever were any) and reward them with options, because that would result in more favorable tax treatment when they took their profits as capital gains. And with the hot market, they could make fortunes with their options, even if there were no business profits. That made the stock price the sole measurement of their personal wealth. This also led to the endemic fraud where deceptive accounting methods were chosen that would inflate the apparent profits, and thus the value of the stock, simply because the stock price was where the executive's bread was buttered, not the company's real bottom line.

Also, millions of Americans had no idea that they were pouring their money into an inflated bubble and a fragile stock market when they poured their money into stocks, mutual funds, and their 401(k)s, thinking they were simply buying into a safe savings program that would go up 20 percent a year. The ignorance was appalling, even bizarre. I can't tell you how many *Ruff Times* subscribers, knowing I was bearish, would assure me, "I'm not in the stock market, I'm in mutual funds," or a 401(k), or whatever. Wall Street propaganda reinforced these dysfunctional attitudes, telling everyone to "buy on dips" and assuring them that the stock market always went up over "the long term," whatever that was. They were burying the fact that even in many companies' published projections, there was no chance of enough profit to justify even current stock prices, let alone the higher prices bigger-fool theorists were betting on. Wall Street's institutional memory had poured down the memory hole the fact that past secular bear markets (long-lasting broad declines) had in some cases lasted as long as 15 to 20 years. If you bought near the top of the previous bull market, it could take that long to simply break even. There is an old Bible-derived adage which I have adapted to make my point: "There is a time to sow and a time to reap" . . . and a time to run like hell, and it was now running time.

Optimism was the word of the day at the peak of the market in March and April of 2000. As I told you in Chapter 7, 98 percent of the recommendations coming from Wall Street analysts and investment advisors were "buy," or "hold," and less than 2 percent were "sell." At that pivotal time, 98 percent "sells" would have been a much sounder strategy, as the falling tide lowered even the sounder boats, even as a bear market was still unthinkable on Wall Street. Most of the "analysts" making these calls were obsessed with the commissions they earned when people bought stocks, including the special deals the brokers got for selling an IPO to a customer. Most of these decisions were made by young whippersnappers who weren't even brokers during the last bear market and had no idea what happened historically during bear markets. To them, the traditional valuations of sales, earnings, and dividends were old-fogy ideas that weren't even in their vocabularies.

I recently had dinner with a very bright young man who told me he had put money in the stock market and his portfolio had fallen big time while he kept hoping for a rebound. He asked me what he should do. I told him to sell and put the money into Treasury Bonds because interest rates were going to fall even lower, and bonds always go up when interest rates go down. He said, "I can't do that. I would take a 50 percent loss."

I said, "You have already taken your loss. I'm just asking you to face up to it and do something about it. There is only one legitimate question to ask yourself: 'Given that I have a portfolio worth $XXXX, would I buy the stocks I own today? I have to avoid further losses and gain some profits.' The paper losses you have now are history. The beginning of wisdom is to face reality."

He then said, "Well, I'm just going to wait and see if I can get it back," which told me that now the total purpose of his investing was to break even, which is not a really smart attitude for an investor when a stock has to double just to break even. You can break even with a lot less risk by putting the money in your mattress. The market dropped another 10 percent while the T-bonds rose 12 percent while yielding 6 percent interest or more!

The out-of-sight traditional market measurements of valuation drove me to recommend in February and March of 2000 that everyone should sell all their stocks, even the "good companies," because the falling tide would lower even the sound boats. I was laughed at by a thousand investors who thought I was a fool when I said this at a major investment conference, and frankly, I felt pretty stupid at the time, even though I knew it was the right thing to do. I told them that the Nasdaq was headed for 1,500 or less. It was about 5,000 at the time, and investors were betting that trees would grow to the sky (see Figure 8.1). Meanwhile, the

Figure 8.1 Nasdaq NMS Composite Index as of August 8, 2002. (Copyright 2002 Yahoo! Inc., http://finance.yahoo.com)

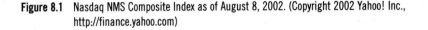

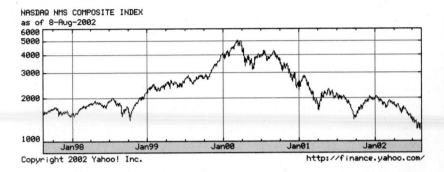

Dow Industrials had peaked at 11,219 in January (see Figure 8.2) and had begun the slide that I believed would not end until it reached 4,500—possibly as low as 2,000, which was where it would go if the market returned to average historical valuations as measured by price/earnings, price/dividend, and price/sales ratios—which history said it would.

The Nasdaq has met my initial target, which I have now lowered to 1,000. The Dow hasn't hit my target yet as this is written, but has been down to just above 8,000, nearly 30 percent below where it was when I made my forecast. (See Figure 8.2.) (Late

Figure 8.2 Dow Jones Industrials Average Index as of August 8, 2002. (Copyright 2002 Yahoo! Inc., http://finance.yahoo.com)

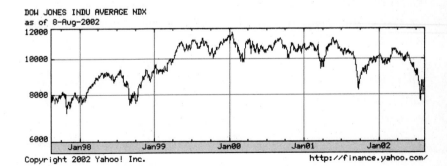

note: during 1983 the Dow rallied over 10,000. Even during secular bear markets, half the years are up years. The bear was just
hibernating.)

We were way above the average valuations over the history of
the market and a heck of a lot further away from the values that
prevailed at the bottom of past bear markets. History taught me
that this bear market would not end until it bottomed out at or
below traditional valuations when pessimism was universal and
it became irresistible to long-term investors because it was nearly
riskless measured by price alone. If it bottomed well short of
these levels, it would be the first bear market that ever ended
without returning to real sanity.

WHY BUY STOCKS?

The purpose of buying stocks has changed dramatically in the
last few years. Historically, you bought a stock to benefit from the
growth of sales and profits. You were betting on the company and
its management, not the market. Now investors (I hesitate to call
them investors—they're really speculators) weren't investing in a
company or a group of companies to participate in increased
sales, and above all, profits. They weren't investing in companies,
they were speculating on stock prices, assuming that trees would
continue to grow to the sky and that the current psychology of
investors would continue into the indefinite future, despite sur-
real valuations.

When the Nasdaq market started to collapse, some money
managers started looking for "value." At least most of the companies in the Dow Jones Industrial Average had some profits,
whereas very few of the companies in the red-hot Nasdaq index
had any or even the prospect of having any. So "sophisticated"
money began to migrate from the Nasdaq to the Dow. But there
was one hitch: Even though there was some value in the Dow
stocks because they had real sales and earnings, they were also

grossly overvalued by traditional measures. The bottom was a long way away, and the market would crash either in one fell swoop or in a slow-motion decline over the next months or even years, like being nibbled to death by ducks.

In the old fuddy-duddy days, if you invested in a company, you assumed the price would take care of itself if sales and earnings grew, so you bet on a management team that knew something more than financial engineering and were interested in something more than today's market value of their options. Wal-Mart is a great example of a company that treasures its bottom line. As this book is written, it is still overvalued, so I wouldn't buy it now, but they have the right idea—market effectively, make money, and eventually the market will reward you. Wal-Mart is on my list of future prospects when the price is right. The only thing wrong with Wal-Mart at the moment is the price.

What does all this boil down to? *Be an investor, not a speculator,* and especially not a "momentum investor"—or at least know what you really are. The odds are against the speculators, especially those who think they are investors but aren't. Don't buy stocks unless there are genuine values as measured by historical standards in the market as a whole, as well as the stock you are buying.

What are those standards and how do you measure them? When the market is finally fairly valued, the world will be on the bargain table. You will be able to tack *The Wall Street Journal* to the wall, throw darts at it, invest in the holes, and make money. Just be patient!

I would suggest that the price/earnings ratio (PE) for the whole New York Stock Exchange at historic bottoms is around 7/1. As this is written, the PE is about 32/1. At the bottoms, dividends yielded around 4 percent. As this is written, the yield is closer to 1 percent. When the market approaches these traditional historical bottoms, I'll report it in *The Ruff Times* (www.rufftimes.com). (See Appendix A.)

Chapter 9

Worshipping the Golden Calf

Too many investors become Gold Bugs and fall in love with their investment. Sometimes it's a great investment, and sometimes it's a sure loser; here's how to tell the difference, when to buy it, and, more important, when not to.

I n Chapter 2 I discussed the folly of worshipping the false and deceptive god Mammon. Now I want to persuade you that it is an expensive mistake to worship any investment, but especially the Golden Calf. This is one of the rare times I learned something important by getting it right!

When I first came onto the investing landscape in 1975, I saw nothing but inflation ahead of us for several years at least, and became a vocal advocate for gold and silver as inflation hedges. My best-selling book, *How to Prosper During the Coming Bad Years*, was the first popular best-seller to alert the public at large to gold and silver as an inflation hedge. Gold subsequently soared to more than $850 an ounce in 1980, up from $120 an ounce in 1975 when I first recommended it. I have been told that because the book sold more than 3 million copies, it was a major factor in creating that spectacular gold and silver bull market and legitimatizing gold and silver as popular mainstream investments.

I thought of gold as an appropriate investment for the times, but I soon found out that for millions of Americans (not to mention Germans, Swiss, etc.) it was a near religion, with its own dogma. Massive investment conferences attended by thousands of true believers were built around gold, such as the annual National Committee for Monetary Reform (NCMR) conference in New Orleans, and dozens of my newsletter colleagues jumped on the golden bandwagon for reasons of their own—some well thought out and some out of mob psychology. I was nearly canonized as a high priest of the Gold Bug Church by the media, which made me a mite uncomfortable. (Actually, I didn't protest as loudly as I should have because I enjoyed the attention, and it was good for my newsletter business.)

But in 1980, gold soared to irrational heights of over $750 an ounce (it eventually shot up to $850, but only for a day or two) and silver shot up from its low of $1.80 to $35 (it soared to $50, but only for one day). I had temporarily lost faith in gold for a little while in 1978, but had gotten back in and ridden it to the top. But now I decided this was really time to sell; inflation had peaked at 18 percent, and I believed that the combination of Ronald Reagan's tax cuts and Paul Volcker, the tough-minded, inflation-fighting chairman of the Federal Reserve, meant that inflation would be under a serious assault. So I put out a sell recommendation to my more than 150,000 newsletter subscribers, suggesting that gold would come back down to $400 and silver below $10. And all hell broke loose. It was as if the Pope had committed apostasy and become a Southern Baptist. (I exaggerate, but not much; my apologies to John Paul II.) Of course, the rest is history. When gold finally broke $400, I was invited to appear on *Nightline* with Ted Koppel and explain why I was so smart—which, of course, I thought I was.

But this was when I learned that gold was a religion with millions of devotees, and I was castigated as an apostate by the believers. I was denounced in print in no uncertain terms by many of my colleagues, and suddenly was in much less demand on the investment conference circuit, which was not much fun. But I have had the last laugh—gold has done hardly anything for investors for more than two decades, and hasn't been in the headlines for years and years, with only occasional trading rallies.

So why was I so smart? Although I had been a passionate advocate of gold as an investment, I was never a passionate Gold Bug, and therein is the lesson I would like to teach you.

Philosophically, I looked at gold in three different ways:

1. I believed, and still do, that gold should be the centerpiece of the world's monetary system, because if the currency was backed by a finite amount of gold, national treasuries and monetary authorities would have to be very cautious about how much money they printed if it was redeemable in gold, for fear of losing it to redemptions. In a world where inflation was a serious threat to the stability of our personal wealth, we needed the discipline only gold would provide. On this subject I was passionate, and still am, but that had nothing to do with gold as an investment.
2. I recommended some gold and silver coins, no matter what the gold and silver markets are doing, and still do, as a part of my calamity-insurance core holdings, along with cash savings and an emergency supply of vital commodities, including a food storage program. This is not an investment program, but an insurance program explained in more depth in Chapter 12. That has not changed in 25 years.
3. Gold is a potentially valuable investment if bought and held when certain economic conditions create a gold-friendly environment, and gold stocks are even better.

Confusing these three reasons for owning gold can lead to ill-timed purchases and market losses, and that has been the case most of the time for two decades. A love affair with gold was a big loser, or at least a going-nowhere investment for most of that time.

So, when is the right time to invest in gold? There are three conditions that are favorable for gold. At least two of them must be present for gold to have a chance, and three is better:

1. *Rising inflation:* Inflation to classically trained economists, especially those of the Austrian School, is not rising prices; it is an increase in the money supply that dilutes the value of each dollar and creates an instinctive flight by investors, especially abroad, to the stability of gold as an inflation hedge. Rising prices are an indicator of inflation, but calling rising prices inflation would be like calling a hurricane falling trees. All during these two lackluster decades for gold, inflation has been stable but slightly positive, or falling slightly, a condition called *disinflation,* which means there is still some price inflation, but at a lesser rate. So what could cause a new outburst of inflation?

   - Exploding government spending because of a war, or more social spending to buy votes for the politicians to stimulate the economy out of an incipient deflation/depression, creating a need to fund rising deficits without paying the political price of raising taxes, causing the Fed to increase the money supply in excess of increases in productivity.

   - Failure of the government to face the inevitable consequences of a shrinking Social Security Trust Fund (even though it is phony), and the burden of fewer and fewer workers to support more and more retirees. The choices are stark: Increase payroll taxes to as high as 40 percent, causing a war between the generations, or print the money (which is the option the government will choose), which will be immensely inflationary.

2. *Repeated big-time terrorism and/or war:* A series of cataclysmic events that throw a serious cloud over the potential survivability of the U.S. economy will revive gold's classic role as a calamity hedge.

3. *A falling dollar in relation to foreign currencies, especially the euro and the yen:* This is the indispensable condition that must be met along with at least one of the preceding events to trigger a true gold bull market. The dollar can fall as soon as foreign investors lose confidence in dollar-denominated investments (stocks, U.S. Treasury securities) as a safe haven against troubles with their own monetary system, or lose confidence in the stability of the American political and economic system. It can also be the consequence of low U.S. interest rates, making dollar investments less attractive to foreign investors.

BUYING GOLD

There are several easy ways to buy gold:

Gold Bullion Coins

The most acceptable and widely owned and most liquid coins are the South African krugerrand, the Canadian maple leaf, the Australian nugget, and the American gold eagle. They are all available in one-ounce coins, and there is little to choose between them, although the gold eagle has one advantage. When Congress authorized IRAs, they made it illegal to buy gold bullion or coins in an IRA, probably as a sop to the antigold forces in the banking system. But when they later authorized the production of the eagle, they specifically authorized it for IRAs and other retirement accounts, because eagles were minted from the U.S. gold reserves, and they wanted the sale to be successful.

These coins can be bought from coin dealers in any quantity, and there will be a modest premium above the price of the ounce of gold, so shop around and compare prices and premiums. You will get it back when you sell the coins.

You should have $2,000 to $3,000 worth of gold and silver coins of a variety of sizes and denominations for each family member as part of your core financial calamity hedge right now, regardless of the current gold market, but don't think of this insurance stash as part of your investment program.

Gold Bullion Bars

These are useful for bigger investors, and you will usually leave them in the depository from which you bought them so that when they are eventually sold, they do not have to be authenticated or assayed. It's a very convenient way to buy gold, if the depository is honest and has a history of dependability. There were several big frauds in the early 1980s, including one I exposed where the gold that was allegedly stored for the customers did not exist, and they lost a lot of millions.

Gold in the Ground

Perhaps the most convenient way to buy gold is while it's still in the ground, by buying the shares of gold-mining companies. This is a good idea when we are in a true gold bull market, and it introduces several variables that you don't have when you buy bullion or gold coins, such as cost of production, management skills, and so on. One of the biggest advantages is that the law allows any securities in an IRA, so the way to make an IRA bet on gold is to buy gold-mining shares. Also, you don't have to store them like coins or insure them.

There is much more risk and more potential profit or loss in a gold-mining stock than in coins or bullion. You are investing in a business enterprise that should be weighed like any other industrial company. As the price of gold rises and falls, the value of their reserves in the ground rises and falls accordingly, and so do their profits per ounce of gold mined, as their costs remain fairly constant as the price rises.

For example, let's say you bought gold at $400, and it went to $500. You would have a 25 percent profit. But if at the same time you bought stock in a company that had a cost of production of $350, and gold was selling at $400, the mine would have a $50 an ounce profit. If gold then went to $500, the profit per ounce would triple to $150, and it is likely the stock would triple also. So gold stocks are leveraged to the price of gold, are much more volatile up and down, and in a gold bull market are much more profitable than bullion or coins.

In a gold bull market, the lowest-cost producers rise first, followed by the higher-cost producers, followed by the exploration companies with proven reserves but no production yet, followed finally by the holes in the ground surrounded by liars, often called *penny golds*.

A rising gold tide truly raises all boats. I have listed my preferred mining stocks by category in Appendix B.

WILL GOLD RISE AGAIN?

Yes, it will. My best guess is that if deflation or economic downturn gets serious—which is a possibility as this is written—to stave off deflation and recession/depression, the Fed will expand the money supply to stimulate the economy and Congress will also step up spending to alleviate financial distress. Consequently, inflation will soar, the dollar will fall further, and gold will rise again. There is a great future for gold, but not until the forces that will drive it are all in place.

How far will it go, and when? It's like what you get when you combine an elephant and a rhino, "Elephino!" These events could happen at any time, maybe before you read this book. I track gold closely in my newsletter, *The Ruff Times.* You can get subscription information from Appendix A or on my Web site at www.rufftimes.com. I will put out a buy or hold signal when my indicators say so, which may have happened even before you read this. Don't buy gold or gold stocks until you check out my recommendations in *The Ruff Times*, as the world is always in a state of flux.

So don't fall in love with gold or worship it when you invest in it. Buy some coins now as a calamity hedge against sudden surprises, and root for a return to the gold standard, but only invest in gold when the preceding investment conditions are right, and include silver in the same calculations. Any other gold strategy can be an expensive mistake.

Late Note (January 2004):

It's happened. Just before I passed the deadline for completing my page proofs, we got a firm buy signal. We are now officially in a gold bull market that will last for some years, driven by the imploding dollar, among other things. Gold bought now at around $400–$450 per ounce and held for two to five years will earn you several times your money if you are patient and hang on. Silver will be several times more profitable, and mining stocks will do even better. See Appendix B, and *The Ruff Times* (Appendix A), for current gold stock recommendations.

Chapter 10

The Financial Death Wish

Buying high and selling low is like a universal plague—most everyone does it. Here are the surprising reasons why you do it, and how to stop.

I doubt that anyone will consider "buy low, sell high" to be a brilliantly controversial idea. It's self-evident, isn't it? Who would do otherwise? Most investors, that's who, because most stock market investors lose money in the markets, even in bull markets. It's an almost universal phenomenon. Most investors have done it at least some of the time. What they don't know is why they did such a dumb thing. There are several definable and avoidable reasons:

- *Ignorant timing:* Investors usually have no clue as to real intrinsic value, so they do the stupid thing described in Chapter 8—they pay too much for an overvalued stock because it's "hot" or in the news (which means the pros have already bought), and then when it inevitably returns to a more realistic valuation, they get discouraged and sell out for less than what they paid for it, so they bought high and sold low. They don't realize that profit is predetermined at the time you buy, much more than when you sell. If you don't buy right, the odds are you will sell low.

- *Emotions:* Emotions are usually a huge factor in stock losses. Investors who make unemotional decisions are rare (if they do, they're usually hardened professionals), and the emotions that can distort judgment are legion: enthusiasm, the desire to not be left out (otherwise known as *herd mentality*), ego, and the ever popular fear and greed.
- *Bad luck:* Sometimes you buy just before some unforeseen piece of bad news hits and the stock tanks. That's not your fault, but it can be an opportunity in disguise that you will probably miss.

Let's look at these mistakes one at a time.

IGNORANT TIMING

I called this *ignorant* rather than *bad* for a reason. It usually happens because you haven't taken the time and trouble to do your homework, starting with a study of the price history of the company and a careful examination of historical valuation ratios (price/earnings, price/sales, etc.), both for the company and its industry group. Even a good company is a lousy investment if it costs too much, as is even the strongest company in a weak industry group. If the price is out of whack with historical values, you are just about to buy high, sell low.

Emotions are the investor's worst enemy, because they skew judgment, often in ways that you aren't even aware of. Let's look at a few reasons why:

- *Love.* I don't know how many times I have had an investor defend a decision to hold onto a losing stock position by saying, "But I love this company!" I can assure you that the company doesn't return your affection. A stock is not a spouse, a child, or a puppy, it's an inanimate thing, and you should be as unemotional and impersonal toward it as it is to you. Go back and read Chapter 9 again.

- *Ego.* This usually manifests when all the objective data say it's time to sell, but you hang on while the losses mount, not willing to admit you made a mistake. Sometimes selling at a small loss seems like a personal insult: "I'll be damned if I'm going to let this stock tell me what to do." Ruff's First Law of Limiting Losses is, "He who refuses to take small losses will take big losses," and ego is the main reason why you don't face unpleasant reality and cut your losses. This principle really won't prevent a loss, but it will avoid big losses.

- *Fear and greed.* We will talk about these two emotions together because they are the two sides of the problem that go together. We fear we will be left out, so we buy after a run-up. We fear we won't think of ourselves as smart if we don't get on board. Greed causes us to hang on too long and ride a stock over the top and down the far slope, for we fear we will leave some money on the table. Fear of loss will also cause us to unload before a promising company has had a chance to prove itself, even if the fundamentals are still promising.

- *Enthusiasm.* This admirable quality is one emotion no investor can afford to indulge when making buy, sell, or hold decisions. It's usually what sucks you into the herd mentality. During the late, lamented dot-com bubble, I heard enthusiasm from individual investors, from stock analysts on CNBC, and from economists touting the new economy and telling us how the old standards no longer apply. Enthusiasm sucks unsophisticated investors into doomed start-ups because they are excited about a new widget that will revolutionize something or other. Enthusiasts emotionally buy into the story, but objective realists ignore the enthusiasts. They want to know if the management team has the skills, knowledge, and balance to turn a great idea into a real company. They want to know if the company will have enough cash to make the necessary capital expenditures, do the market research, and then drive the company to success. They want to see the business plan to determine if the founders and management have really thought through the process of turning a great idea into a great company (see Chapters 17 and 18).

BAD LUCK

We all experience some bad luck from time to time, but smart investors insulate themselves from potential bad breaks so they are minimized. How?

- *They diversify broadly.* I had very little sympathy for the Enron employees who were caught in the sudden collapse of their employer. I watched a parade of them on the TV news as they told their sad stories about how their entire 401(k)s were invested in Enron stock, so their whole future retirement was wiped out overnight. If they had diversified, they would have been hurt but they wouldn't have been wiped out. Investors should look at their portfolio like the portfolio manager of a mutual fund looks at his or hers. Even the best are wrong about 30 percent of the time, and the managers know it. They prune out the losers without a backward glance, unlike a lot of investors who watch a stock more closely after they sell it than they did when they owned it, just to see if they made a mistake. It is unlikely that bad luck will sink your whole portfolio at once if you are broadly diversified. But broad diversification is more than meets the eye. If your diversification is across a narrow spectrum of related investments, like industry groups that will be affected by the same forces in the same direction, that is not diversification, it's what Robert Kiyosaki calls *"de-worsification."* Real diversification might look like this: some income-producing real estate, some gold and silver or gold-mining stocks, some commodities, some land, some undervalued, dividend-producing stocks, a few promising start-ups using the guidelines in Chapter 18, and some T-bonds or foreign bonds and stocks. It is unlikely that they would all go south in a bear market or be crushed by the reprehensible actions of the management of one company, such as Enron.

- *They buy shares of only a single mutual fund.* This is one way to de-worsify. You should divvy up your money between several different types of mutual funds, such as a growth fund, a financial institutions fund, an oil fund, a real estate investment trust (REIT), and a gold fund. That might work and spread the risk.

- *They turn lemons into lemonade.* If bad luck hits one of their investments and it crashes and burns overnight, they reevaluate it and see if they haven't been presented with a chance to buy real value at a big discount. The only reason stocks are cheap is because potential buyers are pessimistic about the future of the company or the market and are selling. The only cheap stocks are out-of-favor stocks, so your piece of bad luck can be a new opportunity in disguise. As Baron Rothschild said, "The time to buy is when the blood is running in the streets." That's a great concept as long as you can determine whether or not the blood is flowing from a mortal wound. But if you diversify over several companies, the odds are that the bad decisions will be more than balanced out by the good ones, especially if you quickly prune the bad decisions from your portfolio as things become clearer.

Chapter 11

Buying on Margin

Buying on margin is a highly leveraged way to buy stocks, but it's just as leveraged on the way down as it is on the way up. It's not for amateur investors, but for sophisticated professionals with nerves of steel. My dad thought he was one, and it wiped him out.

My dad was a gambler at heart, so he sold the stock in the company he had helped to build and went to New York to *really* get rich speculating on stocks on margin. Unfortunately, it was 1929, and on that historic black day in October when the market crashed and Wall Street became a falling-body zone, he lost every penny.

Buying stocks on margin means you borrow money to buy stocks. In 1929, margin buying was the big reason the market had soared. All you needed was 10 percent margin money, which meant you could open a margin account with a broker and buy stocks by only putting up 10 percent of the cost of the stock in cash, with the broker loaning you 90 percent. This multiplied the investor's buying power by 10, driving the market ever higher. Fortunes were made overnight—sometimes in minutes—as a 10 percent move upward would double your money.

That meant that if you wanted to buy 1000 shares of ABC Widgets at $10 a share ($10,000), you only had to put up $1 a share

($1,000), and the broker would put up $9 a share ($9,000). If the stock went up $1 to $11, you doubled your money, because you could sell for $11,000, pay the broker his $9,000 loan, and pocket $2,000. That worked great only when the market was going up. The problem was that the market crashed by more than 10 percent in that one black day in 1929, so margin investors got the only piece of unsolicited advice they were sure to get from their broker—a "margin call." To protect the loan, the broker would require you to put up more margin money. If you didn't "meet the margin call," the broker would sell your stock and liquidate your position. This put the investor in an agonizing position—put more money at risk in a falling market, or sell and take the losses on the chin.

On that fateful day my dad met his margin calls, and as the crash gained momentum, he was wiped out again. This happened to uncounted numbers of investors, as the market powers that be (brokers) kept issuing optimistic statements about the overall health of the economy and the market in an attempt to forestall the selling and suck more margin money out of the hands of their clients. They were wrong big time, and bodies began to fall out of tall buildings as speculators lost their life savings and the panic gained momentum, triggering more selling, and the market continued to plunge.

I don't know how many margin calls my dad met; all I know is that Mom said there were margin calls, and she didn't even know what the term meant. Because she was honorably released from life some years ago, I can't ask her.

With that debacle in mind, the Securities and Exchange Commission (SEC) now sets margin requirements much higher than 10 percent: It's currently 50 percent, which makes another 1929 less likely but still means you can lose money twice as fast on margin than you would if you owned the stock with 100 percent of your own money. So even though buying on margin is less risky than in 1929 with its 10 percent margin requirements, it will still double your risk. If the stock falls 25 percent, wiping out half your margin, you will get a margin call. If you don't meet it, the broker will "sell you out," a term that now has the generic meaning of *betrayal*—which is exactly what it feels like.

When the market started its implosion in March 2000, margin selling was a factor in the continuing slow-motion crash. A lot of margin calls were met, a strategy that had worked in the previous few years when declines were brief and corrected themselves quickly; but this time the market had risen so high that it was just too vulnerable.

Buying on margin is not for amateurs; it doubles the volatility, and it doubles the impact of market moves, either up or down. Don't do it. I may change that advice when the stock market has finally bottomed out at near-riskless levels a lot lower than it is now, but until that day, it's a no-no.

MEET A MARGIN CALL?

One of my basic rules of investing is, Never meet a margin call. Jim Dines has said wisely, "A trend in motion will remain in motion until it ends," which means that you should never buy in a falling market. He also said, "Never try to catch a falling safe," which means essentially the same thing. These maxims sound simplistic and self-evident, but these basic principles will limit your losses, which leads me to one of my wiser maxims: *Avoiding losses is the first rule of investing.*

Chapter 12

Thinking the Unthinkable

You have life insurance, homeowner's insurance, medical insurance, and so on to compensate you in case of common but unforeseen events. But there are other worst-case events no traditional insurance can protect us against, for which we have to create our own insurance. The prosperity or wealth strategies in this book can be endangered or totally aborted by such unexpected events. Here is the insurance you need, and why you need it.

America has never been more vulnerable to such unthinkable surprises, nor have they ever been more likely, and they are always to the downside. Here's a list:

- Unexpected loss of income. You can lose your income and your retirement if you are laid off because your employer is threatened by a recession or depression, sudden interest-rate changes, supply problems, war, unexpected changes in regulations or tax laws, the death of a founder, a hostile takeover, sudden foreign competition, corporate misjudgments, wildcat strikes, hurricanes or earthquakes, power-grid failures, terrorist attacks, or an underfunded pension plan. Your employer might sell out to another company, and your department might be wiped out or transferred to Saskatchewan. You may have gone to work for a big company for safety and security, only to find out there is no security when other people can make unilateral decisions about you unrelated to your competence.

- An attack by terrorist-inspired and -financed hackers that disrupts the economy and normal distribution of goods and services, and can cause a breakdown or even the disappearance of the dollar and the world's monetary system. More about this later.

- Disabling health problems that abort your prosperity or wealth program, such as a heart attack, accidents, cancer, or other serious disease.

To protect yourself and your family in case of any of these unexpected troubles, there are three insurance steps you should take:

1. Accumulate approximately six months of cash (dollars) in reserve, sufficient to pay the mortgage, installment payments, and operating expenses for a car, as well as fresh food.
2. Have an emergency commodity stash, including a six-month supply of food.
3. Own roughly $2,000 to $3,000 worth of gold and silver coins per family member.

Let's discuss these one at a time.

WHY SIX MONTHS OF CASH?

If your income is cut off for any reason, you need enough to cover your essential needs for about six months, which would probably be enough to pay the bills until you were able to right your financial boat. This can be in a local bank, unless a banking collapse is threatened.

WHY AN EMERGENCY COMMODITY STASH?

What if the August 2003 power blackout wasn't over in two or three days? What if it had been caused by a strategic terrorist hacker attack and you couldn't buy common goods because the electronic cash registers wouldn't work? You would wish you had a supply of nonspoilable, canned, dehydrated, and freeze-dried food, water for drinking and cooking, flashlights and batteries, diapers, prescription drugs, first-aid supplies, toilet paper and paper towels, motor oil, soap and laundry detergent, battery chargers, 5- and 10-gallon cans of gas, warm clothes, candles, charcoal and a grill, a battery-operated radio, and so on.

But why? Back in the Introduction I told you about my 1968 bankruptcy when I went to work rich and came home broke, which ruined my whole day. Some months prior to that calamity, a cousin had come through town looking for work, so Kay hired him to build some shelves in the garage for the food-storage program we were going to start. It was a standard principle for Mormons to have at least a six-month supply of food on hand, but I had always pooh-poohed the idea to Kay, telling her, "When you have money, you can always go down to the store and buy food." I felt we were at least very prosperous with my booming speed-reading school. But then my franchise was canceled overnight, my office doors were locked, and my bank accounts were frozen, and I had less than $20 in my pocket. We went out to the garage and stood by the shelves that were stocked with food items Kay had squirreled away using money squeezed out of the food budget, and as we embraced in the garage, we shed tears of gratitude.

I had always thought that food storage was for some possible future time when there might be big, generalized problems for society at large and everyone was in trouble. It had never occurred to me that there might be much more personal and close-to-home reasons for a food storage program. There was no generalized economic problem in our town, nor was there any on the horizon, but there was a potential famine at 27 Arroyo Drive in Moraga, California, and we used our food storage for several months until I got my cash flow rolling again.

Ever since then, I have been a passionate advocate for food-storage programs for America, and never has there been a time when this prudent, riskless, conservative idea made more sense than it does today. There are some serious vulnerabilities and some very credible threats to our smoothly functioning society and no shortage of motivated and well-financed enemies willing and eager to exploit them.

Even without external threats, we live in an age where layoffs and business failures are more and more common. There is also a rising tide of bankruptcies, as described in Chapter 4, and many find themselves in need of charitable help because they can't help themselves. The Mormon idea of personal food storage is at least in part a moral decision that if you are prepared for financial trouble before it materializes, you will not have to dip into other people's pockets through the taxing power of government when trouble actually shows up.

VULNERABILITIES

What if hackers, paid and motivated by America-hating terrorists, launched a virus or other electronic gremlin that disabled the nation's computer systems for even a week or two? What if the ATM machines weren't working for a week or two, as happened for only two or three days in New York, Buffalo, Toronto, Detroit, and places in between in the 2003 power blackout? What if the cash registers at your local supermarket didn't work and you couldn't buy anything? What if your credit and debit cards couldn't be accepted and cash prices tripled? What if terrorists contaminated your local water supply? (We know they have been exploring that possibility.)

Distribution of food and other commodities is becoming more and more computerized and interdependent, and just-in-time purchasing and delivery are common business practices. If the trucks don't roll as scheduled, there will be instant shortages, aggravated and accelerated by panic buying.

The number of Muslims who have been radicalized into becoming America haters has been growing by the millions. They call us the Great Satan, and we seem to be doing everything we can to affirm their perceptions. Did you know that the most-watched TV reruns in the Muslim countries are *Baywatch* and *Jerry Springer?* Millions of Muslims think that these shows are honest representations of the real America. Millions of young Muslims believe that when they kill Americans, they are doing God a favor. And their technological expertise is growing by leaps and bounds. What if they launched a virus that spread to most of America's computers and servers, and they brought down the power grid?

OASES OF STABILITY

The August 2003 blackout is a cautionary tale. While millions of people were scrambling to buy food, water, and flashlights, there were tens of thousands of oases of stability everywhere—the Mormons! I promised that I wouldn't turn this book into a religious tract, but one Mormon practice spills over into the broader social arena—food storage—and you don't have to agree with our theology or join us to benefit from this principle. For Mormons, this is not an apocalyptic thing; it's just the natural outgrowth of the nineteenth-century self-sufficiency attitude that is a part of the Mormon cultural heritage. And we love to share the idea with neighbors and friends, because if this practice became universal, the communities our families live in would be safer and more stable.

Let me tell you what happened for two or three days in August 2003.

The blackout across the Northeast and Midwest was a great test of personal and family preparedness for the Mormons, as several days without electricity or water came unexpectedly and in many forms, and the Mormons have been advised for several years by church leaders to have a personal preparedness program. Whatever else you may think of Mormonism (The Church of Jesus Christ of Latter-Day Saints), it is an eminently practical church. As a result, Mormons from Connecticut to Michigan and Toronto to Ohio generally fared well when the lights went out and all power failed. Reported one bishop (the functional equivalent of a pastor), "A few minutes after the blackout began, I implemented our 72-hour emergency plan, which includes verbal communication with each family, paying particular attention to widows, children, and the disabled . . . various members offered to assist needy families with electricity from backup generators."

A common observation among local church leaders was that there was a sense of calm, much of which had to do with being prepared. Said one bishop, "Being fairly well prepared certainly made a big difference in how we reacted." Another bishop echoed what others had learned—that cordless phones don't work when the power is out.

Many church members who worked in Manhattan and lived 20 or 30 miles away spent the night in the Manhattan Stake Center (a Stake is the Mormon equivalent of a diocese), as did visitors to the city whose electronic hotel keys no longer worked. In Grand Rapids, Michigan, a single mother with two children offered to bring widows to her home where she could feed and care for them. She walked to her non-Mormon neighbors to offer food and assistance. When the blackout hit, the Mormons watched calmly as others scurried to grocery stores. Some areas were without power for up to three days.

Some years ago, one of my subscribers, in a lame attempt at

humor, said, "I will have a food storage program; I will just buy a gun and move next door to a Mormon." Ha ha! There is a better way; do it yourself!

WHY GOLD AND SILVER?

This is a much more complex question and answer. Gold and silver are your protection against runaway inflation, war, international currency exchange problems, a devastating hacker attack on the world's monetary system (which is a real threat, and very likely) and a collapse or devaluation of the dollar through inflation, which we saw less than three decades ago. In the inflation of the late seventies and early eighties, gold went up more than 700 percent, and silver more than 2,500 percent.

In almost all ages, these metals have been real money. All paper currencies eventually die; and the world is littered with dead paper currencies; but there has never been a time when gold and silver were not valuable, either as a means of exchange or as a store of value, or both. They would replace or substitute for all paper currencies if the dollar were to take its place alongside the defunct deutschmark. If the dollar survives all these potential assaults and you need some dollars, there is a ready market for your coins at any neighborhood coin dealer, probably at a profit, as gold is in the early stages of a long bull market even as I write.

You need a variety of gold and silver coins in various weights and denominations, which I will elaborate on later. I have also discussed gold in Chapter 9. Look there for more details.

TERRORISM AND GOLD

The terrorist attack on the World Trade Center was really more than just an attempt to spread terror: It was an assault on the monetary system of America and the rest of the Western World. Ten years ago, the consequences worldwide would have been beyond imagination. In order to understand why, you have to understand the nature of money.

The dollar is mostly in cyberspace; less than 5 percent of all dollars are minted, printed, or coined. All those trillions of dollars (no one knows exactly how many) exist only as computer entries and can be sent around the world with a computer keystroke. A decade ago, nearly all of these computers were in New York, a lot of them in the World Trade Center. Then, a few years ago, the powerful institutions that operate most of the computers that are the heart of the New York Stock Exchange, the Nasdaq, currency trading, and the Treasury- and municipal-bond markets began to decentralize their computer operations. Many of them were moved across the Hudson River to New Jersey, so even as the world watched the World Trade Center collapse, the world's markets hardly missed a beat. One of the world's largest bond traders lost 85 percent of its employees when the buildings crumbled, but trading went on worldwide.

The world's top terrorists are not fools, and they have learned from experience. I believe they now know that America could be brought to its knees if they could contaminate or destroy the software and hardware that runs the Western World.

Much of the multinational banks' international operations are run in Panama in the former Canal Zone without oversight or regulation. How did this happen? America's chief negotiator during the Jimmy Carter canal giveaway, Sol Linowitz, a member of the board of Chemical Bank, was given an interim appointment of one day less than six months so he would not need Senate confirmation. Not only was the deal with Panama signed just one day short of the end of Linowitz's term, but bank buildings were already springing up like mushrooms all over the Canal Zone for months in anticipation of the Canal Zone becoming a free banking zone, which it is now. Three billion dollars in American bank loans to Panama were made good as Panama seized control of the canal revenues.

I'm not a computer expert, but I have been given reason to believe by people who are experts that the computer systems in Panama are much more vulnerable to attack than those in America, and even more important.

But what does this have to do with gold and silver?

Until quite recently in the history of money, gold was the ultimate money—a means of exchange and a store of value. We still say "as good as gold," one of our sports heroes might still be called "the Golden Boy"; retirement is called "the Golden Years." Until Nixon closed the gold window, our money was backed by gold. Now we take a worthless piece of paper and try to make it valuable by merely applying ink. But what happens when the computers go down and we can't get the ink-engraved paper or use our credit or debit cards? Gold and silver coins will be considered real money everywhere in the world. The Germans still remember the inflation that devastated them after World War I, when a wheelbarrow full of money wouldn't buy a loaf of bread, but an American dime would. The Swiss still have a gold-backed currency. In India, people wear much of their wealth around their necks in the form of gold chains. Gold is part of the monetary holdings of nearly all of the world's central banks. The Chinese are still big fans of gold, and in America we are only two decades away from the days when a gold rush drove the price of gold from $120 an ounce to $850, and silver from $2 to $50.

This chapter is not about gold and silver as investments, although that may be a darn good idea, as explained in Chapter 9. I am arguing for each family to have $2,000 to $3,000 in gold and silver coins as a hedge against the possible day when dollars are not available and you need a means of exchange.

I have asked Jim Cook, president of Investment Rarities (www.investmentrarities.com, 800-828-1860), to suggest a coin portfolio of about $3,000 for your consideration for each family member. Jim has served tens of thousands of my subscribers over the years. I have also asked him to create a Howard Ruff Core

Package. I have no financial interest of any kind in this recommendation. Jim suggests ¼ bag ($250 face value) of pre-1965 silver dimes or quarters, worth about $1,000), three rolls (200 coins per roll) of U.S. silver eagles (worth about $450), and four 1-ounce gold coins (krugerrands, eagles, or maple leafs) worth about $1,600. You should have one such portfolio for each family member.

I believe America's biggest terrorist threat is not airplane hijacking but terrorist-inspired computer hacking. If I wanted to disable America, I would simultaneously detonate dirty nuclear devices in Northern New Jersey and the Canal Zone to make them uninhabitable and all those computers inaccessible because of nuclear contamination, and launch a nightmare horde of viruses at the Internet and the servers and computers that manage the world's money supply.

Is this a prophecy? Not at all; I'm no prophet. It's merely a statement of growing possibilities, and an argument to be prepared with a stash of cash, gold and silver coins, and essential commodities. Then relax and sleep well again.

But what if none of these worst cases ever materializes? Well, unlike the money you spend on premiums for term insurance or health insurance, you can eat or otherwise use the stored commodities, or liquidate the gold and silver for dollars—most likely at a profit, as gold responds to war, inflation, and other calamities, and I believe that at least some of these things are likely in our future. In the meantime, proceed with your prosperity or wealth program, knowing you are prepared in case everything else goes to hell for awhile. And don't use the fears I may have aroused as an excuse to ignore everything I may have taught you about how to become Safely Prosperous or Really Rich. If you just stand pat with your life as it is now, you are far more vulnerable to these fearsome theoretical possibilities than you would be if you were out of debt.

Book II

The Secrets of the Rich—The Most Important Things Rich People Always Do

The easy way to get rich is to choose your parents very carefully, but it's too late for that now. This section is about how to leap the gulf between the Safely Prosperous and the Really Rich. For the Really Rich, the rules are different from the ones followed by the Safely Prosperous as described in the preceding chapters. Sometimes they are the exact opposite. For the Safely Prosperous, borrowing is usually bad; for the Really Rich, borrowing is essential. For the Safely Prosperous, mistakes are to be avoided at all costs; for the Really Rich, mistakes and failures aren't stumbling blocks, they are essential stepping stones on the way to wealth.

The Really Rich are really different in other ways, and it's not just how much money they have. Their attitude toward risk is one big factor. The Safely Prosperous are disciplined and make few mistakes with their money, but they take no chances. They live well within their means, and are very comfortable with a riskless lifestyle—and that's OK, God bless 'em. But the Really Rich usually got rich by taking risks all the time and making mistakes they learned from. They aren't gamblers, except with a small part of their fortune, just for the fun and excitement of gambling. They are comfortable with risk, but it is always calculated risk, usually where they can determine the outcome, and it has to return far more than market rates. They are often driven, sometimes by greed, sometimes by grand ideas, sometimes to show someone they are someone too. But most of all, they see risk as measurable and controllable, and they enjoy the game. They also use leverage, sometimes without labeling it as such. They use money leverage, people leverage, and alliance leverage. Without it, they wouldn't get rich.

In the parable of the talents, Jesus told about three servants who were given some money to care for by their master. One was given five talents (more money than most men could earn in a lifetime), one two talents, and one was given only one talent. When the master returned and asked for an accounting, the men who had been given five and two talents had both doubled their money, and were praised and promised great rewards. However, the man with one talent, knowing his master was a hard man, had buried it in the ground, and had no increase. The reward for his no-risk strategy? The master gave his talent to the man who had had five. The Really Rich go even farther than the first two servants; they want returns of 5-fold or 10-fold.

The following chapters tell you the things rich people have always done with their money that you don't do. In good times or bad—no matter how bad—smart people still get rich, and these are their secrets. I will not only tell you how to get rich, I will teach you how to stay rich. Some of the strategies can also be adopted by the Safely Prosperous. The irony is that anyone can get rich if they know how, and I will teach you how.

Chapter 13

Surprising Ways Rich People Get Rich with Leverage

All Really Rich people I know use several kinds of leverage, including some you never heard of. Unlike buying stocks on margin, the way they do it lowers their risk.

Archimedes the Greek, usually given credit for the discovery of the principle of the lever, once said, "Give me a big enough lever and a place to stand, and I could move the world." He understood that a lever was a tool for multiplying your strength beyond its natural limits. He also knew that the bigger the lever, the greater the increase in strength.

Unfortunately for the uninformed, the lever can be another cliché, a two-edged sword. Used unwisely, the wrong kind of leverage not only can multiply your upside, it can work with equal efficiency on the downside and can increase your risk.

Most people who think they understand leverage think it applies only to the use of borrowed money to buy stocks on margin (dangerous) or using a mortgage to buy a home or investment real estate (safe). My father is my Exhibit Number One on the dangerous side of leverage (see Chapter 11), but his story doesn't invalidate my premise that if you want to be Really Rich, leverage is critical to your get-rich program.

Remember, a lever is only a way to multiply your strength. There are three forms of leverage that count, and you should use all of them wisely: money leverage, people leverage, and time leverage. I defy you to show me a rich person who didn't use at least one of them. (I am ignoring movie stars who get $20 million a picture and athletes who make millions of dollars a year for a few years. They don't count, because you aren't one of them.)

NO LEVERAGE?

Most people have no leverage in their earning picture, and that is the probable reason they are not rich. Is there a difference between a $6-an-hour McDonald's counter clerk and a $300-an-hour lawyer? Not as much as you think. In both cases, if they don't work, they don't get paid. Their income is limited by how many hours they work.

And it's even worse than it looks; personal income is taxed at the highest tax rate imposed on any kind of income. If you depend on personal income from your own labors only, you are like a salmon swimming upstream carrying a barbell on its back. One facet of the get-rich strategy is to be personally poor or in modest circumstances, making the smallest amount possible of highly taxed personal income, while controlling enterprises that produce fat profits at much lower tax rates.

If you employ leverage wisely, you will work less and earn more. You will make money even if you can't work, because your money will work for you, your employees will work for you, your partners will work for you, and your money will do double-, triple-, and more duty for you.

Now let's look at the various forms of leverage.

Money Leverage
The old cliché says that it takes money to make money, and that's true, but it doesn't mean it has to be your money. Everyone uses

leverage when they take out a mortgage to buy a much nicer home than they could buy out of their savings. Rich real-estate investors couldn't get rich unless they could borrow money to buy properties. Banks are not just in the money business, they also manufacture levers, and the government is your friend in this case. Unlike buying stocks on margin, no government agency enforces real-estate margin-call rules against you. If real estate hits a soft spot and the appraised value of your home falls below the balance owing on your mortgage, you don't have to put up more money to protect the lender. Make your payments, and it remains yours. This is because of effective lobbying by the real-estate industry.

And how about rich businessmen like Bill Gates? He used lots of leverage, increasing his earnings and the safety of his business and the value of his assets. He raised a lot of investor money by selling some of his stock, and used that leverage to grow his company. His corporate stock is the vast majority of his $60 billion wealth. That's leverage. When Ted Turner was asked how rich he was, he said, "I must be really rich; I owe a lot of money."

There is good debt and bad debt. Consumer debt is always bad debt. Business debt is good debt if you use it properly. Way back in Chapter 4 I said it was OK to borrow money to buy assets that produced enough cash flow to service the debt and then some. So let me elaborate on the rules for deciding whether a debt is a good debt or a bad debt.

Bad Debt
- Money borrowed to buy something that flits out of existence as soon as you use it—such as a vacation—leaving only the debt.
- Money borrowed to buy a money-eating alligator. It could be a vacation or a motor home, or even the bigger, better

home you live in (which is the best argument for buying a smaller home than your credit score would qualify you for, because it means lower mortgage payments, property taxes, and utility and repair bills). If you redefine an asset as something that produces positive cash flow, then your home is not an asset, as it is a negative-cash-flowing alligator.

- Money borrowed to buy a generally depreciating item, such as a car or boat. I'm talking about real depreciation here, meaning true loss of market value, not phantom depreciation, like the tax deductions you can take on an investment property when it is really appreciating.

Good Debt

I won't make a list, because there is only one kind of good debt— borrowed money that goes to work for you to build income-producing assets and that produces enough cash flow to pay the interest and systematically reduce the principal. Rich people always use debt as a business tool.

More Money Leverage

Borrowed money is not the only kind of money leverage. When entrepreneurs sell some equity to finance the company by selling some corporate stock in a private placement or going public in one of the ways I describe in Chapter 18, they are using money leverage, but that's always a financial calculation. If they can sell 10 percent of their companies and thereby produce cash that will double the sales and/or profits, it's a good deal, and they would be fools not to do it. They are then richer, because the value of their remaining stock becomes greater than it was when they owned 100 percent of the stock, and they have working cash to invest in their companies. Such cash is a lever that increases their strength.

People Leverage

I have met businesspeople who still work 12 to 15 hours a day because they don't trust other people to do their job right. That probably reflects more on the entrepreneur than it does on the staff. If staff members are competent, let them do their jobs; if they aren't, get rid of them and hire those who are. Such entrepreneurs don't understand the principle of people leverage. Smart entrepreneurs will hire people to do all the things that they can do better than they or that wouldn't get done if they didn't have the time to do it, so they can spend all their working hours doing only the things that they can do better than their staff, plus providing the leadership and strategic direction for companies that only they can provide.

Not only is people leverage profitable, but the lack of it can sign the death warrant of a company. No one can do everything. If they try, they will burn out, drop a ball they didn't have time to secure, miss something that will slip through the cracks and ruin the company, or be so bogged down in detail they can't stay up to date with developments in their industry and thereby miss opportunities.

THE CEO MENTALITY

Businesspeople who use people leverage by assembling a complementary team of real executives who know their stuff in their specialties and are allowed to use their skills can become very rich in short order. A real chief executive officer (CEO) will tell his or her team what the business objectives will be, set the policies and the battle plan, and get their concurrence with the plan. Then he or she will let the team go to work within the guidelines and budget he or she approved, while monitoring their performance very carefully and helping them make course corrections as necessary. The CEO's monitoring tools are budgets and financial reports.

One reason I liked George W. Bush in the 2000 election is that he has shown he knows how to act as a CEO. The president of the United States is the CEO of the biggest enterprise the world has ever known. Bush had been the CEO of an oil company and a major-league baseball team. I knew he would pick a blue-chip cabinet and team of gifted advisors, get their agreement on the policy objectives of his administration, set up the monitoring systems, and then let them do the jobs for which they were better qualified than him. His political philosophy is not the issue here; it's his management style. Only time will prove if he is an effective CEO, and the intractable issues he has tackled may infuriate enough people to sink his presidency, but, as this is written, so far, so good.

Compare this with the failed presidency of Jimmy Carter. He was a fine Christian gentleman with a good heart, and was very bright. He could immerse himself in the smallest details of government and policy as well as anyone, but he forgot that he had been hired by the electorate to be the CEO of the biggest enterprise the world has ever known. The big picture got away from him and created the worst combination of high interest rates, inflation, and unemployment in our history, and that sank his presidency. To his credit, he has been a pretty good ex-president, with his Habitat for Humanity program. He can hammer a nail with the best of them, as the media have never tired of showing us, but we hired him to be our CEO, not our building contractor.

I have been the founder and CEO of one network marketing company and the top distributor of another. That's where I learned this principle of people leverage. If you built a team of distributors who were always building their teams, you were making money you didn't have to earn with your own sales. You had passive income whether or not you worked yourself or made sales. I personally don't like doing multilevel marketing. It takes a kind of temperament that I don't have, but it's great for the right kind of person and a great way to learn to apply people leverage. But I believe in the principle of people leverage with a passion. It's an essential strategy you must use if you ever want to be rich and secure, especially if you want to earn more and work less.

LEVERAGE IN A NUTSHELL

Let's sum up the principal of leverage. Leverage means making money from the use of money contributed by others or loaned to you, and also making money from the efforts of employees, partners, and business associates. It means making money you did not have to earn by the sweat of your own brow, earning money by the sweat of other people's brows as they work hard to make you rich.

Chapter 14

Getting Rich by Banishing Fear

There are a lot of great products and great business ideas that never become great fortunes. Why? Usually fear. Yielding to fear cost me two fortunes. Here's how to get rich by facing your fears.

A few years ago, after some years of adopting a lower profile, I accepted an invitation to speak at the giant Blanchard investment conference in New Orleans, which I hadn't done for several years. As I rode in the elevator at the hotel that was housing the conference, a woman looked at me and said, "You look just like Howard Ruff." I responded, "You're the fourth person who has told me that today." She replied, "That must be a real drag. Whatever happened to Howard Ruff?" I had no answer, but I realized that day how fleeting fame can be. Now I'd like to answer that woman, and hope she reads this embarrassing story.

I have lost two fortunes and ruined my businesses twice by taking counsel of my fears. Back in the early eighties, I was riding high. My newsletter, *The Ruff Times*, was the biggest, most influential newsletter in the known universe. My book, *How to Prosper During the Coming Bad Years*, had been solidly ensconced at the top of the best-seller list for two years. My cash flow was terrific. I had great political influence in Washington and in Utah because of Ruff PAC and Free the Eagle. We had bought a 10,000-square-foot mansion in Mapleton, Utah, and added 10,000 more feet to contain a near-Olympic-size pool, a racquetball court, a huge garage to house my boat and motor home, and a spare apartment. We were also spending money like water. I was on top of the world, and even bragged to my wife how we were in the top one-half of one percent of wealthy Americans. We had a million-dollar turboprop aircraft and a professional pilot on a generous full-time salary in case I needed to fly to my California office or just wanted to go fishing.

This is exactly the time I allowed my fear to make the fateful decision that began the years-long downslide that eventually cost me my business and my fortune.

Let me share the most embarrassing thing I could ever admit—embarrassing because it shatters the carefully nurtured image I had created (and believed) that I was a wise, successful businessman and a great marketer.

THE WAGES OF FEAR

Direct mail was the tool that had made me rich. I had written a very successful piece to sell *The Ruff Times* and was mailing to about 200,000 rented mailing list names every month. The mailing consisted of an eight-page sales piece, a business reply envelope (BRE), and an order form in a number 10 envelope. We would test a list by mailing to a few thousand names. Then, if it broke even, producing enough revenue to pay for the printing, postage, list rentals, and the "fulfillment cost," we would roll it out, mailing to the list as many times as we could until it failed to break even. Obviously, printing and mailing costs were a big factor in this decision. The only limitation was the number of names I could rent that would break even or better.

Then one day I learned about the web press. Using this new technology, we could produce a "self-mailer" that incorporated the BRE and order form and eliminated the need for a number 10 envelope. Because this reduced the cost of the package by almost half, the break-even cost came way down. This meant that the universe of mailing lists that could produce a break-even or better was hugely expanded. I could get even better list rental prices because of the huge volume and use even more lists if I was willing to print 2 million pieces at a time. The only problem was, I hadn't set aside enough capital to print and mail 2 million pieces. Because of this, I had to do the printing on credit so I would have enough cash to pay the postage, because Uncle Sam didn't offer any credit. The risk was huge, and the upside was hard to quantify exactly, although my gut told me it was acceptable. My decision to do this terrified my staff, who all advised against doing it because if it failed, the company would be broke and they would all lose their jobs. I ignored their fears and plunged ahead.

So far, so good! It worked like a charm. For years America's mailboxes were flooded with self-mailers that asked on the front page, "Can You Afford to Be without This Man's Advice?" and the money rolled in. I mailed 1 to 2 million pieces every month for several years. Then, in the late 1980s, suddenly results started falling off. We were no longer breaking even, and the universe of mailing lists that would produce at break-even or better was shrinking. I soon figured out why; every competitive newsletter publisher had figured out what I was doing and was doing the same thing. Mailboxes all over America were stuffed with self-mailer newsletter solicitations, and mine was getting lost in the general clutter. Also, the competitors were hiring a new breed of talented marketing writers who were writing more compelling copy than mine, and paying them huge amounts of money, which I was unwilling to do. After all, wasn't I the greatest direct-mail copywriter in the world? This is when I made a fateful stupid decision. I decided to cancel my direct mail campaign and concentrate on marketing other products and services to my subscribers.

In other words, out of fear of losing money, I abandoned the business idea that had made me rich—direct mail—and I never got back to it. I didn't use the experience and marketing smarts I had developed in my own head and heart to come up with new marketing methods as I had done in the past. Instead, I was stuck in the past and afraid to bet the company and take a chance. Once the epitome of business courage, now I had become risk-averse—or, in other words, gutless.

In the meantime, my competitors, instead of pulling in their horns like I did, were exploring new methods, such as the "magalog," a sales piece that looked like a magazine but was only a poorly disguised sales pitch. The concept worked like crazy. But it was so expensive to develop, print, and mail that I was too scared to try it.

During the years-long downhill slide that followed, I lost my subscribers at the rate of 25 percent a year, by far the lowest attrition rate in the industry—but the ultimate sure road to failure, given the inexorable math and the nature of time—while some of my tougher and more savvy competitors are still in business with varying degrees of success. Some of them are very rich now: One lives most of the year in his restored chateau in France, while my wealth became a mere shadow of what it once was. As the list of followers shrank, so did the sales of the other products and services I offered them that I was counting on, until in 2002 my list had shrunk to only about 3,000 faithful followers. And how about my glorious Mapleton mansion? I lost it to foreclosure, as I became unable to pay the $8,000-a-month mortgage and the $2,000-a-month maintenance and utilities costs. Yielding to my fears had destroyed my business and personal finances. As I relate this story, I can't even begin to tell you how stupid I feel. Because of fear of loss, the world's greatest direct-mail marketer could no longer market himself out of a wet paper sack.

I can see in retrospect that there was a time when I could have decided to make a few bold moves and end the attrition, but about then (1991) I discovered I had cancer—a slow-growing but incurable non-Hodgkin's lymphoma—and it demoralized me still further as it dominated my thinking, paralyzed me, and fed my fears. (I am cancer-free and in good health now, but how I achieved that is another story for another time.)

DOING IT RIGHT

My story is a horrible example of what not to do, but there are contrasting stories that tell you what you can accomplish if you refuse to take counsel of your fears. As this is written, we've been in a recession for three years, and still may be when you read this. In any recession, hundreds and thousands of companies fail. But hundreds of their competitors do just fine in exactly the same businesses, because, for them, a recession is the chance of a lifetime. They always do well in good times or bad, whichever the economy dumps on their doorstep. If they don't take counsel of their fears, that attitude opens up avenues of thought and creativity that make them successful in good times or bad.

The examples that follow don't only apply to businesspeople. The principle also applies to investors, college graduates making a career decision, and so on.

So what's the difference? What separates the winning sheep from the losing goats in uncertain times (and the times are usually uncertain)? Guts and optimism! They don't make fear-driven mistakes. In business, the failed competitors may have equally good products—sometimes even better. They may have more capital and more skilled financial management. But when times get tough and the goats have pulled in their horns, the winning sheep will have courageously outmarketed the losing goats! They will have made louder noises in a quieter environment, and they will have made money when their competitors were just sitting there paralyzed by fear and being nibbled to death by ducks, year after year.

Procter & Gamble is a classic example. P&G was a small seller of soap when the Depression of the early thirties hit. All of P&G's competitors, driven by fear of loss, cut their marketing budgets and hunkered down to wait for better times, and that's what most of Procter & Gamble's shareholders wanted them to do. After all, financially strapped customers were defecting to cheaper brands. P&G's sales dropped 28 percent in 1933, and their stock fell more than 70 percent.

But P&G was blessed with one of the most gifted presidents in American business history, Richard Deupree. Deupree noted that despite the Depression, some companies were prospering, and consumers were even buying luxury items like radios—and they still needed soap. To make a long story short, Deupree decided to ride the crest of this new wave—the radio—and use it as a new advertising medium. He knew that in that day, before the invention of all of our labor-saving devices, housewives had hours of backbreaking and tedious work, with little to break the boredom—until radio. He decided to use it to pitch soap, and, after a series of experiments, hit on the serial soap opera, which captured a growing army of hardworking housewives who had to know what was happening to Ma Perkins, Our Gal Sunday, or Mary Noble, Backstage Wife. The characters used Oxydol and Ivory and Rinso White, listeners bought it by the carloads in preference to cheaper generic brands, and Procter & Gamble became one of the giants of American industry. The company is still an icon of marketing to be studied at MBA schools.

The point is, all of P&G's cheap competitors are gone, and P&G owns the cleaning products industry—all because one man decided to not take counsel of his fears and marketed aggressively and creatively in the face of the worst depression in American history.

A cat that has been burned on a hot stove won't get on another one, but it won't get on a cold one either. But what about you? You aren't Procter & Gamble, or even Howard Ruff. How does this lesson apply to you? Here are a few examples.

Let's assume you were one of the new stock investors that got burned in the recent and still ongoing stock market collapse. This may have been your first venture into the stock market. You followed the advice of your stockbroker. And why not? He's a professional, isn't he? He was following the advice of the analysts working for his employer, and they were uniformly dead wrong. In fact, just as the market was peaking in March 2000, 98 percent of the recommendations of Wall Street analysts were bullish. Then we found that some of these positive recommendations were for the stocks of companies that were big consulting clients of the broker. Then, to add insult to injury, we found that hundreds of companies were fudging—to put it mildly—their earning reports with accounting methods way beyond the abilities of the typical investor to even understand, let alone analyze. TV scenes of handcuffed Wall Street executives on their way to jail were not exactly confidence-building. It was a big shock to find out that the executives of the companies we invested in were really crooks.

So, will you ever get back into the market again? After your losses, will you even have the money to do it if you wanted to? Should you? Most people won't. They are too scarred and scared by their experience. They are afraid. But should they be?

Markets go up and markets go down, and money is made by savvy people no matter what, but you shouldn't jump in unless you are willing to burn the midnight oil to become self-educated. The stock market is no place for people who don't know what they are doing, and sometimes the right thing to do is to wait on the sidelines until the risk/reward ratio is right. That takes patience. Every bear market is followed by the opportunities of a lifetime. But will you be on the sidelines because you are patiently waiting for an opportunity or because you are scared? If it's just fear, when the opportunity comes you won't even see it. Those whose vision isn't dimmed by fear will make fortunes.

OTHER VICTIMS OF FEAR

Let's assume you are the typical middle-class American with the typical $150,000 house and to-the-hilt mortgage, a secure job (you hope) at a big company, and the typical 2.2 kids. The odds are that you are ridden with fears. What are you afraid of? Getting laid off in hard times? Not getting that raise? Worried about your pension plan and its big investments in the stock market? Worried about your debts? (See Chapter 4.) How will you pay for 2.2 college educations starting in 8 or 10 years?

Those fears may have chained you to your own job treadmill like a hamster on a wheel, which runs and runs and never gets anywhere. You think you are only prudent, that starting a business is too risky. You choose security above all. You are afraid of losing money. Yet, every rich man or woman I know, without exception, was willing to cast off the golden handcuffs and launch out into the unknown, armed only with a desire to be rich, faith in God and themselves, and the belief that the world needed what they had to offer that was apparently of no interest to their employer. They believed, as does best-selling author Robert Kiyosaki, that they shouldn't work for money; their money should work for them. Besides, how secure are you if you put your present and future in the hands of a heartless, downsizing corporation that decides you must be sacrificed in the interests of preserving their profits or shrinking their losses?

The ones who will survive hard times are those who realize there is no security when your destiny is in the hands of other people. There is no security when J.O.B. stands for "Just Over Broke."

If you won't stop listening to your fears, you will never be rich. Your only hope is to have a good job and work hard enough to be indispensable to your employer. You pretend to work hard, and your employer pretends to pay you a lot, while you pretend to be rich while piling up consumer debt. Maybe if that's good enough for you, that's what you should do. There's nothing immoral about it; after all, we're not talking about right and wrong here, just about professional and financial choices. If it wasn't for the fact that most people have made that decision, I wouldn't be able to hire the workers I need for my business. If you follow the counsel in the first four chapters, you can be prosperous and much more secure, even if you decide not to take a chance by leaping the gulf that separates the Safely Prosperous and the Really Rich. That's OK. You can stop reading here and go back to Book I.

YOUNG CHOICES

Let's assume you're in college deciding what course your life will take from here on. Will you prepare for a good job with a big, safe corporation—like, say, Enron—or will you be laying the foundation for an independent life in business? Will you prepare for security and possible prosperity, or do you want to be rich and truly independent?

Here's what I would do if I were in college. It's a darn good idea to go to college and learn the academic lessons of discipline and hard work necessary to get good grades. Just bear in mind that most of us end up doing something quite different from what our degrees prepared us for. I majored in music education, but the classes that helped me the most were those that dealt with written communication and research, like freshman English. Just make sure you acquire the skills you will need wherever you find yourself: basic accounting (if only to help you analyze and keep track of your own personal financial progress), computer skills, and communications (English literature, creative writing—the most valuable skills and disciplines will be acquired when you write a term paper). You will need all these skills whether or not you offer yourself in the job market or plunge into the maelstrom of entrepreneurial life.

Take a job with a company that will give you the experience you will need to draw on when you decide to become an independent businessperson, and learn everything you can from them. Then stay out of debt. Live a lifestyle below that which you could achieve with the liberal exercise of credit, and accumulate a stake that will give you the independence to choose the life you really want and support yourself while a new venture finds its legs. Above all, don't take counsel of your fears. Independence and calculated risks can be exhilarating fun and immensely profitable.

My favorite character in all of literature and musical theater is Don Quixote. He saw virtue where others only saw vice. He wasn't afraid to follow his impossible dream, despite the ignorance and criticism of those who were "only thinking of him." He was even willing "to march into Hell for a Heavenly cause." He marched to music others could not hear. And above all, he was courageous. There was no place in his heart for fear, as he pursued his single-minded quest of virtue. And that mad quest changed all the lives he touched as people found in themselves deep wells of goodness and courage they and all who knew them didn't know they had—even the common slut, Aldonza, who literally became the Lady Dulcinea.

I repeat: No rich person I know of took counsel of his or her fears.

THE GODS MUST BE CRAZY

One of my favorite movies of all time is *The Gods Must Be Crazy*. A game biologist in Africa is studying elephant dung to analyze the animals' diets. One night as the biologist is camped out in the jungle around a small fire, a rhino runs into the camp, destroying the tent, then stamps out the fire and runs off. According to the script, rhinos are Africa's self-appointed fire control officers, stamping out little fires before they can become big fires. (I can't vouch for the truth of this, but it helps make my point, so let's not be too critical here.)

The world is full of rhinos willing to stamp out your creative fires when they are still small. If you have big dreams, stay away from the rhinos in your life when the fire is still small. Don't listen to the naysayers who are always willing to feed your fears and tell you why you are a fool to abandon the allegedly safe, well-traveled rut you are in. Only share your fire with those who can contribute real insights that can help you correct course, and only when necessary.

Don't be afraid of failure; the road to wealth is paved with failures. J. C. Penney failed in business five times before he finally made it. Abraham Lincoln lost every elective race he entered before he was elected President. When, after testing 1,000 substances as filaments for his electric light bulb without success, Edison was asked about his project, he said, "It's wonderful. I now know a thousand things that won't work." It's a very rare and lucky guy who strikes oil in his first well. Remember the Linkletter Principle: "I never learned a thing from my successes. Everything I know I learned from my failures." (See Chapter 15 for the Linkletter story.)

So where am I now? I have written this book. I am the board chairman of a company started by my son Larry, which helps people get out of debt, including their mortgage, in nine years or less. I have launched a company that sells a natural product called Hi-Q that has been the result of an almost obsessive interest in nutrition to stave off mental decline in the golden years. By the time you read this, it may have made me rich again. Each one of those things involved taking a calculated risk when I could have just sat on what I had and nursed it until I died. But if I hadn't done those things, I am convinced I would die a few years sooner, and my final years would be ones of mental, emotional, and physical decline and terminal (literally) boredom. I am not interested in a comfortable but penurious retirement, always counting my pennies. If any of these ventures fails, I will just pick myself up and try again, and find joy in the trying, as long as God gives me breath.

We are all vulnerable to fear when we are exploring the unknown, and well-meaning but lesser humans are pointing out all the dangers that might be lurking in the darkness. Don't listen to them! I was approaching an airport the other day and saw a sign with an arrow that read, "Terminal." I wonder if that's why people are often afraid to fly!

Chapter 15

The Rich Person's Mind-set

The Really Rich think differently. While the Safely Prosperous get that way by avoiding mistakes and debt, the rich are heavily in debt, and cheerfully make a lot of mistakes. The Safely Prosperous avoid risk like the plague, but the Really Rich take carefully calculated risks by the carload. The difference? The mind-set!

Art Linkletter is one of my most treasured friends. He is undoubtedly the best investor in start-ups in the world, and he is one of Hollywood's richest men. Once when he was on a cruise with us, he told me something that has changed my life.

"Howard," he said, "I have invested in a lot of deals. Some worked out, and some didn't. When we had a good one and we got together with other investors to get our payoff, we toasted each other and congratulated ourselves for being so smart. To tell the truth, I can't even remember what most of them were. For sure, I never learned anything.

"But if the deal failed, we would get together for as much as two weeks for a postmortem and try to find out why it didn't work out for us. Sometimes it was the entrepreneur we were betting on who failed. Sometimes it was just bad luck. Sometimes it was an idea whose time had not yet come. Sometimes it was poorly executed or a bad idea. But as we dissected the corpse, we learned and learned.

"Howard, I never learned a thing from a success. Everything I know I learned from my failures."

RICH PEOPLE'S MIND-SETS #1 AND #2

Don't Be Afraid to Fail, and, if You Do, Treat It as a Learning Experience
I'm not talking about the stupid, common mistakes with money discussed in Book I, such as letting compound interest eat your income. I'm talking about errors in judgment when taking carefully calculated risks, an entirely different matter. In our society, we penalize people for their mistakes, starting in the first grade. Our wrong answers were not treated as learning experiences, but as reasons to give out bad grades, and we were punished for them. Business is different; mistakes and failures are your best teachers, and real entrepreneurs aren't afraid to venture, because they know a temporary failure—even a spectacular one—is a chance to learn something they would never have known otherwise. Every Really Rich person I know has left a trail of failures behind him or her before he or she made it big.

I think the best classroom for me was my two years spent as a Mormon missionary. It was there I learned to live with rejection. It was truly the school of hard knocks on tens of thousands of doors. Day after day we had to endure dozens of rejections, sometimes with courtesy, but often with hostility and profanity. I even had a German Shepherd sicced on me. The acceptances were infrequent, but all the sweeter for the rejections we had experienced, even next door. Two years, tens of thousands of doors, and only 25 convert baptisms, representing only eight families! So what kept me going into the teeth of rejection? The money? No, my mother sent me $50 a month to live on. It was passion, the unshakable conviction that their lives would be enriched if they allowed me to share with them what I knew.

This same kind of passion drives all business pioneers onward into the teeth of skepticism, rejection, and failures. Without it, they would probably quit just short of the promised land of success when things got tough or even hopeless—and most every rich man I know had a time when all seemed hopeless, his back was to the wall, and the wolves were circling. Without that passion, sooner or later, he was dead meat. And even if that project failed, he was ready to attack another one with even more passion.

I remember the day when my speed-reading school franchise was canceled. I had gone to work rich and I came home broke. I told Kay, "I've just had a bad day; Tomorrow will be better." And if you will allow me a rather loose definition of "tomorrow," it actually took me two years until I was clearly on the comeback trail.

Resilience is a part of the rich people's makeup. When they fail, they mourn what could have been for a day or two, then they bounce back, armed with undented confidence and new lessons learned.

RICH PEOPLE'S MIND-SET #3

You Can't Leap a Deep 10-Foot Ditch in 1-Foot Jumps

Business success requires grand efforts. Successful businessmen have dared greatly, unlike the "timid souls" Teddy Roosevelt told us about, "who know neither victory nor defeat."

RICH PEOPLE'S MIND-SET #4

They Pride Themselves on Providing Good Jobs for Good People

When the rich hire people who are willing to work very hard to make them rich, they reward those people well when success arrives on the doorstep. It would be a difficult world for me if everyone bought the rich people's mind-set, as where would I get the worker bees I have to have to make things work? Only a few of the people who read this book will be clear enough on the concept and determined enough to apply these principles to make themselves rich, instead of their employer. But if one of them does catch the spirit of the rich people's mind-set, you might want to consider investing some of your money in his or her start-up, as described in Chapter 18.

RICH PEOPLE'S MIND-SET #5

They Are Willing to Endure Deprivation along the Road to Riches

The rich don't take a big salary at the cost of business success. I remember when I was trying to build *The Ruff Times* in the early years, and in order to succeed we had to pour every penny back into marketing, even when we were behind on the family bills. When Kay would ask me when we would have the money to pay the back bills, I would tell her that if we would take care of the business, eventually the business would take care of us, and that's exactly what happened. Because the rich believe passionately in their future, they are rich even before they get rich.

RICH PEOPLE'S MIND-SET #6

They Are by Nature and Inclination Futurists

These people are not building a business for today, but for tomorrow. They see a future that others cannot see. In my discussions with such rich people, I used to ask them what they read. After the usual and expected *Wall Street Journal*, the daily local paper, the newsmagazines, the newsletters, the professional journals, and other financial publications, in an amazingly high percentage of cases, they loved and read science fiction.

When I was three years old, my brother, Jim, became enamored of a radio show called "The Quiz Kids." These were little kid geniuses who would answer hard questions that even the adults couldn't answer. Jim decided to make me a quiz kid and taught me how to read. Even before I started the first grade, I was already way beyond the usual smart-kid books, and was tackling the daily newspaper and adult-level books with an all-consuming passion. I don't remember how it happened, but I stumbled across *Twenty Thousand Leagues under the Sea* by Jules Verne, and the science fiction pulp magazines of the day. This was the start of a lifelong love of science fiction. By the time I was eight, I had read all the works of Jules Verne and H. G. Wells and many other pioneers of the genre. I believe that was the basis of my success as a financial forecaster and entrepreneur. Science fiction trained me to instinctively extrapolate the present trends into the future, to think outside the box, just as those authors did.

Even a moment's consideration will convince you that successful businesspeople must be somewhat prophetic. If they aren't, their competitors will eat their lunch. Even the near future will be different from today. In the modern age of information, a trend that in the last century would have taken decades to develop will now show up in months, if not weeks. The rich person must be emotionally able to change all of his or her basic premises in the blink of an eye, and the science-fiction view of "the future that can be" is a big help. It was for me.

RICH PEOPLE'S MIND-SET #7

They Have Burned Their Bridges behind Them

If Columbus had had an easy way out, would he have discovered the New World? What if he was not willing to lose sight of the Azores before he was willing to venture into the trackless sea? The Really Rich will not ask other people to invest in their ventures until they have all their own chips on the table and have closed a backdoor exit. Smart investors will demand just that.

RICH PEOPLE'S MIND-SET #8

They Are Passionate Believers in Their Ventures

Until they have this passion, they are just dilettantes playing around with an idea, and not committed. And their passion has to be more than money. Thomas Edison became one of the richest men in the world when he founded General Electric. His biographers tell us he loved money and enjoyed being rich, but that was not what drove him. It was his passion for his projects and inventions that made him work ungodly hours.

RICH PEOPLE'S MIND-SET #9

They Happily Take Carefully Calculated Risks

They risk their own money and other people's money. But they are not gamblers, relying on chance or forces beyond their control, unless their reading of the future is very compelling. They need a favorable risk/reward ratio. My benchmark for that is 1 to 10 in your favor.

Perhaps the simplest form of risk/reward analysis is to compare the money that could be lost (usually all of the start-up capital) against the potential upside profit. If I am going to put $10,000 into a venture, there has to be a high-probability upside for me of at least $100,000. When I am looking at deals to invest in, I know that despite everyone's best efforts, at least a few of them will fail. That means I have to have a high enough upside to make up for the losers. I then look at the principles I will enumerate in Chapter 18 to see how many of the desirable qualities in that particular venture outnumber the missing elements of success by at least 2 to 1.

The following is an updated article I wrote for *The Ruff Times* a few years ago. It applies here.

NO BACKDOORS

The successful entrepreneur is truly another breed of cat. He or she has a compulsion for growth and success. He or she happily takes risks and is undefeatable.

Here's my list of the things you must have to become Really Rich, roughly in descending order of importance. Without most of them, you won't make it. You might still make it without one or two of them, but I doubt it.

- *A supportive spouse.* Nothing is more destructive to a marriage or a business than a spouse who is not willing to endure years of deprivation, chronic cash shortages, and fear (the sky-is-falling feeling when you wake up to worry at 4:00 A.M.). Needed is an almost Christlike willingness to refrain from nagging or criticism when success takes longer than expected. Without that attitude, the emotional price to be paid will cause either the marriage or the business to fail.

  If your spouse adds unnecessary emotional burdens to the already intolerable new-business pressures, you will be less effective. Or, in your desire to please your spouse, you cannot, or will not, make the sacrifices necessary for success.

  Kay was always totally supportive. She believed in me with all her heart, and did her best to make home a heaven on Earth. Without the support of your spouse, starting a new business is next to impossible. More than once, Kay offered some advice that I ignored, but I have since learned that she has good instincts and that more than once I should have listened.

  Remember the lessons of Chapter 2: A good marriage is worth a lot more than being Really Rich. If push comes to shove, settling for Safely Prosperous might be just fine.

- *No backdoors.* Starting a small business is an all-consuming, frustrating, exhausting effort. If you have an easy out—a terrific job to go back to, a lot of cash, or a rich dad to fall back on—you probably won't hang in there when it is tempting to give up.

Almost every successful business has had occasions when all seemed lost. Those who refused to give up made it. If you have a backdoor, you are much more likely to quit when things seem hopeless. If you really want to succeed in business, burn your bridges so there is only one way to go—forward. The Japanese learned early in World War II that a kamikaze was more likely to complete his mission if the wheels of his plane fell off as he took off.

- *Incurable optimism.* Small businesses rarely succeed when the founder is a pessimist or overly cautious with an "accountant-like mentality." I'm not knocking accountants; any business needs good ones as part of a successful team to help you understand the tax or profit possibilities of proposed courses of action, and to provide the financial statements that will tell you how things are really going. Not all of them have accountant-like mentalities. I mean the timid souls who see only problems where the entrepreneur sees opportunities.

  When real entrepreneurs see an opportunity, they pounce on it. If they keep their eye on their objective, obstacles are merely exciting challenges. They believe in themselves, their products, and their mission, despite everyone else's pessimism.

  Napoleon Hill's great book, *Think and Grow Rich,* says, "No great enterprise will ever begin if all obstacles must first be overcome." That is the entrepreneur's creed. Optimism ultimately prevails because skepticism eventually crumbles under the relentless pressure of an incurable optimist. Nobody will follow a skeptic very far. The optimists sweep others away with their enthusiasm and spur them to greater performance heights by giving them a sense of mission. Optimists have to hire some pessimists to keep the books and deal with the banker, but they should keep the pessimists out of their lives as much as possible because they will stifle the entrepreneur's dream. A start-up business without incurable optimism is dead meat.

- *The ability to postpone gratification.* Budding entrepreneurs must be willing to deprive themselves now to get the big rewards later. If they insist on taking a big salary out of the budding business, they will suck it dry before it matures.

  When my sons bring me a new business plan with a big salary for themselves, I toss it back. They won't have the sense of desperation that forces them to land that contract now, to make that sale now, to rush that project to completion now!

  Postponement of gratification is the surest sign of maturity. Many (not most) successful entrepreneurs live high lifestyles—big cars, big houses, flashy rings, and so on—as the postponed payoff for years of deprivation when they hardly knew what they were going to eat, let alone which car to buy. They enjoy it to the fullest when rewards come, because they paid the price first. Perhaps this satisfies some subconscious, deep need to flaunt their success before the cynics who said it couldn't be done—rubbing their noses in it as a sort of delicious revenge. The conspicuous consumption is understandable after the years of self-denial—and very common.

- *Intellectual honesty.* Real entrepreneurs maintain a delicate balance between rampant optimism and realism. They admit it when their product falls short of expectations and needs to be improved. When they look at accounting numbers, they don't allow their optimism to cloud their good judgment. They face their problems and deal with them, while never allowing problems to convince them that "it ain't gonna work." Because they are honest with themselves, they are also honest with others. When they hire people, they candidly lay out the risks and rewards, but their optimism still shines through.

They rely on their accountants for real numbers, but don't allow those numbers to destroy their dream when they look bleak, because they believe that through hard work and ingenuity, they can change the numbers. But they face the truth as it is.

If an entrepreneur isn't intellectually honest, sooner or later some fact he or she refused to face will rise up and bite him or her. Optimism won't save him or her if it is built on the sand of unfaced facts. Pessimists distort this principle to justify their pessimism. They say, "Here are the facts. It's terrible. There's nothing you can do about it. Give up." The intellectually honest optimist says, "Here are the facts as they are. I acknowledge that, but I can change them, and I will."

- *A friend or partner.* Usually entrepreneurs have skills in one or two areas, but are woefully lacking in others. They might be great salespeople, but know nothing about production or accounting. They might be an electronics genius or inventor who couldn't sell worms to fishermen, and to them, accounting is witchcraft. They need a business associate who shares their dream and supplies the skills they do not have. All my major successes have been shared with such a partner.

  When I started my Reading Dynamics school, which, despite my subsequent failure, was very successful for several years, I shared my dreams with John Manson, who believed in them and helped me execute them. When I founded *The Ruff Times* in 1975, I had Terry Jeffers, an administrator and computer expert from IBM. I concentrated on reading, writing, and marketing, and Terry ran the business. I could dump my dreams all over Terry and John, and they reinforced and supported them. They weren't fire-control rhinos and they believed in me. They supplied skills that enabled me to concentrate on what I do best.

One of my most important business strategies is to assess my deficiencies and my strengths, then spend my time doing only the things I do best. That takes intellectual honesty. I either hire or affiliate with people who can do the things I do not do well. Once you honestly acknowledge that you don't do some things well, and turn those things over to competent people who can share your dream, you are unleashed. It's people leverage.

Some people have a strong enough ego to stand alone, but most of us do a heck of a lot better with someone shoulder to shoulder with us, to plug the holes in our defenses.

- *A strong ego.* I don't know any successful businessman who isn't an egotist, although some are better than others at concealing it. There is a crucial difference between a big, strong ego and a big, fragile one. I know some very talented people in my business who get offended easily and are constantly on the alert for slights and insults, real or imagined. People with strong egos simply shrug off most criticism and only counterattack when good business judgment says they must. They usually just sail serenely on their self-confident way.

  My ego is at least as big as that of anyone in my business. Without it, I never would have believed that my deathless prose or unorthodox economic views were worth charging for, but whenever I would let my ego affect my business judgment, disaster lay dead ahead.

  The clearest sign of a strong, secure ego is the ability to laugh when the joke is on you, to take a lot of kidding without pain, and to never doubt yourself despite the ridicule of the majority. I know my ego rubs some people the wrong way, but being 73 years old, I seriously doubt if my personality will change much. My family helps me keep my ego under some control. If Dad gets too pompous, my kids are wonderfully creative at bringing me down to earth. Around the Ruff house, the joke is usually on me.

Only a person with a secure ego will face reality, admit mistakes, cut losses, and change directions. A strong ego reflects itself in many ways, some of them rather obnoxious; but usually the braggart or the temperamental artist has a fragile ego, not a strong one. A wise person once taught me the true definition of temperamental: 9/10 temper and 1/10 mental.

Secondary, But Still Important

Here are a few more points that may not be as fundamental as the preceding ones, but can increase the success odds of a small business.

- *You need a business plan.* A business plan isn't just an idea or a narrative. It's a concept reduced to numbers on a month-by-month projection. It realistically projects expenditures and income monthly for two years and quarterly after that. It's usually done on a computer spreadsheet. You can also play "what if" business "war games." Sometimes these exercises will tell you that an idea isn't worth it, even if it comes out as expected.

  Without a business plan and spreadsheet, you don't have the slightest idea whether or not your project is even worth doing. You don't know how much capital you need or where your potential pitfalls are.

  A good computerized business plan can be revised constantly with a few keystrokes as the real numbers come in and become more and more accurate. Without a business plan and spreadsheet, you need a lot more dumb luck. I'd rather be lucky than smart, but I'd hate to have to bet on it.

- *You need a position.* A position is a simple concept that focuses on a relatively narrow segment of the market. When people bring me business deals, they often emphasize how their concept is for everyone. Successful businesses usually have found a relatively narrow market segment and have had a relatively simple product or service to offer it. The right name or advertising slogan can automatically define that position.

One example of positioning was Free the Eagle's fight against the IMF funding several years ago. Our position was simple: "They're bailing out the big banks with your tax money." Not only was it true, even though the issue was more complicated than that, but it clicked into place in people's heads and it was very difficult to drive out. That simple position won the battle of public opinion. We killed the bill.

The more specific and specialized your product or service, the more likely it is to be successful. In this great nation, even a narrowly focused concept should be big enough to make you rich. A concept that tries to be all things to all people is a 100-pound marshmallow; no one knows where to start eating. It generally does not cause people to flock to your door.

You can broaden your concept later, but only within your position. (More about this in Chapter 19.)

Chapter 16

Financial Winners in Bad Times

Hard times are loaded with opportunities for the Really Rich. That's when they find bargains in the stock market, good but cheap companies to buy, and talented people to hire at reasonable wages. It's also when competitors are pulling the bedclothes over their heads, so they don't even see you as you steal their market share.

It was in the depths of the Depression of the thirties that Joe Kennedy laid the foundations of the fortune that created a political dynasty and elected a president. He is a perfect example of how wealth can be created when the rest of the world is bemoaning hard times.

Joe Kennedy was a big-time stock-market speculator who had a big pile of paper profits in the margin-buying stock mania of the late 1920s. He had liquidated his stock holdings in 1928, lived at the estate he had bought with his profits, and was thinking of getting back into the market in 1929. One day he walked out of the New York Stock Exchange and stopped for a shoeshine, and the shoeshine boy started giving him stock tips and bragging about how much money he had made speculating on 10 percent margin. Joe paid the boy, went back into the exchange, and canceled his buy orders; if even the shoeshine boys had become expert stock pickers, the market had become irrational, and the top was near.

To understand how gutsy this was, you have to understand the times. We had just gone through The Roaring Twenties, and the Crash of 1929 and the Depression of the 1930s were still in the future. People were prosperous and there wasn't a pessimist in sight, and amateurs were making paper fortunes every day. But even so, Joe stayed out. For weeks he was a laughingstock as the market kept going up and up, but then came the historic crash that would traumatize America for decades. In one week the market was lower than where it was when he had walked away, and Wall Street became a falling-body zone, and they stopped laughing at Joe.

As the subsequent depression deepened, Joe patiently bided his time for three years, waiting out false market rallies. Then, as the depression deepened, real estate crashed and foreclosures were everywhere. But Joe had cash, and he waited for the right deal. His patience was finally rewarded when opportunity pounded on his door.

The Merchandise Mart in Chicago was a huge, mausoleum-like building with a rabbit warren of rooms where manufacturers and wholesalers displayed their goods and retailers went to buy. But business had crashed, and so had the tenants and their customers. As the building could be bought for pennies on the dollar, the risk/reward ratio was right. In 1932, three years after the market crash and at the bottom of the subsequent real estate depression, Joe bought the Merchandise Mart dirt cheap from its distressed owners for cash. In the inevitable economic recovery that followed, the building again filled up, and Joe became richer than he had ever dreamed of being. And that was just the beginning of his fortune. (For our purposes, a discussion of his bootlegging career is not relevant.)

So what did Joe have that his colleagues didn't? Three things: lots of patience, lots of guts, and cash—and cash was king. Sometime in the not-too-distant future, we will see a similar time; the stock market will be full of historic bargains, even for the little guy, and cash will again be king. That will be a historic opportunity for the Safely Prosperous to make the leap to becoming Really Rich.

But can you prosper or even get rich like Joe Kennedy did in hard or uncertain times, like now when we are in a recession that might get a lot worse? Hundreds of thousands of people have become rich in any financial climate. They don't seem to be any different from the Safely Prosperous—no smarter, no more famous—but something sets them apart, and it was worthy of study. Fortunately I had a ready-made laboratory and database with *The Ruff Times*, and out of that study, I have identified the not-so-obvious intangible things that made these people rich. It was a rich mix of personal attitudes, hard work, calculated risk taking, lots of study, and a firm grasp of the leverage and capitalist principles that have made people rich throughout the centuries. They understood the mystique of capitalism, the rules of people and money leverage, marketing, and the role that character, resilience, tenacity, and patience had to play.

They all understood that adversity was just another disguise for opportunity. Sometimes they had to wait awhile for the right opportunity, like the cat that patiently crouches by the mouse hole for hours, ready and waiting for the chance to pounce. Sometimes opportunity was wrapped in uncertainty and scare headlines in *The Wall Street Journal*. Sometimes it was hidden in a sudden event that dropped out of nowhere, and they acted when everyone else was struggling to get their bearings.

First, let's look at the different kinds of hard times you may have to face.

RISING INFLATION

The inflation hedge choices for investors are obvious: gold and silver, plus gold and silver mining stocks. Real estate is another obvious choice—all kinds of real estate, even though in normal times it varies a lot by locality or region. You remember the

, "Location, location, location." But rising inflation will
bail you out of your mistakes in choosing properties.

Generally speaking, I lean toward income-producing properties (rentals), and residential properties are best in hard times.
Commercial properties have one big vulnerability; when times
get tough, many small companies have to shut down, and many
big companies will slash expenses, sometimes by closing branch
offices, leaving the landlord holding the bag. But people have to
live somewhere, and rent is one of the last things they will fail
to pay.

When inflation is raging, collectibles seem to do well, although
they require specialized knowledge and experience that I don't
have; I seem to always buy antiques and sell junk, and there are
lots of pitfalls. Inflation seems to bring out the rare coin hucksters;
however, grading, which determines value and price, is so subjec-
tive, you shouldn't mess with this unless you have a dependable,
stable, years-in-business vendor you can trust. If so, this can be
part of your inflation hedge portfolio. In the past when inflation
was raging, the Swiss franc was a very profitable investment,
because Swiss currency is gold-backed and the Swiss are very
inflation-conscious.

At times like this, business debt, if the money is wisely
deployed, makes a lot of sense. After all, as the dollar diminishes
in value, it is in effect helping you to pay off your debts in shrinking dollars.

DEFLATION AND DEPRESSION/RECESSION

These three terms are almost synonymous, and the rules on debt
become the exact opposite. You should avoid either side of the
creditor/debtor relationship. As Shakespeare said, "Neither a
borrower nor a lender be." Borrowers have trouble servicing their
debts and creditors have trouble collecting their money.

As prices fall, the purchasing power of cash rises, and it is a fine investment holding. When the economy is slowing down dramatically, businessmen have trouble maintaining their prices, let alone raising them. More and more talented people are out of work, making this a buyer's market for employers. This is a great time for solvent companies to raise the quality of their talent pools.

Here are a few good deflation choices:

- *Residential rental property.* This is the only kind to even consider and that very carefully.
- *Government bonds and notes.* Remember the discussion of how bond and note prices go up when interest rates are falling? Interest rates always fall when deflation, recession, or depression hits, so bond prices go up (see Chapter 3). In the 1930s, rates fell so low that for a short time, T-bonds had negative yields to maturity. This is why I had my subscribers in T-bonds and notes from March 2000 to June 2003. We made a lot of money, even as the stock market was in a free-fall.

FOR BUSINESSPEOPLE ONLY

Recession/depression is the time for gutsy businesspeople to make a big leap forward. Go back and reread the story of Procter & Gamble in Chapter 14. It is a classic tale of how to make hay in hard times. Also read my personal cautionary tale in the same chapter. It will tell you how fear turns hay into manure.

Stock Bear Markets

There are a lot of ways to make money when you are caught up in a bear market. Some are pretty sophisticated, like "going short." Others are pretty easy, like buying shares of the Prudent Bear Fund, which takes the short side of the market and tends to go up as the general market goes down. Just be careful you are sure the market will be falling before you buy.

Chapter 17

The Capitalist Manifesto: Creating Wealth Out of Thin Air

Capitalists aren't just rich plutocrats on Wall Street. America has millions of them, and you can become one too. The strategies I will teach you in this chapter have created more millionaires than any other get-rich strategy.

The year was 1990, during the Gorbachev era and the days of glasnost and perestroika. Gorbachev was engaged in his ill-fated and naive attempt to save the unsavable Communist empire by reforming what he perceived to be the worst evils of the Communist system. Among other things, he thought he could improve the Communist state by introducing a whiff of the free market and a little bit of political freedom to a society that was ignorant of the barest rudiments of the genius of capitalism. Unfortunately for Gorbachev, that whiff of freedom was just enough to eventually destroy the Soviet system, which was held together only by terror and total oppression. The syndicated columnist Jack Anderson and I took 140 of my newsletter subscribers on a three-week tour of Russia and Ukraine to observe this dramatic and unprecedented history in the making.

Jack and I had dinner in an ill-lit room in one of the first privately owned restaurants in Moscow with a small group of men who were in the vanguard of the new, emerging Russia, including two who had just been elected to the Soviet parliament. They were bursting with enthusiasm for the new world being created around them as they told us of their dreams for their country. As we huddled around the table in the candlelit restaurant, I felt like we were in a bad B movie, portraying revolutionaries plotting the overthrow of the government. Six months earlier, we would have been in serious danger of being picked up by the KGB.

Productivity had just plummeted as millions of Russians were watching with incredulous wonder the all-night rebroadcasts of the sessions of the new, freely elected parliament and were too tired to go to work the next day. They had seen with their own eyes a newly elected representative, a colonel in the army, tear into a KGB general in a hearing on state oppression. The general had no choice but to sit there and take it while the nation watched with amazement and wonder.

It quickly became obvious that these enthusiastic, newly minted revolutionaries at our dinner table had no clue about the American free-enterprise capitalist system. They had been taught all their lives that capitalism only meant the rich grinding the faces of the poor as they exploited them, and they had not been given any reason to doubt that this was so. There wasn't a single basic accounting class in any high school or college in all of the Soviet Union. There was no body of commercial law to protect businesses from a predatory government or organized crime, and there was no patent law to be enforced by a system of independent courts. There was a solid wall of ignorance and inertia in a society that had been hostile to its fictitious version of these ideas for many decades. The Soviet people still believed that the only way to get rich was through graft by government officials or by being a member of the rapidly expanding, vicious Russian Mafia—and at that moment of history, in that place, they were probably right.

As an example of their enthusiastic naiveté, they enthusiastically proposed to Jack and me the revolutionary (to them) idea that Russian farmers should be allowed to own their own farms as private property. That sounded at first like a great leap forward— until they explained that, of course, farmers wouldn't be allowed to sell or transfer their property except by inheritance to their offspring. That meant that if Boris had a farm, he would have to leave it to his kids when he died. "But," I asked, "what if Boris had only one daughter and she was a ballerina with the Kirov ballet company and had no interest in farming? What then?" That hadn't occurred to them. They had no clue!

As I listened to these very sincere men who expected us to be blown away by their revolutionary embrace of "capitalism," I realized that not only didn't they know a thing about the genius of capitalism, but Americans don't either, even as they dine at the bounteous capitalist table.

I was to conduct a seminar for a bunch of Russians in a few days. I knew that my monumental task was to explain to them just exactly what capitalism was, and I had to think it through myself. I was like a goldfish that swims in its tank, never thinking of the chemistry of the water it breathes that keeps it alive; it just breathes. And now I had to teach a water chemistry lesson to a bunch of Russian air breathers. I had to think it through.

I remembered a question I asked my dinner companions: "What does Russia need most from the West?" Their quick answer was, "Capital," meaning loans from Western banks. I responded, "If you need capital, why don't you create your own?" Not only was this statement met with looks of incomprehension, I realized I would have gotten the same looks if I had said the same thing to a group of Americans.

CAPITALIZING INCOME

Something dawned on me that I already knew, but didn't know why I knew it. And that's what this chapter is about: *Capitalism is the act of creating real wealth out of nothing by capitalizing income.* It is by far the most productive route to becoming Really Rich, creating more millionaires than any other route. It's the magic yellow brick road to wealth followed by those who become rich in business and real estate. It's the ultimate leverage. It is the most important lesson I can teach you if you want to get rich comparatively quickly. It's why Bill Gates is the richest man in the world, worth $60 billion! He doesn't have $60 billion in cash in the bank, he has $60 billion worth of Microsoft stock in his portfolio, and he created that $60 billion value out of nothing by capitalizing his income! He simply sold some of his corporate stock to the public and let the marketplace determine its value and the prospects for the company. As investors got more and more impressed with the growth prospects of Microsoft, the stock sold at a higher and higher multiple of its prospective earnings per share. Not only did Bill Gates make a ton of capital gains at low tax rates by selling some of his stock to the public, but his portfolio of Microsoft stock on his balance sheet, where his real wealth is, soared in market value. So did the portfolios of his early investors and employees who accepted stock and options as part of their compensation: hundreds of them are now millionaires. Gates did as capitalists do and used his stock to attract a world-class management team.

Neither you nor I will ever be as rich as Bill Gates, but you can become rich beyond your wildest dreams in the same way Bill Gates did, by creating income and capitalizing it, which means letting investors determine what your stock is worth on the free market by going public. If you do it right, you can be rich by anyone's measurements in 2, 3, 5, or 10 years. Then you can have passive income as you get your money to work for you, instead of you working for your money. Not only is capitalism not exploitation of the poor by the rich, it is a cornucopia of wealth that feeds everyone, rich and poor alike. And it can create real millionaires in a hurry. This great capitalist secret has created more Really Rich people than any other get-rich strategy.

CAPITALISM 101

The day for my seminar had finally come, and I was standing in front of a group of skeptical Russians and some equally skeptical Americans from our tour group. Here is what I taught them:

> The essence of capitalism is creating income and then capitalizing that income, thus creating capital out of thin air. You want capital? You want the Western banks to loan you money? Then you must become loanworthy the capitalist way. Here's how. Let's use real estate as an example.
>
> You can create capital with real estate, but not until you make it fully transferable at a price dictated by the free market. You need an army of Red Carpet real-estate salespeople [that needed explaining] freely buying, brokering, and selling real estate, with the free market deciding how much it's worth. No bank will loan you capital if they can't assume ownership of the property you borrow against if you don't repay them, then recapture their loan by selling it. [These commonplace American ideas blew their minds. Moving right along . . .]
>
> Let's look at the story of Boris and Ivan. They have adjoining farms of about the same size. Boris works hard all day on his farm, while Ivan drinks a liter of vodka a day [there was a ripple of recognition in the crowd] and only produces half as much wheat or corn or pigs as Boris.
>
> Because real estate is not transferable, Boris's financial stake is doomed to remain small because he can't buy Ivan's farm and expand his operations and turn Ivan's unproductive land into a profitable piece of his farm.

But if real estate were transferable in a truly free and widely recognized market, some bank would loan Boris the money to buy Ivan's farm (cheaply, because of its low profitability) and make it productive with the efficiencies he could introduce by working hard and buying better and newer machinery, plus the economies of scale he could achieve by buying seed and feed and fertilizer cheaper in bigger quantities. The bank would loan him the money to buy it, based on the property's potential income. And what would the value (price) of Ivan's farm be? Under capitalism, the farm would be valued at some multiple of its profits. Maybe five times, maybe more. So if Ivan's farm was making 1,000 rubles a year in profits, the farm would have a fair market value of at least 5,000 rubles. And if Boris could double the productivity and profits to 2,000 rubles a year, Ivan's former land would be worth 10,000 rubles now, and Boris could borrow even more money to buy Alexei's farm across the road.

Boris would have become a capitalist. Did he exploit anyone? No, everyone benefited. Ivan can now take his 5,000 rubles and drink his liver into mush if he wants too, and Boris would have a more efficient and profitable and growing farm on his balance sheet, which is where he would measure and keep track of his growing wealth, because the fair market value of his farm would be a multiple of his farming profits. He would have capitalized his income. This wouldn't work unless there was some way to measure the value of his property. This requires a free market—a capitalist market.

I then explained how Americans create profitable businesses, sell some of their stock to the public, and become wealthy based on the fair market value of the stock they still hold. Instead of making $100,000 a year from their 100 percent privately held business, they could own perhaps 75 percent of it, but this asset would be worth 10 or 20 times as much as they were earning every year. If they needed some cash, they could sell some or all of their stock and pay capital gains taxes at about half the rate of their former ordinary income.

AMERICAN APPLICATIONS

I have no recollection of anyone at my seminar coming up to me and telling me I had revolutionized their thinking, but I hope I can revolutionize yours. (Actually, I vividly remember the looks of incomprehension. It must have been due to an incompetent translation, right?) The big question is, How can you create and capitalize your income and get rich fast?

Here is a simplified listing of the steps to real wealth:

1. Start a business enterprise.
2. Raise some capital by selling some of your equity (a portion of the company's stock) in a private placement to investors.
3. Use capital to build the business into a profitable venture, on a small scale at first, but with a healthy growth curve.
4. As the profits grow, capitalize them by becoming a publicly owned entity in any one of several ways, listed either over the counter or on a stock exchange, with the free market determining the price of your stock. It will probably be worth 10 times (more or less) your share of the earnings (profits), or even more if your growth-rate curve is very steep.
5. This can be done in several ways: (a) doing an initial public offering (IPO); (b) selling your company to an existing bigger company for its fair market value in cash; (c) merging with a larger existing public company by exchanging your private stock for their public stock in a tax-free exchange; or (d) doing a "reverse merger." Each of these alternatives has its pluses and minuses. To go public by

any of these approaches, your private company must also have audited financial statements going back three years, so you need good accounting from day one.

6. Your personal stock then goes on your balance sheet as an asset at the fair market price, which then produces passive income for you through dividends and corporate pretax personal benefits. (There are many things your corporation can do for you with pretax dollars that are not taxable income for you.)

7. As the years go by, every dollar of increased earnings per share will add $10 or more to your balance sheet. That's leverage!

8. As your balance sheet net worth grows, you are able to borrow more money to buy assets that produce more for you than the loan costs you in interest, adding to your income and wealth until you don't have to work for money any more, as your money works for you instead.

Voilà! You are Really Rich.

Is it really this easy? No. It's that *simple*, but not that *easy*. There are many things you need to learn to make it work that don't require an MBA or PhD, just a lot of hard study and reading on your own. The hardest part is building a profitable business, as described in Chapter 18, but that has been done by millions of people, so it must be achievable, and you must believe it is achievable by you as well.

The one thing that separates the Really Rich from the poor or Safely Prosperous is knowledge. The Really Rich must know more to do the things they do, but this is not rocket science. I would be a liar if I told you that you can get rich knowing only what you know now, but it is within the capacity of anyone who is smart enough to read this book, understand these concepts, and go on from there. The amazing thing about the Really Rich is how few of them have college degrees. Most people are born with the inherent ability to be successful if they are willing to pay the price in self-discipline and study to learn the techniques and acquire the attitudes and mind-sets that create wealth and then apply them. If you are trying to build a business that requires highly specialized skills, as many high-tech companies do, a college degree can be necessary, but in this world of millions of pedestrian, successful businesses, the knowledge necessary to be successful is not always found in the Ivy League, but more often in the school of hard knocks, and it's also for sale or rent. In fact, most of what an MBA will teach you is how to climb the ladder in an already-established Fortune 500 company.

You will have to know how to run a computer spreadsheet and to read a profit and loss statement and a balance sheet. You will have to grasp the basics of leadership to forge an effective business team. You will have to understand the essential elements of marketing, or hire those who do, and learn enough to understand what your team is telling you. There is nothing here that you can't learn in commercial seminars or night school classes at the local junior college, or by working for two or three years for a successful company in the field you wish to attack.

Is there a less tiring and more painless way to accomplish the same thing, or close to it? Yes, there is. It's not as good, but still OK. You can find a promising entrepreneur, apply the standards in Chapter 18 to evaluate him or her, invest in the company at a cheap price in a private placement (wholesale) before it goes public, and ride it to wealth when it does go public at a higher price. The real money is not made by those who buy in the public offering (retail) or on the public market after the IPO; it is made by those who buy the stock cheap *before* the company goes public.

This is not a handbook on the tactics of how to build a successful business. There are plenty of fine books to teach you that. This is a handbook on the strategy of real wealth. Just make sure you don't try this without understanding the principles in Chapter 18 as they apply to you, the entrepreneur.

HOW TO BECOME A PUBLIC COMPANY

First, your business must become a corporation. Then you must register with the state and federal SEC and the National Association of Securities Dealers (NASD). There are several ways to do this.

Starting a corporation is a simple matter of registering with the state in which your corporation will be a legal resident. Nevada corporations have several legal advantages:

- There is no corporate income tax.
- There are no taxes on corporate shares.
- There is no franchise tax.
- There is no personal income tax.
- There is no information-sharing agreement with the IRS.
- There is no public record of shareholders.
- There are minimal reporting and disclosure advantages.
- Stockholders, directors, and officers need not live in or hold meetings in Nevada, although a trip to Las Vegas for "corporate meetings" is tax-deductible.
- Officers and directors can be protected from personal liability for lawful acts of the corporation.
- Nevada corporations may issue stock for capital, services, personal property, or real estate, including leases and options. The directors may determine the value of any of these transactions, and their decisions are final.
- Best of all, this can be set up for under $1,000.

For more specific information about the companies and law firms that can provide all these setup services, go to Google.com and type in "Nevada Corporation." There are a zillion Web sites there to help you.

Then you have to issue shares to the potential shareholders, based on the money they contribute or the talent they bring to the party. Corporate stock is an incomparably valuable tool for attracting executives and investors. It will be a temptation to try to borrow the money instead and pay high interest and save the equity for yourself, but that is usually a mistake. The debt is a drag on the balance sheet and a burden on the cash flow. Equity money never has to be paid back, and is more attractive to more sophisticated investors who know that having an equity stake in a successful start-up is many times more profitable than interest, even with a very high interest rate. They also understand the leverage inherent in being a shareholder. You should be able to develop the team and raise the capital and still keep control of the majority of the voting stock, anything from 51 percent to 80 percent. Bill Gates owns less than 5 percent of Microsoft.

FOR BUSINESS OWNERS ONLY

The world is full of small-business owners who have never gone public and seem to be satisfied. I have heard all their reasons: "I don't know how to go public," "I don't want to be answerable to other stockholders who might meddle with my management decisions," "I don't want to do all the legally required reporting because I treasure my privacy," "My business is profitable enough that I am satisfied with my level of wealth," "I love my business so much that I would never want to turn loose of even a little of it to a stranger or even a friend." And the biggest one: "I don't want to have to deal with SEC bureaucrats!"

These are all perfectly good reasons to stay private, and you might be happier doing just that, but compared to what? These negatives must all be measured against the financial leverage inherent in going public. We're talking here about getting Really Rich. If you wish to be Safely Prosperous, stay private—your choice—but first consider the following example.

Let's say you have a small business that earns you $100,000 a year in dividends after paying you a decent salary. You will have

$100,000 plus your salary to live on or spend each year, and that's better than a poke in the eye with a sharp stick.

Then let's say you decide to go public by selling 20 percent of the stock to investors in a public offering, pocketing a few hundred thousand dollars in proceeds from the sale but reducing your annual dividend to $80,000 a year (80 percent ownership). But because the market quotes your stock at a price/earnings ratio (PE) of 10 (10 times earnings), your stock is worth $800,000. If your company is growing fast, you might realize 20 times earnings, making your stock worth $1.6 million. You have become much richer by owning less, instead of remaining Safely Prosperous.

Although Bill Gates only owns a tiny percentage of Microsoft, his $60 billion is almost all in the value of his stock. Being rich doesn't consist of how much cash you have in the bank; it consists of how much in assets you have on your balance sheet, and how much passive cash income those assets throw off.

ONE WAY TO SKIN A CAT: AN IPO

Most people think that to go public you have to have an IPO through a Wall Street underwriter, and that it always has to take hundreds of thousands of dollars and a year or two of preparation. Not so. There are other ways to do it at nominal cost that are also a lot faster. First let's look at the pluses and minuses of a traditional IPO.

The Pluses

- You raise money in the underwriting, either to add to the company's capital or to put in your own pocket if you sell some of your personal stock.
- There is usually publicity, which can be good for the stock price and for business.
- Participating Wall Street brokers will sell some of the IPO

to their clients, so the broker will have to follow the company and "make a market" in the stock. This increases the odds of higher trading volume and increases the price.

The Minuses

- It is costly. Even a small offering can cost upward of $250,000, possibly as high as $1 million. There are underwriting fees, sales commissions to the selling brokers, legal fees (a lot), and accounting fees.
- It is a slow process. Plan on at least a year, and lots of time-consuming and expensive exchanges between your lawyers and accountants and the SEC and NASD.
- You could work on an IPO for a year and spend a lot of money on it, then run into a bad market environment when IPOs are hard to sell and have the underwriter back out.
- Your IPO could be a "best-efforts" deal, and the offering might not sell out.

A SECOND WAY TO SKIN A CAT: A MERGER

You can sell your company to an already existing public company. If you pick your merger partner carefully, you can receive a combination of cash and your new partner's stock. If you get all cash, it is all taxable income at the much lower capital gains rate, but if you accept stock, you can do a tax-free exchange, postponing any tax consequences until you sell your stock for cash. You are then a minority shareholder of the surviving company, usually worth a multiple of several times your old company's earnings per share. This, of course, is a balance sheet item, which makes you supremely bankable, meaning you can borrow money at near prime rates to make other investments, using some of your stock as collateral. You can also sell some of your stock if you decide you want or need cash, and you will pay the lower capital gains rate rather than the ordinary income rate, which is as much as double.

There are many pluses in going the merger route; however, in most mergers you generally must give up control of your business, and your new partners can now tell you how they want your company to be run. You could even be fired if you haven't protected yourself in the merger contract. If you can see the new partners might want to get rid of you, you can usually negotiate a golden parachute and take comfort that the transaction has made you rich, even if you no longer have a job. You will have to consider these factors when you are weighing the trade-offs for increasing your wealth.

A CHEAPER, FASTER WAY TO SKIN A CAT: A REVERSE MERGER

There is a less-known way to go public that gets the job done in a fraction of the time and at a fraction of the cost but makes you every bit as much a public company as an IPO. It's called a *reverse merger*. This is the low-rent district of underwriting, and has not enjoyed the best of press; but it is cheap, and if done right, it happens fast and provides you most of the benefits of being public. It can also be full of pitfalls if you choose the wrong people to manage the merger for you, but I will have suggestions on what the pitfalls are and how to avoid them.

A reverse merger combines your private company with an already existing, usually small but viable public company already being quoted on one of the Nasdaq quotation systems. The company will have a small operating business going nowhere fast and the management has decided to give up majority control of the public company, usually 80 percent or more, to a larger operating private business in pursuit of growth. It doesn't have to be in the same industry as your business.

Previously, reverse mergers were done with a *corporate shell*— a public company that has no operating business, but once did.

The company is still registered with the SEC and the NASD and may or may not be currently trading.

Recently, however, the NASD has upgraded the rules for trading on its Nasdaq stock quotation system and will only allow viable operating companies to be quoted. I would strongly suggest that you not consider merging with a nontrading or nonoperating public shell; the costs and the risks are just too great.

Mechanically, here is how a reverse merger works. First, you find a small public company being quoted on the Nasdaq that is looking for a larger private company to acquire. You can put feelers out through your broker or securities attorney or place a small ad in *The Wall Street Journal*. There are also promoters who specialize in putting together reverse mergers. (One competent professional I trust is Gary McAdam of Denver, Colorado, 303-791-1188). They usually know of public companies looking for a merger partner. Once you find one, a dating game ensues. To still be trading, the small public company must maintain audited financial statements and current quarterly and annual registration statements with the SEC. Having access to these SEC filings will also provide you with both the historical and financial information you need to decide whether this is a company you'd like to have your private company merge with. It is much like a marriage. First you want to get to know each other to see if you both want the same things out of life.

The next step is to negotiate the percentage of dilution your private company is willing to give up in order for you to go public through this backdoor process. It usually requires you to leave between 5 and 10 percent with the public company's shareholders. It will depend somewhat on your negotiating skills as well as on how large your private company is and how much the management of the public company believes in your company's potential future growth.

Once the managements of both companies agree on the ownership percentages for both companies' shareholders after the merger is consummated, attorneys prepare summaries of a merger agreement, including financials for the approval of shareholders of both corporations. The type of registration the company used to go public will determine whether the merger will require the companies to wait for comments back from the SEC to complete the merger; most do not. Your SEC attorney will guide you. You should hunt for a 15 D reporting public company, which does not require the SEC's involvement for approval. You simply file a report telling the SEC what the two companies have agreed to. An honest promoter like Gary McAdam will walk you through the whole process.

The End Result

In a reverse merger, there is not actually a complete merger. Once the merger agreement is approved by both sets of shareholders, an exchange of stock takes place between both companies as follows.

Let's suppose the agreement was that postmerger, your private company's shareholders (you) would own 90 percent of their outstanding shares and all the public company's shareholders would own 10 percent. Let's further suppose the public company had 1 million shares authorized. In this scenario, the public company would issue the private company 9 million shares to be divided proportionally with the existing private company's shareholders (you) in exchange for 100 percent of the outstanding shares in the private company. This is called a "tax-free stock-for-stock exchange." Instead of an actual merger, the private operating company has become a wholly owned subsidiary of the public company. You wind up maintaining two separate but united corporations. It is like a married couple's joint tax return; their financial records are merged or consolidated and reported as one. The management team and directors of the public company usually simultaneously resign and are replaced with the private company's management team and/or directors, and the shareholders change the corporate name to be more consistent with the company's new business—probably the old private company's name. The new public/private entity is now run by the private company's management team.

The Pluses

- You can go public quickly—usually in 30 days or less, as opposed to a year or more.
- You can go public inexpensively, generally for $25,000 to $50,000 in total legal, accounting, and mailing costs, as opposed to hundreds of thousands of dollars.
- You immediately have a public trading market value for your shares to provide you with currency for acquisitions or key-employee recruiting.
- You can raise money privately or publicly based on your stock's trading value, not on negotiations with a brokerage firm that would try to keep your company evaluation down in an IPO for the benefit of its customers. The private money source for a private company will usually try to price the stock based on book value. If you are public, negotiations begin at market value, which, if the private company has a good growth curve, will be a whole lot higher.

The Minuses

- You will be giving up dilution (5 to 10 percent) without receiving new capital, as in an IPO, although raising money is now much easier and on better terms than when you were private.
- You will not have a brokerage firm or syndicate of brokers who would have raised your IPO money to make markets in your company's shares or to tell your story to the public on an ongoing basis.
- There is some credibility temporarily lost in the securities

industry by going public through a reverse merger—but a bit of time cures that completely, and it doesn't matter anyway.

One key is who you choose to guide you through the process and what added services they will provide, such as raising capital, developing the trading syndicate, and so on, all of which can be managed by competent professional promoters.

I can't caution you enough to work with experienced professionals—accountants, lawyers, promoters—who specialize in reverse mergers. Their mainstream equivalents will either not understand the process or will pooh-pooh it in favor of a time-consuming, expensive IPO and the handsome professional fees it generates.

In summary, creating a public company is the most lucrative of all the routes to wealth, but it requires guts, a creative and venturesome spirit, a drive to succeed, and a healthy helping of tenacity.

Chapter 18

Getting Rich by Investing in Start-ups

If you don't want to go through the trouble and worry of becoming a capitalist yourself, there are ways to invest in those who do. Most start-ups fail, but you can separate the sheep from the goats. I will show you how and when to jump in, and when to run like hell.

Investing in start-ups is one path to real wealth. The problem is that if you don't know how to sort out the sheep from the goats, it can be a freeway to the poorhouse. It's usually an all-or-nothing proposition: You either make a lot of money or lose your whole investment. Capital investing has serious risks, but if you know what you're doing, they are acceptable calculated risks.

Wouldn't you like to have been one of the hundreds of millionaires created by Microsoft? Sure, Microsoft is one in a million, but there are little Microsofts being created every day. Other than starting your own business, investing in start-ups has more upside potential than any other get-rich strategy. It can be as much a part of your get-rich plan as the stock market or real estate, but only if you do it right—and because there are a zillion ways to do it wrong, they can all make you poor if you don't know what you're doing.

Where did I learn this stuff? First, I have watched hundreds of start-ups and invested in some of them, including some losers. Second, I have started several new business ventures myself; some were winners, some were losers. Much of what I know about the subject I learned by stepping in it; my failed ventures and start-up investments have been my real teachers. The most important lesson I have learned is that all successful start-ups have some things in common, no matter how different the businesses seem to be. And there are other things the failures all have in common.

THE ONE INFALLIBLE RULE OF START-UP INVESTING

Let's get the most important rule of start-up investing out of the way up front: *Don't lose your money in start-ups that really never had a chance.* These are a lot easier to identify than you might think. Ignoring the rules in this chapter gives you odds that are far worse than the slots at Vegas. In my experience, 9 out of 10 start-ups either fail completely, taking the investors' money with them, or they never amount to anything. However, once you have eliminated the sure losers, the odds improve to better than 50-50.

On the other hand, because successful start-ups can return as much as $10 to $100 for each dollar invested, if you spread your choices over at least 10 new companies you can absorb the five losers and still be ahead of the game. Even with careful adherence to the rules in this chapter, you will be doing a really good job if as many as half of your choices survive.

Don't put all of your eggs in one start-up basket; set up a start-up portfolio. It's a numbers game, pure and simple. Even with a 50 percent success ratio, you can average more than 100 percent per year return on your total investment and change raw gambling into calculated risk-taking with a great risk/ reward ratio.

Now let's look at the "never-do's" of start-up investing. Avoiding these pitfalls can save you a fortune.

THE SEVEN NEVER-DO'S

Never-do #1: Never invest in a start-up that doesn't have a carefully thought-out, written business plan, complete with pro-forma projections. If they don't have one, that's a clear sign that they lack the sophistication and know-how to create a real company. And you must challenge the assumptions in the spreadsheet to see if they can hold up under assault. I've discussed this in more detail in Chapter 15.

Never-do #2: Never invest in a "good idea" that is "for everyone." If it's for everyone, it's usually for no one. Successful start-ups almost always focus on a narrow market that can be exploited on a cost-efficient basis.

Never-do #3: Never invest in a one-man gang. Although most successful start-ups are the result of the drive and leadership skills of one intrepid entrepreneur, successful new companies have a well-balanced, talented support team to provide all the necessary skills and experience the entrepreneur doesn't have.

Never-do #4: Never put your money into an undercapitalized company. Invariably, it costs more and takes longer. Without enough capital—and then some—the company will fail, but not before sucking you into more and more investment in a vain effort to save it before it goes down the tubes.

Never-do #5: Never invest money you can't afford to lose, because some of your picks *will* fail.

Never-do #6: Never invest without an exit strategy. How will you get your money back or realize your profits? If the entrepreneur does not envision a future IPO or a merger, or a possible sale of the company to a larger company, and tells you how you will double or triple your money with profits and dividends, run, because that never happens.

Never-do #7: Never invest in a start-up without a well-conceived marketing plan focused on a narrow market, with a predetermined, cost-efficient path to the potential customers.

Just by never doing these seven things, you've already increased the odds from 1 in 10 to about 5 in 10!

THE PERFECT START-UP

The perfect start-up, which probably doesn't exist in nature, will look a lot like the following. (Where I use the masculine *he* in the generic sense, it could very well be a *she*.)

1. The Entrepreneur

The entrepreneur's character and personality is the major limiting factor in start-up success. Ideally, he will have all or most of the following characteristics:

- He will have had experience working for a company that required the same skills he will need this time.
- He will understand that he is not just developing a hot idea; he is starting a business that must be built from scratch like any other business, with all the standard, routine business functions needed by any company, such as accounting, sales, marketing, collections, information technologies, and so on.
- He will have strong skills in one of the critical areas needed by this and any other business, such as communications, marketing, sales, relevant technology, accounting, capital raising, and so on.
- He will have leadership skills, and will build a team of talented people who share his dream, respect him, and supply

the essential skills he doesn't have. At a minimum, he must have a computer-savvy controller to produce the financial statements needed to analyze the start-up's progress, a marketing VP, a sales manager, and an office or operations manager.

- He must have a supportive spouse, or no spouse at all, and to a great extent that's up to him. No one can be at his best on the job when he is being hassled at home. Start-ups require so much time and dedication that the spouse must understand the pressures the entrepreneur is under and provide a safe harbor so that if he comes home, his emotional batteries will be recharged instead of further drained. To earn that support, despite the long hours he must work, he must not become a compulsive workaholic. He must set aside dedicated, predictable time for spouse and family and never fail to keep his family commitments. If a wife knows that she can have Friday night as a date night, she will not hassle her husband during the week, and if the kids know that Dad will always be there for recitals and games, they will feel supported.

- He must have a big, strong ego, as opposed to a big weak one, so he doesn't feel threatened when it turns out he has made a bad mistake and needs to change course. Big, weak egos make people so defensive about the inevitable mistakes made in new businesses that they won't make essential course corrections, and they will lead the company down the hole that leads to business hell.

- He will be a reader, keeping up with relevant information in his industry and the marketplace as a whole. I hesitate to invest in an entrepreneur who doesn't read *The Wall Street Journal*, including the editorial and opinion pages.

- He will be a realistic optimist (or an optimistic realist, if you prefer). That means he can face the facts as they are, and if they are negative, he will believe he can change them.

- He will be intellectually honest, which is different from just being honest. An honest person won't lie to you, but an intellectually honest person will never lie to himself. Self-deception is the cause of countless business failures. Self-liars always fail, because they will not admit it when they are wrong and change course in time.

- He will have clear, well-articulated long-term goals. Course changes and refined and altered objectives are fine as the company gains experience in the real world, but without a clear objective in mind, the entrepreneur will be at best a tactician, not a strategist—and tacticians don't build successful companies.

- He will not drain the company's capital to support himself. He will have independent income, or some savings, or a willingness to live on short rations so he is an asset, not a liability, for the company. He and his family must be willing to live modestly and not care about the dishonest facade of success. There will be time to show off when the company has really made it and there is plenty of money.

- He probably will have failed at least once, and is a lot smarter for it and has demonstrated his resilience and stubborn persistence. That's good!

- He must not be greedy. He must be willing to share the equity to attract and build a top-flight management team, and that must be their focus, not just a salary. Also, managers who are willing to work for equity in the form of stock, convertible bonds, and options have the right motivation to build a real company so they can get rich too.

2. The Product

The best products and services to bet on usually aren't revolutionary; they are simple improvements on an already accepted product or service—a better, faster, or cheaper way of doing old things or providing useful services. It doesn't have to be a hot consumer product; sometimes it is sold to businesses. It needs to be the solution to a problem, and it is a lot easier if you don't have to convince people they have a problem, just that you have a simple-to-grasp solution to a problem they already know they have. The best, safest, and also most profitable start-up companies don't have to be dramatic or in the hot market du jour. They are usually dull and prosaic, and often very low-profile.

3. The Marketing

Marketing is an essential skill for a start-up. Marketing isn't just advertising, direct mail, or selling; it's an amalgam of a lot of disciplines. When I launched Hi-Q, a brain-food supplement, we had to figure out how to sell it. We tested direct mail, and it worked OK but not well enough, so we are testing direct-mail appeals. We are testing a 30-minute radio infomercial, preceded by numerous 10-second promos to draw listeners to the show, a personal talk-show appearance on the same station, one-minute radio spots, and a simultaneous major direct mail campaign. We are also looking at point-of-sale display racks in health-food stores and a book on nutrition and the brain. We'll test everything in a small retirement community, throw out what doesn't work, and then pour money into everything that does work in city after city. Now that's marketing!

PICKING LOSERS

Most potential investors who come to me to excite me about some venture don't have the slightest idea how or whether the entrepreneur meets the preceding requirements. They haven't asked these questions, and they probably don't even know what questions to ask. They are just excited about a product or idea, and believe the company will make them rich because "everyone needs (or will want) one" or "there is no competition." It is rare that these enthusiasts really know whether or not they are investing in a real business—and much more often than not, they aren't.

THE PROFILE OF A SUCCESSFUL START-UP INVESTOR

If you as an investor don't have most of the following attitudes, you should probably put your money into T-bonds.

- You must think long term. If you think there will or must be a quick profit, you will be wrong. This is a dysfunctional attitude. It also means that you must be a patient, long-term investor, with no fixed deadline when you will need your money. You must be willing to look at least five years ahead.

- You must demand monthly financial statements and be willing to read every number. I am amazed at how many start-up investors don't insist on this rudimentary requirement, or wouldn't even understand the statements if they got them. If the company won't give you statements every month, it tells you that either the company doesn't know how it is doing, or it is doing badly and doesn't want you to know. If all you get is optimistic reports from management, not backed up by good financials, you know that they aren't being honest with you, or maybe even with themselves. If the plan is to go public or sell to a bigger company someday, the buyer or underwriter will require statements going back to day one. Trying to reconstruct accurate financial statements going back to the beginning is a nightmare, and you can forget about an IPO.

- You must get the stars out of your eyes. They obstruct your vision. You don't have to become a money-grubbing Scrooge, but you must know not just the upside but also the downside of the company. You must treat this as an investment, not an exciting romance. Money will not love you, but you must at least care about it, and you must be objective and realistic about it.

- Have a piece of the real action. Don't just loan money to the start-up because it is your son or daughter or cousin Bob, or a pewmate from church, or a product that excites you. Insist on making any loans convertible to common stock, or at least on options to buy common stock as a kicker that are exercisable at a very cheap price. Remember, start-ups are usually an all-or-nothing proposition. If the company fails, you will lose everything. If it succeeds, it could be worth a lot of money, so you should have an upside commensurate with the risk. This is called the risk/reward ratio, and it should be at least 10 to 1—that is, the potential profit should be at least 10 times the potential loss. This is the only way I know to buy stock wholesale and someday sell retail. Successful venture capitalists always do this.

- Get collateral if possible. This may not be as good as it sounds. If the entrepreneur is someone you love, such as one of your offspring, and the collateral is a mortgage on their home, it is of no value if when push came to shove you wouldn't be willing to foreclose.

- Be sure the company is raising enough money. Optimism is an essential characteristic of an entrepreneur, but it can kill a company if optimism causes the entrepreneur to believe his own starry-eyed projections and grossly underestimate how long he will have to be paying the overhead until the cash flow turns positive. Look at his estimated cash needs, double them, then double them again, and it might be just enough.

- Check out the entrepreneur for previous failures. If he has failed once or twice, that can be a positive if he learned from it. Ask him what he learned from his failures. If he failed because of a lack of intellectual honesty and won't admit it, run!

FOCUS

What is the primary focus of the company? Is it on a product or idea, or is it on building a real business with a high-probability, well-thought-out plan for becoming a wealth vehicle? If it isn't the latter, it is doomed to fail. The founder's eyes must be firmly fixed on the long-range goal, which is to maximize the value of the stock for the stockholders. If that's not the goal, you don't want to be a stockholder.

It all comes back to where we started: Avoid the obvious losers, and that's not hard to do.

Chapter 19

Marketing

The last great reason the Really Rich got that way

In good times and bad, hundreds and thousands of companies fail, especially young ones. But hundreds of their competitors get rich in exactly the same businesses, because for them a recession is cherry-picking time, and good times mean an endless assembly line of hot fudge sundaes. They do well no matter what the economy dumps on their doorstep. How do they do it? Marketing!

Great entrepreneurs create their own capital through marketing, and the better they are at it, the less capital they need. I should know, because when I started *The Ruff Times*, I was broke, and successful marketing, along with some gutsy, calculated risk-taking, turned us profitable in short order. When I became rich and famous in the late 1970s and early 1980s, it wasn't because I had a monopoly on good newsletters. There were some very competent competitors. Some were very talented writers, and some had just as good a track record of successful market calls, or even better, but I was a better marketer. Because of that, I dominated the financial newsletter industry for many years.

In the Introduction I told you that in the late 1970s and early

1980s I became rich and famous, but I didn't tell you how I got that way. Then, in Chapter 14, I told you how I lost my fortune—by failure to market aggressively when times turned bad in my industry. Now I'm going to give my failure a postmortem and share the inside story with you.

With the help of my partner, Terry Jeffers, *The Ruff Times* was the first publication in our industry to turn direct mail marketing from a shot in the dark into a by-the-numbers science, and now that's the way everyone does it. We first made the calculated decision that it was easier to sell a personality than a publication, so we made my name into a household word by the sheer volume of direct mail, supplemented by an aggressive publicity campaign conducted by Michael Baybak (4515 Ocean View Boulevard, Suite 305, La Canada, CA 91011, 818-542-6880) and a very carefully crafted TV show called *Ruffhou$e*, an interview and financial commentary show featuring yours truly as the host. We bought the air time for it in the markets we wanted and sold the advertising to offset the costs, but it was never profitable—in fact, it lost a lot of money. But we carefully tracked the direct mail results in the zip codes where the show was airing, and the increased mail results justified the losses on the TV show and then some.

Exploiting Terry's IBM background, we were the first in our industry to lease an IBM mainframe and track the results of our test mailings by lists. We also tested headlines on the mailing pieces, offers, and various prices, and carefully measured, quantified, and compared the results. If our tests showed the results of a partial list to be break-even or better, we rolled out the whole list and repeated the mailings until the results dropped below break-even, assuming that the profits would show up at renewal time. It was a numbers game, pure and simple. It was scientific marketing.

My job was to make sure *The Ruff Times* gave real value in

financial education and good forecasting and market calls and was fun to read, because good marketing of an inferior product, or one that was not an honest representation of the product (me), would implode with high cancellation rates and low renewal rates. It had to also be honest marketing, which is the only kind that has staying power. We didn't promise anything I wasn't sure we could honestly deliver.

So it's time to admit that, although I am a real person, and what you see is what you get, the public Howard Ruff is a marketing creation, and you will have to decide from my writing whether I can justify the hype. If I hadn't spent a lot of productive money on marketing, you would never have heard of me.

I've gone into this detail to show you that, when it comes to marketing, I know what I'm talking about. Marketing is a science, but most attempts at marketing don't work because they are run by amateurs who don't understand the science. If you take the trouble to learn the science, you dramatically raise the odds of business success.

Marketing separates the winning sheep from the losing goats in any environment. Marketing is the last remaining great secret of the Really Rich who got that way in business. Without this secret, they either are among the majority of new ventures that fail, or they just limp along in the business twilight called "muddling through."

I saved this chapter for last because until you have made the decision to become rich through capitalism—starting your own business and taking it public—it probably won't be of any value to you. A real education on marketing would take several books and audio tapes, so I have a limited objective here—to stimulate you either to learn all you can about the subject or to bring into your company someone who really knows the subject. I also want to guide you to the sources that can teach you the most about this pivotal subject, and not just academically; most academic marketing courses are useless, even MBA-level courses, unless you just want to be trained to work in the bowels of the marketing department of a Fortune 500 company.

If you decide to hire that marketing talent, be sure it is someone with a real-world track record in small-company marketing. Sometimes there is a good marketing class at your local junior college. Often these are taught by real-world businesspeople or marketers. The experience of the real-world instructor is all-important. Maybe you can hire him or her.

WHAT MARKETING IS SUPPOSED TO DO

Marketing has several objectives, such as sales, differentiating yourself from your competitors, and finding hidden corporate assets that can make money. Marketing includes public relations and publicity, labeling, finding cost-efficient ways to penetrate market segments, pricing, sales, product bundling, product design, advertising, direct mail, image making, positioning, franchising and licensing, customer development (back-end sales), and a host of other factors. Marketing also includes joint ventures, risk reversal, and underexploited asset deployment strategic alliances, unique selling propositions (USPs), and dozens of other mind-blowing concepts that will seem ridiculously obvious only after you hear them. In effect, marketing will teach you how to reshape your business as you see it through the eyes of the public and potential customers to produce several times the results, and it will all be called "Marketing."

Your competitors may have equally good products—sometimes even better. They may have more capital and more skilled financial management. But when times get tough, the winning sheep will outmarket the losing goats! They will have made louder noises in a quieter environment as other marketers foolishly pulled in their horns—and they will have made money when their competitors are losing theirs.

A PATH TO YOUR DOOR?

If I had a dollar for every time an enthusiastic new entrepreneur, or a *Ruff Times* subscriber who has just invested in one or is related to one, has told me, "This product (or service, or idea) will sell itself." That is nonsense; nothing sells itself. The old cliché says, "If you create a better mousetrap, the world will beat a path to your door." That alleged mousetrap is claptrap! That attitude will kill a new company faster than anything I can think of. Marketing is the only way to get the world to beat a path to your door. The world won't even know you exist until you tell them about your gee-whiz product or service, and that requires marketing.

I seriously doubt that you will become a successful capitalist until you can convince customers to come into your establishment (advertising), pick out your product from the shelf in preference to your competitors' products right next to it (packaging), or overcome their skepticism enough to try out a new product they've never heard of risk-free (risk reversal), without one or more of the many forms of marketing.

For example, I was able to pioneer the no-risk guarantee using the risk reversal principles I learned from my friend, marketing genius Jay Abraham. Subscribers could get all their money back at any time they decided they did not like *The Ruff Times* for any reason. At that time, hardly anyone had even heard of me. Sales soared, and, strangely enough, cancellations dropped. Using the same principle, we offered my latest book as a premium, and subscribers could keep the book if they asked for a refund. These were revolutionary methods in the late 1970s and early 1980s, and they still work today.

Here are a few great examples of creative marketing I learned about from Jay, who is the best marketing educator of them all:

- He taught a dry cleaner how to license his very effective ads to thousands of other dry cleaners in other towns. The dry

cleaner made more on licensing fees than on dry cleaning—
hundreds of thousands of dollars every year.

- One of Jay's clients had a local lumberyard doing a modest
amount of business and a unique kiln-drying process for
his own lumber. Jay taught the client how to teach 200 other
lumberyards how to use this process and then license them
to use it. The client made $1.8 million a year in license fees.
- Another client had a car wash and an effective system for
increasing the number of customers who asked for a hot
wax. Jay convinced him to license his methods to 2,000
other car washes, and he made more from the licenses than
from his own car wash.

You can design irresistible sales offers where you assume the
risk, not the customer, and prospects see that it is obvious they
will be worse off if they don't respond to your offer.

You can develop your own unique selling proposition (USP)
that can be expressed in a few words to ring a bell in the potential
customer's mind ("We're Number Two—We Try Harder"). Nothing is more important in establishing you and your product or
service—not just in the marketplace, but especially in the customer's mind—as the only viable solution, not just a better one.

You can package complementary products together to get a
bigger unit of sale and much bigger profits per transaction.

You can raise your prices, even in a weak market, and
increase the market's perception of your product's value to them
and increase your sales.

You can develop a back end of profitable sales of other products to your existing or inactive customers. You spent a lot of
money to get them, and now you can "monetize" them for life.
Your business can generate additional multiple income streams
year after year from those same customers. It doesn't matter what
you sell, the principle will work.

You can make money by joint-venturing, endorsing, recommending, introducing, or representing other products and services

that you don't usually sell that might be attractive to your customers. You may have built up a good name and reputation and a list of customers who know who you are and have a good opinion of you. There is a huge pile of cash for you in understanding and exploiting this unrecognized asset.

CREATIVE MARKETING CASE STUDIES

Here are a few case studies gleaned from Jay Abraham's files.

Case #1: David Beal took a single office-suite leasing company, figured out what other products and services he could sell, lease, or rent to his tenants, and obtained the right to be their commercial broker when they grew and moved out. Beal's operation grew to 480 locations in 17 countries with gross annual revenues of more than $600 million.

Case #2: Mark Victor Hansen and Jack Canfield got the idea for the many spin-offs of the *Chicken Soup For the Soul* books and built a $40 million publishing empire with *Chicken Soup* for just about everything and anyone.

Case #3: An Australian software company was selling very expensive software ($15,000 to $250,000) and only converting about 1 out of every 200 leads. But they realized that fully 75 percent of the leads needed the software—they just couldn't afford it. They found another piece of software that did the same basic job, acquired it on a royalty basis, and offered it for between $2,000 and $5,000. They were able to close one-third of the people they couldn't close at the higher price and made as much money on the ancillary product as they did on the main one.

SEND ME A MAN WHO READS

You need to read two books to start on your marketing education: *Positioning,* by Al Ries and Jack Trout (Warner, 1928; available in paperback at any good bookstore, and the best marketing book ever written), and *How to Get the Most Out of Everything You've*

Got, by Jay Abraham (St. Martin's Press, 2001). Jay also has audio tapes and special marketing reports that are loaded with mind-blowing concepts and well worth a lot of hours of study.

Jay's advice is ordinarily very expensive. People pay him $5,000 an hour ($40,000 a day) for his personal help. His seminars go for $25,000 a person. His tape sets run as high as $5,000 per set. But at my request he has prepared a complete marketing education of extraordinary audio tapes, expensive books, and special reports for a modest $500 for readers of this book. They are easily worth 10 times that amount. It includes a live audio tape of a seminar for which the attendees paid $5,000, a book worth $400, and a series of special reports.

If you phone my office (801-224-3660) or e-mail me (howard @rufftimes.com), I will forward your order on to Jay.

THE END OF THE ROAD

As the preacher said, "Thus endeth the lesson." In this book, I haven't told you everything I know, just the essence of what I thought was important to get you started. If I have only helped you to choose which path you want to take, and you are happy with it, I'm pleased. If I haven't, I still wish you well.

Chapter 20

Was It Worth It?

Now that you have read the whole book, it's time to make a decision. Do you want to be Safely Prosperous or Really Rich? There are several things you ought to consider seriously.

Way back in Chapter 2 I told you about my ethical trepidation over writing about how to get rich, because of the real risk of worshipping Mammon and losing things that are more important than money in the headlong pursuit of riches. Now that you understand that you have a real choice of two achievable objectives—Safely Prosperous or Really Rich—it's time to consider some soul-searching questions.

1. Can you really resist the temptations that the pursuit of money always brings and that always lead to unhappiness amid wealth—especially if you are on the Really Rich track? These temptations are always easier to resist on the Safely Prosperous track, as you can usually get the cooperation of your spouse, and it becomes a family joint venture that can help you to build a successful marriage.
2. If you decide to become Really Rich, ask yourself why. Do you just want riches to feed your ego, to compete with the

Joneses, to have more toys, or so you can climb the social ladder as we did in the 1960s? Those are not only dubious motives, but can be truly soul destroying. If your answer is yes, seriously reconsider the Safely Prosperous route.

3. I'm a big fan of entrepreneurs who are driven to start and build businesses. There is a big difference between an entrepreneur and a small-business owner. The latter just wants to be his or her own boss and own a bar, a beauty salon, or a fast-food franchise. But one who has caught the real entrepreneurial spirit and has invented a widget wants to become McWidgets. However, if the entrepreneur is solely money-driven, rather than a passionate believer in what the product or service can do to bless lives or change the world, I don't like that person much. Nothing will test your character and spirituality like the pursuit of money. And when you do have a lot of it, will you love it? It won't love you back.

4. When you succeed, are you truly willing to be generous and give thanks to God, who has blessed you abundantly, by helping His children when they need that help? As mentioned before, our family used to pray to God to "bless the poor, the sick, and the afflicted." One day a question struck me: Why were we throwing back to God the assignment He gave us, especially when He has given us the means to be very generous? Ever since that epiphany, my family has prayed for God to help us to find those who need our help so *we* can bless the poor, the sick, and the afflicted. Since then, it is truly amazing how many people with real needs I have stumbled over, and how good we felt when we have blessed their lives. Remember my account of my great-grandfather Mayberry, who learned he couldn't give it away faster than God would bless him with it. I truly believe in the law of compensating returns. It has been said that at the time of death, you can't take it

with you. So what can you take with you? I believe you can only take with you what you have become and the character that you have achieved by giving it away.

5. We are also setting up a family-help fund to aid those who really need and deserve temporary help. I and some of the more affluent family members are providing the start-up capital for the fund, and we are asking all the family to contribute something every month according to their ability, even if it's only a tiny amount.

6. Kay and I try to live modestly, following the principles in Book I. We are comfortably well off, and someday I might be half as rich as everyone thinks I am. If that happens, nothing in our lives will change, except our ability to be generous. We have no consumer debt. I only use my credit cards for necessary travel, and pay them off in full every month. Our cars are all paid for. One of them is three years old with 80,000 miles on it, and the other is seven years old with 200,000 miles, but they're both in great shape, and I will drive one of them until we have to shoot it to put it out of its misery. We owned a 20,000-square-foot mansion in the past, but we have found we are just as happy in our lovely 3,000-square-foot home; and the small mortgage is the only personal debt we have. I do have a small bass boat that is fully paid for, and it's my only indulgence except for dinner out at a modest but nice restaurant two or three times a week with Kay. We live very comfortably on no more than $3,000 a month, although we could afford a lot more. What's more, we have learned to like our lifestyle, and are comfortable with it, so we are trying to practice what I have preached in these pages.

7. Do you want to be rich so you can leave your kids a lot of money to prove you love them? Serious studies have demonstrated that the first generation after you will start to dissipate inherited fortunes, and the next generation will

finish the job. I intend to leave my kids everything I had as a child—including poverty. If you truly love them, you want them to be happy, and real happiness is always hard-earned. Struggle and surmounted obstacles are the real happiness builders, and inherited wealth is a happiness destroyer. No matter how rich you become, don't spoil your kids with unearned things. One of the great lessons of life that can bless your kids is learning how to work hard for the things they want. We tried to do this by having our kids work hard in the family businesses for the same wages as any other laborer. It seems to have paid off, and the lessons seem to have been passed on to our grandchildren.

8. I intend to set up a trust fund for the grandchildren's college education. It will pay for tuition, fees, books, and lodging if it's away from home. I will require their parents to match as much of the funds as they are able.

In essence, you need to make a family decision about exactly what you really want out of life. What would make you truly happy? I have been both rich and poor—each more than once—and I can honestly say we have been happy no matter what the bank balance when we have kept our eyes fixed on the things that lead inexorably to happiness. Much of the misery we have experienced has been the direct result of the violation of the principles taught in this book. If you have learned nothing else from my scribblings, I hope you learn this. God bless!

Appendix A

The Ruff Times Newsletter

Do not run out and execute the market recommendations in this book as soon as you read it. We have a very dynamic economy, and time can change things. Some recommendations may be good ideas for which the right time has come and gone or the propitious time has not yet arrived. Throughout 2004 I will provide a brief, free update of any recommendations that may have changed since this book was written. You can get this update by calling 1-801-224-3660 between 8:00 A.M. and 5:00 P.M. MST (e-mail howard@ rufftimes.com).

The best way to keep up with things is to subscribe to *The Ruff Times,* which is written every three weeks, as I track all these recommendations very closely.

WHAT YOU GET

The Ruff Times has several specific departments.

The Markets
I track the stock market, looking for that elusive day when you can throw darts at *The Wall Street Journal* and invest in the holes and make money. I also follow gold and silver very closely because I believe their time is coming again—perhaps soon, if it is not here already. I also track very carefully the trends in interest

rates, as this affects your total return on safe, interest-bearing investments such as bonds. Actually, despite my reputation as a gold prognosticator, my track record on interest rates is better.

Investing for Income

There are lots of above-average returns just waiting to be discovered. I will dig them out for you. This will help you take the compounding route to prosperity, as described in *Safely Prosperous or Really Rich*. For older Americans, this is crucial information to help them enjoy their golden years, knowing that Social Security is a Ponzi scheme that may not be there when they really need it.

Ruffonomics 101

Most of the economics you hear from Wall Street is just swill. Not only will I teach you *real* economics, I won't go down deep and come up dry. If you don't understand the economics of a market call, you shouldn't do it.

Disneyland on the Potomac

I have a free-market, libertarian political philosophy: I love my country, but sometimes I fear and distrust my government. Rarely does it meet or exceed expectations. Everything Washington does will inevitably affect your financial life. They spend 45 percent (and counting) of the gross national product and taxes are an avoidable fact of American life. They don't spend money like a drunken sailor—a drunken sailor spends his own money. I track proposed legislation on Social Security and Medicare. The political content is rarely partisan. I have a lot of respect for George W. Bush—he has been a tower of strength in defending our security against those who hate us, and as commander in chief that is his primary responsibility—but I am not a blind, partisan worshipper. Bush has also caved in to the big spenders, and this has given us the largest deficits in the history of the known universe. However, if Teddy Kennedy or Tom

Daschle are your kind of guys, and you believe Bill Clinton and Jimmy Carter were great presidents, you probably won't like me. If you believe government must do more for us, rather than get out of our way and leave us alone, you will be uncomfortable here. If you believe we are undertaxed, you might as well go away now. Government is a terrible threat to all of us who aspire to be something more than a lockstep dependent of Uncle Nanny. I am an aggressive advocate of lower taxes and a smaller government.

How, and How Much?

You can sign up for **one year for $139,** or for **two years for $230.** You will receive another copy of this book to give to a friend or relative for each year. In either case, it is riskless, as I will refund your money in full if you ask for it within 90 days of the start of your subscription, and you may keep the issues you've received and the book.

How to Save Some Real Money

If you are willing to receive your subscription via the worldwide Web or e-mail, You can subscribe for only **$99 a year,** because we save a lot of money on postage and printing. This method of delivery has one big advantage for you—time! If you get *The Ruff Times* in the regular mail, it will arrive in your mailbox as many as 10 days after it is written, because of the time involved in printing, addressing, and mailing—to say nothing of delays caused by Uncle Sam's snail mail. If you get *The Ruff Times* electronically, it will come the day after it is written. Also, if I have an urgent bulletin between regular issues, you will get it immediately, *but only electronically.*

How to Subscribe

You can subscribe by telephone (1-801-224-3660), via e-mail (service@ rufftimes.com), or via regular mail (P.O. Box 41, Orem, UT, 84059).

THE PRINCIPLES OF A MAVERICK

What I write grows out of deeply held principles, and here
they are:

- I am a passionate believer in and defender of the capitalist
  free-market system.
- I believe that when government passes laws or regulations, it expands into space formerly occupied by freedom.
  Thomas Jefferson called government "a singularly dangerous beast, and it must be chained; and we have chosen to
  chain it with the Constitution." I believe the beast is bursting its chains.
- I believe you should prepare for an independent life that
  does not depend on a government check, and I will help
  you do just that.
- I believe that God rules in the universe, and that his laws
  are eternal, and there is an appropriate place for him in the
  public square.
- I believe that our children are the hope of the future. We
  must neutralize the perverse doctrines taught them in the
  public schools and teach them about the founding and history of this great democratic republic and the virtues of the
  free-market capitalist system. If we don't, we are only one
  generation away from losing history's greatest experiment
  in human freedom.
- I believe that the real heroes of our society are the entrepreneurs who, like Columbus, are willing to lose sight of
  the safe, known shore to search for better solutions to life's
  problems; and that government should not penalize their
  success by taxing it. The rule is simple: If you want less of
  something, tax it, and that's just what you'll get. I am an
  entrepreneur and so are several of our children. I have
  started six companies; three of them failed, and three
  worked out just fine. I believe that success is rooted in the

stubborn failures of this world who are willing to pick themselves up, brush off the dust, and dive back into the business fray with undiminished enthusiasm. That is the *real* America.

- I am a student of Austrian economics, which tells us how the real world works and touts gold as the appropriate centerpiece of the world's monetary system. I will teach you about this in terms that any reasonably bright high school graduate can understand.

Welcome aboard!

Appendix B

Recommended Vendors

ADVISORY NEWSLETTERS

DELIBERATIONS on World Markets by Ian McAvity, Deliberations Research Inc., P.O. Box 182, Adelaide Station, Toronto, Ontario, M5C 2J1 Canada; phone 416-964-1359; e-mail www.chartguy.com/deliberations.htm.

Forecast & Strategies by Mark Skousen, One Massachusetts Avenue N.W., Washington, DC 20001; phone 800-777-5005; www.mskousen.com.

Gold Mining Stock Report by Bob Bishop, P.O. Box 1217, Lafayette, CA 94549; phone 925-284-1165; fax 925-891-9188; www.goldminingstockreport.com.

The McAlvany Intelligence Advisor Publishers Management Corp., P.O. Box 84900, Phoenix, AZ 85071; phone 800-528-0559 or 602-252-4477; fax 602-943-2363; www.publishers-management.com.

Remnant Review by Gary North, Publishers' Management Corp., P.O. Box 84900, Phoenix, AZ 85071; phone 800-528-0559 or 602-252-4477; fax 602-943-2363; www.publishers-management.com.

Richard Russell's Dow Theory Letters, P.O. Box 1759, La Jolla, CA 92038; www.dowtheoryletters.com. (One of my favorites, written by a wise old pro. An excellent source of market information.

The Ruff Times, P.O. Box 441, Orem, UT 84059; phone 877-665-6818 or 801-491-4075; www.rufftimes.com. (See Appendix A.)

Safe Money Report by Martin Weiss, P.O. Box 31689, Palm Beach Gardens, FL 33420-9905, e-mail safemoneyreport.com.

WORLD WIDE WEB SITES

www.beprepared.com Emergency Essentials, a leader in providing prepackaged dehydrated and freeze-dried food-storage units.

www.drudgereport.com Site of the infamous cyberjournalist Matt Drudge. I check it out at least twice a day, as it is constantly updated.

www.economist.com *The Economist* magazine.

www.opinionjournal.com From *The Wall Street Journal.* I love the editorial page and the marketing section.

www.rufftimes.com *The Ruff Times* newsletter.

www.washtimes.com *The Washington Times.*

INFORMATION ON HOW TO PREPARE YOUR OWN
SURVIVAL PROGRAM

http:/bekkal.tripod.com/food/ Personal Web site by a Mormon woman who really knows about food storage.

www.nat.usdaq.gov/fnic/ The Food and Nutrition Center. Links to several government information sites, with the usual establishment nutritional bias, but useful.

www.survival-center.com/food Most frequently asked questions about food storage.

DEBT REDUCTION COMPANIES

No More Mortgage. 365 East 1200 South, Orem, UT 84058; phone 888-239-3765; e-mail info.nomoremortage.com. I am chairman of the board and have a financial interest. My son Larry Ruff is president.

PRECIOUS METALS DEALERS

Investment Rarities Inc., 7850 Metro Parkway, Minneapolis, MN 55425; phone 800-328-1860 or 612-853-0700; www.investmentrarities .com. (They have helped my subscribers for 25 years.)

Camino Coin, 851 Burlway Road # 202, Burlingame, CA 94010; phone 800-348-8001 or 650-348-3000; www.caminocoin.com. (Very dependable and competitive.)

BOOKS

The Boy Scout Handbook (Boy Scouts of America). Great reference material on basic survival skills. Available from any local store that sells Boy Scout supplies.

Don't Get Caught with Your Pantry Down by James Talmage Stevens (Historical Publications, 1998; $29.95). Includes the most complete directory of preparedness vendors. Available in most bookstores and at 888-925-2555.

Getting Everything You Can out of All You've Got by Jay Abraham (Griffin, 2001). Jay is an authentic marketing genius. Available at bookstores.

Making the Best of Basics: Family Preparedness Handbook by James Talmage Stevens (Origin Books, 1997; $19.95). This is the best-selling book ever on basic storage programs for everyday necessities. Available in most bookstores, and at 888-925-2555.

Multiple Streams of Income by Robert G. Allen (Wiley, 2000). A terrific book by one of my favorite authors and best friends.

The One Minute Millionaire by Robert G. Allen (author of *Nothing Down* and *Multiple Streams of Income*) and Mark Victor Hansen (author of the fabulous *Chicken Soup* series) (Harmony Books, 2002).

Positioning by Al Ries and Jack Trout (McGraw-Hill, 2000). One of the best books ever written on marketing. It's an idea-packed thin paperback available at any bookstore.

NUTRITIONAL PRODUCTS

Hi-Q Nutrition (Howard Ruff), 877-665-6818; www.hiqnutrition.com. I have created a revolutionary brain food that is also a complete multi-supplement. Contains 58 vitamins, chelated minerals, trace minerals, herbs, and other botanicals that are known to nourish the brain, and especially stave off brain aging.

Meleleuca (Tim Ruff), 888-846-7833. Tim is my son, but I have no financial interest. They have a complete line of fine natural supplements.

Neo Life (Norvel and Joann Martens), 800-824-7861. Neo Life manufactures a line of high-quality supplements. I've done business with them for more than 30 years.

Usana (Aaron Allen), 801-376-6508. Aaron represents this fine supplement company. I especially like their vitamin C.

GOLD MINING STOCKBROKERS

National Securities 800-532-7574.

GOLD MINING AND SILVER STOCKS

Gold stocks fall into several categories. We have only listed a few of my favorites as of February 1, 2004, with many thanks to two newsletter writers I have known for almost a quarter of a century. They are Ian McAvity, who writes the *DELIBERATIONS on World Markets* newsletter (Deliberations Research Inc., P.O. Box 182, Adelaide Station, Toronto, Ontario, M5C 2J1 Canada; phone 416-964-1359; www.chartguy.com/deliberations.htm) and Bob Bishop, who writes the *Gold Mining Stock Report* (P.O. Box 1217, Lafayette, CA 94549; phone 925-284-1165; fax 925-891-9188; www.goldminingstockreport.com). For a one-time-only free updated list, visit our Web site at www.rufftimes.com or call *The Ruff Times* at 801-491-4075.

Closed-end mutual funds are traded like stocks (often on an exchange) at a price that is rarely the same as the value of its portfolio, but usually close:

ASA LTD (ASA). Mostly invested in South African shares.
Central Fund of Canada Ltd. (CEF). Listed on the American stock exchange, it is a pure bullion fund owning gold and silver at a fixed ratio of 50 ounces of silver to 1 ounce of gold, held in a Canadian bank. It is a useful proxy for gold whose shares can be held in an IRA, Keogh, or other tax-protected plan where bullion ownership is prohibited.

No-load, open-end mutual funds, which are structured like orthodox mutual funds, are priced daily at the real market value of the portfolio. I recommend only the no-load variety, where no sales commission is paid to the broker (these commissions can be as much as 8 percent). These are usually best for less active investors:

Tocqueville Gold (TDLDX)
American Century Global Gold (BGEIX). Probably has the lowest
  expense ratios.
Fidelity Select Gold (FSAGX)

The majors are the big gold producers, usually exchange-traded:

Newmont Mining (NEM-NYSE). If you own only one gold stock, this
  is the one.
Barrick Gold (ABX). Has sold a lot of future production forward in the
  futures market, which is a good idea if you expect lower gold
  prices. A fine company, but they have lost the futures bet. Not my
  favorite, but a fine company.
Placer Dome (PDG). Half of their reserves are in South Africa, with
  some political risk.

Second-tier companies include **Buenaventura, Harmony,
Goldcorp, Kinross Gold, Glamis,** and a raft of others, including
many exploration companies that are not yet into production but
have proven reserves in the ground just waiting for higher gold
prices to start digging. Some of Bob Bishop's preferred exploration
companies are **Nevsun Resources (NSU.T), Orezone Resources
(ORZ.T), Almaden Minerals (AMM.T),** and **Northern Lion
Resources (NL).** I also like **Madison Resources (CDNX:MNP.V),**
which I have recommended for some time.

Pure silver mines may be the best performers of all the mining
stocks because of the greater potential of silver over gold. You
should probably divide your silver-mining money among at least
three of them. They are **Pan American Silver (PAAS), Apex Silver
(SIL), Silver Standard (SSRI),** and **Western Silver (WPZ).**

Index